DAYS OF BATTLE

ARMOURED OPERATIONS NORTH OF THE RIVER DANUBE, HUNGARY 1944-45

Norbert Számvéber

Translated by Blanka Gálné Bíró

Edited by Dr Frederick P. Steinhardt, MS, PhD.

Helion & Company

Helion & Company Limited
Unit 8 Amherst Business Centre
Budbrooke Road
Warwick
CV34 5WE
England
Tel. 01926 499 619
Fax 0121 711 4075
Email: info@helion.co.uk
Website: www.helion.co.uk
Twitter: @helionbooks
Visit our blog http://blog.helion.co.uk/

Published by Helion & Company 2013. Reprinted in paperback 2018
Designed and typeset by Farr out Publications, Wokingham, Berkshire
Cover designed by Farr out Publications, Wokingham, Berkshire
Printed by Hobbs the Printers Ltd, Totton, Hampshire

Originally published as *Pancelosok a Felvideken, Pancelosutkozetek a Dunatol eszakra, 1944–1945* (Nagykovacsi: Puedlo Kiado, 2008).

ISBN 978-1-912174-26-3

British Library Cataloguing-in-Publication Data.
A catalogue record for this book is available from the British Library.

For details of other military history titles published by Helion & Company Limited contact the above address, or visit our website: http://www.helion.co.uk.

We always welcome receiving book proposals from prospective authors.

Contents

List of maps

In colour section

List of tables

Glossary of German Military Terms

Abteilung	detachment/battalion (dependent upon context)
Abteilungskommandeur	detachment/battalion commander
Abteilungsarzt	detachment/battalion doctor
Armeekorps	Army Corps
Artillerie	artillery
Arzt	doctor
Aufklärung	reconnaissance
Aufklärungsabteilung	reconnaissance detachment
Aufklärungszug	reconnaissance platoon
Aufstellungsstab	formation staff
Ausbildungs	training
Ausbildungs und Ersatz	training and replacement
Bataillon	battalion
Bataillonsarzt	battalion doctor
Batterie	battery
Befehlshaber	senior area commander
Chefsarzt	head surgeon
d.R. (der Reserve)	reserve grade officer
Divisionsarzt (IVb)	divisional doctor
Divisionsbegleitkompanie	divisional escort company
Divisionsstab	divisional staff
Einheit	unit, could be a generic term, or refer to a specific, often temporary unit, e.g. *Einheit "Krause"*
Einsatzstab	operational staff
Ersatz	replacement
Feldbrückekolonne	field bridging column
Feldlazarett	field hospital
Flak	anti-aircraft
Generalstabsoffizier	General Staff Officer
Gruppe	squad
Gruppenführer	squad leader, also an SS General officer rank
Halbzugführer	half platoon leader
Hauptmann beim Stabe	battalion staff head
Heeresgruppe	Army Group
Hilfsarzt	assistant doctor
Ia	first staff officer (*1.Generalstabsoffizier*)
Ib	supply officer
Ic	intelligence officer
IIa	adjutant
IVa	administrative officer
IVb	doctor

V	engineer
Infanterie	infantry
Inspekteur	Inspector
Instandsetzungsabteilung	maintenance detachment
Kampfgruppe	battle group (temporarily assembled)
Kommandeur	commander
Kompanie	company
Kompanie Chef	company commander (permanent)
Kompanie Führer	company leader (not permanently designated, although they often were later)
Korps	corps
Kraderkundungszug	motorcycle reconnaissance platoon
Kradmelderzug	motorcycle dispatch rider platoon
Kradschützen	motorcycle riflemen
Kradschützenzug	motorcycle platoon
Krankenkraftwagenkolonne	ambulance column
Lehrgruppe	teaching group
leichte	light
Major beim Stabe	regimental staff head
MLR	main line of resistance (in German, *HKL, hauptkampflinie*)
Nachschubdienst	supply service
Nachschubtruppen	supply troops
Nachrichten	signals/communications
Nachrichten Offizier	signals officer
Nachrichtenzug	signals platoon
Nachrichtenabteilung	signals detachment
NPEA	*Nationalpolitische Erziehungsansalt*, National Political Education Institute
O1	ordnance officer, assigned to Ia
O2	ordnance officer, assigned to Ib
Offizier	Officer
Ordnungspolizei	Order Police (uniformed)
Ordonnanz Offizier	ordnance officer
Panzer	armour/tank
Panzergrenadier	armoured infantry
Panzergrenadierschule	armoured infantry school
Panzerjäger	tank hunter
Panzerjägerzug	tank hunter platoon
Panzerjäger Abteilung	tank hunter detachment
Panzerkorps	armored corps
Pionier	engineer
Pionier Bataillon	engineer battalion
Regimentsarzt	regimental doctor
Regimentskommandeur	regimental commander
Sanitäts	medical

Sanitätsabteilung	medical detachment
Sanitätskompanie	medical company
Sanitäts Staffel	medical group
Scheinwerfer	searchlight
Schirrmeister	NCO for motor vehicles
Stab	staff/HQ
Stabsbatterie	staff battery
Stabschef	Chief of Staff
Stabskompanie	staff company
Stabsscharführer	senior designated NCO
Sturmgeschütz	assault gun (limited traverse armored vehicle)
TFK	Technical Officer for Vehicles
TFW	Technical Officer for Weapons
Truppführer	squad leader
Truppenübungsplatz	troop training area
Unterführeranwärter Lehrgang	non-commissioned officer-candidate instruction course
Versorgungskompanie	supply company
Verwaltungsführer	officer responsible for administration
Verwaltungsoffizier	administrative officer
Werfer	rocket projector
Werkmeister	maintenance foreman
Werkstattkompanie	repair company
Werkstattzug	repair platoon
Wirtschafts Abteilung	administrative detachment
Zahnarzt	dentist
Zug	platoon
Zugführer	platoon leader
II.Zugführer	2nd platoon leader

Introduction

There is a line of events within the course of the history of the battles in Hungary during 1944-45 that has been studied thoroughly up to this day. The issue of the areas of Felvidék (Upper Hungary) that were returned to Hungary between 1938-1945 have usually been left out of the discussions of military history written during the period between 1945-1989. The reason for this was that, based on the historical situation following 1945, military historians have seen this territory as being part of Czechoslovakia, and, after the front lines crossed the borders that had been set for the countries before 1938, they usually stopped their research.

There can be no attempt made at thorough elaboration of the complete combat history of the Felvidék (Upper Hungary) in 1944-45. For now, we cannot even try to fit the combat history of the area within our narrow field of research, armoured warfare. At present we can only examine those engagements and battles in which both the Germans and Soviets deployed a large number of armoured fighting vehicles.

The first of these is the battle fought along the Garam [Gran] and the Ipoly rivers in the last third of December 1944. The deployment of the Hungarian Division "*Szent László*" constituted part of this battle, which, after thorough examination of archive sources, became more detailed and complete.

The second part deals with the history of the battle for Komárom, fought between 6-22 January 1945 and is an integral sequel to the first part, both in chronological and operational means.

In the third part we deal with the German operation "*Südwind*" that took place in February 1945. Based on newly found sources and data the combat history of "*Südwind*" was considerably extended and more detailed, compared to the study published in 2000 in my book *Nehézpáncélosok (*Heavy armour*)*.

The fourth part summarizes the battles going on at the end of March 1945, concentrating on the units of both sides in which armoured fighting vehicles played the prominent roles.

In the course of writing this book the help of László Némedi was priceless. I received generous help from a number of people, including Péter Andráš, Péter Barnaki, Dénes Bernád, Dr. Attila Bonhardt , Dr. Csaba B. Stenge, Mirko Bayerl, András Palásthy, Lieutenant Colonel Dr. János Suba, Zoltán Weimper and Mrs. Sándorné Karai. I express my heartfelt gratitude to all of them.

This was not the first time I have taken advantage of my dear wife's and family's patience; again they had to endure while I turned our home into a "battlefield". I thank you all for all of your support!

Norbert Számvéber

1

Armour along the Ipoly and the Garam (11-31 December 1944)

Loss of the Ipolyság corridor

Until the first week of December 1944, continuous combat brought battle casualties in swiftly increasing numbers, which, at last, convinced the Soviet military leadership that the weakened forces of the 2nd Ukrainian Front, commanded by Marshal Rodion Yakovlevich Malinovski, would not be able to eliminate the German—Hungarian *Armeegruppe "Fretter-Pico"*[1] standing in defence around Budapest and carry out the swift capture of the Hungarian capital on their own. The 4th Ukrainian Front, its left flank originally turned towards Budapest, was nowhere close to the capital at that time. Therefore, in its Directive issued on 12 December 1944, the Soviet Supreme High Command ordered that the forces of the 2nd and 3rd Ukrainian Fronts were to work in close cooperation and launch simultaneous attacks from the North and South to encircle and smash the German and Hungarian forces around Budapest and capture the capital. The Fronts were given until 19-20 December to prepare for the offensive.

The corridor at Ipolyság was the key to the western half of Felvidék (Upper Hungary). If the Soviet 2nd Ukrainian Front had managed to capture this territory, it would have gained the opportunity of possibly cutting the German *Heeresgruppe Süd* in half. Ipolyság and its immediate vicinity were situated exactly on the boundary between *Armeegruppen "Fretter-Pico"* and *"Wöhler"*. As was so often the case at such boundaries, neither group prepared for the defence of that area.

In the afternoon of 7 **December** the main forces of the Soviet 6th Guards Tank Army were engaged north of Vác and southwest of Balassagyarmat. Its advance troops were already in the area of Nógrád, west of Diósjenő and southeast of Nagyoroszi. Therefore, on 8 December, *Heeresgruppe Süd* ordered the Hungarian 2nd Armoured Division (Colonel Endre Zádor) to close the corridor at Ipolyság with its full strength, basing its defence on the village and the *Margarethen-Stellung* (Line) to its south. The task of the division was to prevent Soviet forces from breaking through to the west. The defence was to be centered along the mountain road leading from Diósjenő towards Kemence. The division was attached to the *IV. Panzerkorps* of *Armeegruppe "Fretter-Pico"*. The *Armeegruppe* commanded the forces on the Dunakanyar – Ipolyság (excluded) section. Any and all combat-ready units and *Alarmtruppen* in the area behind were to be immediately deployed on this section of the *Margarethen-Stellung* (Line), including the armoured fighting vehicles and heavy weapons under repair. The field police officers of the *Feldjäger-Kommando I* were ordered to establish a blocking line along the Ipoly and to draft every single combat-ready soldier and all available weapons into the defence.[2] Thus the German *Feldstrafabteilung 18*

1 The army group consisted of the German *6. Armee* and the Hungarian 3rd Army. Its commander was *General der Artillerie* Maximilian Fretter-Pico. The army group was commanded by the German *6. Armee*.

2 HM HIM *Hadtörténelmi Levéltár*, Budapest, microfilm archives, *Kriegstagebuch Ia der Heeresgruppe Süd*,

(Field Penal Detachment 18) was also committed to defend the Ipoly.

On **9 December** the Hungarian 2nd Armoured Division had four battalions, two combat-ready *Panzer* IV tanks, five *Toldi* light tanks, seven *Nimród* armoured self-propelled anti-aircraft guns, five towed 7.5cm anti-tank guns and six light anti-aircraft guns, as well as 18 10.5cm field artillery pieces with which it was to carry out the given order.

The first units assigned to defend the entrance of the corridor were detached from the German *24. Panzer-Division/IV. Panzerkorps* (*Generalmajor* Gustav-Adolf von Nostiz-Wallwitz). Beginning on 8 December 1944, the Ipolyság corridor was defended by the German *III. (Abteilung)/Panzer-Regiment 24*[3], the *II. Abteilung/Panzergrenadier-Regiment 26* and elements of *Panzer-Aufklärungs-Abteilung 24/24. Panzer-Division.*[4]

As of 13 December, these forces were attached to *Divisionsgruppe "Rintelen"* fighting on the left flank of the *Armeegruppe "Fretter-Pico"*.

On **11 December, 1944**[5], attacking westward, the Romanian forces broke through the line of defence in the sector of *Korpsgruppe "Breith"* in the south-eastern part of Gödöllő, and crossed the Gödöllő–Isaszeg railway line. Units of the Hungarian 10th Infantry Division and the 12th Replacement Division retreated in the wake of an attack by a Soviet rifle regiment. As a result of this, a 3km gap opened in the German—Hungarian defence.

The 2nd and 3rd Tank Battalions of the Soviet 27th Independent Guards Tank Brigade, in cooperation with the forces of the 155th Rifle Division, proceeded with the attack toward Csomád–Fót. According to Soviet reconnaissance data, the line Hill 220 (one kilometre southeast of Csomád) – Hill 213 – in front of the Veresegyház railway station, was defended by elements of the *46. Infanterie-Division* and elements of *Panzergrenadier-Regiment 93/13. Panzer-Division*. That day Soviet forces observed 10 German armoured fighting vehicles active along this front line, which was further reinforced by anti-tank ditches and minefields.

Soviet armour and infantry occupied the eastern sector of Csomád at about 1200 hours. At 1300 hours the 1st Battalion/27th Independent Guards Tank Brigade succeeded in bypassing the anti-tank ditch in the area of Veresegyház, and, at about 1600 hours, two of its tanks advanced along the road 2km east of Hill 213. Meanwhile the 2nd Battalion/27th Independent Guards Tank Brigade remained on the eastern edge of Csomád, and repulsed counterattacks of the German infantry, supported by armour, from the direction of Hill 220.

The German *Luftwaffe* carried out raids on the same day against the 27th Independent Guards Tank Brigade with formations of 10-20 aircraft. The ground-attack aircraft destroyed

Ia Nr. 13590/44 *geh.*, 8. 12. 1944 (roll no. 627. image no. 7210982).

3 The *Abteilungskommandeur* of the *III. (Abteilung)/Panzer-Regiment 24* was *Hauptmann* Kuls. On 9 December 1944 the unit had, altogether, two combat-ready *Panzer* IV tanks, six *StuG.* III assault guns and *StuH.* 42 assault howitzers, although four of the latter were fighting in the area of the German *8. Jäger-Division*.

4 Senger und Etterlin Jr. v. F. M. Dr., *Die 24. Panzer-Division vormals 1. Kavallerie-Division 1939–1945* (Neckargemünd, 1962), pp.280-281.

5 Weather: frost during the night, 6° Celsius during the day, generally bright, good visibility conditions; the unpaved roads were drying out.

two T–34 tanks and one SU–85 self-propelled gun with bombs, and a further two T–34s were knocked out by cannon fire. Apart from this, the Soviet Guards Tank Brigade lost one T–34 tank and two SU–85 self-propelled guns to the German forces (these were burnt out), and a further SU–85 ran over a mine. Thus the 27th Independent Guards Tank Brigade suffered considerable losses that day, losing a total of lost nine armoured fighting vehicles.[6]

Between Csomád and Alsógöd the forces of the Soviet 25th Guards Division and the 409th Rifle Division launched a new attack toward the south-west with the support of approximately 61 T–34 tanks of the 20th Guards and 21st Guards Tank Brigades. With the help of the assault units created from the force of the 73rd and the 78th Rifle Regiments, the tanks finally succeeded in crossing the anti-tank ditch and proceeded approximately 3km south, after breaking into the defence of *Panzer-Division "Feldherrnhalle"* by opening a 4-5km gap.

The *2.* (armoured personnel carrier) *Kompanie* of the division's *Panzer-Aufklärungs-Abteilung* carried out a counterattack with the support of the *StuG. III* assault guns of *Panzerjäger-Abteilung "Feldherrnhalle"*, but was only able to halt the Soviet troops temporarily. The German units claimed to have knocked out 20 Soviet armoured fighting vehicles (five of these were knocked out by infantry in close combat, with handheld anti-tank rocket-launchers).

In consequence of the Soviet attack, the Germans had to pull their MLR [main line of resistance] back to the Kisalag north – Alag north – Dunakeszi area. However, the defence positions there were still under construction. Between the right flank of *Panzer-Division "Feldherrnhalle"* and the left flank of the *13. Panzer-Division* yawned a 4km gap.[7]

That same evening, the frontline of the Soviet 5th Guards Tank Corps, the 25th Guards– and the 409th Rifle Division, extended along the line three kilometres north of Alag – 500 metres south of Csomád.[8]

On that day, the independent *Maschinengewehr-Bataillon "Sachsen"*, which was marching from Szentendrei island to the new MLR, units minus one company, was attached to *Panzer-Division "Feldherrnhalle"*. *III. Panzerkorps* requested a further *Panzergrenadier-*regiment and a number of *Panther* tanks from the replacement armour arriving in the Dunántúl (Transdanubia) area in order to be able to strengthen the defence; however, in order to avoid disrupting the forces, the request was denied the *Armeegruppe*.[9]

As no further reserve forces were available, and *Panzer-Division "Feldherrnhalle"* was already engaged and was unable to provide assistance, at around 1800 hours the *Armeegruppe* permitted the defence of the *III. Panzerkorps* to fall back to the line extending along the north-eastern corner Isaszeg– Hill 329 – northern outskirts of Kisalag – northern border of Alag.

Between Ipolyság and Kismaros, on the mountain front line of the Hungarian 2nd

6 Combat report of the 27th Independent Guards Tank Brigade to the commander of the 7th Guards Army tank and mechanized troops (a copy owned by the author), 11 December 1944. The operational armoured fighting vehicle strength of the unit in the evening consisted of seven T–34 tanks, one SU–85 and one SU–76M self-propelled guns.

7 HM HIM *Hadtörténelmi Levéltár* (Budapest), microfilm archives, *Kriegstagebuch Ia der Heeresgruppe Süd, Kriegstagebuch vom* 11. 12. 1944 (roll no. 626. image no. 7210805).

8 *Budapestskaya Operaciya*. Contemporary composition of the 2nd Ukrainian Front. A copy owned by the author, p.101.

9 HM HIM *Hadtörténelmi Levéltár* (Budapest), microfilm archives, *Kriegstagebuch Ia der Heeresgruppe Süd, Kriegstagebuch vom* 11. 12. 1944 (roll no. 626. image no. 7210815).

Armoured Division, both sides conducted reconnaissance. Half of the deployed forces of the Hungarian 4th Motorized Rifle Battalion went over to the Soviet troops.

At Kismaros the defence tasks were transferred to *Kampfgruppe "Lehner"*. The *Kampfgruppe* was named after the company commander of the *3.* (armoured personnel carrier) *Kompanie/Panzer-Pionier-Bataillon "Feldherrnhalle"*, *Oberleutnant* Lehner. Apart from his own company, one company of *Maschinengewehr-Bataillon "Sachsen"*, a Hungarian platoon, and a group of Hungarian anti-tank guns and anti-aircraft guns (presumably from the Hungarian 2nd Armoured Division) were also attached to *Oberleutnant* Lehner's group. Following a short artillery preparation, the spearhead of the *Kampfgruppe* reached the Kismaros-Kóspallag road by 2100 hours.

In order to support the ongoing combat activity in the area, the naval units of the German Danube Flotilla were also attached to *Korpsgruppe "Breith"*.

The spearhead of the 46th Guards Tank Brigade/9th Guards Mechanized Corps of the 6th Guards Tank Army[10] launched its attack from the western outskirts of Drégelypalánk in order to capture and control Ipolyság, approached Hont and came within 700 metres of the village.

Following the above-mentioned events, the 46th Guards Tank Brigade and the 31st Guards Mechanized Brigade of the corps captured Hont in heavy combat. During the fighting for the village, a female army medic, Ljubov Dzjuba, earned fame and respect for moving in line with the armoured fighting vehicles with her armoured first-aid carrier vehicle and rescuing casualties without regard for her own safety. She rescued twelve tank crew members and six infantry machine gunners from the firing-line; she was awarded the Medal "For Courage".[11]

On that same day, the 46th Guards Tank Brigade, the 31st Guards Mechanized Brigade and their M4A2 tanks thrust forward between the Ipoly river and the railway, reaching the southern outskirts of Ipoly. Armour of the 2nd Battalion/46th Guards Tank Brigade occupied Homok, established defence positions there and repulsed ongoing counterattacks by German infantry that were supported by two to three armoured fighting vehicles and five to six assault guns.

The tank destroyer ground-attack aircraft of the *I. Fliegerkorps* launched a concentrated attack in the hours around noon against the Soviet tank wedges that had reached Ipolyság. According to Soviet sources[12], the initial combat actions were carried out by nine *Ju* 88 aircraft, then a further two formations arrived. It is more likely, however, that these were *Hs* 129 B2 tank destroyer aircraft from the *14. Staffel/Schlachtgeschwader 9.* The aircraft spent approximately 90 minutes in the air, circling over the Soviet troops, some of whose armoured fighting vehicles fled from the road to seek cover under the trees. After Germans knocked out 10 Soviet armoured fighting vehicles from the air, and a further five were damaged, the Soviet troops withdrew eastwards.[13]

According to Soviet sources one of the M4A2 tanks of the 46th Guards Tank Brigade

10 The advance troop consisted of one company from the 1st Battalion/46th Guards Tank Brigade, with 30 infantry soldiers riding on the M4A2 tanks.

11 Loza, Dimitry Fjodorovich, "A szovjet csapatok felszabadító harcai Nógrád megyében", (Liberating battles of the Soviet troops in Nógrád county. December 1944) in: *Hadtörténelmi Közlemények,* issue 1967/4, p.613.

12 Loza, Dimitry, *Commanding the Red Army's Sherman Tanks* (Lincoln NE, 1996), pp.62-63.

13 HM HIM *Hadtörténelmi Levéltár* (Budapest) microfilm archives, *Kriegstagebuch Ia der Heeresgruppe Süd, Kriegstagebuch vom* 11. 12. 1944 (roll no. 626. image no. 7210806).

(tank commander: Guards-Lieutenant G. Verbovoy) drove up to the railway embankment and shot down an attacking *Ju* 88 aircraft with its gun.[14] However another source (although the same author) states that this German aircraft was shot down by the 37mm cannon of the 388th Guards Anti-Aircraft Artillery Regiment positioned in the area of Homok village.

These automatic anti-aircraft guns played an important role in the fighting against the six armoured fighting vehicles that were advancing from the direction of Bernecebaráti towards Homok. The 37mm guns knocked out all of them in a short time from a distance of a couple of hundred metres.[15] Presumably these were Hungarian *Toldi* light tanks or *Nimród* armoured self-propelled anti-aircraft guns, if the 37mm anti-tank rounds were effective against them.

The 18th Guards Mechanized Brigade/9th Guards Mechanized Corps, carrying out a night manoeuvre, succeeded in entering Ipolyvéce in the morning hours and occupying the village.[16]

That day the German *Luftwaffe* claimed destruction of a total of 22 tanks, one self-propelled gun, 70 cars and 50 horse-drawn wagons, damage to a further 12 armoured and 60 motor vehicles. It also claimed to have downed 15 aircraft and destroyed two more on the ground between Vác and Ipolyság. Furthermore, it scored a number of direct hits on the military bridge at Ercsi.[17]

Upon approval of the *Oberkommando des Heeres* (*OKH* or Supreme High Command of the Land Forces), with the regrouping of the *SS-Sturmbrigade "Dirlewanger"*, an *SS-Regiment* (*Regimentsstab*, two reinforced *Sturmbataillone*, two light artillery batteries and a *Nebelwerfer* battery) was transferred to the Ipolyság area in order to strengthen the defence forces. The regiment was to be deployed under its own command. Considering the "special"[18] nature of the unit, it was not possible to move it in small units, because its soldiers would then have had better opportunities to get away. This part of the brigade was attached to *Armeegruppe "Fretter-Pico"*. One battalion launched an attack towards Hont.

In the sector of the *IV. Panzerkorps,* the Germans, in general, eliminated the Soviet bridgehead on the Ipoly north of Balassagyarmat.

On **12 December 1944**[19]**,** the forces of the Soviet 68th Guards Rifle Division/46th Army repulsed an attack launched in the *Korpsgruppe "Breith"* sector by the *22. SS-Freiwilligen-Kavallerie-Division*; the attack, from the direction of Soroksár, was carried out in regimental strength by infantry supported by five armoured fighting vehicles.[20]

14 Loza, 1996, p.63.

15 Loza, 1967, p.613. The source contains unit number 338 as the consequence of a mistyping error.

16 *Budapestskaya Operaciya*. Contemporary composition of the 2nd Ukrainian Front. A copy owned by the author. p.120.

17 HM HIM *Hadtörténelmi Levéltár* (Budapest), microfilm archives, *Kriegstagebuch Ia der Heeresgruppe Süd, Kriegstagebuch vom* 11. 12. 1944 (roll no. 626. image no. 7210808).

18 Earlier, the unit had consisted of convicted criminals. However, at this time it also included those convicted by the court martial of the *Waffen-SS*, men who were given the opportunity to "prove" their military virtues. Apart from them, soldiers arrived here from all units of the *Wehrmacht*. What is more, it even allowed prisoners coming from concentration camps who had been imprisoned because of leftist thinking, as well as convicted criminals, to enter.

19 Weather: frost during the night, 6° Celsius during the day, generally foggy and rainy; the condition of the unpaved roads worsened.

20 HM HIM *Hadtörténelmi Levéltár* (Budapest), *Szovjet iratmásolatok gyűjteménye a Budapest körüli*

The German—Hungarian forces retreated into their newly established securing positions along the line southwest of Isaszeg – 2.5km southwest of Gödöllő – 2.5km northeast of Mogyoród –Northern edge of Kisalag.

Following the repeated battalion-strength attacks, the Soviet troops occupied Kisalag. *Panzer-Division "Feldherrnhalle"* did not have enough *Panzergrenadier* infantry forces to launch the necessary counterattack, although seven *Alarmkompanien*[21] had already been created from the strength of the *Nachschubtruppen* [supply train elements].

German reconnaissance observed 40 Soviet tanks moving from the direction of Alsógöd towards Vác. A truck column with infantry was spotted moving in the opposite direction.[22]

The 5th Guards Tank Corps had turned over its frontline sector to the 25th Guards Rifle Corps/7th Guards Army on the night of 11/12 December. With 87 operational T–34 tanks, it started a 60km march northward. It then assembled in the area of Érsekvadkert and Nagyoroszi. The corps did not take part in combat until 20 December. The 4th Guards Motorcycle Regiment marched from the area of Vác to Tereske.[23]

The 2nd Battalion/27th Independent Guards Tank Brigade launched its attack from the grove 600 metres from Veresegyház at 2000 hours toward Fót-Rákospalota, in cooperation with the 786th Regiment/155th Rifle Division. Their task was to reach the area of the Rákospalota–Rákosszentmihály road by the end of the day.

During this combat action the Soviet troops succeeded in breaking into the lines northeast of Mogyoród with a battalion-strength unit, supported by five armoured fighting vehicles. However, the attack bogged down in artillery fire from the direction of Hill 279 (2.5km northeast of Fót) and Hill 266 (2km northeast of Mogyoród), and tank gun fire from the direction of Mogyoród. The defenders launched a counterstrike and knocked out a Soviet T–34 tank. According to the records of the Soviet Guards Tank Brigade, one armoured personnel carrier and 20 soldiers were destroyed and three additional armoured personnel carriers captured.[24]

In the morning, Soviet armour and infantry reached the northern edge of Fót. The defenders forced them back to the northern edge of Kisalag with concentrated fire of anti-tank guns. Northeast of Fót, Soviet troops penetrated the wooded area of Fóti-Somlyó northeast of the town. The *Sturmbataillon* that had been activated from the strength of the Budapest Police was attached to *Panzer-Division "Feldherrnhalle"* to cover the gap on the right flank of the division. The next day the *Sturmbataillon* was deployed to secure the hill north of the road between Fót and Mogyoród.

Both sides conducted reconnaissance on the right flank and in the center of the sector of the MLR held by the Hungarian 2nd Armoured Division.

The Soviet 18th Guards Mechanized Brigade/9th Guards Mechanized Corps crossed

harcokról. A 2. *Ukrán Front hadijelentései*, 1944. December 12.

21 Four such *Alarmkompanien* were fighting in the *13. Panzer-Division*.

22 HM HIM *Hadtörténelmi Levéltár* (Budapest), microfilm archives, *Kriegstagebuch Ia der Heeresgruppe Süd*, *Kriegstagebuch vom* 12. 12. 1944 (roll no. 626. image no. 7210822).

23 *Budapestskaya Operaciya*. Contemporary composition of the 2nd Ukrainian Front. A copy owned by the author. pp.119-120.

24 Combat report of the 27th Independent Guards Tank Brigade to the commander of the 7th Guards Army tank and mechanized troops (a copy owned by the author), 12 December 1944. The operational armoured fighting vehicle strength of the unit in the evening consisted of 13 T–34 tanks and one SU–76M self-propelled gun.

the Ipoly during the night of 11/ 12 December with two battalions at Ipolyvece and one battalion at Ipolyhídvég, and, in cooperation with units of the 303rd Rifle Division, captured Ipolyhídvég.[25]

The Soviet troops knocked out three assault guns at Ipolyvéce, which had kept the crossing point under concentrated fire. The 83rd Guards Tank Regiment provided support from the southern bank of the Ipoly with gun and machine gun fire to establish the bridgehead on the other bank.[26]

The 46th Guards Tank Brigade and the 31st Guards Mechanized Brigade of the corps occupied Homok once again, and resumed its combat activity in the area of Ipolyság in order to cross the Ipoly river. The 30th Guards Mechanized Brigade and the 14th Motorcycle Battalion were stationed in the area of Drégelypalánk.[27]

During the morning Soviet forces launched an attack from Hont toward the northwest, supported by 15 tanks. One tank was knocked out by the defenders and the attack was repulsed. In the afternoon the Soviets concentrated their infantry and, bypassing Ipolyság to the south and north, resumed their advance. Attacking along the road leading from Nagyoroszi and from the Hont area, by 1600 hours the Soviets approached within 3km of Bernecebaráti from the east and southeast.

The staff of the 2nd Hungarian Division was, according to the Germans, apparently incompetent to command in the present extremely complex situation. Therefore the task of command was assigned to the *357. Infanterie-Division*.

In the sector of *IV. Panzerkorps/Armeegruppe "Wöhler"*, the Soviet Cavalry Mechanized Group "Pliev", after a heavy artillery preparation, attacked Szécsény in successive waves from west and southwest with infantry and 30 tanks.

Two assault units were formed in each motorized rifle battalion of the 4th Guards Mechanized Corps during the night of 11/12 December. These consisted of a rifle platoon, two light machine guns, two 82mm mortars, one gun and an engineer platoon. At 1000 hours, following a short artillery preparation, the forces of the 4th Guards and the 6th Guards Cavalry Corps launched a general assault. However, the attackers suffered severe losses and did not gain ground.[28]

The Soviet rapid response group occupied Rimóc and Nagylóc south of Szécsény. A 10th Guards Cavalry Division/4th Guards Cavalry Corps was engaged in the area of Szécsénykovácsi to gain ground for crossing the Ipoly.[29]

On **13 December 1944**[30], in the area of the Börzsöny hills, command was transferred from the staff of the Hungarian 2nd Armoured Division to the commander of the *357. Infanterie-Division, Generalleutnant* Josef Rintelen.

25 *Budapestskaya Operaciya*. Contemporary composition of the 2nd Ukrainian Front. A copy owned by the author. p.120.

26 Loza, 1967, p.614.

27 *Budapestskaya Operaciya*. Contemporary composition of the 2nd Ukrainian Front. A copy owned by the author. p.120.

28 Loza, 1967, p.618.

29 HM HIM *Hadtörténelmi Levéltár* (Budapest), *Szovjet iratmásolatok gyűjteménye a Budapest körüli harcokról*. A 2. *Ukrán Front hadijelentései*, 1944. December 12.

30 Weather: 3° Celsius during the day, medium high cloud base, local rainstorms, occasional snow in the area of the *2. Panzerarmee*, the condition of the unpaved roads was unfavourable.

A chief of staff of the 1st Battalion/46th Guards Tank Brigade of the 9th Guards Mechanized Corps, Guards Captain N. N. Bogdanov initiated a bold reconnaissance action during the night of 12/13 December with his M4A2 tank to the area of Bernecebaráti and Kemence in order to recconnoiter the German—Hungarian defence systems southwest of Ipolyság. The Guards Captain spoke German very well; he and his tank driver put on German uniforms, the gunner and the loader remained in their Soviet uniforms. The extremely windy weather at night was advantageous for the lone vehicle entering enemy territory. The radio was to be used only in emergencies, as the German radio detection system constantly monitored Soviet radio traffic and the exact location of the broadcaster could be swiftly determined.

At about midnight Guards Captain Bogdanov spotted an armoured fighting vehicle standing still on the road between Bernecebaráti and Kemence. The M4A2 tank stopped a little distance away and the chief of the battalion staff calmly came closer. He recognized the vehicle as a German assault gun equipped with night vision devices. He addressed them in German, and two heads emerged from the open escape hatch. Bogdanov learnt that the engine of the vehicle was out of order and that the commander had returned to Kemence to his unit's command post with two of his crew. The Guards Captain introduced himself as a communications officer of the German *6. Panzer-Division* and, claiming an order that had to be communicated immediately, lured the crew out of the assault gun. When they got out, the Soviet soldiers captured them. The two prisoners were taken into the Soviet armoured fighting vehicle, the Soviet loader sat in the towed captured vehicle. With considerable difficulty, they succeeded in towing the seized assault gun back to the Soviet front line with the M4A2. Two weeks later Guards Captain Bogdanov received the Order of the Red Banner.[31]

During the day Soviet forces attacked from the direction of Hont and Homok toward the southwest, reaching the southern edge of Bernecebaráti. However, a German—Hungarian counterattack drove them back from this area.

North of the Ipoly, the Soviet forces thrust forward to the northern edge of Ipolyság. According to an uncertain report, the Soviet troops crossed the Ipoly at about 1100 hours on the repaired bridge that existed at Ipolyhídvég and were already advancing with 17 armoured fighting vehicles. This was the 18th Guards Mechanized Brigade/9th Guards Mechanized Corps which was advancing on the Ipolyhídvég–Tesmag march route and approached to within 600 metres of Ipolyság by 1300 hours. The 46th Guards Tank Brigade, attacking from the northwest, joined the assault. However, the action failed to capture the village.[32]

German reconnaissance identified an attack position with approximately 1000 Soviet soldiers in the area of Ipolyszécsényke.

The main body of the Hungarian 2nd Armoured Division, consisting of 25 rail wagons, loaded with most of the German and Hungarian manufactured armoured fighting vehicles and other vehicles of the unit, was re-routed, for no known reason, to Gumpertsdorf near Oppeln, Silesia, instead of its Hungarian unloading place. A German armoured equipment centre was located in this village. The Hungarian crews escorting the vehicles were ordered off the vehicles in Breslau and were turned back home. *Heeresgruppe Süd* intervened with

31 Loza, 1996, pp.56-60.

32 *Budapestskaya Operaciya*. Contemporary composition of the 2nd Ukrainian Front. A copy owned by the author. p.121.

the military authorities responsible in order to immediately redirect the consignment back to Nyergesújfalu.[33]

On the front line sector of the *IV. Panzerkorps/Armeegruppe "Wöhler"*, the defenders repulsed an attack at Tótgyarmat that was launched by battalion-sized Soviet forces.

The Soviets fired a 30-minutes artillery preparation, followed by a renewed assault with ground-attack aircraft support in order to capture Szécsény. The assaults were repeated several times and were also supported by a number of armoured fighting vehicles. However, the defenders repulsed all of the attacks.

The Germans identified a Soviet attack position (with approximately 30 armoured fighting vehicles) southwest of Szécsény, in the so-called Káprási-erdő. Concentrated artillery fire prevented the Soviet tanks from attacking and destroyed three of them. Five more were presumed destroyed.[34]

According to German radio intelligence, five Soviet cavalry regiments were gathering south of Szécsény, in the area of Rimóc. From this, the Germans concluded that a new assault against Szécsény or an eastwards facing Soviet attack was impending. The Germans listened in on the staff of the Cavalry Mechanized Group "Pliev" which contacted the 23rd Tank Corps for the first time.[35]

On **14 December 1944**[36], elements of the Soviet 9th Guards Mechanized Corps assaulted Ipolyság at 1300 hours in the sector of *Divisionsgruppe "Rintelen"*.[37] The 18th Guards and the 31st Guards Mechanized Brigades of the Corps, with fire support provided by the 46th Guards Tank Brigade, swung into action from the direction of Hont. The Soviet units captured the entire town by 1600 hours.

During this time the 30th Guards Mechanized Brigade was attacking south-westwards toward Bernecebaráti and gained control of the road leading to the village.[38] With this, the Soviets controlled the entrance to the Ipolyság corridor, through which the 6th Guards Tank Army could launch its attack westwards.

The 9th Guards Mechanized Corps established a circular defence around Ipolyság during the day and repulsed German—Hungarian counterattacks launched from the direction of Kistúr and point no. 282 (3.5km east of Középtúr). By that point, the Soviet corps had only 110 operational tanks and self-propelled guns left.[39]

---

33 HM HIM *Hadtörténelmi Levéltár* (Budapest), microfilm archives, *Kriegstagebuch Ia der Heeresgruppe Süd, Ia Nr.* 13849/44 *geh.*,13. 12. 1944 (roll no. 627. image no. 7211062).

34 HM HIM *Hadtörténelmi Levéltár* (Budapest), microfilm archives, *Kriegstagebuch Ia der Heeresgruppe Süd, Kriegstagebuch vom* 13. 12. 1944 (roll no. 626. image no. 7210840).

35 HM HIM *Hadtörténelmi Levéltár* (Budapest), microfilm archives, *Kriegstagebuch Ia der Heeresgruppe Süd, Kriegstagebuch vom* 13. 12. 1944 (roll no. 626. image no. 7210849).

36 Weather: slightly cloudy, but altogether clear, 2-4° Celsius during the day, rain and snow, vehicle traffic was extremely difficult because of the unpaved roads.

37 This consisted of the German *Stab* of the *357. Infanterie-Division*, the *Kampfgruppe* containing the remnants of the *Division*, parts of the *SS-Sturmbrigade "Dirlewanger"* and the Hungarian 2nd Armoured Division, reinforced by a number of German and Hungarian anti-aircraft artillery units. The latter were mainly deployed in the anti-tank block position north of Kemence.

38 *Budapestskaya Operaciya*. Contemporary summary of the 2nd Ukrainian Front about the operations around Budapest. (A copy owned by the author.) p.121.

39 *Budapestskaya Operaciya*. Contemporary composition of the 2nd Ukrainian Front. A copy owned by the author. p.122.

The strength of the German—Hungarian troops defending Ipolyság was considerably reduced by the fact that the German *II. Abteilung/Panzergrenadier-Regiment 26* of the *24. Panzer-Division* was transferred from that area. This battalion-sized unit represented a considerable combat force, for on that day alone it had knocked out nine Soviet tanks north of Hont (seven of which were knocked out by anti-tank weapons), repulsed all of the attacks launched by the Soviet forces and prevented them from breaking through. *Feldwebel* Julius Pöppel, platoon leader of the *5. Schwadron/Panzergrenadier-Regiment 26* destroyed four armoured fighting vehicles with *Panzerfäuste* on his own within two hours.[40] He was awarded the Knight's Cross of the Iron Cross for this achievement on 31 December.

The German *II. Abteilung/Panzergrenadier-Regiment 26*, which, at times, had a combat strength of only 60 soldiers, destroyed a total of 40 Soviet armoured fighting vehicles during the defence of the Ipolyság corridor by 14 December; most of them in close combat.[41]

According to the war diary of *Heeresgruppe Süd*, the relief of the *Panzergrenadier*-battalion on the night of 13/14 December by the incoming *SS-Sturmbrigade "Dirlewanger"* was not carried out properly, and this fact may have contributed to the loss of Ipolyság. The *SS*- battalion assigned to relieve the unit remained in the woods southeast of the village. Thus the weak securing forces defending Ipolyság were easily assaulted by the Soviet units after the *II. Abteilung/Panzergrenadier-Regiment 26* left the area.[42]

At 1400 hours in the afternoon, the *II. Sturmbataillon/SS-Regiment 1* of *SS-Sturmbrigade "Dirlewanger"* launched a counterattack from the northwest, and units of the *I. Sturmbataillon/SS-Regiment 1* of *SS-Sturmbrigade "Dirlewanger"* counterattacked from the northeast toward Ipolyság. The attack of the *I.* and *III. Sturmbataillon/SS-Regiment 1* from the Felsőtúr–Palást area reached the *Margarethen-Stellung (Line)* at the south-eastern outskirts of Kelenye and the area to its southwest.[43] The latter two battalions were presumably supported by the tanks, assault guns and *Jagdpanzers* of the *III. (Abteilung)/ Panzer-Regiment 24* that were standing by at Palást.

The commander of the 6th Guards Tank Army, Colonel General Kravchenko was at the command post of the 30th Guards Mechanized Brigade when the German counterattack reached the headquarters of the Soviet large military unit. Later he was informed that the Germans had cut the communication landlines between the army commander's command post and the reserve army commander's command post. Now Kravchenko, himself, was able to hear the sound of the engines of the approaching German armoured fighting vehicles[44]. Upon his orders the Soviet engineer troops blew up the bridges that were still standing on the Ipoly river. During these combat actions the commander of the 30th Guards Mechanized Brigade, Guards Colonel M. V. Sutov, was also severely wounded.[45]

The German—Hungarian air force flew a total of 260 sorties that day, mainly against

40 HM HIM *Hadtörténelmi Levéltár* (Budapest) microfilm archives, *Kriegstagebuch Ia der Heeresgruppe Süd, Tagesmeldung vom* 18. 12. 1944 (roll no. 627. image no. 7211818).

41 For this, see: Senger und Etterlin, 1962, p.281.

42 For this, see: HM HIM *Hadtörténelmi Levéltár* (Budapest) microfilm archives, *Kriegstagebuch Ia der Heeresgruppe Süd, Kriegstae buch vom 14. 12. 1944* (roll no. 626. image no. 7210863).

43 HM HIM *Hadtörténelmi Levéltár* (Budapest) microfilm archives, *Kriegstagebuch Ia der Heeresgruppe Süd, Kriegstagebuch vom* 14. 12. 1944 (roll no. 626. image no. 7210855).

44 These armoured fighting vehicles were presumably part of the armoured *Kampfgruppe* of the *24. Panzer-Division*.

45 Armstrong, Richard N., *Red Army Tank Commanders – The Armored Guards* (Atglen PA, 1994), p.434.

the Soviet attack positions identified between Ipolyság and Szécsény. In the meantime the aircraft destroyed a bridge on the Ipoly river east of Ipolyság, destroying approximately 50 horse-drawn wagons and motor vehicles, and shot down 17 Soviet aircraft.[46]

On **15 December 1944**[47], west of Nagyoroszi, on the front line of *Divisionsgruppe "Rintelen"*, Soviet units, by the light of night searchlights, dismantled the anti-tank obstacles established on the road.

Northeast of Bernecebaráti a considerable gap opened in the German—Hungarian front line. The reason for this was the fact that approximately 200 soldiers from the *III. SS-Sturmbataillon/SS-Regiment 2* of the *SS-Sturmbrigade "Dirlewanger"* left their positions. The Germans were informed by intercepted Soviet radio communications that the Soviets had taken 160 prisoners there. From this the Germans concluded that the missing soldiers had deserted and changed sides.

The attack of two battalions of *SS-Sturmbrigade "Dirlewanger"* from northwest and northeast to recapture Ipolyság failed. Armour of the Soviet 9th Guards Mechanized Corps came round Ipolyság from the east, advanced through Középtúr toward the north as far as the southern outskirts of Palást, westward to Gyerk, and occupied Pereszlény in the course of the combat.

The battalions of *SS-Sturmbrigade "Dirlewanger"* that were defending north and northwest from these positions retreated frantically toward the west. They were assigned new covering positions between Kistompa and Szalatnya. The organization thereof was assigned to *Generalmajor* Emmo von Roden, a General of *Heeresgruppe Süd* for special tasks [*z.b.V.*]. Northeast of Ipolyság, a battalion of *SS-Sturmbrigade "Dirlewanger"* was still attempting to occupy the section in the *Margarethen-Stellung (Line)* southwest of Kelenye.[48]

The combat situation was considered to be extremely dangerous for the German troops, therefore the *Oberbefehlshaber* [commander in chief] *der Heeresgruppe Süd, Generaloberst* Friessner also visited the command post of *"SS-Sturmbrigade "Dirlewanger"* and ordered that the wooded area northeast of Ipolyság be held at all costs.

Generalleutnant Helmuth von Grolman, Chief of Staff of *Heeresgruppe Süd* ordered that anti-aircraft guns were to be transported to the area of penetration from the area of Esztergom; that the full strength of the Hungarian 2nd Armoured Division (including all armoured fighting vehicles still under repair) was to be deployed on the Ipolyság front line, and that the *357. Infanterie-Division* was to relocate its command post from Vámosmikola closer to the penetration point in order to maintain better communication.[49]

Early in the afternoon the *Heeresgruppe* informed *Armeegruppe "Fretter-Pico"* that the (self-propelled) *leichte Flak-Abteilung 77* was also be employed at Ipolyság. It also stated that one battalion of the *357. Infanterie-Division*, which had been committed elsewhere, and units of *Artillerie-Regiment 357* had also been transferred there. Two companies of

46 HM HIM *Hadtörténelmi Levéltár* (Budapest) microfilm archives, *Kriegstagebuch Ia der Heeresgruppe Süd, Kriegstagebuch vom 14. 12. 1944* (roll no. 626. image no. 7210856. and next image).

47 Weather: 0-2° Celsius during the day, cloud cover, snow; minor roads and the terrain were sodden, tracked vehicles were moving with considerable difficulties.

48 HM HIM *Hadtörténelmi Levéltár* (Budapest) microfilm archives, *Kriegstagebuch Ia der Heeresgruppe Süd, Kriegstagebuch vom 15. 12. 1944* (roll no. 626. image no. 7210871. and next image).

49 HM HIM *Hadtörténelmi Levéltár* (Budapest) microfilm archives, *Kriegstagebuch Ia der Heeresgruppe Süd, Kriegstagebuch vom 15. 12. 1944* (roll no. 626. image no. 7210880. and next image).

the battalion were immediately committed that afternoon in a counterattack to secure and close the gap northeast of Bernecebaráti. The village itself was under German—Hungarian control.

The anti-tank blocking position established in the area was attacked by the Soviet 30th Guards Mechanized Brigade/9th Guards Mechanized Corps from the south-western outskirts of Homok; eight of their 22 tanks were knocked out by the defenders and the attack itself was repulsed.[50] Five of the knocked out armoured fighting vehicles (one T–34/85 and four M4A2s) were knocked out by the German anti-tank-guns of *Divisionsgruppe "Rintelen"*.

It became necessary to establish a *Korps* command in order to provide better command and control, and, above all, to maintain unified command of the artillery. Therefore, the German *LXXII. Armeekorps*, which also had its own *Artilleriekommandeur* (Artillery Commander, or *Arko* 472), received its orders that same day to assume command and control of the area between the northern side of the Pest bridgehead and the left boundary of the sector of the German *6. Armee*, the Slovak-Hungarian border. *Korpskommandeur Generalleutnant* August Schmidt then visited the command post of *Divisionsguppe "Rintelen"* at Vámosmikola, to be briefed on the combat situation. The Chief of Staff of the *Armeekorps* remained at the former command post at Alcsút in order to handle further details of the transfer of the former front line sector with the *LVII. Panzerkorps*.

Late at night, after 2200 hours, *Generalleutnant* Grolman and *Generalmajor* Heinz Gaedcke, Chief of Staff of *Armeegruppe "Fretter-Pico"*, discussed further details of the possibilities for solving the problem of Ipolyság. In Gaedcke's opinion the following possibilities could be taken into consideration:

1. It seemed meaningless to deploy the units of the Division *"Szent László"* that were assembling at Mór and at Ipolyság, because the unit was defenceless against strong tank formations;
2. Relief of the German *1.* and *23. Panzer-Division*, their replacement by the Division *"Szent László"*, and their deployment at Ipolyság was impossible, since the area of Székesfehérvár had to be secured at all costs in order to prepare for the coming great Soviet offensive;
3. Transfer of the German *8. Panzer-Division* to Ipolyság had the inherent danger that Soviet forces might break through between the Velence Lake [*Velencesee*] and Budapest;
4. The joint deployment of the Division *"Szent László"* and a German *Panzer-Abteilung*, supported by *Panther* tanks, under command of the *13. Panzer-Division* or of *Panzer-Division "Feldherrnhalle"* would have reduced the probability of success of the planned German counterattack at the Dunántúl (Transdanubia).

Generalmajor Gaedcke wanted to equip the 25 *Jagdpanzer* 38(t) tank destroyers, intended to be assigned the next day to the Hungarian 2nd Armoured Division, with German crews, and wanted them to be immediately deployed at the penetration point. In the end the two Generals agreed that *Divisionsguppe "Rintelen"* was to try to hold and contain the further western and south-western Soviet advance in the area of Ipolyság, and

50 HM HIM *Hadtörténelmi Levéltár* (Budapest) microfilm archives, *Kriegstagebuch Ia der Heeresgruppe Süd, Kriegstagebuch vom* 15. 12. 1944 (roll no. 626. image no. 7210882).

that the northern direction was to be covered by the German *24. Panzer-Division* as far as the railway extending along the north-western side of the village; furthermore, together with the attached units of *SS-Sturmbrigade "Dirlewanger"*, it was to prevent the Soviet forces from entering Slovakia. Any decision regarding transfer of German armoured troops would be made the next day, if they received a more precise picture of the situation and the intentions of the Soviet troops.

The Soviet troops had been continuously attacking Szécsény for days on the front line of the *IV. Panzerkorps/ Armeegruppe "Wöhler"*. Cavalry Mechanized Group "Pliev" was reinforced that day with units of the 72nd Guards Rifle Division.[51]

The Soviet troops again committed tanks. 1.5km southwest of Szécsény, in the area of Hermina farm, the 15th Guards Mechanized Brigade, together with 15 armoured fighting vehicles of the 36th Guards Tank Brigade, broke into the German defences in a surprise attack and, by 1600 hours, occupied 15 houses on the south-western side of the town. At this time the 14th Guards Mechanized Brigade was in combat 900 metres north of Szécsény. At 1700 hours the Germans launched a counterattack with infantry, armoured fighting vehicles and armoured personnel carriers against the units of the 14th Guards and the 15th Guards Mechanized Brigades and drove them back. The 15th Guards Mechanized Brigade had to abandon the houses that it had already occupied.[52]

From west, southwest and south, infantry assaults in battalion-strength were successively launched against the town.[53] The units defending Szécsény, namely, the German *46. Infanterie-Division*[54], reinforced by units of the *18. SS-Panzergrenadier-Division*[55] and the troops of the *24. Panzer-Division*[56], repulsed all of the attacks.

On **16 December 1944**[57], at 0000 hours, the Commander in Chief of the *LXXII. Armeekorps, Generalleutnant* Schmidt, took over the command and control on the front line along the Ipoly.[58] The most critical point was located west of Ipolyság, where units of the Soviet 6th Guards Tank Army had already entered.

On the night of 15/16 December, the assigned new front line of *LXXII. Armeekorps* was still defended by the *Divisionsgruppe "Rintelen"*. *Divisionsgruppe "Rintelen"* planned to hold its retreating infantry along the line 1.5km southwest of Kistompa – point no. 125 along the Selmec-patak – Felsőszemeréd – Királyfia line, where they were to be employed

51 HM HIM *Hadtörténelmi Levéltár* (Budapest), *Szovjet iratmásolatok gyűjteménye a Budapest körüli harcokról. A 2. Ukrán Front hadijelentései,* 1944. December 15.

52 Loza, 1967, p.618.

53 HM HIM *Hadtörténelmi Levéltár* (Budapest) microfilm archives, *Kriegstagebuch Ia der Heeresgruppe Süd, Kriegstagebuch vom* 15. 12. 1944 (roll no. 626. image no. 7210872).

54 Of the *StuG* III assault guns of the *46. Infanterie-Division*, three were in combat-ready condition.

55 Of the 10 assault guns and *Jagdpanzers* of the *SS-Panzergrenadier-Regiment 18*, five were combat-ready, and, of the 26 armoured fighting vehicles of the *SS-Panzergrenadier-Regiment 4,* 13 were combat-ready.

56 That day, of the 27 *Panzer* IV tanks and *Panzer* IV/70 (A) *Jagdpanzers* of the *24. Panzer-Division,* only four were in combat-ready condition. None of the nine assault guns were combat-ready. See: *Bundesarchiv–Militärarchiv* (Freiburg im Breisgau), *RH 2 Ost Lagekarten 5231.*

57 Weather: frost during the night, 3° Celsius during the day, the sky was cloudy; the minor roads and the terrain were thoroughly soaked, tracked vehicles were moving with difficulty.

58 *Bundesarchiv–Militärarchiv* (Freiburg im Breisgau), RH 24–72, *Kriegstagebuch Ia des LXXII. Armeekorps,* 15. 12. 1944.

in the defence of a new MLR.[59]

The Hungarian 2nd Armoured Division was assigned to further defend its MLR and prevent Soviet troops from penetrating the positions along the Danube and in the gap between the left flank of the German *II. Bataillon/Pionier-Regiment 52* and the right flank of the Hungarian 4th Motorized Rifle Battalion[60]. The Soviet forces that had already broken in were to be destroyed and the former positions of the *III. SS-Sturmbataillon/SS-Regiment 2* were to be regained.

In order to carry out this task a new German unit was provided to the division, *Kampfgruppe "Hafner"*[61], two companies of which carried out a successful counterattack east of Kemence and in the area of Bernecebaráti. The most important task of the Hungarian unit was to prevent the Soviets from outflanking the blocking position that had been created with anti-aircraft guns north of Kemence.

According to data as of 16 December, the Hungarian 2nd Armoured Division had the following combat strength to carry out the task:

- 4th Motorized Rifle Battalion with 147 men;
- 5th Motorized Rifle Battalion with 949 men (full combat strength);
- 6th Motorized Rifle Battalion with 951 men (full combat strength);
- 2nd Reconnaissance Battalion with 82 men;
- 2nd Armoured Engineer Battalion with 128 men;
- German *Kampfgruppe "Miedeck"* with 300 Germans and 103 Hungarians;
- German *Kampfgruppe "Hafner"* with 450 Germans and 61 Hungarians;
- German *Kampfgruppe "Struchtemayer"* with 350 Germans and 99 Hungarians;
- German *Kampfgruppe "Zirke"* with 264 men;
- Two combat-ready *Panzer* IVs and four *Toldi* tanks, five *Nimród* armoured self-propelled anti-aircraft guns, six 7.5cm anti-tank guns, 19 10.5cm light field howitzers.[62]

The remnants of the *357. Infanterie-Division* were to establish new defence positions along the Selmec-patak and secure the crossing points with anti-aircraft and anti-tank guns.[63] The division had to rely exclusively on the following units to carry out this task: 270 soldiers of the remnants of *SS-Sturmbrigade "Dirlewanger"* and four 7.5cm anti-tank guns of *Panzerjäger-Abteilung 357*, two 10.5cm howitzers of the Hungarian 2nd Towed Artillery Battalion, and eight of the 5th Artillery Battalion, and two mortars of the German *schwere Artillerie-Abteilung 736*.

59 *Bundesarchiv–Militärarchiv* (Freiburg im Breisgau), RH 24–72, *Morgenmeldung der Div. Grp.Rintelen, Ia an AOK* 6, 16. 12. 1944.

60 From the Battalion, significant forces (300 men, led by 1st Lieutenant Imre Koós) went over to the Soviet side. See: HM HIM *Hadtörténelmi Levéltár (Budapest), Fővezérség meghatalmazott tábornoka naplója* (Diary of the appointed General of the High Command) p.25.

61 *Hauptmann* Otto Hafner was the commander of the *Kampfgruppe* composed of the various German and Hungarian elements and the remnants of the two battalions of *SS-Sturmbrigade "Dirlewanger"*.

62 *Bundesarchiv–Militärarchiv* (Freiburg im Breisgau), RH 24–72, *Fernschreiben an Armeegruppe Fretter-Pico, 17. 12. 1944, Anlage Nr. 1030.*

63 *Bundesarchiv–Militärarchiv* (Freiburg im Breisgau), RH 24–72, *Korpsbefehl für die Übernahme des Befehls über den Abschnitt der Donau und ungarisch-slowakischen Landesgrenze durch LXXII. A.K., 16. 12. 1944.*

That same day *LXXII. Armeekorps* has established its command post at Vámosmikola. During the afternoon a discussion took place between the Commander in Chief of the German *6. Armee, General der Artillerie* Maximilian Fretter-Pico and the *Korps* Commander considering the situation.

During the day, at 0730 hours in the morning, a counterattack was launched on the front line of the Hungarian 2nd Armoured Division[64], attached to the *Korps*, toward Kinszky farm; the farmstead was recaptured by 1000. Hill 386, 6km south of Ipolyság, and Irtványi Hill south of the Csitári-puszta (Hill 363) were attacked by a battalion-sized Soviet unit. At about 1500 hours the Soviet units occupied Hill 455 (2km south of Irtványi Hill), and Irtványi Hill itself at 1630 hours. Soviet troops also exerted heavy pressure on both sides of the Nagy Valley in the direction of Kemence.

At the end of the day the Hungarian 2nd Armoured Division had one combat-ready assault gun, two 7.5cm anti-tank guns and four 8cm anti-aircraft guns. Six *Nimród* armoured self-propelled anti-aircraft guns and two of the division's 8cm anti-aircraft guns were destroyed during the day's fighting.[65]

During the previous night, the Soviet 9th Guards Mechanized Corps advanced through Kistúr and occupied Palást with two tanks groups, escorted by infantry, and advanced through Gyerk with a third tank group to take Kistompa. The Soviet tank and mechanized brigades did not advance further, but occupied the villages that had already been taken or that were already behind them. This way, Kistúr, Középtúr, Felsőtúr, Palást, Szalatnya, Kistompa and Gyerk went over to Soviet hands on 16 December.[66]

The German commander in Slovakia planned to deploy *Alarmtruppen* against the Soviet units that were attacking from Palást toward the north, and a number of tanks and assault guns from those that were under repair were to be deployed at Krupina (Korpona).[67]

Only two to three companies of Soviet infantry attacked the front line of *Divisionsgruppe "Rintelen"* that day, supported by five to six tanks. The Germans knocked out one armoured fighting vehicle using a *Panzerfaust*.

The combat strength in the *Divisionsgruppe* was only 130 men. The *Flak* units had two 8.8cm guns, three 3.7cm and five 2cm cannon. These units secuered 4km east of Deménd, between points no. 200 and 204, after they had been driven back toward Deménd by the Soviet forces.

The *I.* and *III. SS-Sturmbataillon/SS-Regiment 1* deployed between Ipolyság and Kelenye were, according to the report by the *Ordonnanz* of the *SS-Sturmbrigade "Dirlewanger"*, assaulted by considerable Soviet infantry and tank forces at about 1200 hours. Both *SS-* battalions retreated northwards into the woods.[68]

The Soviet tank crews questioned civilians about the quality of the roads leading to Korpona. At about 1500 hours 20 Soviet tanks were observed assembling in Felsőszemeréd.

---

64 The Hungarian 2nd Armoured Division reported to the *LXXII. Armeekorps* via the German communications unit *D.V.K.* 149 assigned to them.

65 *Bundesarchiv–Militärarchiv* (Freiburg im Breisgau), RH 24–72, *Kriegstagebuch Ia des LXXII. Armeekorps, Tagesmeldungen unterstellter Einheiten vom* 16. 12. 1944.

66 HM HIM *Hadtörténelmi Levéltár* (Budapest), *Szovjet iratmásolatok gyűjteménye a Budapest körüli harcokról. A 2. Ukrán Front hadijelentései,* 1944. December 16.

67 HM HIM *Hadtörténelmi Levéltár* (Budapest) microfilm archives, *Kriegstagebuch Ia der Heeresgruppe Süd, Kriegstagebuch vom* 16. 12. 1944 (roll no. 627. image no. 7211109).

68 *Bundesarchiv–Militärarchiv* (Freiburg im Breisgau), RH 24–72, *Kriegstagebuch Ia des LXXII. Armeekorps, Tagesmeldungen unterstellter Einheiten vom* 16. 12. 1944.

Soviet reconnaissance units, supported by tanks, appeared in Egeg. Gyűgy and Alsóterény were occupied by weak German securing forces.

That same day the *3.* (armoured personnel carrier) *Kompanie/Panzer-Pionier-Bataillon/Panzer-Division "Feldherrnhalle"*, the *3. Kompanie/Maschinengewehr-Bataillon "Sachsen"*, the Hungarian 5th Light Artillery Battalion and the *Stab/schwere Artillerie-Abteilung 809* were attached to *Divisionsgruppe "Rintelen"*.[69]

Generalleutnant Schmidt and his staff had the impression that the Soviet infantry was going to try to advance westward and attack the blocking position that had been established north of Kemence, which was defended to the rear by *Flak* units.

During the morning, the Chief of Staff of *Heeresgruppe Süd*, *Generalleutnant* Grolman made his decision about solving the problem of Ipolyság. At about 1025 hours, *Armeegruppe "Fretter-Pico"* received orders to relocate the German *8. Panzer-Division*[70] – for the time being, minus its *I. (Abteilung)/Panzer-Regiment 10* – together with its *Panzergrenadiers*, artillery, anti-tank guns and *Jagdpanzers*, to the south-western outskirts of Ipolyság, whence the division was to attack and retake the village. The prerequisite for the successful assault was that elements of *SS-Sturmbrigade "Dirlewanger"* had to hold the wooded area northeast of Ipolyság. In this way, theoretically, it became possible to close the Ipolyság corridor and to cut the supply line of the Soviet troops that had already broken into the area.

According to records of the Hungarian General Staff, the following units were attached to *LXXII. Armeekorps*: two artillery batteries of the *153. Feldausbildungs-Division*, a Hungarian assault artillery battalion with *Jagdpanzer* 38(t) tank destroyers and two tank battalions of the Hungarian 2nd Armoured Division. These forces were to be employed to repulse the Soviet forces that were entering the Ipolyság corridor.[71]

Approval of the divided use of the *8. Panzer-Division* was requested by *Generaloberst* Friessner at about 1300 hours, during a situational report from Chief of Staff of the *Heer* (*Chef des Generalstabs des Heeres*) *Generaloberst* Heinz Guderian. Guderian first asked if the *Luftwaffe* would be able to solve the situation emerging at Ipolyság. The Commander in Chief of *Heeresgruppe Süd* answered that all possibilities had been taken into account, and that a more effective intervention than air raids was needed. *Generaloberst* Guderian then approved divided deployment of the *8. Panzer-Division*: the larger part of the forces to be committed at Ipolyság while the unit's armoured *Kampfgruppe* was to be held in ready reserve behind the *Margarethen-Stellung (Line)*.[72]

Based on the above-mentioned facts, it can clearly be seen that the idea of splitting up the *8. Panzer-Division*, although born of necessity, originated with the high command of *Heeresgruppe Süd*, and that *Generaloberst* Guderian had only given his approval. *Generaloberst* Friessner hoped that the *8. Panzer-Division* would swiftly accomplish its tasks along the Ipoly and would be able to return to the Dunántúl (Transdanubia) soon,

69 HM HIM *Hadtörténelmi Levéltár* (Budapest) microfilm archives, *Kriegstagebuch Ia der Heeresgruppe Süd, Tagesmeldung vom* 16. 12. 1944 (roll no. 627. image no. 7211801).

70 The *8. Panzer-Division* had on that day 24 combat-ready *Panther* and eight *Panzer* IV tanks, six *Jagdpanzer* IV tank destroyers and eight *Marder* tank destroyers. Combat strength of their *Panzergrenadiers* counted to approximately 2100 men.

71 HM HIM *Hadtörténelmi Levéltár* (Budapest), *VKF Fővezérség hadműveleti osztályának napi helyzettájékoztatója*, 1944. December 16., p.2.

72 HM HIM *Hadtörténelmi Levéltár* (Budapest) microfilm archives, *Kriegstagebuch Ia der Heeresgruppe Süd, Kriegstagebuch vom* 16. 12. 1944 (roll no. 627. image no. 7211106-7211108).

because the unit was also needed for Operation "*Spätlese*".

Command and control of the defensive fighting north of Ipolyság was transferred that day from the *24. Panzer-Division*[73] to the *18. SS-Freiwilligen Panzergrenadier-Division "Horst Wessel"*, with command post established on Korpona.

On the front line of *IV. Panzerkorps/Armeegruppe "Wöhler"*, the Soviet 4th Guards Mechanized Corps/Cavalry Mechanized Group "Pliev" renewed its attacks from the southwest and south against the German forces defending Szécsény. These attacks were repulsed and three Soviet armoured fighting vehicles knocked out.

The Soviets regrouped their cavalry forces, then broke into the weak securing line south of Nagylóc. Elements of the 6th Guards Cavalry Corps occupied Nagybárkány and Kisbárkány. The cavalry division at the head of the 4th Guards Cavalry Corps reached Hollókő around 1800 hours.

On the night of **16/17 December 1944**[74], *Generalmajor* Gottfried Fröhlich, Commander of the *8. Panzer-Division*, arrived at the *LXXII. Armeekorps* command post and discussed the planned employment of his division on 17 December. The first relocated units of the *8. Panzer-Division* had already arrived during the night, and were immediately sent to their attack positions.[75]

Following an extremely quiet night, there were only minor local engagements on the front line of *LXXII. Armeekorps* during the day. According to the morning report, the following units had been attached to the Hungarian 2nd Armoured Division:

- 2nd Reconnaissance Battalion (six officers, 176 enlisted men);
- 4th Motorized Rifle Battalion (14 officers, 133 enlisted men);
- German *Kampfgruppe "Zirke"* (three officers, 472 enlisted men);
- German *Kampfgruppe "Miedeck"* (14 officers, 389 enlisted men);
- German *Kampfgruppe "Hafner"* (13 officers, 498 enlisted men);
- German *Kampfgruppe "Struchtenmayer"* (six officers, 301 enlisted men);
- 2nd Towed Artillery Battalion (11 10.5cm light field howitzers);
- 6th Towed Artillery Battalion (eight 10.5cm light field howitzers);
- One combat-ready assault gun and two 7.5cm anti-tank guns.[76]

However, there was considerable Soviet combat activity on the right flank of the *Armeekorps*. Forces of the 53rd Rifle Division approached Kismaros from the west and were only 2km away from the village. West of the village the strength of the defence consisted of only 100 German soldiers and some Hungarian anti-aircraft and anti-tank guns. The German—Hungarian reconnaissance troops identified Soviet artillery and rocket launcher positions at Nógrádverőce and units amounting to the strength of two battalions of the

73 The *24. Panzer-Division* had on that day one combat-ready *Panzer* III command tank, two *Panzer* IV tanks and two *StuG.* III assault guns. Combat strength of their *Panzergrenadiers* was approximately 800 men.

74 Weather: frost during the night, 5° Celsius during the day, cloudy sky in the area of *Armeegruppe "Fretter-Pico"*, otherwise the sky was clear, minor roads and terrain were drying up.

75 *Bundesarchiv–Militärarchiv* (Freiburg im Breisgau), RH 24–72, *Kriegstagebuch Ia des LXXII. Armeekorps*, 16. 12. 1944.

76 *Bundesarchiv–Militärarchiv* (Freiburg im Breisgau), RH 24–72, *Kriegstagebuch Ia des LXXII. Armeekorps, Morgenmeldungen unterstellter Einheiten vom* 17. 12. 1944. (Combat strength in brackets).

409th Rifle Division at Szokolya. The defenders repulsed the westward facing attack of a company-sized unit of the latter.

That same day, the Soviet 27th Independent Guards Tank Brigade assembled in the Őrszentmiklós area in order to march to Szokolya, as had been previously ordered. At 1630 hours in the afternoon, the 1st and 2nd Tank Battalion and the motorized battalion of the brigade commenced their march through the villages of Vácrátót, Vácduka, Rád, Keszeg, Ősagárd, Nőtincs and Berkenye with nine T–34s, four SU–85s and one SU–76M self-propelled gun. In order to maintain communication with the armoured fighting vehicles, the mobile radio stations of the brigade staff were also deployed. In the evening, the units stopped at Felsőpenc in order to be able to carry out necessary maintenance works on the armoured fighting vehicles.[77]

The Soviet attacks on Hill 421, 6km east of Kemence, also failed. The German—Hungarian troops reoccupied Irtványi Hill south of the Csitári-puszta at 1130 hours in the morning, but it was lost again to three new Soviet assaults carried out by battalion-sized forces. Kinszky farm, 3km southwest of Ipolyság, was attacked by a battalion-sized Soviet unit with fire support from artillery, anti-tank guns and tanks. However, the attempt was halted by the fire of the German—Hungarian artillery, anti-aircraft guns and cannon. According to Soviet data they lost at least 40 dead. According to Hungarian reports 30 Soviet tanks gathered in the area of Homok and the Pereszlényi-puszta.

At 1710 hours German reconnaissance identified five Soviet tanks of the 9th Guards Mechanized Corps which entered Egeg and then advanced toward Gyűgy. A further 20 Soviet armoured fighting vehicles were observed coming from the direction of Szalatnya and advancing north-west toward Egeg.

Although *Divisionsgruppe "Rintelen"* ordered the German *I. Bataillon/Pionier-Brigade 52* to blow up the stone bridge at the northern outskirts of Egeg and mine the crossroads south of Gyűgy, the execution of the order was prevented by the German *24. Panzer-Division*. According to other sources the bridge was saved from destruction by two *leventes*[78] from Egeg, who, unnoticed, pulled the wires out of the detonator. The Germans intended to destroy the bridge by using a total of a 12 anti-tank mines, but failed. The mines remained in their positions until 1967.[79]

The blocking position east of Deménd, organized by *SS-Hauptsturmführer* Harald Momm in front of the sector of *Divisionsgruppe "Rintelen"*, reporting a combat strength of only 100 men, was still holding out, although it was repeatedly assaulted by company-sized Soviet units.[80]

77 Combat report of the 27th Independent Guards Tank Brigade to the commander of the 7th Guards Army tank and mechanized troops (a copy owned by the author), 17 December 1944.

78 The so-called "*Levente* Movement" was a combination of movements dedicated to prepare 12-21 year old boys of Hungarian nationality for military training and to educate them along the national principles. The *Levente* organizations were established on the basis of the Act LIII of 1921 on physical exercises (1921: LIII. *törvénycikk: a testnevelésről)*. The Act II of 1939 on national defence (1939: II. *törvénycikk: honvédelmi törvény*) assigned the *Levente* training among the military and national defence obligations of boys from the age of 12 until entering military service: it constituted a 10-month training course each year, with four hours of exercises per week, in groups selected on the basis of age. After the seizure of power by the Arrow Cross Party on 16 October 1944 the *Leventes* were also thrown into combat, equipped mostly with handheld anti-tank weapons.

79 Recollections of local residents as communicated to the author by Mr. Andráš Péter in writing.

80 *Bundesarchiv–Militärarchiv* (Freiburg im Breisgau), RH 24–72, *Kriegstagebuch Ia des LXXII. Armeekorps,* 17. 12. 1944. On 15 December, *SS-Hauptsturmführer* Momm, after suppressing the panic spread among

That same day, the main body of the *8. Panzer-Division* arrived (minus the armoured *Kampfgruppe* left near Székesfehérvár) and prepared to launch an assault on the night of 17/18 December to capture the Ipolyság gateway.

However, the arrival of *Panzerjäger-Abteilung 43,* which was entraining in Bicske as of 0600 hours could not be anticipated before the afternoon of 18 December, because, in the absence of sufficient wagons, the unit was still stranded in Bicske at about 1500 hours. The *Jagdpanzers* and tank destroyers of *Panzerjäger-Abteilung 43* comprised the majority of the division's armoured fighting vehicles intended for deployment along the Ipoly. Their delay was extremely disadvantageous for the planned assault by the *8. Panzer-Division.*

At the same time, however, radio communication was established with the *24. Panzer-Division,* which was to attack from the Kelenye area, advancing toward the south-west toward the units of the *8. Panzer-Division* that were heading northeast. According to the plans, this attack of the two *Panzer* divisions would have cut the supply lines of the Soviet forces that had broken into the Ipolyság gateway toward the northwest, thereby facilitating the destruction of these units.[81]

The command post of the 8. *Panzer-Division* was at Ipolyszakállos. The unit had, for the time being, only eight combat-ready *Panzer* IV tanks and 14 towed 7.5 anti-tank guns. *Kampfgruppe "Grosse"*, which was attached to the unit had no winter battledress, therefore the commander requested 500 camouflage pattern battledress from the *Armeekorps.*

LXXII. Armeekorps' battle plan for the *8. Panzer-Division* attached the division to *Kampfgruppe "Fröhlich"*. According to this plan, the *Kampfgruppe* was to set off from its positions east of Bernecebaráti on the night of 17/18 December and vanquish the Soviet forces positioned in the northwestern outskirts of the Börzsöny. It was to start from the rear and eliminate the anti-tank area established southwest of Ipolyság, and, as an immediate objective, was to reach the Hont – Ipolyság line. Two *Panzergrenadier* battalions were to be deployed. The task of the third battalion was to eliminate the anti-tank positions at Ipolyság. After the *Kampfgruppe* occupied Ipolyság and established a blocking position to the north and west, and following the regrouping and arrival of the armoured fighting vehicles of *Panzerjäger-Abteilung 43*, the attack was to continue toward the east, with a subsequent objective of occupying Drégelypalánk and Ipolyhidvég and blocking the corridor toward the southeast, east and northeast. Following this the armoured units of the *Kampfgruppe* were to attack through Ipolyság toward the west – northwest in order to attack the Soviet forces from the rear and destroy any units that might have have arrived there.

The flanks of *Kampfgruppe "Fröhlich"* were covered by the units of *Kampfgruppe "Grosse"*, the Hungarian 2nd Armoured Division on the right, and *Divisionsgruppe "Rintelen"* on the left. The reinforced *II. (Abteilung)/Flak-Regiment 24* supported *Kampfgruppe "Fröhlich"*, and was to establish an anti-tank blocking position facing north and north-west

the soldiers of the *SS-Sturmbrigade "Dirlewanger"*, improvised a front line 1km west of Kistompa with 27 soldiers, three light anti-tank guns and one 8cm mortar. The well-directed and concentrated fire of this small formation made it extremely difficult for the Soviets to rebuild the demolished bridge east of Kistompa, and to advance further westwards. Thus the formation helped strengthen the German blocking position at Deménd. Momm was an *Oberst* in the *Heer* earlier, but was degraded in consequence of his comments on the attempt to kill Hitler on 20 July, and because of his friendship with *Oberst Graf* Claus Schenk von Stauffenberg. In retribution he was appointed as commander of one of the battalions of *SS-Sturmbrigade "Dirlewanger"*.

81 *Bundesarchiv–Militärarchiv* (Freiburg im Breisgau), RH 24–72, *Kriegstagebuch Ia des LXXII. Armeekorps*, 17. 12. 1944.

after occupation of the Ipolyság bridgehead. The reinforced *I. (Abteilung)/Flak-Regiment 48* was to support *Divisionsgruppe "Rintelen"*, in case the front line was assaulted by Soviet tanks.[82]

The artillery of *LXXII. Armeekorps* consisted of 47 combat-ready guns that day. The Hungarian 5th Towed Artillery Battalion was positioned in the Deménd area with two batteries, the German *II. (Abteilung)/Panzer-Artillerie-Regiment 80* stood near Csarnapuszta, and the *III. (Abteilung)/Panzer-Artillerie-Regiment 80* was positioned near László-puszta. The *2. Batterie/schwere Artillerie-Abteilung 736* switched positions toward Ipolyszakállos.[83]

The previous evening, the Soviet units occupied Pásztó on the front line of the *IV. Panzerkorps* of *Armeegruppe "Wöhler"*. The units of the *Armeekorps* established new defence positions on the Mátra west – tari szűkület (Tar-gorge) – Nagybárkány east area.

During the morning, the Soviet units launched a new attack against Szécsény with strong infantry forces supported by 16 armoured fighting vehicles. The attackers broke into the town, but the German defenders sealed the gap with a counterattack and knocked out four tanks. During the afternoon, repeated Soviet attacks were launched with battalion-sized forces from the west and south in order to occupy the town. However, they failed, as the defenders repelled all combat actions initiated by the Soviets.[84]

Until dawn on **18 December 1944**[85], the front line of the Hungarian 2nd Armoured Division remained quiet, except for two small-scale Soviet attacks which were repelled. During the morning the division reported the following strengths:

- 2nd Reconnaissance Battalion (six officers, 176 enlisted men);
- 4th Motorized Rifle Battalion (14 officers, 131 enlisted men);
- German *Kampfgruppe "Zirke"* (80 men);
- German *Kampfgruppe "Miedeck"* (10 officers, 290 enlisted men);
- German *Kampfgruppe "Hafner"* (11 officers, 350 enlisted men);
- German *Kampfgruppe "Struchtenmayer"* (five officers, 304 enlisted men);
- German *II. SS-Sturmbataillon/SS-Regiment 2* (two officers, 252 enlisted men);
- German *II. SS-Sturmbataillon/SS-Regiment 3* (two officers, 79 enlisted men);
- 6th Towed Artillery Battalion (eight 10.5cm light field howitzers);
- Two combat-ready *Panzer* IVs and four *Toldi* tanks, five *Nimród* armoured self-propelled anti-aircraft guns and six 7.5cm anti-tank guns.

The *8. Panzer-Division* launched its attack before sunrise, even though *Kampfgruppe "Amsel"*[86], based on *Panzerjäger-Abteilung 43,* had not arrived yet. The division had eight

82 *Bundesarchiv–Militärarchiv* (Freiburg im Breisgau), RH 24–72, *Korpsbefehl für den Angriff der Gruppe Fröhlich zur Gewinnung der Enge von Ipolyság*, 17. 12. 1944.

83 *Bundesarchiv–Militärarchiv* (Freiburg im Breisgau), RH 24–72, *Kriegstagebuch Ia des LXXII. Armeekorps, Tagesmeldungen unterstellter Einheiten vom* 17. 12. 1944.

84 HM HIM *Hadtörténelmi Levéltár* (Budapest) microfilm archives, *Kriegstagebuch Ia der Heeresgruppe Süd, Kriegstagebuch vom* 17. 12. 1944 (roll no. 627. image no. 7211117).

85 Weather: 5° Celsius during the day, fog, with possible rain and snow; minor roads and terrain were again thoroughly soaked, therefore, inaccessible for tracked vehicles.

86 The *Kampfgruppe* was commanded by the commander of *Panzerjäger-Abteilung 43*, *Major* Georg Amsel.

combat-ready *Panzer* IV tanks and 14 towed 7.5cm anti-tank guns. In addition, for the attack it was also reinforced with nine combat-ready *Panzer* IV tanks of the *10. Schwadron/Panzer-Regiment 24* of the *24. Panzer-Division* (Oberleutnant Pilder).[87]

At the same time that the attack of the *8. Panzer-Division* was launched, units of the 25th Guards Rifle Corps/Soviet 7th Guards Army also swung into action on the right flank of *LXXII. Armeekorps*, advancing westward from the Kismaros–Szokolya line on a broad front.

The German—Hungarian securing forces of the Hungarian 2nd Armoured Division were locally forced back, but some units continued to hold in their well-chosen mountain positions and repulsed the attacking Soviet forces.

The hills north of Nagymaros remained in German—Hungarian hands, although Soviet troops attacked from the direction of Klöcki Hill at about 0830 hours and drove the 2nd Reconnaissance Battalion back toward Kóspallag. Forces of the Soviet 409th Rifle Division reached the eastern outskirts of Kóspallag at about 1515 hours. They then attacked from the south, east and north with regiment-sized forces and, after heavy street fighting, occupied the village at about 1800 hours. The new German—Hungarian blocking position was established 500 metres west of Kóspallag on the hills along the road leading toward Márianosztra.

Kampfgruppe "Zirke" was attacked twice by battalion-sized forces of the 53rd Rifle Division from the western outskirts of Kismaros and from the Jánosdomb; the Germans therefore retreated to the line extending between the Hills 104 and 225. In order to strengthen the *Kampfgruppe*, *LXXII. Armeekorps* sent three companies of the German *Maschinengewehr-Bataillon "Sachsen"* and one *Flak* unit with six 3.7cm and two 2cm guns. The commander of the latter was *Hauptmann* Bode. The mission of these units was to reinforce the defence of the southern flank.

The Germans managed to halt the battalion-sized attacks of the Soviet 141st Rifle Division/27th Guards Rifle Corps 3km northwest of Diósjenő and 2km west of Kámor (Hill 662).

The Soviet units could not advance further on the hills east of Kemence. The German—Hungarian forces that were attached to the Hungarian 2nd Armoured Division also suffered serious losses on that day. Units of German *Pionier-Bataillon 751* from the Budapest bridgehead arrived at the division that same day, and the *3. Kompanie/Maschinengewehr-Bataillon "Sachsen"* arrived at *Kampfgruppe "Zirke"*.

By order of *LXXII. Armeekorps* all usable roads in the Börzsöny were to be blocked by felled trees, hillside demolitions, mines and camouflaged demolition charges. The trees were felled by civilian work crews.[88]

The Soviet 27th Independent Guards Tank Brigade continued its march and concentrated at Szendehely at about 1600 hours with 12 operational T–34 tanks, four SU–85 and one SU–76M self-propelled guns to support the forces of the 409th and the 53rd Rifle Divisions.[89]

---

87 *Bundesarchiv–Militärarchiv* (Freiburg im Breisgau), RH 24–72, *Kriegstagebuch Ia des LXXII. Armeekorps, Morgenmeldungen unterstellter Einheiten vom* 18. 12. 1944.

88 *Bundesarchiv–Militärarchiv* (Freiburg im Breisgau), RH 24–72, *Gen. Kdo. LXXII. A.K. Ia Nr. 2884/44 geh. 18. 12. 1944, Anlage Nr. 1040.*

89 Combat report of the 27th Independent Guards Tank Brigade to the commander of the 7th Guards Army tank and mechanized troops (a copy owned by the author), 18 December 1944.

The reinforced *28. Panzergrenadier-Regiment/8. Panzer-Division* launched its attack at 0630 hours in the morning from attack positions east of Bernecebaráti. The battalion that was deployed on the right flank met only weak Soviet resistance and advanced quickly. However, the battalion on the left flank ran into heavy resistance during the elimination of the Soviet positions in the area of Hill 284 (Nagy Szuha) and point no.225, and in the woods west of the latter. It was only able to reach the road 1.5km southwest of Homok by about 1530 hours, in cooperation with *Kampfgruppe "Hafner"*. After a short preparatory time, the two battalions on the right flank launched an assault to occupy Parassapuszta and Homok, but became engaged in heavy combat under fire of Soviet anti-tank guns and mortars.

The armoured *Kampfgruppe* of the division, (*Panzer-Aufklärungs-Abteilung 8*[90], reinforced with nine *Panzer* IV tanks of the *10. Schwadron/Panzer-Regiment 24*), moved out at 1410 hours along the road leading to Homok to eliminate the Soviet anti-tank strong point that had been established between the railway and the road. Under heavy fire from Soviet anti-tank guns and tanks, the armoured *Kampfgruppe* reached the bridge 1km southwest of Homok, which was found to have already been blown up and mined. The German attack was halted.

After the bridge was restored, the main body of the *8. Panzer-Division*, which constituted *Kampfgruppe "Fröhlich"*, continued its march. Despite heavy Soviet resistance the group managed to reach the borders of the woods south and southeast of Homok, the railway embankment south of the village and the road bend 1.5km southwest of Homok. The attack to occupy Ipolyság and Homok was planned to be resumed at about midnight, following completion of regrouping. The division had seven combat-ready *Panzer* IV tanks that evening.

LXXII. Armeekorps artillery supported the German counterattack launched in the area of Homok and Ipolyság with a total of 660 rounds. At the end of the day, 48 guns were combat-ready and in position.

During the morning, *Gruppe "Momm"* of *Divisionsgruppe "Rintelen"* (with a combat strength of 266 men) was driven from its securing positions stretching 4km east of Deménd by a company-sized unit of Soviet pioneers and six T–34 tanks attacking from the direction of Felsőszemeréd and Kistompa. The German unit was forced back to a line stretching east of the village, directly along the roadside. Here one of the anti-tank guns of the *357. Infanterie-Division* knocked out a Soviet armoured fighting vehicle. In the course of this battle, the Hungarian 3rd Battery/2nd Towed Artillery Battalion was attacked by the Soviets. One 15cm howitzer was knocked out and another was captured in combat-ready condition.

It was only by direct, personal action that *General* Rintelen, pistol in hand, managed to stop the infantry that were flowing backwards toward the west via Deménd, and force them to occupy a narrow securing position 1km east of the village. The firepower of the defenders was enhanced by a number of 8.8cm anti-aircraft guns, heavy anti-tank guns and a 2cm self-propelled anti-aircraft cannon. Because it was impossible to hold the positions with the few and unstable infantry available, *General* Rintelen decided to abandon Deménd at twilight. The Germans began to evacuate the village at about 1630 hours, as the dusk was falling.

At 1710 hours, German troops blew up the bridge west of the village, over the Búr-

90 The commander of *Panzer-Aufklärungs-Abteilung 8* was *Hauptmann* Hans-Joachim Sell.

patak (Búr creek), and established a further blocking position south, west and north of the village. This mainly included anti-aircraft artillery units, which were secured by weak infantry positions. The Soviets attacked again. This time they captured Deménd.

It was mainly due to the *3.* (armoured personnel carrier) *Kompanie/Panzer-Pionier-Bataillon "Feldherrnhalle"* that the new securing position was held. The company, commanded by *Oberleutnant* Lehner, dismounted from their armoured personnel carriers and supported the weak, panic-stricken resistance of the *SS-Sturmbrigade "Dirlewanger"* in dismounted combat.

During the battles around Deménd it was again proven that the remnants of *SS-Sturmbrigade "Dirlewanger"* had little combat value. In the meantime an inspection found out that, with the exception of three soldiers, the whole *10. Kompanie/SS-Sturm-Regiment 2* of the *Brigade* had deserted and gone over to the Soviet units on 15 December. Therefore, *Generalleutnant* Schmidt ordered that German machine guns were to be positioned behind the *SS-Straftruppen* and were to open fire immediately in case of desertion. Nevertheless the *Generalleutnant* himself could not expect a significant outcome because of the terrain of hills and wooded areas. *Generalleutnant* Rintelen was concerned that these *SS* troops might shoot their officers in the back.[91]

Effective at midnight, command and control was to be taken over by *LXXII. Armeekorps* within the area south of the Danube (at the northern side of Szentendrei island) as far as the northern front line of the Budapest bridgehead. Accordingly, the command post of the *Armeekorps* was relocated to Béla. However, *Generalleutnant* Schmidt remained at the detached command post in Vámosmikola in order to closely observe the assault of the *8. Panzer-Division*.[92]

Early in the evening, the position of the right flank of the Soviet 7th Guards Army was as follows:

- 27th Guards Rifle Corps (Major General Evgeniy Stepanovich Alehin)
    - 227th Rifle Division between Balassagyarmat (exclusive) Ipolyszög;
    - 303rd Rifle Division between Hídvégipuszta (exclusive) Hont Ipolyság Kistúr;
    - 141st Rifle Division between Nagyoroszi Hill 662 (Kámor) Diósjenő;
    - 36th Guards Rifle Division in the Hont area, in march toward Borsosberény;
- 25th Guards Rifle Corps (Major General Ganij Bekinovich Safiulin)
    - 6th Guards Airborne Division between Diósjenő (exclusive) Királyrét;
    - 409th Rifle Division between Szokolya Hill 480 (Fekete Hill), engaged in battle at Kóspallag and for the possession of Hill 361 (Peres Hill);
    - 53rd Rifle Division engaged in battle at the Kismaros Kismaros west 2kms road line.[93]

---

91 *Bundesarchiv–Militärarchiv* (Freiburg im Breisgau), RH 24–72, *Generalkommando LXXII. A.K. Abt. Ia/III Nr. 2837/44 geh., 18. 12. 1944, Anlage Nr. 1048.*

92 *Bundesarchiv–Militärarchiv* (Freiburg im Breisgau), RH 24–72, *Kriegstagebuch Ia des LXXII. Armeekorps*, 18. 12. 1944.

93 Daily combat reports of the Soviet 7th Guards Army to the command of the 2nd Ukrainian Front (a copy owned by the author), evening report, 18 December 1944

On **19 December 1944**[94] Soviet forces attacked the broad front line of the Hungarian 2nd Armoured Division, attached to *LXXII. Armeekorps.*

The forces of the Soviet 53rd Rifle Division overcame the securing units and bypassed the positions of the German *Kampfgruppe "Zirke"*, then reached the northern outskirts of Zebegény at about 1600 hours. *Kampfgruppe "Zirke"* prepared all-around defence positions in Nagymaros. An attack of a battalion-sized unit of the Soviet 409th Rifle Division was repulsed east of Márianosztra. *Pionier-Bataillon 751,* which had just arrived during the night without its *2. Kompanie,* improvised a blocking line 1.5km east of the town. The Soviet units outflanked a Hungarian reserve company that was defending at Kisirtáspuszta and, except for four soldiers, captured the company; they then approached to within 1.5km of Nagybörzsöny from the southeast. The latter town, the south-eastern side of which was secured by elements of German *Panzer-Aufklärungs-Abteilung 8* and forces of the Hungarian 2nd Armoured Division, was engaged in fire by Soviet mortars, and was captured by elements in the strength of two to three companies.

At 1400 hours in the afternoon, the Hungarian 5th Motorized Rifle Battalion arrived at Szob, and was deployed at Bridge 142, 2.5km northeast of the town. The 2nd Reconnaissance Battalion, the 6th Towed Artillery Battalion and the German *Pionier-Bataillon 751* defended Márianosztra. Two *Panzer* IV tanks, two *Toldi* tanks and four *Nimród* armoured self-propelled anti-aircraft guns of the Hungarian 2nd Armoured Division were also engaged there. The 2nd Reconnaissance Battalion suffered 30% losses that day.[95]

In the evening the German *3. Batterie/ Flak-Abteilung 181* of *Flak-Regiment 104* marched from Letkés to Helemba and established positions at the crossroads northwest of Szob. One unit of the German (self-propelled) *leichte Flak-Abteilung 77* was also in the area of the Hungarian Division; another of its units was engaged together with *Divisionsgruppe "Rintelen".*

In the *8. Panzer-Division's* sector of the front line, Soviet units could not advance further south of the Kemence-patak. However, on the right flank, south of Homok, the tank-supported counterattack of the Soviet 30th Guards Mechanized Brigade forced the Germans back into the woods. *LXXII. Armeekorps* ordered that the tank crews of the Hungarian 2nd Armoured Division which had been employed as infantry were immediately to be withdrawn, and that preparations were to be made for the withdrawal of the remaining approximately 60 soldiers of *Panzer-Pionier-Bataillon 2.*

The German *8. Panzer-Division,* besides securing its right flank, was engaged in combat in the direction of Ipolyság along the road to Homok. The forces of the Soviet 30th Guards Mechanized Brigade established their defences in a horseshoe between the northern edge of the wooded hills south of Homok, the southern edge of Homok, southwest of Ipolyság, and point no. 142. Their firepower was provided mainly by anti-tank guns and armoured fighting vehicles. Eighteen off the latter were identified by the Germans at the south-western edge of Homok and seven more at Gyerk.

In the morning hours, the attack of reinforced *Panzer-Aufklärungs-Abteilung 8* against the Soviet defensive positions 2km southwest of Homok bogged down.

94 Weather: 5° Celsius during the day, solid cloud cover, parting in some places, with occasional rain; good visibility; some of the minor roads were drying up, the condition of others worsened.

95 *Bundesarchiv–Militärarchiv* (Freiburg im Breisgau), RH 24–72, *Kriegstagebuch Ia des LXXII. Armeekorps, Tagesmeldungen unterstellter Einheiten vom* 19. 12. 1944.

During those same morning hours, the *II. Bataillon/Panzergrenadier-Regiment 28* captured Pereszlény in a surprise attack and succeeded in holding the village during the day. The *Panzer* IV tanks of the *I. (Abteilung)/Panzer-Regiment 10* also participated in the combat activity around Homok and Pereszlény.[96]

At about noon, *Generalleutnant* Schmidt visited the command post of the *8. Panzer-Division* at Ipolyszalka. *Generalmajor* Fröhlich briefed Schmidt on the situation, and claimed that, to that point, four Soviet tanks had been knocked out (one by *Panzerfäuste*). However, half of the allocated *Panzerfausts* failed to function. According to the *Heeresgruppe Süd* war diary, the command and control system of the *8. Panzer-Division* was not working properly, especially in the case of lower rank commanders.[97]

After the leading elements of *Panzerjäger-Abteilung 43* arrived at the armoured *Kampfgruppe* that was based on reinforced *Panzer-Aufklärungs-Abteilung 8*, it was further reinforced by the *I. Bataillon/Panzergrenadier-Regiment 28*. At about noon, the division had four combat-ready *Panzer* IV tanks, four *Jagdpanzer* IV tank destroyers and eight Marder tank destroyers. At the same time, the combat strength of the *II. Bataillon/Panzergrenadier-Regiment 98* was approximately 230, the *I. Bataillon/Panzergrenadier-Regiment 28* was 250 and the *II. Bataillon/Panzergrenadier-Regiment 28* was 200 men.

German ground-attack aircraft units incessantly attacked Homok, Ipolyság and Gyerk from 0930 hours onwards. The Soviets deployed only 18 fighter aircraft and three Il–2 ground-attack aircraft in the area. In the meantime, *Generalleutnant* Schmidt was at the command post of the *8. Panzer-Division* and witnessed the German ground-attack aircraft attacking Homok, where they met heavy Soviet anti-aircraft fire.

That day the German—Hungarian air force flew 190 sorties, the majority in the Ipolyság area. The airmen claimed to have knocked out two tanks and three anti-aircraft guns, besides others.[98]

At 1400 hours, following an artillery preparation by twelve German and Hungarian batteries, the armoured *Kampfgruppe*, reinforced by the *I. Bataillon/Panzergrenadier-Regiment 28*, launched a new assault toward Homok. The oblique fire of the Soviet defence however stopped the Germans once again. The armoured fighting vehicles attacking at the spearhead lost one *Panzer* IV tank and three *Jagdpanzer* IV tank destroyers to the fire of the Soviet anti-tank guns and tanks.

The Germans destroyed six Soviet tanks during that fighting (four with *Panzerfäuste*, in close combat), and three more were immobilized. The Soviet forces had considerable battle casualties (120 confirmed and 350 estimated deaths, three captives) and lost eight anti-tank guns, five machine guns and six trucks.

By evening, *8. Panzer-Division* had only three combat-ready *Panzer* IV tanks, one *Jagdpanzer* IV tank destroyer and nine *Marder* tank destroyers.[99]

During the day, the Soviet troops continued to receive reinforcements. Tank and infantry units of considerable strength were concentrating at Gyerk. The Germans observed

96 Haupt, Werner, *Die 8. Panzer-Division im Zweiten Weltkrieg* (Friedberg, 1987), p.379.

97 HM HIM *Hadtörténelmi Levéltár* (Budapest) microfilm archives, *Kriegstagebuch Ia der Heeresgruppe Süd, Kriegstagebuch vom* 19. 12. 1944 (roll no. 627. image no. 7211156).

98 HM HIM *Hadtörténelmi Levéltár* (Budapest) microfilm archives, *Kriegstagebuch Ia der Heeresgruppe Süd, Kriegstagebuch vom* 19. 12. 1944 (roll no. 627. image no. 7211150).

99 *Bundesarchiv–Militärarchiv* (Freiburg im Breisgau), RH 24–72, *Kriegstagebuch Ia des LXXII. Armeekorps, Tagesmeldungen unterstellter Einheiten vom* 19. 12. 1944.

approximately 50 armoured fighting vehicles moving from Homok via Ipolyság toward the north.

German—Hungarian field artillery and *Flak* directed harassing fire against six Soviet tanks observed at the south-eastern edge of Deménd in the area of *Divisionsgruppe "Rintelen"*. This artillery fire, at the same time, hindered the restoration of the bridge that had been demolished west of the village.

According to the *LXXII. Armeekorps* assesment, the Soviet units also noticed the weakness of the defence of the Hungarian 2nd Armoured Division, and attempted at all costs to gain control of the Vámosmikola–Párkány road, which was essential to the German—Hungarian troops for all of their operations in the area.

The German *6. Armee* promised major reinforcements for the *Armeekorps*. *Generalleutnant* Schmidt sent 17 of his staff officers to meet the anticipated reinforcement troops in order to direct them by the shortest roads possible so that they could arrive as soon as possible. However, only three heavy howitzers had arrived by the early morning of 19 December. Thus, the *Armeekorps* had to halt the west-north-west advance of the units of the 7th Guards Army and the 6th Guards Tank Army with its former resources. These were the following[100]:

Table 1 – Strength of *LXXII. Armeekorps*, 19 December 1944

Units	Anti-aircraft artillery	Field artillery	Combat strength of securing infantry	Armament of securing infantry
Divisionsgruppe "Rintelen"	14 x 8.8cm 3 x 3.7cm 9 x 2cm	10 x 10.5cm	299[1]	19 machine guns 2 heavy machine guns 3 medium mortars 4 heavy anti-tank guns 6 armoured personnel carriers
8. Panzer-Division	18 x 8.8cm 10 x 3.7cm 22 x 2cm	24 x 10.5cm 13 x 15cm 2 x 21cm	1221[2]	No data
Hungarian 2nd Armoured Division	4 x 4cm	8 x 10.5cm	380[3]	16 machine guns 1 heavy machine gun 4 medium mortars

1 The German *Feld-Strafbataillons "Ehlert"* and *"Steinhauer"* (presumably the *12.* and *18.* respectively) with 180 and 84 men, and the *3.* (armoured personnel carrier) *Kompanie/ Panzer-Pionier-Bataillon "Feldherrnhalle"* with 35 men.

2 The German K*ampfgruppe "Miedeck"* with *403, Kampfgruppe "Hafner"* with 511 and the *Kampfgruppe "Struchtenmayer"* with 307 men, respectively. The *8. Panzer-Division's* own forces were deployed in combat, therefore they are not added to this table.

3 The Hungarian 2nd Reconnaissance Battalion with 180 men and the German K*ampfgruppe "Zirke" with 200 men.*

100 *Bundesarchiv–Militärarchiv* (Freiburg im Breisgau), RH 24–72, *Kriegstagebuch Ia des LXXII. Armeekorps, Anlage Nr.* 1060, 19. 12. 1944.

During the day the independent German *Pionier-Bataillon 751*, the Royal Hungarian River Guard (*Magyar Királyi Folyamőrség)* and the naval units of the German *Donauflotille* were also attached to *LXXII. Armeekorps*[101]. With this the *Armeekorps* artillery consisted of 58 tubes, four of which were naval guns.

During the day, *Armeegruppe "Fretter-Pico"* planned to attach the following units to *LXXII. Armeekorps* in order to reinforce the Börzsöny area:

- Division *"Szent László"*;
- The main body of the German *Maschinengewehr-Bataillon "Sachsen"*;
- The main body of the German *Pionier-Bataillon 751*;
- The regimental *Kampfgruppe* of the *357. Infanterie-Division* deployed elsewhere;
- Two battalions and eight tanks of the Hungarian 2nd Armoured Division;
- 25 *Jagdpanzer* 38(t) tank destroyers from the Esztergom training facility intended for assignment to the Hungarian assault artillery troops.

The Germans planned to assign a total of 75 *Jagdpanzer* 38(t) (*Hetzer* tank destroyers) to Hungarian forces. Of these, *Heeresgruppe Süd* was committed to form the first assault artillery battalion (25 *Jagdpanzers*) as soon as possible. In order to achieve this it was ordered that the assault artillery crews of the "Billnitzer" group that were fighting as infantry in the Budapest bridgehead were to be withdrawn from the front line. The second third of the vehicles were to be used to outfit the assault artillery battalion of Division *"Szent László"*. The third of such units was to be organized with the help of the Hungarian 1st Assault Artillery Battalion.[102]

The war diary of the German *LXXII. Armeekorps* mentions a group of 25 Hungarian Jagdpanzer 38(t) tank destroyers for the first time on 19 December 1944. The *Stabsoffizier* responsible for anti-tank issues of the *6. Armee* (*Stopak*), who was, at the same time, commander of the Hungarian *Hetzer*-training, *Oberstleutnant* Thams, reported at 1500 hours to the Chief of Staff of *LXXII. Armeekorps*, *Oberst* Möller, that the 25 crews that were in training in the Esztergom training facility under his command would be ready for deployment in three to five days.[103]

This probably referred, to the so-called Assault Artillery Battalion "Bernolák", combining elements of the 16th and 24th Assault Artillery Battalions. The improvised unit was named after the commander of the 16th Assault Artillery Battalion, Major *nemes* Pál Bernolák of Haraszt.

In theory, the 20th Assault Artillery Battalion (commanded by Major József Henkey-Hőnig) was a combat element of the Division *"Szent László"*, but was not yet in combat-ready condition. According to data from 21 December, the staff of the unit, which consisted of 15 officers, 550 non-commissioned officers and enlisted men, was stationed in Kővágóőrs with 25 *Jagdpanzer* 38(t) tank destroyers. The crews were in Győr undergoing re-training.

---

101 Two Hungarian patrol boats (*Szeged, Kecskemét*) with 8cm guns, and two German gunboats with 7.5cm guns were attached to the *Armeekorps*.

102 HM HIM *Hadtörténelmi Levéltár* (Budapest) microfilm archives, *Kriegstagebuch Ia der Heeresgruppe Süd, IaF Nr. 4892/44 g. Kdos. vom* 19. 12. 1944 (roll no. 627. image no. 7211433).

103 *Bundesarchiv–Militärarchiv* (Freiburg im Breisgau), RH 24–72, *Kriegstagebuch Ia des LXXII. Armeekorps, Anlage Nr. 1052, KTB-Notizen* 19. 12. 44.

The battalion did not have any vehicles and thus was completely immobile. [104]

As a consequence of the advance of the Soviet troops between Vác and Ipolyság and of the attack of the 8. *Panzer-Division* bogging down, *Heeresgruppe Süd* was forced to carry out significant regroupings north of the Danube in order to defend the Ipolyság corridor. Moreover, according to information gathered by German reconnaissance, the units of the Soviet Cavalry Mechanized Group "Pliev" had also relocated from the Szécsény area, and it was feared that these forces were going to be deployed northwards along the Ipoly, or westwards, through the Ipolyság corridor.[105]

Generalmajor Gaedcke informed *Generalleutnant* Grolman at about 1225 hours that the Division *"Szent László"* would be committed together with the *8. Panzer-Division* at Ipolyság. When Grolman inquired about the possible necessity of ordering more armoured fighting vehicles to Ipolyság, Gaedcke answered that the terrain would prevent armoured fighting vehicles from being able to fan out at the corridor in front of Ipolyság.[106] With this the Chief of Staff of *Armeegruppe "Fretter-Pico"* abandoned the possibility of reinforcement by their own units.

After the Division *"Szent László"*, which was assembling in the Mór area, had left, *Armeegruppe "Fretter-Pico"* did not have any infantry reserves left on the front line between Lake Balaton and the Danube. Therefore *Heeresgruppe Süd* proposed that the newly arriving *Kavallerie-Brigade 4* be ordered to the Székesfehérvár area as reserves. OKH, however, ordered that this unit be transported to the *2. Panzerarmee* because Hitler was concerned about the oilfields in Zala County in the rear of the *Armee*. Therefore the units that had already unloaded in Veszprém were also directed west of the Balaton.

At about 1530 hours in the afternoon, the Chief of Staff of *Heeresgruppe Süd* was informed via the *Operationsabteilung* [operations section of the staff] of the *Oberkommando des Heeres* of the proposal by *Generaloberst* Guderian, namely that the problem near Ipolyság should be solved by involving the German *3.* and *6. Panzer-Division*, although with divided forces, as was the case with the *8. Panzer-Division*. The armoured *Kampfgruppen* of the *Panzer* divisions would remain behind the section of the *Margarethen-Stellung (Line)* between the Balaton and the Danube.

Five minutes later Grolman and Gaedcke discussed the proposal. In the opinion of the Chief of Staff of *Armeegruppe "Fretter-Pico"*, the relocation of two other *Panzer* divisions northwards would be extremely difficult and time-consuming in the mountain terrain with few roads. Nevertheless the proposal was accepted and execution thereof began immediately. Command of the two *Panzer* divisions was assigned to *LVII. Panzerkorps* (*General der Panzertruppe* Friedrich Kirchner).

Accordingly, command and control over the northern sector of the front line of *LXXII. Armeekorps* was taken over by the *LVII. Panzerkorps,* as ordered by *Heeresgruppe Süd*. This *Panzerkorps* had, for the time being, the main body of the German *3.* and *6. Panzer-Divisions* at its disposal (although without their armoured *Kampfgruppen*). The

104 HM HIM *Hadtörténelmi Levéltár* (Budapest), *Honvéd Vezérkar főnöke iratai, Fővezérség meghatalmazott tábornokának hadinaplója, 56. melléklet: A „Szent László" hadosztály helyzete 1944. december 21-én 11 órakor.*

105 HM HIM *Hadtörténelmi Levéltár* (Budapest) microfilm archives, *Kriegstagebuch Ia der Heeresgruppe Süd, Kriegstagebuch vom* 19. 12. 1944 (roll no. 627. image no. 7211153).

106 HM HIM *Hadtörténelmi Levéltár* (Budapest) microfilm archives, *Kriegstagebuch Ia der Heeresgruppe Süd, Kriegstagebuch vom 19. 12. 1944* (roll no. 627. image no. 7211157).

two *Panzer* divisions were not only ordered to prevent the Soviet troops gaining ground through the Ipolyság gateway toward the southwest and northwest, but they were also to launch their own assault toward the east.[107] After 2200 hours *Generaloberst* Guderian told *Generalleutnant* Grolman that "he hopes the losses of the *Panzergrenadiers* employed at Ipolyság without the armour will not be too severe".[108]

The *3. Panzer-Division* (*Generalleutnant* Wilhelm Philipps) was to cross the Danube on the Esztergom bridge and assemble in the area of Vámosmikola. The *6. Panzer-Division* (*Generalleutnant* Rudolf *Freiherr* von Waldenfels) was to advance via the Komárom bridge to Szete. The German *6. Armee* had informed *LXXII. Armeekorps* of this by 2000 hours in the evening. At the same time, it was necessary to relocate at least one regimental-sized *Kampfgruppe* of the *24. Panzer-Division/IV. Panzerkorps* from the east to the area of Ipolyság for the defence of the right flank of the German *Armeegruppe "Wöhler"*.

The units of the *SS-Sturmbrigade "Dirlewanger"* were also ordered to take part in closing the Ipolyság corridor. The *SS-Sturmbrigade* was attached to the *18. SS-Freiwilligen Panzergrenadier-Division "Horst Wessel"*, reinforced by elements of the German *Sturmgeschütz-Brigade 228*. The other half of the *Sturmgeschütz-Brigade*, together with the *Sturmgeschütz-Brigade 286*, was attached directly to *IV. Panzerkorps*.[109]

That evening the position of the units on the right flank of the Soviet 7th Guards Army were:

- 27th Guards Rifle Corps
    - 227th Rifle Division in the area of Kóvár;
    - 303rd Rifle Division between Kistompa Gyerk;
    - 36th Guards Rifle Division on the line Hont Homok Bernecebaráti two kilometres northeast of Bernecebaráti;
    - 141st Rifle Division between Hill 436 (Döbre-bérc) Diósjenő;
- 25th Guards Rifle Corps
    - 6th Guards Airborne Division between Hill 571 (Kegyes-hegyorom) and Hill 509 (Kis-Koppány);
    - 409th Rifle Division engaged in battle for the possession of Márianosztra;
    - 53rd Rifle Division was engaged in battle north of Zebegény.[110]

Attached to the 7th Guards Army, the 27th Independent Guards Tank Brigade, directly supporting the infantry, arrived that same day from the direction of Szendehely and was ordered to support units of the 25th Guards Rifle Corps. The brigade had, at that time, 41 T–34 tanks, 12 SU–85 and four SU–76M self-propelled guns. However, only nine T–34s, four SU–85s and one SU–76M were in operational condition. Eight additional repaired T–34s were *en route* to the unit.

At about 1145 hours the 1st Guards Tank Battalion/27th Independent Guards Tank

107 *Bundesarchiv–Militärarchiv* (Freiburg im Breisgau), RH 24–72, *Kriegstagebuch Ia des LXXII. Armeekorps*, 19. 12. 1944.

108 HM HIM *Hadtörténelmi Levéltár* (Budapest) microfilm archives, *Kriegstagebuch Ia der Heeresgruppe Süd, Kriegstagebuch vom* 19. 12. 1944 (roll no. 627. image no. 7211160).

109 *Bundesarchiv–Militärarchiv* (Freiburg im Breisgau), *RH 2 Ost Karte 5229.*

110 Daily combat reports of the Soviet 7th Guards Army to the command of the 2nd Ukrainian Front (a copy owned by the author), evening report, 19 December 1944

Brigade reached the Nagy creek southwest of Szokolya, and crossed it at about 1500 hours with the help of engineers of the 409th Rifle Division. The 3rd Guards Tank Battalion/27th Independent Guards Tank Brigade went into action at that same time, advancing southwest of Kismaros toward the anonymous terrain feature 700 metres west of Hill 104.[111]

As ordered by the 2nd Ukrainian Front, the 6th Guards Tank Army received assault missions on a 12km wide, independent front line. The direct objective was to capture Szántó, the important traffic junction. Liaison officers from the 5th Air Army had arrived at the army staff and two of its corps, in order to insure effective cooperation between the ground forces and the aircraft units, especially regarding close support.

Colonel General Kravchenko planned to deploy his troops in one single echelon. Only artillery and engineer units remained in the army commander's reserve. The 6th Guards Tank Army had, at that time, a total of 220 operational tanks and self-propelled guns.[112]

The 9th Guards Mechanized Corps was to launch an attack in the morning of the next day toward Szalatnya, Gyűgy, Hontnádas and Dolné Zemberovce, and to occupy Hontvarsány, Hontfüzesgyarmat and Szántó by the end of the day. Its advance troop had to occupy crossing points on the Garam in the area of Garamtolmács. The 9th Guards Mechanized Corps had concentrated in the area of Szalatnya – Felsőtúr – Kistúr in order to carry out the attack, with 107 operational tanks and self-propelled guns. The brigades of the corps took the following positions to prepare for the following day:

- Main body of the 18th Guards Mechanized Brigade in Felsőtúr, in defence, advance troop in Palást;
- Main body of the 31st Guards Mechanized Brigade in Kistompa, advance troop in Szalatnya;
- 30th Guards Mechanized Brigade engaged in battle in the Bernecebaráti area;
- 46th Guards Tank Brigade was the Corps Commander's reserve in the area of Homok.

The 5th Guards Tank Corps was gathering in the area of Felsőszemeréd – Egeg. According to the orders issued it was to attack in the forthcoming morning toward Egeg, Deménd, Szántó, Hontfüzesgyarmat, Vámosladány and Léva, and was to occupy Léva, Nagykálna, Garamszentgyörgy and Hontfüzesgyarmat by the end of the day. The advance troop of the corps was to occupy crossing points on the Garam at Nagykálna. There were a total of 89 operational T–34 and T–34/85 tanks of the 5th Guards Tank Corps waiting for the assault.

The flank of the tank army between Palást and Gyűgy was covered by the 4th Guards Motorcycle Regiment, reinforced by the 1426th Light Artillery Regiment.[113]

The following day, the 6th Guards Tank Army was to attack toward Nyitra, and was to occupy positions approximately 200km northwest of Budapest, in the area of

111 Combat report of the 27th Independent Guards Tank Brigade to the commander of the 7th Guards Army tank and mechanized troops (a copy owned by the author), 19 December 1944.

112 Armstrong, 1994, p.435. There were altogether 196 operational tanks and self-propelled guns in the two corps. In addition, there were 10 Mk IX Valentine tanks and some SU–57s (57mm anti-tank guns mounted on half-track armoured personnel carriers) in operational condition in the 4th Guards Motorcycle Regiment, and seven IS–2 heavy tanks in the 49th Guards Heavy Tank Regiment.

113 *Budapestskaya Operaciya*. Contemporary summary of the 2nd Ukrainian Front about the operations around Budapest. (A copy owned by the author). p.123.

Gímeskosztolány, Nyitra and Verebély between 25-28 December, 1944.[114]

On the front line of the 2nd Ukrainian Front, Soviet troops had, by 19 December, swiftly penetrated into the operational depths of *Armeegruppe "Fretter-Pico"* with the 6th Guards Tank Army and the Cavalry Mechanized Group "Pliev" and had successfully occupied the Ipolyság corridor. However, the flanking of Budapest in the northwestern direction and the encirclement of the German—Hungarian troops was not successful. The failure of the 5th Guards Tank Corps south of Vác, and that of Cavalry Mechanized Group "Pliev" at Szécsény contributed to the slowing down of the pace of the attack.

On **20 December 1944**[115] combat activity continued along the entire front line of *LXXII. Armeekorps*. The *8. Panzer-Division* was forced into defence. In the morning, the division reported the following combat strength and armament:

- *I. Bataillon/Panzergrenadier-Regiment 28* with 273 men;
- *II. Bataillon/Panzergrenadier-Regiment 28* with 297 men;
- *II. Bataillon/Panzergrenadier-Regiment 98* with 285 men;
- *Panzer-Aufklärungs-Abteilung 8* with 490 men;
- *Kampfgruppe "Grosse"* with 874 men;
- One combat-ready *Jagdpanzer IV* tank destroyer, nine *Marder* tank destroyers and 14 towed 7.5cm anti-tank guns.

Kampfgruppe "Amsel" of the German unit (reinforced *Panzerjäger-Abteilung 43*) launched an attack during the morning from the northwest aimed at the recapture of Nagybörzsöny, which was held by two Soviet companies (presumably of the 6th Guards Airborne Division). The Germans pushed the Soviet units back, but their advance bogged down north and west of the village.

That evening units of the *8. Panzer-Division* launched a counterattack against the battalion-sized unit of the 141st Rifle Division that had broken into Perőcsény from the southeast, and against the forces of the 36th Guards Rifle Division that had reached the southeastern edge of Bernecebaráti. The *8. Panzer-Division* claimed that the Soviet forces lost 90 dead, three prisoners, two mortars, one machine gun, two anti-tank guns and one tank knocked out on the road northwest of Ipolyság in that day's fighting.

The Vámosmikola–Párkány road was secured by the newly arrived units of the German *Panzer-Aufklärungs-Abteilung 3* after they had repulsed the units of the Soviet 409th Rifle Division that had reached the road at Ipolyszalka. Some of the light armored reconnaissance vehicles of the unit were deployed that day west of Lelédhidipuszta, at the hunter's cottage on the other side of the Ipoly. The accomplishments of *Oberfeldwebel* Friedrich, serving in the *Stabskompanie/Panzer-Aufklärungs-Abteilung 3* was mentioned in the daily combat reports.[116]

The Soviet troops advancing westwards in the section of the Hungarian 2nd Armoured Division were more or less successfully halted; heavy fighting was going on for Szob and

114 Zavizion, G. T. & Kornyushin, P.A., *na Tiknom okeane...* (Moscow, 1967), p.126.

115 Weather: 6° Celsius during the day, complete cloud cover at times, parting cloud cover at other times; minor roads were drying up.

116 *Geschichte der 3. Panzer-Division Berlin-Brandenburg 1935–1945* (Berlin, 1967), p.502.

Márianosztra. The division had three combat-ready *Nimród* armoured self-propelled anti-aircraft guns and two combat-ready 7.5cm anti-tank guns. The fighting units of the division were concentrated in the *Kampfgruppe* of Colonel Jenő Altorjay, commander of the 3rd Motorized Rifle Regiment. The 2nd Reconnaissance Battalion, commanded by armoured Captain *nemes* Dezső Dorner, was also part of this group.

Parts of the Hungarian 2nd Battalion/1st Parachute Regiment, the first elements of Division *"Szent László"*, attached to *LXXII. Armeekorps*, that were arriving in the area recaptured the hills east of Letkés.[117] By that time, the following elements had arrived: 5th Company/1st Parachute Regiment, 1st Platoon of the 6th Company/1st Parachute Regiment, the heavy weapons company and the machine gun company of this Battalion.[118] The majority of these forces, entering action from the line of march, repulsed the attack of elements of the Soviet 409th Rifle Division at Ipolyszalka. The Soviet forces pursuing the remnants of the Hungarian 2nd Armoured Division were already on the bridge when the paratroopers surprised them. Almost 90 Soviet dead remained on the bridge and in the village of Letkés, which the paratroopers soon entered in a counterattack. At least 180 prisoners and considerable amounts of seized material were taken without losses to their own side.[119]

The commander of the Division *"Szent László"*[120] was Staff Colonel *vitéz*[121] Zoltán Szügyi. According to the order of the day of the commander of the division, the Air Force Rifle Regiment [122] that was coming from Úrhida on trucks had to assemble in Letkés with its lead battalion. The battalion transported in the second echelon, together with the regimental units, had to assemble in Ipolyszalka. The staff of the 1st Battalion (Captain György Pályi) of the Air Force Rifle Regiment and reached Ipolyszalka around midnight on 19 December, and then set off for Letkés with orders to relieve the 2nd Battalion/1st Parachute Regiment fighting in the bridgehead.[123]

117 The paratroopers may have arrived to Ipolyszalka at about 1600 hours on 19 December 1944.

118 See HM HIM *Hadtörténelmi Levéltár (Budapest), Fővezérség meghatalmazott tábornoka naplója,* p.26.

119 HM HIM *Hadtörténelmi Levéltár (Budapest), Tanulmányok és visszaemlékezések gyűjteménye* (Collection of studies and recollections), nr. 3138., Martin Kornél: *Néhány adat és emlék a „Szent László" felderítő osztály életéből,* 1944. XI. 17.–XII. 27. (Kornél Martin: Data and memories from the life of the Reconnaissance Battalion *"Szent László"*, 17 November – 27 December 1944), p.20.

120 The Division reported to the command of *LXXII. Armeekorps* via the German communications unit *D.V.K.* 118 assigned to them.

121 The *Vitézi Rend* (so-called Order of Valiants) was founded by Governor Miklós Horthy in 1920. The *Vitézi Rend* welcomed persons into its ranks who were awarded military decorations for bravery shown in combat (First and Second World Wars), or possibly performed other kinds of services for the Hungarian nation. The members of the *Rend* received estates, and were entitled to use the denomination *"vitéz"*, which, however, was not a mark of nobility.

122 The Regiment was composed of the volunteering officers, non-commissioned officers and the soldiers coming from the Air Force itself. During combat ground training the soldiers received live ammunition. Emphasis was put on the use of the *Panzerschreck* and the hand grenades. In consequence, one of the soldiers was killed (due to a *Panzerschreck* accident) and more were wounded (due to hand grenades detonating). For this, see HM HIM *Hadtörténelmi Levéltár (Budapest), Tanulmányok és visszaemlékezések gyűjteménye* (Collection of studies and recollections), nr. 3064, *Pályi György: A Szent László hadosztály repülő lövészezredének története, 1944. október – 1945. december.* (György Pályi: History of the Air Force Rifle Regiment of the Division *"Szent László"*, October 1944 – December 1945), p.4.

123 HM HIM *Hadtörténelmi Levéltár (Budapest), Tanulmányok és visszaemlékezések gyűjteménye* (Collection of studies and recollections), nr. 3064 *Pályi Görgy: A Szent László hadosztály repülő lövészezredének története, 1944. október – 1945. december.* (György Pályi: History of the Air Force Rifle Regiment of the

The lead battalion of the grenadier regiment was directed to Leléd. The battalion arriving in the second echelon and the regimental elements were ordered to Bajta. The main task of the division was to establish a bridgehead on the eastern bank of the Ipoly, east of Letkés, and to secure the deployment of *LVII. Panzerkorps* by holding the bridgehead. The bridgehead at Letkés extended along the following line: Ipoly east bank – Liliom-puszta – Hill 206 – Hill 254 – Dávidrévi-puszta – Ipolytölgyes north. The 1st Battalion of the Air Force Rifle Regiment that arrived first had to occupy the whole bridgehead on 21 December in a series of strong ponts and hold it until the arrival of the additional elements.[124]

As of 1100 hours in the morning, the position of the units of the Division *"Szent László"* was:

- 1st Battalion/1st Parachute Regiment around Balatonszentgyörgy in process of entraining;
- 2nd Battalion/1st Parachute Regiment had arrived and deployed, attached to the Hungarian 2nd Armoured Division;
- 1st Battalion/Air Force Rifle Regiment had arrived at Letkés;
- 2nd Battalion/Air Force Rifle Regiment had arrived at Ipolyszalka with its units;
- The position of the Grenadier Regiment was uncertain, presumably directed to the Győr Komárom march route; six German officer patrols and one courier aircraft were sent to look for it;
- Reconnaissance Battalion *en route*, the arrival of its cavalry company was anticipated for 24 December;
- 1st Mortar Artillery Battalion (16 12cm mortars) *en route* from Székesfehérvár with scarce ammunition;
- 76th Light Artillery Battalion with three horse-drawn batteries (12 10.5cm field artillery guns) deployed around Tahitótfalu;
- 9th Artillery Battalion with three horse-drawn batteries (12 8cm guns) deployed at Csepel;
- VIII Medium Towed Artillery Battalion with three towed batteries (12 15cm field artillery guns) to arrive in the evening of 21 December at Bajta;
- 20th Assault Artillery Battalion with 25 *Jagdpanzer* 38(t) tank destroyers in Kővágóőrs, retraining of the crew in progress in Győr, not ready for marching orders because of absence of vehicles;
- Tank Destroyer Battalion with six towed 7.5cm anti-tank guns, which, due to lack of prime movers, were towed by trucks of the Grenadier Regiment;
- 53rd Pioneer Battalion was *en route* by train from Budapest.[125]

The main body of the German *Panzer-Pionier-Bataillon 59/8. Panzer-Division*, which was attached that day to the Hungarian 2nd Armoured Division, together with Hungarian paratroopers, forced the battalion-sized forces of the 6th Guards Airborne Division from

Division *"Szent László"*, October 1944 – December 1945), p.7.

124 See HM HIM *Hadtörténelmi Levéltár (Budapest), a „Szent László" hadosztály tüzérparancsnokának naplója és mellékletei. 55. sz. melléklet: 320./Szent László ho. I. A.44.XII. 20. szám: Intézkedés a ho. felvonulására és annak biztosítására.*

125 See HM HIM *Hadtörténelmi Levéltár (Budapest), Fővezérség meghatalmazott tábornoka naplója és mellékletei, 56. sz. melléklet: A „Szent László" ho. helyzete 1944. XII. hó 21-én 11h.*

Ipolytölgyes, recaptured Széppatakpuszta and forced them back to the east, thereby clearing the Letkés–Ipolytölgyes road.

During the heavy fighting that day the units that were attached to the Hungarian 2nd Armoured Division prevented Soviet units from breaking into the German—Hungarian positions on the wooded mountain terrain and occupying the Ipoly valley. Paratrooper Cadet Sergeant Sándor Pethő whose unit was closing the road leading from Letkés toward Ipolytölgyes, observed six Hungarian light tanks retreating from the north, which were, however, knocked out by the Soviet forces. "It was sad to see the six tanks not even trying to set up a formation. They went on like sheep led to the slaughter."[126]

The 1st Battalion/27th Independent Guards Tank Brigade, supporting the Soviet 25th Guards Rifle Corps, with three operational T–34 tanks in his strength, arrived at Kóspallag at about 1200 hours.[127]

The units of the Soviet 5th Guards Tank Corps/6th Guards Tank Army launched an attack at 0800 hours in the morning, after an artillery preparation fire of only 10 minutes, with approximately 80 armoured fighting vehicles, on the left flank of *LXXII. Armeekorps* toward the northwest. The 20th Guards Tank Brigade attacked toward Szántó, Hontfüzesgyarmat and Vámosladány. The 22nd Guards Tank Brigade set off for Szántó, Csánk and Hontvarsány.

The *Divisionsgruppe"Rintelen"*, reporting a combat strength of 280 soldiers, fighting intensely with its 14 8.8cm anti-aircraft guns and one 7.5cm anti-tank gun, was attacked by 35 Soviet tanks that approached from the direction of Deménd. The armoured fighting vehicles of the 5th Guards Tank Corps stormed the positions of the German anti-aircraft guns at Hévmagyarád and destroyed two guns. Two T–34 tanks were knocked out during the combat. The Soviet armoured fighting vehicles that turned toward Szántó entered the village at about 1100 hours. Nine tanks turned toward Hontfüzesgyarmat, supported by infantry; the others continued their advance toward the northwest.

The German *Kampfgruppe* was preparing for the defence of Hontfüzesgyarmat, but, at 1230 hours, Soviet infantry attacked with the fire support from tanks and entered the northern part of the village. The three 10.5cm field artillery guns of the Hungarian 2nd Battery/5th Artillery Battalion positioned on the northern edge of Hontfüzesgyarmat were seized by the Soviets at 1500 hours in intact condition.

The *Divisionsgruppe "Rintelen"* retreated as far as Garamszentgyörgy, where the defenders were wedged into a narrow bridgehead. The forces of the Soviet 22nd Guards Tank Brigade reached the eastern and southern edges of Léva with 17 tanks and tank-rider riflemen at about 1430 hours, after a 32km advance. They then began to burn the town. The units of the brigade, together with the forces of the 20th Guards Tank Brigade occupied the town at about 1520 hours. The advance troop of the 20th Guards Tank Brigade, with 10 T–34 tanks and the entire machine gun battalion of the brigade reached the Garam near Garamszentgyörgy.

The crossing points on the Garam, west and northwest of Léva, were to be secured by a battalion of the *Division "Tatra"* attached directly to the German Commander-in-chief in

126 Martin Kornél & Ugron István, „Fejezetek a Szent László hadosztály történetéből. I. rész." (Chapters from the history of the Division *"Szent László"*, Part I.) in: *Hadtörténelmi Közlemények*, issue 1995/3, p.112.

127 Combat report of the 27th Independent Guards Tank Brigade to the commander of the 7th Guards Army tank and mechanized troops (a copy owned by the author), 20 December 1944

Slovakia. However the unit did not arrive in time.

The advance troops of the 20th Guards Tank Brigade approached Nagykálna, where the bridge on the Garam was blown at 1630 hours, before three Soviet T–34 tanks could cross it to the western bank. However, lacking orders for its destruction, the German *Pioniers* were unable to destroy the railway bridge.

The *II. (Abteilung)/Flak-Regiment 24* and *Panzer-Aufklärungs-Abteilung 6/6. Division* were assigned as reinforcements to *Divisionsgruppe "Rintelen"* in defence there. The arrival of both units was anticipated for next day. In the evening the *II. (Abteilung)/Flak-Regiment 24* was ordered to the sector between Kiskálna and Garamszentgyörgy, the *I. (Abteilung)/ Flak-Regiment 48* was ordered southeast of that area. According to German reconnaissance the infantry of the 6th Guards Motorized Rifle Brigade was soon engaged on the east bank of the Garam, in the area of Garamszentgyörgy.

The 9th Guards Mechanized Corps launched its attack at 1100 hours. The 46th Guards Tank Brigade set off from the area of Szántó and advanced toward Bori and Kálnaborfő. Which latter was taken by the end of the day. The 31st Guards Mechanized Brigade reached Csánk and Hontvarsány.

In the sector of the *IV. Panzerkorps*, which was engaged on the right flank of *Armeegruppe "Wöhler"*, units of the 9th Guards Mechanized Corps attacked with 35 tanks from Egeg toward the north and north-west. However, the attempt of the 18th Guards Mechanized Brigade was temporarily thwarted by the Germans at the crossroads 1km north of Egeg, who knocked out 10 armoured fighting vehicles.[128]

The defenders placed two (anti-tank and/or anti-aircraft) guns and four machine guns east of the road at no. 179 (Gesztence), directly by the basin of the Kénesfürdő at Gyűgy which kept the road from Egeg to Gyűgy under fire. After combat activity in the area ceased, the local civilians observed more than three holes in some of the Soviet armoured fighting vehicles. Nine of the knocked out tanks burnt out on the road and one on the road crossing leading to Egyházmarót.[129]

Despite heavy losses, the 18th Guards Mechanized Brigade renewed its attack and finally reached the area of Apátmarót by the end of the day. According to the combat report of the 2nd Ukrainian Front, the 9th Guards Mechanized Corps/6th Guards Tank Army occupied Apátmarót by the end of the day and continued its attack toward Hontnádas. The 5th Guards Tank Corps occupied Hévmagyarád, Szántó, Csánk, Hontvarsány and Léva. As the day ended, its advance troops were engaged in combat for Nagykálna, with one of its brigades fighting for Vámosladány.[130]

In the *LXXII. Armeekorps* sector, the *Luftwaffe* liaison officer that had been assigned reported that a total of 25 heavy fighter, 15 ground attack, 10 fighter and one reconnaissance aircraft sorties had been completed; 11 Soviet aircraft were claimed as shot down, with four losses on the Axis side.[131]

128 HM HIM *Hadtörténelmi Levéltár* (Budapest) microfilm archives, *Kriegstagebuch Ia der Heeresgruppe Süd, Kriegstagebuch vom* 20. 12. 1944 (roll no. 627. image no. 7211165).

129 Recollections of local residents as communicated to the author by Mr. Andráš Péter in writing. After the fighting on December 1944, local residents counted a total of 13 destroyed Soviet tanks between Egeg and Gyűgy, and one at Egeg.

130 HM HIM *Hadtörténelmi Levéltár (Budapest), Szovjet iratmásolatok gyűjteménye a Budapest körüli harcokról. A 2. Ukrán Front hadijelentései, 1944. december 20.*

131 *Bundesarchiv–Militärarchiv* (Freiburg im Breisgau), RH 24–72, *Kriegstagebuch Ia des LXXII. Armeekorps, Anlage Nr. 1065*, 20. 12. 1944.

During the day *LXXII. Armeekorps* also received considerable reinforcements. The missing elements of the Hungarian 2nd Battalion/1st Parachute Regiment arrived and were immediately committed, as was also the case with elements of the *Kampfgruppe* of the German *357. Infanterie-Division* that had previously been attached to other units, the main body of *Maschinengewehr-Bataillon "Sachsen"*, the missing elements of *Pionier-Bataillon 751* and three 21cm howitzers of the *8. Batterie/Heeres- Artillerie-Brigade 959.* The main body of the Division *"Szent László"*, two batteries of *Artillerie-Regiment 357*, the *3. Batterie/Flak-Abteilung 278* and one battery of *Flak-Abteilung 299* were expected to arrive soon.[132]

LXXII. Armeekorps had already assigned a mission to the Division *"Szent László"*, even though it was still *en route*. The Hungarian unit was to move out in the morning of the next day from the eastern outskirts of Letkés toward the northeast and break up the Soviet troops in its area. It was then to advance to the road connecting Kisirtáspuszta and Nagybörzsöny. Thereby, the defenders would cut the supply line of the Soviet 7th Guards Army that was attacking in the Börzsöny. The *Korps* assigned the following objectives to the unit:

- Immediate objective: Sas hill (Hill 403) Sakola-tető (Hill 488);
- Subsequent objective: Nagy-Koppány (Hill 549) Kis-Koppány (Hill 509);
- Final objective: Kisirtás-puszta point no. 250.[133]

With this, the German *Armeekorps* had, essentially, forced the Division *"Szent László"* into the extremely unfavourable terrain of the Börzsöny range. Staff Major Árpád Lajtos, Chief of Staff of the Division *"Szent László"* remembered receiving the orders:

> At about 2100 hours I was ordered via a courier to go to Béla (I was chosen because Colonel Szügyi did not speak German). *Oberst* Möller[134] told me that the attack orders had been prepared and that I should take them, read them, and then execute them. These orders were so typical of the absurd naivety of the German high command those days that I felt it worth recording them in a draft.
>
> After having read the document (six pages of military tactical masterpiece) at first I was shocked with astonishment. The fact that the *Korpskommando* would drive a division into the forest of the Börzsöny, blindfolded, was not the greatest of my astonishments: it was that they simply did not accept the fact that there was no division that could possibly execute such orders. I told Möller that this order was, literally, set in a vacuum. And when I notified him that there were no units of our own, he told me: 'Orders are orders. They are to be executed immediately!' I laughed, though not because I was so happy. At this, *Generalleutnant* Schmidt came over from the next room; I told him why I was laughing. His face became red with anger and he shouted in Möller's face, calling him an idiot: 'You see! I told you that this is meaningless!' I could not help adding, myself: 'But your Excellency has signed it.' A

132 *Bundesarchiv–Militärarchiv* (Freiburg im Breisgau), RH 24–72, *Kriegstagebuch Ia des LXXII. Armeekorps*, 20. 12. 1944.

133 *Bundesarchiv–Militärarchiv* (Freiburg im Breisgau), RH 24–72, *Korpsbefehl für die Kampfführung am* 21. 12. 1944.

134 *Stabsoberst* Möller was the *Stabskommandeur* of *LXXII. Armeekorps*.

dramatic scene ensued during which Möller sprung up and requested that the idiot be withdrawn, because of his rank as a staff officer. Schmidt calmed him down, saying that he was an even greater idiot. It is sad to think that the fate of Hungary lies in the hands of such people.

Following this I asked the *Korps* commander not to issue orders when we do not have any units to execute them. Give us clearly set tasks and we will see what we can do to execute them. At least we are a division command and we have some units, but they do not have anything.

Schmidt then told me that our mission was defend the Ipoly as well as we could, the most important task being that the roads in question be kept open for a day or two. (Another confusing order, because if there was combat activity going on in the Léva and Balassagyarmat area, that must be supplied for a longer period than just a day or two).

I went back to Bajta.[135]

The 1st Battalion/Air Force Rifle Regiment was assigned the mission, after 2100 hours, to attack and extend the bridgehead to the east to Liliom-puszta and Lelédhidi-puszta and to the vineyards northeast of Letkés in the north. The 2nd Company/I Air Force Rifle Battalion set off for the Liliom-puszta, with its right flank resting on the road. The 1st Company/I Air Force Rifle Battalion launched an attack northward toward the vineyard. The 3rd Company/I Air Force Rifle Battalion went into reserve 400 metres behind the 2nd Company. The tank destroyer platoon, made up of two squads, was positioned on the road, behind the 2nd Company, because Captain Pályi anticipated a Soviet tank attack from the direction of Márianosztra. The Hungarian attack was to be executed without preparatory fire in the most silent way possible. The advance surprised the Soviet troops and they retreated from the area of Letkés without offering significant resistance.[136]

However, the commander of the Air Force Rifle Regiment did not maintain separation of the attacks of the 1st and 2nd Battalions. Thus the units became intermixed for a short time. This resulted because the 2nd Battalion had to advance along the road toward Helemba silently, without contacting the enemy, then establish contacts with the remnants of the Hungarian 2nd Armoured Division engaged there, and then return on the same road.

Armeegruppe "Fretter-Pico" ordered that the front line between the *LXXII.* and *LVII. Panzerkorps* be revised. Accordingly, the new sector boundary extended along the Vámosmikola (*LVII.*) – László-puszta (*LXXII.*) Ipolyság (*LVII.*) – Ipolyhidvég (*LXXII.*) – Ipolyvéce (*LXXII.*) line.

LVII. Panzerkorps was assigned to launch an attack within the shortest time possible with units of the *3.* and *6. Panzer-Divisions* from the Szete–Százd line. The reinforced left flank of the *Korps* had to reach the hills south of Palást via Kistompa and Felsőtúr, in order to be able to turn south from there and open the Ipolyság corridor. For that mission the

135 HM HIM *Hadtörténelmi Levéltár (Budapest), Tanulmányok és visszaemlékezések gyűjteménye* (Collection of studies and recollections) nr. 2598., *Lajtos Árpád: Szent László hadosztály (Visszaemlékezés). (Árpád Lajtos*: Division *"Szent László"* (Recollections)). pp.53-54.

136 HM HIM *Hadtörténelmi Levéltár (Budapest), Tanulmányok és visszaemlékezések gyűjteménye* (Collection of studies and recollections), nr. 3064, Pályi Görgy: *A Szent László hadosztály repülő lövészezredének története, 1944. október – 1945. december.* (György Pályi: History of the Air Force Rifle Regiment of the Division *"Szent László"*, October 1944 – December 1945), pp.9-10.

Panzer IV tanks, *Jagdpanzers* and self-propelled anti-tank guns of the *8. Panzer-Division* were all attached to *LVII. Panzerkorps*. *Panzer-Aufklärungs-Abteilung 8* remained attached to *LXXII. Armeekorps* and was ready to enter Ipolyság from the south if *LVII. Panzerkorps* succeeded in its operations.[137]

The assigned units of the German *6. Panzer-Division* moved out toward Komárom at 2330 hours in the preceding night. The main body of the units reached Kisbér at about 0530 hours on 20 December. The last of the wheeled vehicles crossed the Danube at Komárom at about 1645 hours. The *3. Panzer-Division* moved out from Bicske toward Esztergom at midnight on 19 December. The leading elements of its wheeled vehicle column was *en route* at about 1400 hours, east of Tát, at Körtvélyes island.

In the evening, the infantry units of the right flank of the 7th Guards Army were engaged at the following positions:

- 27th Guards Rifle Corps
    - Elements of the 227th Rifle Division occupied Ipolykiskeszi;
    - 303rd Rifle Division occupied Ivánka farm near Százd and was fighting for Százd and Ipolyvisk;
    - 36th Guards Rifle Division at the woods south of Homok engaged in battle for Bernecebaráti;
    - 141st Rifle Division between Hill 449 Hill 741 (Várbükk) Bányapuszta;
- 25th Guards Rifle Corps
    - 6th Guards Airborne Division engaged in battle for Ipolytölgyes and the Ganádi mill;
    - 409th Rifle Division occupied Hill 109 1km north of Letkés and was engaged in battle for the occupation of the village;
    - 53rd Rifle Division occupied Szob, and was engaged in battle along the railway northwest of the town.[138]

On **21 December 1944**[139], on the front line of *LXXII. Armeekorps* in the sector of the Hungarian 2nd Armoured Division, the defenders had been forced back by dawn to the line between the church in the western part of Szob and point no. 234 (Kerek Hill), 2.5km northwest of the church.

According to the morning report of the Hungarian 2nd Armoured Division it had one combat-ready *Turán* 75 and two *Turán* 40 tanks (75mm and 40mm main guns respectively), and five 7.5cm anti-tank guns. According to German archive sources two of the division's 21 *Panzer* IV tanks and two of the four *Panthers* were also combat-ready.[140] The 2nd Reconnaissance Battalion had a combat strength of 65 men, the German *Panzer-Pionier-Bataillon 59* had 152 men. No report had been received from the other attached

137 *Bundesarchiv–Militärarchiv* (Freiburg im Breisgau), RH 24–72, *Armeegruppe Fretter-Pico Ia Nr. 6464/44 geh., Anlage Nr. 1066*, 20. 12. 1944.

138 Daily combat reports of the Soviet 7th Guards Army to the command of the 2nd Ukrainian Front (a copy owned by the author), evening report, 20 December 1944.

139 Weather: temperature alternating between -1 and +4° Celsius, bright, sunny sky; minor roads were drying up.

140 For this, see *Bundesarchiv–Militärarchiv* (Freiburg im Breisgau), *RH 2 Ost Karte 5249 (Panzer-Lage vom 21. Dez. 1944).*

units. The Hungarian 2nd Armoured Division supplemented the above data at 1300 hours. According to this, the unit had the following combat strength:

- 5th Motorized Rifle Battalion with 110 men;
- 2nd Reconnaissance Battalion with 40 men;
- German *Kampfgruppe "Zirke"* with 70 men;
- German *Maschinengewehr-Bataillon "Sachsen"* with 200 men;
- German *Pionier-Bataillon 751* with 130 men.

In the Ipolyszalka area there was intense Soviet air activity that included a number of bombing raids. The bridge over the Ipoly was hit, and a large hole was blown in the middle of it.[141]

The *8. Panzer-Division* held its positions, apart from an area 2.5km east of Kemence, where Soviet troops penetrated the outposts. The penetration was sealed off by the Germans. In the morning the *8. Panzer-Division* had only one *Jagdpanzer* IV tank destroyer and nine *Marder* tank destroyers ready for action.[142]

On the front line of *Divisionsgruppe "Rintelen"*, Soviet troops with weak infantry forces built bridgeheads on the Garam at Nagykálna and Alsóvárad, which were, however, blocked by the enemy. In the latter area, the counterattack by *Panzer-Aufklärungs-Abteilung 6* eliminated the bridgehead. The railway bridges of the two villages were not blown up by the Germans as had been ordered by the *Heeresgruppe Süd.* This was immediately exploited by the Soviet troops.

During the day, forces of the 7th Guards Army launched an assault which was now supported by heavy artillery fire and tanks in the southern area of the Börzsöny, on the right flank of *LXXII. Armeekorps.* There was extremely heavy combat in the Ipoly bridgehead that was held by the Germans and the Hungarians between Szob and Ipolydamásd.

Elements of the Soviet 409th Rifle Division, with support from the 1st Guards Tank Battalion/27th Guards Tank Regiment, launched an attack at 1130 hours along the road toward Bástya. The Soviet company-sized unit attacked with artillery fire and tank support but did not succeed in penetrating the bridgehead. The commander of the German *Maschinengewehr-Bataillon "Sachsen"*, *Hauptmann* Müller, who had earlier been decorated with the Knight's Cross, destroyed two Soviet T–34 tanks with *Panzerfäuste.* The heavy German and Hungarian losses amounted to 30 percent of the combat strength. The loss of the two tanks is also confirmed by the Soviet sources.[143]

The already weak Hungarian 2nd Armoured Division was literally destroyed by the Soviet troops. The above-mentioned list also confirms that, apart from the German forces, there were only 150 Hungarian infantrymen left in the unit.

Northwest of Ipolydamásd, the Soviet forces broke through from the north-east to the Ipolydamásd–Letkés road. Elements of the Air Force Rifle Regiment/Division *"Szent László"* attacked this penetration from the area of Letkés in the afternoon hours toward the

141 Kornél & Ugron, 1995, p.111.

142 *Bundesarchiv–Militärarchiv* (Freiburg im Breisgau), RH 24–72, *Kriegstagebuch Ia des LXXII. Armeekorps, Morgenmeldungen unterstellter Einheiten vom 21. 12. 1944.*

143 Combat report of the 27th Independent Guards Tank Brigade to the commander of the 7th Guards Army tank and mechanized troops (a copy owned by the author), 21 December 1944. In the evening the Brigade had 14 operational T–34 tanks and three SU–85 self-propelled guns.

east and the southeast.

Despite the strong defence put up by the Soviet forces, the concentrated Hungarian assault recaptured Liliom-puszta at about 1730 hours and advanced further to the southeast. At about 1810 hours in the evening, the Air Force Rifle Regiment reached Lelédhidi-puszta, then point no. 114, 500 metres north of Ipolydamásd, at 2015 hours. Elements of these Hungarian units established defence positions on the edge of the woods east of Lelédhidi-puszta.

The German—Hungarian defenders held the hills east of Letkés, as well as Ipolytölgyes and Ganádmajor, 2km to its north. One company (presumably the *2.*) of the freshly arrived *Panzer-Aufklärungs-Abteilung 3*, attached to *LXXII. Armeekorps*, was also committed.[144] This company, together with the Hungarian 2nd Battalion/1st Parachute Regiment, using its 23 *Sd.Kfz.* 250 light armoured personnel carriers, moved out from the direction of Letkés toward the north, cleared the road and the area west of the Dávidrévi-puszta and repulsed the Soviet troops that had already advanced as far as the road.

During the morning, the *3. Panzer-Division* conducted a thorough and extensive reconnaissance in preparation for the attack that was to be carried out in its attachment to *LVII. Armeekorps* A high price was paid for this, however, because many of the unit's high-ranking officers were seriously wounded, including the commander of *Panzergrenadier-Regiment 394*, *Oberst* Schacke, and the commander of the *II. Bataillon/Panzergrenadier-Regiment 394*, *Hauptmann* Schmidt (the latter died shortly thereafter).[145]

During the day, *Panzer-Pionier-Bataillon 59* was attached to the Division *"Szent László"*. The regimental units and the 2nd Battalion of the Parachute Regiment were engaged in battle at Letkés, the regimental command post was at Ipolyszalka. At about noon the Air Force Rifle Regiment and the 2nd Battalion/1st Parachute Regiment were attached to the Hungarian 2nd Armoured Division.

However, not even the Air Force Rifle Regiment was present in full strength at the Ipoly. Two companies of the 2nd Battalion arrived at about 1000 hours in the morning, but other units were still away on the Dunántúl (Transdanubia), at Sárkeresztúr. The immediate transport of these troops required 21 heavy trucks.

LXXII. Armeekorps planned to hold the Szob bridgehead with its remaining forces, to secure the Letkés–Ipolydamásd road while conducting offensive combat activity. Following the arrival of the full forces of the Division *"Szent László"*, which was attached to the *Armeekorps*, it was planned to launch an assault between Letkés and Nagybörzsöny aimed at the destruction of the Soviet forces emerging out of the Börzsöny-hegység. The plan was adversely affected by the fact that the units of the Division *"Szent László"* that had already arrived and that were still *en route* did not have supply troops, and the division artillery, the 20th Assault Artillery Battalion and the 53rd Pioneer Battalion were not available.[146]

The German *Divisionsgruppe "Rintelen"*, concentrating the remnants of the *8. Panzer-Division* and the *357. Infanterie-Division*[147], was reattached to *LVII. Armeekorps*. Effective

144 The commander of the German *2. Kompanie/Panzer-Aufklärungs-Abteilung 3*, *Oberleutnant* Gohle was mentioned in the daily combat report. For this, see: *Geschichte der 3. Panzer-Division Berlin-Brandenburg 1935–1945*, 1967, p.451.

145 *Geschichte der 3. Panzer-Division Berlin-Brandenburg 1935–1945*, 1967, p.451.

146 *Bundesarchiv–Militärarchiv* (Freiburg im Breisgau), RH 24–72, *Kriegstagebuch Ia des LXXII. Armeekorps,* 21. 12. 1944.

147 The *Kampfgruppe* of the *357. Infanterie-Division* had on that day two combat-ready *StuG.* IV assault guns and five out of seven 7.5cm anti-tank gun ready for action.

at 1200 hours, this *Armeekorps* assumed command and control on the former northern flank of *LXXII. Armeekorps*. The *3.* and *6. Panzer-Divisions*, which were *en route,* were delayed by heavy raids by Soviet ground-attack aircraft. As a result of these air raids, the planned assault was not launched until 1800 hours.

German reconnaissance identified 70 Soviet armoured fighting vehicles in the area of Hontfüzesgyarmat, which could have launched an attack against the north-western flank of *LVII. Panzerkorps* at any time.[148]

At about 1500 hours the commander of the 6th Guards Tank Army ordered the 21st Guards and 22nd Guards Tank Brigades/5th Guards Tank Corps and the 46th Guards Tank and the 30th Guards Mechanized Brigades/9th Guards Mechanized Corps to turn south and attack toward Hontfüzesgyarmat, Garamsalló and Zalaba in order to prevent the German *8. Panzer-Division* from attacking the right flank of the 7th Guards Army.[149] At that time, the 21st Guards and 22nd Guards Tank Brigade had a total of 54 operational T–34 and T–34/85 tanks.[150]

Consequently, the Soviet tank and mechanized brigades were given orders to turn to the south even before the Germans could actually launch their attack with the three *Panzer* divisions toward Kistompa. Although the reason for the Soviet manoeuvre was the activity of the *8. Panzer-Division*, its consequences were soon to be felt by both of the other *Panzer* divisions too.

The forces of the three *Panzer* divisions of *LVII. Panzerkorps* were:

Table 2 – Strength of the three *Panzer* divisions of *LVII. Panzerkorps*, 21 December 1944

	3. Panzer-Division	***6. Panzer-Division***	***8. Panzer-Division***	**Total**
Armoured fighting vehicles	*Pz-Jäger-Abt. 543 1.Kompanie/Pz-Ausfklärungs-Abt. 3*	*II. Pz.-Abt./Pz.-Rgt. 11 Pz-Jäger-Abt. 41*	Two *Komp. of I. Pz. Abt./Pz. Rgt. 10 Pz-Jäger-Abt. 43*	5 *Abteilungen*
Armoured personnel carriers	*Pz-Aufklärungs-Abteilung 3*	*Pz-Aufklärungs-Abteilung 6*	*Pz-Aufklärungs-Abteilung 8*	3 *Abteilungen*
Panzergrenadiers	*II. Bataillon/Pz.-Gren.-Rgt. 3, I. and II. Bataillon/Pz-Gren.-Rgt. 394*	*I. and II. Bataillon/ Pz.-Gren.-Rgt. 4, I. Bataillon/Pz-Gren. Rgt. 114*	*I.* and *II. Bataillon/ Pz.-Gren.-Rgt. 28, II. Bataillon/Pz-Gren. Rgt. 98*	9 battalions
Artillery	*I.* and *III. Abt.s/ (towed) Pz.-Art-Rgt. 75*	*II.* and *III. Abt.s/ (towed) Pz.-Art-Rgt. 76*	*II.* and *III. Abt.s/ (towed) Pz.-Art-Rgt. 80*	6 *Abteilungen*
Pioniers	two *Kompanien* of the *Pz.-Pionier-Btl. 39*	two *Kompanien* of the *Pz.-Pionier-Btl. 57*	two *Kompanien* of the *Pz.-Pionier-Btl. 59*	6 Companies
Flak	*Flak-Abteilung 314*	*Flak-Abteilung 298*	*Flak-Abteilung 286*	3 *Abteilungen*

148 HM HIM *Hadtörténelmi Levéltár* (Budapest) microfilm archives, *Kriegstagebuch Ia der Heeresgruppe Süd, Kriegstagebuch vom* 21. 12. 1944 (roll no. 627. image no. 7211196).

149 *Budapestskaya Operaciya*. Contemporary summary of the 2nd Ukrainian Front about the operations around Budapest. (A copy owned by the author). p.124.

150 Zavizion & Kornyushin, 1967, p.131.

On 21 December the German group above possessed the following combat-ready armoured fighting vehicles[151]:

- *3. Panzer-Division*
  - *Panzerjäger-Abteilung 543 with* 17 *Jagdpanzer* tank destroyers;
  - *1. Kompanie/Panzer-Aufklärungs-Abteilung 3* with 25 *Aufkl. Panzer 38(t)* reconnaissance tanks;
- *6. Panzer-Division*
  - *II. Abteilung/Panzer-Regiment 11* with 25 *Panzer IV* tanks;
  - *Panzerjäger-Abteilung 41* with 13 *Jagdpanzer IV* tank destroyers;
- *8. Panzer-Division*
  - Two (1st and 3rd) mixed companies of the *I. (gemischte) Abteilung/Panzer-Regiment 10* with all *Panzer IV* and *Panther* tanks in repair;
  - *Panzerjäger-Abteilung 43* with four *Jagdpanzer IV* tank destroyers and nine *Marder* tank destroyers.

This gave a total of 93 combat-ready German armoured fighting vehicles, 25 of which, however, could be counted as light tanks (with 2cm guns as main weapons), and nine were tank destroyers with open top and back. In contrast to these figures, the Soviet literature generally speaks of a total of 200 attacking German armoured fighting vehicles of the three *Panzer* divisions.[152] This is by no means confirmed by the German records.

The German *LVII. Panzerkorps* finally launched its attack toward Kistompa at about 1800 hours in the evening. The *8. Panzer-Division* was positioned on the right flank, the *6. Panzer-Division* was in the centre, and the *3. Panzer-Division* took the left flank. The advancing units of the *6. Panzer-Division* that were attacking toward Ipolyvisk and Kistompa were included in *Kampfgruppe "Stahl"*, which was named after *Oberst* Stahl, commander of *Panzergrenadier-Regiment 114*.[153]

By the end of the day, the 9th Guards Mechanized Corps/6th Guards Tank Army occupied the following villages: Hontnádas, Kálnaborfő, Dolné Zemberovce and Horhi, and one of its brigades was engaged in combat south of Kispeszek.

The 5th Guards Tank Corps captured Zsemlér and Nemesoroszi and, at the end of the day, two of its brigades were in combat south of Nemesoroszi.[154]

The 27th Guards Rifle Corps/7th Guards Army captured Pereszlény, Ipolyvisk, Bernecebaráti and Nagycsalomja. The 25th Guards Rifle Corps repulsed the counterattacks of the German—Hungarian forces. The army claimed to have knocked out eight enemy tanks, two *Jagdpanzers* and four armoured personnel carriers, and to have taken 320 prisoners.[155]

By 2200 hours, the Soviet tanks committed toward the south reached Garamsalló on

151 Without the wheeled reconnaissance armoured cars of the *Panzer-Aufklärungs-Abteilungen*.

152 See for example Zaharov, M. V., *A 2. és a 3. Ukrán Front felszabadító hadműveletei Délkelet- és Közép-Európában, 1944–1945* (Liberating operations of the 2nd and 3rd Ukrainian Fronts in Southeastern and Central Europe, 1944-1945), Budapest, 1973, p.226.

153 Paul, Wolfgang, *Brennpunkte. Die Geschichte der 6. Panzerdivision (1. leichte) 1937–1945* (Krefeld, 1977), p.438.

154 HM HIM *Hadtörténelmi Levéltár (Budapest), Szovjet iratmásolatok gyűjteménye a Budapest körüli harcokról. A 2. Ukrán Front hadijelentései, 1944. december 21.*

155 Daily combat reports of the Soviet 7th Guards Army to the command of the 2nd Ukrainian Front (a copy owned by the author), evening report, 21 December 1944.

the newly created left flank of the German *LXXII. Armeekorps*. The German *Armeekorps* had only two assault guns and some infantry that could be dispatched toward the northwest against the penetrating forces. *LXXII. Armeekorps* prepared the bridges on the Garam for demolition and prepared to alert supply troops stationed in the rear area on the north bank of the Danube. Furthermore, the *Armeekorps* requested regrouping of units of the Hungarian *Jagdpanzer* 38(t) tank destroyers that were being retrained in the Esztergom training facility.

That day German—Hungarian units of *Luftflotte 4* supported *Armeegruppe "Fretter-Pico"* with a total of 470 sorties. The activity of the Soviet fighter aircraft and anti-aircraft artillery prevented the exact assessment of losses inflicted on the enemy. The pilots claimed to have destroyed three armoured fighting vehicles, some anti-aircraft guns, two prime movers and approximately 50 horse-drawn wagons.[156] That same day, the Hungarian 102nd Rapid Bomber Group attacked a Soviet car column that was moving on the road between Ipolyság and Deménd.[157]

According to unconfirmed German reports from that same day, Soviet forces continued the assault from Léva toward the northeast and the northwest with two tank formations, together with 30-40 additional armoured fighting vehicles on the front line sector of the *IV. Panzerkorps/8. Armee*. One of their groups reached Pukanec (Bakabánya) in Slovakia, and another reached Garamkovácsi.

It is a well-known fact that reconnaissance elements of the *24. Panzer-Division* were in action with elements of the Soviet 9th Guards Mechanized Corps on the Korpona–Léva road near Dolné Zemberovce (Alsózsember) in Slovakia. At that time, the Germans did not know whether the Soviets wished to cover their main forces from the north or if they really had launched an attack northward.[158] The Selmecbánya–Újbánya road, however, was closed by *Alarmtruppen*.

On the western flank of *IV. Armeekorps* the Soviets captured Aranyosmarót with a battalion-sized force supported by a number of armoured fighting vehicles. At 1500 hours in the afternoon, elements of *SS-Sturmbrigade "Dirlewanger"* and the reinforced regimental *Kampfgruppe* of the *24. Panzer-Division* launched an attack aimed at the recapture of the hills north of Palást and the section of the *Margarethen-Stellung (Line)* west of Balassagyarmat. The *24. Panzer-Division* recaptured Inám and was engaged in battle for Ipolykeszi.[159]

At dawn on **22 December 1944**[160], the forces defending Szob were forced back to the western bank of the Ipoly by the night assault of the Soviets on the front line of *LXXII. Armeekorps*. The attack of the Air Force Rifle Regiment/Division *"Szent László"* via Lelédhidi-puszta reached Ipolydamásd. East of Letkés the Soviets penetrated the outpost

156 HM HIM *Hadtörténelmi Levéltár* (Budapest) microfilm archives, *Kriegstagebuch Ia der Heeresgruppe Süd, Kriegstagebuch vom 21. 12. 1944* (roll no. 627. image no. 7211184).

157 Kindly disclosed by military historian Csaba B. Stenge.

158 HM HIM *Hadtörténelmi Levéltár* (Budapest) microfilm archives, *Kriegstagebuch Ia der Heeresgruppe Süd, Kriegstagebuch vom 21. 12. 1944* (roll no. 627. image no. 7211198).

159 HM HIM *Hadtörténelmi Levéltár* (Budapest) microfilm archives, *Kriegstagebuch Ia der Heeresgruppe Süd, Kriegstagebuch vom 21. 12. 1944* (roll no. 627. image no. 7211183).

160 Weather: temperature alternating between -3 and +5° Celsius, sunny, bright sky, minor roads were drying up.

lines toward the west. The German *Panzer-Pionier-Regiment 59* repulsed advancing Soviet forces north of Ipolytölgyes, at the Ganádi mill.

The crossing points on the Garam at Kéménd and Garamkövesd had been closed by *Flak* units in anticipation of a Soviet tank assault. A Hungarian anti-aircraft battery established its positions North of Nána, and two *Kampfgruppen* of the German *II. (Abteilung)/Flak-Regiment 24* were positioned at Kéménd, with a total of seven 8.8cm guns.

There were eight more 8.8cm anti-aircraft guns in anti-tank positions on the road between Garamkövesd and Kicsind. Staff Major Lajtos ordered the Bicycle Company/ Reconnaissance Battalion of the Division *"Szent László"* that had arrived to defend the anti-aircraft guns. However, if the company was in danger of destruction, it was to retreat to Garamkövesd in time.[161]

Further units of the Division *"Szent László"* arrived by morning, mostly from the grenadier regiment. According to a German report issued at 0730 hours the composition of the regiment was:[162]:

- 1st Grenadier Battalion with a sapper platoon with 80 men;
    - 1st Company with 173 men,
    - 2nd Company with 103 men,
    - 3rd Company with 80 men,
    - Heavy weapons company with 51 men;
- 2nd Grenadier Battalion
    - 4th Company with 170 men,
    - 5th Company with 50 men,
    - 6th Company with 72 men,
    - Heavy weapons company with 150 men.

According to the morning report of the Division *"Szent László"* the unit had the following equipment:

- The 2nd Battalion/1st Parachute Regiment with 318 men (30 machine guns, two heavy 7.5cm anti-tank guns, six 5cm mortars, two 8cm mortars and one heavy machine gun);
- The Air Force Rifle Regiment with 1600 men (no report regarding armament);
- The German *Panzer-Pionier-Bataillon 59* with 151 men and 15 machine guns;
- 2nd Towed Artillery Battalion with nine 10.5cm light field howitzers;
- 6th Towed Artillery Battalion with nine 10.5cm light field howitzers.[163]

The 2nd Battalion/Air Force Rifle Regiment of the Division *"Szent László"* reached the line northern edge of Ipolydamásd – point no. 312 (onekm northeast of Ipolydamásd),

161 HM HIM *Hadtörténelmi Levéltár* (Budapest), *Tanulmányok és visszaemlékezések gyűjteménye* (Collection of studies and recollections) nr. 2598., Lajtos Árpád: *Szent László hadosztály (Visszaemlékezés).* (Árpád Lajtos: Division *"Szent László"* (Recollections)), p.55.

162 *Bundesarchiv–Militärarchiv* (Freiburg im Breisgau), *RH 24–72, Kriegstagebuch Ia des LXXII. Armeekorps, Anlage Nr. 1127, 22. 12. 1944.*

163 *Bundesarchiv–Militärarchiv* (Freiburg im Breisgau), RH 24–72, *Kriegstagebuch Ia des LXXII. Armeekorps, Morgenmeldungen unterstellter Einheiten vom 22. 12. 1944.*

and the 1st Battalion reached the line Lelédhidi-puszta – point no. 206 (Letkés east).

The 2nd Company/1st Battalion of the Grenadier Regiment in reserve (1st Lieutenant Béla Szepesvári) was reinforced with a mortar platoon (four tubes) and two machine guns. It was then ordered to the western bank of the Ipoly to go into defence west of Lelédhidi-puszta. 1st Lieutenant Szepesvári wrote the following in his diary:

> I gave orders to move out at 0600 hours, but, of course, my company was not yet ready, and I was extremely angry. I also took two civilian vehicles for carrying ammunition, but I had troubles with them also, because they [the civilian drivers] were too afraid to come out into the front line. We were feeling about uncertainly in the freezing cold and the pitch black darkness of the night.
>
> It was already dawning, and bullets were spattering about. Damn, it was already going to be morning light when I got to my position! How was I to place my company then? At last, when it was already bright daylight, I reached the Ipoly. There was a little hunter's cottage on the bank, which I entered. I saw that an artillery observer warrant officer slept there in the greatest calmness possible, and there were approximately 50 armoured forces' warrant officers in the barn. I inquired about the situation. They had been there for about a month now, assigned to observe the river. I told them that the vacation was over, the Russians were here. They showed me the defence positions; the left side was well-built and equipped with bunkers but there was nothing on the right side. I placed my company and I also set up my command post on the hilltop (equipped with a bunker, too).[164]

During the day, forces of the Hungarian 2nd Armoured Division and Division *"Szent László"* were engaged in heavy combat with Soviet units attacking from 1300 hours onwards with heavy artillery and mortar fire and air support, and prevented them entering the woods southwest of the Letkés–Ipolydamásd road.

The Division *"Szent László"* assumed command on the front line of the Hungarian 2nd Armoured Division at 1500 hours. The Hungarian 2nd Armoured Division was attached to the division, as well as all attached German and Hungarian units, as well as the German *Flak-Gruppe* positioned in the southeastern part of Kicsind. Both Hungarian units had their command post on Garamkövesd. Staff Colonel Szügyi addressed his soldiers in his order of the day:

> Soldiers of the Div[ision] *"St. László"*! The attention of the whole Hungarian Nation is anxiously [focused] upon you, and courage and resistance is expected from you such as has only been seen in the veteran regiment of the Div[ision], the par[a]tr[oope]r fighters.
>
> An intense battle awaits us, but let us hold on to every single foothold on this land with courage and resolution, because we all want to look into our children's eyes with clear consciences, we all wish to say that we have done everything for our Homeland. This Homeland was defended for a thousand years by our forefathers, and we cannot be less than they were.[165]

164 *A Hazáért mindhalálig. Vitéz Szepesvári Béla háborús naplója. Magánkiadás, é.n.* (For the Motherland, until the end. Wartime diary of *Vitéz* Béla Szepesvári, self-published, n.d.), pp.68-69.

165 HM HIM *Hadtörténelmi Levéltár* (Budapest), *a „Szent László" hadosztály tüzérparancsnokának naplója*

Additional units of the Division *"Szent László"* arrived in the course of the day:

- The full Grenadier Regiment, minus 150 men;
- The Reconnaissance Battalion (minus the anti-tank gun platoon and the cavalry company);
- One company of the tank destroyer battalion with six 7.5cm anti-tank guns.[166]

The commander of the Division *"Szent László"* ordered its troops to hold the bridgehead established at Letkés. The line extended along Hill 109 – 1km southeast of Lelédhidi-puszta – Lelédhidi-puszta – Liliom-puszta – Hill 206 – point no. 182 – Hill 109, then further along the Ipoly to the mouth of the river. Staff colonel Szügyi divided the available forces into two *Kampfgruppen*:

- *Kampfgruppe* of Colonel Jenő Altorjay[167]
    - 5th Motorized Rifle Battalion;
    - 2nd Reconnaissance Battalion;
    - Reinforced 2nd Battalion of the Grenadier Regiment[168];
    - The German *Kampfgruppe "Zirke"*;
    - The German *Maschinengewehr-Bataillon "Sachsen"*;
    - Company-sized group of the German *Pionier-Bataillon 357*;
    - Group of the German *Pionier-Bataillon 751*;
- *Kampfgruppe* of Lieutenant Colonel István Heinrich[169]
    - Air Force Rifle Regiment;
    - 2nd Battalion/1st Parachute Regiment;
    - Units of the Hungarian 2nd Armoured Division;
    - Hungarian 52nd Anti-Aircraft Artillery Battalion.[170]

Southeast of Ipolydamásd, the Soviet 53rd Rifle Division crossed the Ipoly with a regiment-sized unit and advanced from the north to Helemba, where urban combat commenced. The II Grenadier Battalion, attached *Kampfgruppe "Altorjay"*, had to launch a counterattack in the afternoon of 22 December along a track Leléd–Helemba in order to repulse units of the Soviet 53rd Rifle Division that had reached Helemba on the eastern bank of the Ipoly. The German—Hungarian counterattack was soon launched toward Helemba.

és mellékletei. 58. sz. melléklet: 330./Szent László ho. I. A.44.XII. 20. szám: Intézkedés a Szt. László ho. Ipoly-menti első harcfeladatára.

166 *Bundesarchiv–Militärarchiv* (Freiburg im Breisgau), RH 24–72, *Kriegstagebuch Ia des LXXII. Armeekorps, Tagesmeldung an Armeegruppe Fretter-Pico vom 22. 12. 1944.*

167 Colonel Jenő Altorjay was the commander of the 3rd Motorized Rifle Regiment/Hungarian 2nd Armoured Division.

168 The battalion carrying out the counterattack from the northeast toward Helemba was not attached to the *Kampfgruppe* until after the attack had been executed.

169 Lieutenant Colonel István Heinrich was the commander of the Air Force Rifle Regiment of the Division *"Szent László"*.

170 See HM HIM *Hadtörténelmi Levéltár (Budapest), a „Szent László" hadosztály tüzérparancsnokának naplója és mellékletei. 58. sz. melléklet: 330./Szent László ho. I. A.44.XII. 20. szám: Intézkedés a Szt. László ho. Ipoly-menti első harcfeladatára.*

West of Helemba, at the Kovácspatak railway station, the Hungarian forces established a blocking position consisting of two 7.5cm anti-tank guns and two *Nimród* armoured self-propelled anti-aircraft guns that had been reassigned that same day from the armoured platoon of the reconnaissance battalion of the Division *"Szent László"*, under command of 2nd Lieutenant Kornél Martin. At about 1100 hours in the morning, Soviet twin-engine bombers attacked Esztergom. Three of them turned toward the Hungarian blocking position after dropping bombs. The *Nimród* armoured self-propelled anti-aircraft guns opened fire, each vehicle firing three bursts of four rounds each. However, they did not score confirmable direct hits. Soon afterward they came under extremely accurate Soviet mortar fire. The open-top turret armoured fighting vehicles were lucky to avoid damage, but, according to the reminisces of Kornél Martin, the blocking position did not escape undamaged:

> Many were wounded and we had dead too. There was a poor young "*levente*" who carried a *Panzerschreck*[171] whom I pitied the most. There was a wooden box standing at the roadside – the sentry box at the relieving road – he was hiding there. He was killed by the splinters shearing through the box wall like hot knife through butter.[172]

Around noon the two *Nimród* armoured self-propelled anti-aircraft guns were ordered back to Garamkövesd.[173] *Kampfgruppe "Heinrich"* had to hold the bridgehead at Letkés. Despite armoured support, the Soviet attacks against this bridgehead were repulsed by the defenders. The 27th Independent Guards Tank Brigade supported the units of the 409th Rifle Division with three T–34 tanks near Bástya during the crossing of the Ipoly, and a further five tanks attacked toward Lelédhidi-puszta, Liliom-puszta and Letkés.[174]

The 2nd Company/I Grenadier Battalion (commanded by 2nd Lieutenant Szepesvári) gained experience of Soviet tank support that day:

> I had just started looking around from my lookout, when I saw four T–34 and two KV-2 tanks[175] appear on the road at the other bank of the Ipoly with great pounding noise. Somebody from the IInd platoon fired at them with a rifle. What a commotion followed! All six tanks turned out and open fire. The distance was approximately 100 metres. Then, noticing the soldiers from armoured units in the hunter's cottage

171 The "stove-pipe" (*"kályhacső"*) was just one of the names of the handheld anti-tank rocket launcher (*Panzerschreck*, or *"páncélrém"*). At the end of 1944 the direct anti-tank platoons of more than one Hungarian Division were filled out mainly by *"levente"* soldiers.

172 HM HIM *Hadtörténelmi Levéltár* (Budapest), *Tanulmányok és visszaemlékezések gyűjteménye* (Collection of studies and recollections), nr. 3138., Martin Kornél*: Néhány adat és emlék a „Szent László" felderítő osztály életéből, 1944. XI. 17.–XII. 27.* (Kornél Martin: Data and memories from the life of the Reconnaissance Battalion *"Szent László"*, 17 November – 27 December 1944), p.15.

173 HM HIM *Hadtörténelmi Levéltár* (Budapest), *Tanulmányok és visszaemlékezések gyűjteménye* (Collection of studies and recollections), nr. 3138., Martin Kornél: *Néhány adat és emlék a „Szent László" felderítő osztály életéből, 1944. XI. 17.–XII. 27.* (Kornél Martin: Data and memories from the life of the Reconnaissance Battalion *"Szent László"*, 17 November – 27 December 1944), p.15.

174 Combat report of the 27th Independent Guards Tank Brigade to the commander of the 7th Guards Army tank and mechanized troops (a copy owned by the author), 22 December 1944.

175 This is an apparent error. There were no KV–2 heavy tanks in use with any of the fighting Soviet troops. The company commander of the 27th Independent Guards Tank Brigade may have mistaken the T–34/85 tanks for KV–2.

> and my mortar crew arriving later with ammunition, the tanks began to fire at the cottage and soon destroyed it. The armoured crew ran away in every possible direction. The artillery observer warrant officer and three armoured warrant officers ran up to my command post. Now they believed it was war around us! 'No problem', said the artillery observer, 'we shall take revenge'. The lad soon established contact with the battery. While the tanks did not dare to advance further, and they were still face-to-face with us, we opened fire at them with 10.5cm howitzers. At first they did not seem to even notice. But the artillery warrant officer directed the fire very well; the miracle happened and the Göring [the Hungarian nickname for the 10.5 cm towed light field howitzer – the author] hit one of the tanks. What a commotion started among the Soviets! The tank that was hit had its track ripped off. They had serious difficulties in the heavy fire but at last they succeeded in attaching a tow-rope to the damaged tank. Meanwhile another of their tanks was hit; it hid behind the wall of the farmstead in front of us [Lelédhidi-puszta – the author]. The others shamelessly ran away."
>
> Meanwhile Soviet infantry infiltrated Lelédhíd farm in front of us. We quickly blew the farmstead away – the artillery lad fired exceptionally well. I also ordered the mortars to open fire but their aim was much worse. The current situation was quite confusing. I did not have the slightest idea who was where. The *zászlósok* were sent on a reconnaissance mission... [...] The armoured crew ran away at the sight of the tanks. I could hardly gather 25 of the 50 of them. Brave soldiers, if I may say... I placed those who remained near my command post as reserves. I requested anti-tank guns from the division in order to be able to knock out the damaged tank and any that might come later. The 75mm gun arrived with the twilight. The Soviets were very lucky, for their armoured recovery vehicle arrived at the same time and, following some exciting moments, they succeed in towing the damaged tank away. Our anti-tank gun opened fire but no hit was scored. I placed the gun in a good position.[176]

Ipolytölgyes remained in German—Hungarian hands. A total of 43 Soviet soldiers were captured that day. According to their information, three of their rifle battalions were completely destroyed during that day's fighting. The German—Hungarian troops also suffered considerable losses.

In the course of the day it turned out that the delayed transportation of the units of the Division *"Szent László"* was the Germans' fault. Staff Colonel Szügyi was cut off from the command of the units and the task was assigned to an officer from the *III. Panzerkorps*, *Hauptmann* Beck. He, however, ordered the truck columns of the division to take a wrong road, and as a result of this, the majority of them were forced to take a detour toward Komárom and Győr.[177]

On the night of 21/22 December forces of the Soviet 6th Guards Tank Army tried to gain control of the bridges on the Garam at Zseliz and Kéménd with a bold armoured thrust. 80 tanks moved out of the Hontfüzesgyarmat area toward the south, and the majority of them reached Kisgyarmat.

At about 0530 hours in the morning the armoured fighting vehicles of the Soviet 21st Guards Tank Brigade/5th Guards Tank Corps entered Zalaba and overran six heavy

176 *A Hazáért mindhalálig. Vitéz Szepesvári Béla háborús naplója. Magánkiadás, é.n.* (For the Motherland, until the end. Wartime diary of *Vitéz* Béla Szepesvári, self-published, n.d.), pp.69-72.

177 HM HIM *Hadtörténelmi Levéltár (Budapest), Fővezérség meghatalmazott tábornoka naplója*, p.28.

anti-tank guns that were surprised while being towed into firing positions in the assigned blocking position of the German *LVII. Panzerkorps*.

At Zseliz, five tanks of the Soviet 22nd Guards Tank Brigade were approaching the bridge east of the village when the defenders blew it up at 0520 hours, in accordance with higher orders. On the eastern and southern edge of Zseliz *Generalleutnant* Rintelen surveyed the establishment of defence positions in person, which were taken up by the *3. Kompanie/Panzer-Pionier-Bataillon 57* of the *6. Panzer-Division* and three towed 7.5cm anti-tank guns of the *3. Kompanie/Panzerjäger-Abteilung 41*. The anti-tank guns knocked out three Soviet tanks by the morning of the next day. The Germans also succeeded in establishing blocking positions at Bény and Kéménd.

At about 0930 hours in the morning the *6. Panzer-Division* reported to *LXXII. Armeekorps* that a battalion-sized infantry unit and five Soviet self-propelled guns had found a crossing point on the Garam at Lekér, had crossed the river to the western bank and was attacking Oroszka from the north.

Two *StuG. IV* assault guns of *Panzerjäger-Abteilung 357* were directed to Garamkövesd, along with the *Begleit-Grenadier-Zug*, where the units were directly attached to *LXXII. Armeekorps*.

At about noon, *Panzerjäger-Abteilung 41/6. Panzer-Division*, regrouped via railway, arrived to the Párkány railway station with 13 *Jagdpanzer* IV tank destroyers (11 of which were combat-ready at that time). One company of the *Abteilung* was directed to Kéménd via Nána and Kőhídgyarmat. The other was directed to Garamkövesd.

The units of the German *II. Abteilung/Panzer-Regiment 11*[178] (*Hauptmann* Herbert) arrived from the direction of Komárom, and moved out on the road along the east bank of the Garam. They reached the southern outskirts of Kisgyarmat, where they met Soviet tanks. The *Panzer* IV tanks of the *Abteilung* advanced along the west bank. Supported by a number of assault guns and an *Alarm-Kompanie*, they reached Zseliz, cleared the western bank of the Garam, and re-established communication with *Divisionsgruppe "Rintelen"*.

The previous night, before midnight, *Divisionsgruppe "Rintelen"*, together with *Panzer-Aufklärungs-Abteilung 6*, succeeded in reaching the railway bridge at Nagykálna from the north on their own front line. At the same time, another German attack from the south reached the church in Nagykálna. The Soviets had larger forces in the village than had been assumed by the Germans: 12 T–34 and T–34/85 tanks of the 20th Guards Tank Brigade and a battalion-sized infantry unit were identified in the southern part of Nagykálna, and one to two infantry companies in the northern part of the village. Of the 12 armoured fighting vehicles stationed in Nagykálna, six were destroyed by the Germans by morning.

In the meantime, the Soviets modified the railway bridge to make it suitable for armoured fighting vehicles to cross the river. Therefore the Germans needed to demolish the bridge at all costs. An assault team of officers was organized, which was also joined by *Oberleutnant* Lehner, commander of the *3. Kompanie/Panzer-Pionier-Bataillon "Feldherrnhalle"*, and *Oberleutnant* Hammer, commander of the *3. Kompanie/Panzer-Aufklärungs-Abteilung 6*. The German party finally demolished the bridge at 0535 hours on 22 December. With this, the forces of the Soviet 5th Guards Tank Corps that were engaged in Nagykálna were cut off.

---

178 On 16 December, the German *II. (Abteilung)/Panzer-Regiment 11* had 28 combat-ready *Panzer* IV tanks and two command *Panzer* IV tanks; according to data regarding 18 December the unit had a total of 25 combat-ready armoured fighting vehicles.

However, the Soviet units did not give up the village and, with it, their bridgehead on the west bank of the Garam. Reinforcements were sent over the river via emergency makeshifts, and, at 1150 hours, they launched a counterattack which repulsed the northern group of the Germans.

In the meantime, the southern German group was reinforced with 10 *Jagdpanzer* 38(t) tank destroyers of *Sturmgeschütz-Abteilung 1176*[171799]. In this way the Germans were able to continue the attack. By 1430 hours in the afternoon, Nagykálna was recaptured and cleared of Soviet forces, while all of the Soviet tanks stuck on the western bank of the Garam were destroyed. The defenders knocked out a total of 14 Soviet armoured fighting vehicles, six of these with *Panzerfäuste*. The majority of the remaining eight tanks were knocked out by the *Sd.Kfz.* 251/9 armoured personnel carriers of the *4. (schwere) Kompanie/Panzer-Aufklärungs-Abteilung* of the *6. Panzer-Division*; which had been equipped with short-barrelled 7.5cm tank guns.[180]

LXXII. Armeekorps had almost no reserves; their attention was gradually turning toward the Hungarian Assault Artillery Battalion "Bernolák", which was in training at the Esztergom training facility. At 0325 hours, at dawn on 22 December, *Oberstleutnant* Thams reported as requested by the Chief of Staff of the *Armeekorps,* that the *Hetzers* were not yet combat-ready because their guns had not yet been ranged. According to his opinion the Hungarian *Jagdpanzers* might not be ready for combat until the evening of 22 December, at the earliest, following a live fire practice carried out in the course of the day. However, their deployment needed the approval of *Heeresgruppe Süd*. According to the German plans, in the event that Esztergom was threatened by any Soviet attack, the Assault Artillery Battalion would establish contact with the combat commander in Esztergom, and place its forces at his disposal.[181]

However, the pressure exerted by the Soviet troops increased. Therefore, on 22 December, at 2240 hours, one of the officers of the *Artillerie-Kommandeur* of *LXXII. Armeekorps* set off to *Oberstleutnant* Thams in the Esztergom training facility with orders that, because of the disadvantageous enemy situation, he was to immediately send seven fully filled up *Jagdpanzers* with combat-ready crew and supplies for three days toward Kéménd, under command of a capable German (!) officer; the unit was to arrive at Kéménd by 0600 hours in the morning of 23 December.[182] However, *Oberstleutnant* Thams did not send the Hungarian *Hetzers*.[183]

The offensive of the *3.* and *6. Panzer-Division/LVII. Armeekorps* from the southern outskirts of Százd toward the northeast made good forward progress. According to the Soviets the attacking unit consisted of only 15 armoured fighting vehicles and a regiment-

179 The unit was originally a company of *Panzerjäger-Abteilung/76. Infanterie-Division*.

180 *Bundesarchiv–Militärarchiv* (Freiburg im Breisgau), RH 24–72, *Kriegstagebuch Ia des LXXII. Armeekorps, 22. 12. 1944.*

181 *Bundesarchiv–Militärarchiv* (Freiburg im Breisgau), RH 24–72, *Kriegstagebuch Ia des LXXII. Armeekorps, Anlage Nr. 1127, KTB-Notizen 21./22. 12. 44.*

182 *Bundesarchiv–Militärarchiv* (Freiburg im Breisgau), RH 24–72, *Kriegstagebuch Ia des LXXII. Armeekorps, Anlage Nr. 1127, KTB-Notizen 22. 12. 44. Blatt 5, and Anlage Nr. 1170.*

183 Therefore, the *Armeekorps* ordered the commander of the German garrison at Esztergom, *Hauptmann* Buchenau, at 0445 hours on 23 December, to make the *Oberstleutnant* write a report explaining why the seven *Jagdpanzers* had not yet moved out. The report was going to be part of the documentation of the inquiry initiated by the *Korpskommandeur, Generalleutnant* August Schmidt.

sized infantry unit.[184] The *I. Bataillon/Panzergrenadier-Regiment 4* of the *6. Panzer-Division* (*Major* Reimar) temporarily occupied Kistompa[185], and the German units reached the hills south, southwest and southeast of Alsószemeréd.

Meanwhile, the main body of the 4th Guards Mechanized Corps (Lieutenant General Vlagyimir Ivanovics Zsdanov) arrived from the Ipolyszög area. That large military unit had, by 1000 hours in the morning, organized its defence as follows:

- 36th Guards Tank Brigade in the area of point no. 225 (Bakasztó Hill);
- 15th Guards Mechanized Brigade on the northern edge of Egeg;
- 14th Guards Mechanized Brigade engaged in battle with the Germans on the southeastern edge of Kistompa.

With the support of the 36th Guards Tank Brigade, the 14th Guards Mechanized Brigade attacked from the south and east, and the 46th Guards Tank and the 30th Guards Mechanized Brigades of the 9th Guards Mechanized Corps launched their respective attacks from the northeast, from the area of Deménd, and recaptured Kistompa by the end of the day.[186] In extremely heavy combat, the village changed hands four times on that single day, and finally remained in Soviet hands.[187]

After that, the 30th Guards Mechanized and the 46th Guards Tank Brigades attacked southward, occupied Százd, and advanced to the northwestern edge of Ipolyszakállos. A number of Soviet tanks advanced to the command post of the German *3. Panzer-Division*, which was located at Lontó, despite the containing fire of the *III Panzer-Artillerie-Abteilung/ Panzer-Artillerie-Regiment 76* of the *6. Panzer-Division*. The soldiers of the *1. Kompanie/ Panzer-Nachrichten-Bataillon 39* knocked out three Soviet tanks with *Panzerfäuste*. The command post of the division was then relocated to Ipolyszakállos, where the commands of the *6.* and the *8. Panzer-Divisions* had also been stationed.[188]

With support of the 22nd Guards Tank Brigade, Soviet infantry thrust forward from the area of Garamsalló toward the southeast, and reached the western edges of Vámosmikola.[189]

Because Soviet tank and mechanized units were in the rear of the German *Panzer* divisions, *LVII. Armeekorps* advised the *Kampfgruppe* via *Armeegruppe "Fretter-Pico"* that the front line was to be pulled back to the Bernecebaráti–Ipolyvisk–Lontó–Garam line. The *Kampfgruppe* went even further and proposed that the *Panzer* divisions should retreat to a Garam bridgehead, the northern front of which would have been in the Vámosmikola area. According to *Generalleutnant* Grolman this plan was impossible to carry out because the opportunity would be lost to close the gap at Ipolyság that extended to the right flank of the German *8. Armee*. As a result, *LVII. Panzerkorps* had to hold the area that had been attained in the area of Kistompa and Gyerk, and the *8. Panzer-Division* on the right flank

184 *Budapestskaya Operaciya*. Contemporary summary of the 2nd Ukrainian Front about the operations around Budapest. (A copy owned by the author), p.125.

185 Paul, 1977, p.438.

186 *Budapestskaya Operaciya*. Contemporary summary of the 2nd Ukrainian Front about the operations around Budapest. (A copy owned by the author), pp.125-126.

187 Paul, 1977, p.438.

188 *Geschichte der 3. Panzer-Division Berlin-Brandenburg 1935–1945*, 1967, p.452.

189 HM HIM *Hadtörténelmi Levéltár* (Budapest) microfilm archives, *Kriegstagebuch Ia der Heeresgruppe Süd, Kriegstagebuch vom 22. 12. 1944* (roll no. 627. image no. 7211203).

was to attempt to recapture Bernecebaráti and the hills extending south of Ipolyság.[190]

In the evening the units of the 5th Guards Tank Corps/6th Guards Tank Army were engaged in battle on the following front line sections:

- 21st Guards Tank Brigade north of Zalaba;
- 22nd Guards Tank Brigade east of Zseliz;
- 20th Guards Tank Brigade at Léva;
- 6th Guards Motorized Rifle Brigade between Nagykálna (exclusive) and Garamszentgyörgy on the east bank of the Garam.

At the same time, forces of the 9th Guards Mechanized Corps/6th Guards Tank Army occupied the following positions:

- 30th Guards Mechanized Brigade engaged in battle with German armoured fighting vehicles at Lontó;
- 46th Guards Tank Brigade engaged in battle with German armoured fighting vehicles at Lontó;
- 18th Guards Mechanized Brigade in the area of Dolné Zemberovce;
- 31st Guards Mechanized Brigade covered the main bady of the corps from the north.

Reconnaissance of the Soviet 6th Guards Tank Army identified 50 enemy armoured fighting vehicles at Lontó, 16 at Nagykálna and six in the area of Kiskoszmály.[191]

In the meantime, the Soviet 6th Guards Tank Army formed an anti-tank group from an anti-tank rifle regiment [192] (12 x 100mm M 1944 BS–3 field guns) and six IS–2 heavy tanks of the 49th Guards Heavy Tank Regiment in order to act against the attack of the right flank of *LVII. Panzerkorps*. The command of the unit was assigned to Major Kochurov, who was the deputy commander of the heavy tank regiment. The guns and the heavy tanks occupied firing positions on the 6km line between the Ipoly and the Börzsöny mountains.[193]

According to Soviet data, the right flank of the 7th Guards Army was attacked on that day by approximately 80 armoured fighting vehicles of *LVII. Panzerkorps* from the north-western outskirts of Ipolyság. The position of the army that evening was:

- 27th Guards Rifle Corps
    - Units of the 227th Rifle Division attempting to restore the former situation at Ipolykiskeszi;
    - 303rd Rifle Division in defence southwest of Alsószemeréd on points no.197, 186 and 189 and the section extending to the Ipoly;
    - 36th Guards Rifle Division at the wood south of Homok and in the

190 HM HIM *Hadtörténelmi Levéltár* (Budapest) microfilm archives, *Kriegstagebuch Ia der Heeresgruppe Süd, Kriegstagebuch vom 22. 12. 1944* (roll no. 627. image no. 7211219 and next image).

191 HM HIM *Hadtörténelmi Levéltár (Budapest), Szovjet iratmásolatok gyűjteménye a Budapest körüli harcokról. A 2. Ukrán Front hadijelentései, 1944. december 22.*

192 The Regiment was presumably part of the 34th Independent Anti-Tank Artillery Brigade.

193 Lykow, Iwan Semjonowitsch, *In bedrohlicher Stunde* (Berlin, 1987), p.306.

Bernecebaráti area;
    - 141st Rifle Division between Hill 449 – Hill 741 (Várbükk) Bánya-puszta;
- 25th Guards Rifle Corps
    - 6th Guards Airborne Division was fighting for Ipolytölgyes and Ganádi mill;
    - 409th Rifle Division engaged in battle for the occupation of Letkés;
    - Elements of the 53rd Rifle Division crossed the Ipoly, captured the railway station of Helemba and were engaged in combat on the eastern edge of Helemba.[194]

The 4th Guards Motorcycle Regiment/6th Guards Tank Army and the 1426th Light Artillery Regiment tried to cover their own forces against the attacks of elements of *SS-Sturmbrigade "Dirlewanger"* on the sector of Palást (exclusive)–Szalatnya northeast.

However, the Germans succeeded in surprising the enemy, breaking into the eastern side of Palást, and taking the hills east of Szalatnya (the Nagy-Kemence and Kis-Kemence). In this situation, the two battalions and the ten armoured fighting vehicles of the *24. Panzer-Division* were not to go round Palást from the east and attack toward the south, but first to enter the village. The forces of *SS-Sturmbrigade "Dirlewanger"* recaptured Szalatnya in the evening of 22 December, and also Palást, at about 2300 hours.[195]

By dawn on **23 December 1944**[196] the Germans also eliminated Soviet resistance in the Alsóvárad area on the front line of *LXXII. Armeekorps*. At about 1700 hours on the previous day, a company-sized Soviet unit of motorized infantry penetrated Felső and Alsóvárad through the ruins of the demolished railway bridge and also by boats. *Divisionsgruppe "Rintelen"* sent two armoured personnel carrier platoons of *Panzer-Aufklärungs-Abteilung 6* and one *Jagdpanzer-Zug* of *Sturmgeschütz-Abteilung 1176* against them. These units cleared out both villages by 0405 hours on 23 December.

Divisionsgruppe "Rintelen" reported its morning combat strength as 420 men, 13 10.5cm light field howitzers, 10 *Jagdpanzer* 38(t) tank destroyers, five 7.5cm anti-tank guns and six 8.8cm anti-aircraft guns. During the day the *3. Batterie/Sturm-Artillerie-Brigade 239* with six combat-ready 10.5cm *StuH* 42 assault howitzers was also attached to the unit.

The Soviet 7th Guards Army continued its assaults on the positions of the German *LXXII. Armeekorps* west of the Börzsöny.

The 2nd Battalion/Air Force Rifle Regiment/Division *"Szent László"* recaptured Helemba during the night of 22/23 December and kept the village during the day. In the evening hours the Soviets succeeded in breaking into the village with minor forces south of the railway, along the Danube.

The 1st Battalion of the Regiment was encircled and attacked from three sides by the Soviets on the night of 22/23 December. However, the battalion was able to break out toward the eastern edge of Letkés, though only by suffering 35% combat casualty ratio.

194 Daily combat reports of the Soviet 7th Guards Army to the command of the 2nd Ukrainian Front (a copy owned by the author), evening report, 22 December 1944

195 HM HIM *Hadtörténelmi Levéltár* (Budapest) microfilm archives, *Kriegstagebuch Ia der Heeresgruppe Süd, Kriegstagebuch vom 22. 12. 1944* (roll no. 627. image no. 7211221).

196 Weather: -3° Celsius, damp, frosty, light snow, minor roads were drying up.

The commander of the Air Force Rifle Regiment, Lieutenant Colonel István Heinrich, planned to retake the former front line of the bridgehead at Letkés. Because the regimental commander was "enthusiastic, but untrained in commanding ground combat", Staff Major Lajtos borrowed Captain Sándor Derestey from the Hungarian 2nd Armoured Division to serve as advisor for Lieutenant Colonel Heinrich. According to the recollections of Árpád Lajtos, from then on, it was Derestey who was really in command of the Air Force Rifle Regiment.[197]

At about midnight on 22 December, Captain György Pályi succeeded in arranging his 3rd Company/1st Air Force Rifle Regiment for a counterattack. Major Lajos Maszlay[198] arrived with four *Nimród* armoured self-propelled anti-aircraft guns as support weapons. According to the recollections of Pályi:

"The counterattack was successful with the assault guns [actually: the *Nimród* armoured self-propelled anti-aircraft guns – the author]. The hill of Letkés-puszta (Liliom-puszta) was again in our hands. However, Soviet resistance was extremely hard as we tried to retake Gallyastető [actually: Galla-puszta, 3km east-southeast of Letkés– the author]. I did not force my men to carry on with the attack, for Gallyastető was bushy terrain, even less clear in the night, and many unpleasant surprises could await us. Maszlay also disapproved of fighting at night on a heavily wooded terrain, so I ordered the 2nd Company to establish defence positions on the hills of Letkés-puszta (Liliom-puszta)."[199]

The German *Panzer-Pionier-Bataillon 59* that was engaged in Ipolytölgyes had also been attacked from three sides by the Soviet 6th Guards Airborne Division. The combat strength of the *Pionier* unit dwindled to only 32 men. According to the morning report of the Division *"Szent László"* it had the following strength:

- 2nd Battalion/1st Parachute Regiment with 160 men;
- 1st Battalion/Air Force Rifle Regiment with 400 men;
- 2nd Battalion/Air Force Rifle Regiment with 500 men;
- 1st Battalion/Grenadier Regiment with 600 men;
- 2nd Battalion/Grenadier Regiment with 500 men;
- Reconnaissance Battalion with a crew of 200 men;
- The 5th Motorized Rifle Battalion with 130 men;
- The 2nd Reconnaissance Battalion with 45 men;
- The German *Maschinengewehr-Bataillon "Sachsen"* with 130 men;
- The German *Pionier-Bataillon 751* with 130 men;

197 HM HIM *Hadtörténelmi Levéltár* (Budapest), *Tanulmányok és visszaemlékezések gyűjteménye* (Collection of studies and recollections) nr. 2598., Lajtos Árpád: *Szent László hadosztály (Visszaemlékezés).* (Árpád Lajtos: Division *"Szent László"* (Recollections)), p.58.

198 Major Lajos Maszlay was the commander of the Hungarian 51st (self-propelled anti-aircraft cannon) Reserve Battalion, and arrived with his armoured cannon from the Esztergom training facility. For this, see Martin Kornél – Ugron István: *Fejezetek a Szent László hadosztály történetéből. I. rész.* (Kornél Martin – István Ugron: Chapters from the history of the Division *"Szent László"*, Part I.) in: *Hadtörténelmi Közlemények* issue 1995/3, p.115.

199 HM HIM *Hadtörténelmi Levéltár (Budapest), Tanulmányok és visszaemlékezések gyűjteménye* (Collection of studies and recollections), nr. 3064 Pályi Görgy: *A Szent László hadosztály repülő lövészezredének története, 1944. október – 1945. december.* (György Pályi: History of the Air Force Rifle Regiment of the Division *"Szent László"*, October 1944 – December 1945), p.16.

- Eight combat-ready 7.5cm anti-tank guns.[200]

The 2nd Battalion/Grenadier Regiment of the Division *"Szent László"* (Captain Miklós Békássy) was committed against the forces of the Soviet 409th Rifle Division that had broken in northwest of Ipolydamásd. The aim of the counterattack was to cut off the Soviet units engaged there from their supplies. Meanwhile, at about 1000 hours, seven T–34 tanks of the 1st Guards Tank Battalion/27th Guards Tank Regiment supporting the 675th Rifle Regiment /409th Rifle Division approached Lelédhidi-puszta from the southeast and were only 500 metres away. However, the Soviet infantry fell behind the armoured fighting vehicles which turned back and waited for the soldiers of 675th Rifle Regiment at the quarry by the roadside. After the infantry rejoined, at 1200 hours, they resumed their advance and occupied Lelédhidi-puszta. The German—Hungarian defenders knocked out a total of two Soviet T–34 tanks there during the day.[201] 1st Lieutenant Béla Szepesvári, commander of the 2nd Company/I Grenadier Battalion recorded the events in his diary as follows:

> The night was relatively calm. I sent out patrols. The Soviets reportedly crossed the Ipoly at the quarry [1.5km southeast of Lelédhidi-puszta– the author]. This was reported by the German *Pioniers* directly to me[202]. They also added that they had repulsed the Soviets. At about 7 o'clock in the morning I heard a huge blast and saw fire rising up. Our anti-tank gun had knocked out a T–34. It was ablaze and suddenly blew up with thunderous sound. My men cheered loudly at the sight. Later the anti-tank gun knocked out a truck and a car packed Soviet officers. My two machine guns located by my command post also opened fire. Down under, my men hunted Soviet officers and shot at the tyres of the cars. The Soviets were also active in the farmstead. Again we engaged them with fire with the help of my artilleryman friend.
>
> No food supplies. We were starving together.
>
> In the afternoon I visited the Germans again. I sent out recon patrols to assess the situation. South of me, around Helemba, fierce combat was going on by the Danube, with huge losses on the Regiment's side. In the afternoon the anti-tank gun was also dealt with, unluckily. It was fired upon so heavily that not even a foothold was left clear. The *Ratsch-bum*[203] also opened fire. The anti-tank gun remained undamaged, but its crew took advantage of the dark and disappeared. Luckily there was no more traffic on the road during the day.[204]

200 *Bundesarchiv–Militärarchiv* (Freiburg im Breisgau), RH 24–72, *Kriegstagebuch Ia des LXXII. Armeekorps, Morgenmeldungen unterstellter Einheiten vom 23. 12. 1944.*

201 Combat report of the 27th Independent Guards Tank Brigade to the commander of the 7th Guards Army tank and mechanized troops (a copy owned by the author), 23 December 1944. The operational armoured fighting vehicle strength of the unit in the evening consisted of 17 T–34 tanks and six SU–85 self-propelled guns.

202 Probably the German *Pionier-Bataillon 751.*

203 After the widely known expression in German military slang (*Ratsch-bum*), the Hungarian soldiers called the Soviet anti-tank guns likewise. The high muzzle velocity of the projectile caused the impact to be heard earlier in the target area than the discharge itself.

204 *A Hazáért mindhalálig. Vitéz Szepesvári Béla háborús naplója. Magánkiadás, é.n.* (For the Motherland, until the end. Wartime diary of *Vitéz* Béla Szepesvári, self-published, n.d.), p.73.

The other knocked out Soviet tank was, presumably, the vehicle that had been rendered immobile by the artillery of the Division *"Szent László"* out of six armoured fighting vehicles that assembled in the Ipoly valley.[205]

The Soviet 675th Rifle Regiment, supported by tanks, was to occupy Letkés by the evening of the same day. Although the Soviets were able to narrow the bridgehead at Letkés, the village itself remained in German—Hungarian hands. The Hungarian 2nd Battalion/1st Parachute Regiment was unfaltering in defending the hills east of the village. In the evening, Soviet pressure pushed the 2nd Company/1. Air Force Rifle Battalion out of the area of Liliom-puszta and forced it back to the eastern edge of Letkés; the company dwindled to no more than 35 men. Late in the evening, Captain Pályi received orders to recapture Liliom-puszta. Therefore, the battalion commander concentrated the heavy weapons company, elements of the 3rd Company/I Air Force Rifle Battalion, the battalion sub-units and his own staff to carry out the counterattack.[206]

The Garamkövesd–Ipolypásztó road was perfectly usable. In the late afternoon hours, small Soviet units crossed the Ipoly southeast of Ipolyszalka. The defenders were also unable to contain and repulse the Soviet advance in the area of Ipolytölgyes. West of this area, Ipolykiskeszi was defended by only 80 older soldiers under command of a reserve 2nd Lieutenant. Their heavy armament consisted of two self-propelled 2cm twin-barrelled anti-aircraft cannon.[207]

The main body of armoured *Kampfgruppe "Scheppelmann"*[208] started off from the area of Keménd at 0900 hours, proceeded via Kisgyarmat and attacked Zalaba with eight *Panzer* IV tanks and 13 *Jagdpanzer* IV tank destroyers. At about 1000 hours the other half of the *Kampfgruppe*[209] was in combat between Kisgyarmat and Zalaba.[210] According to a report issued at 1440 hours, seven Soviet tanks were identified north of Kisgyarmat. The armoured *Kampfgruppe* attacked Kisölved at about 1600 hours and also recaptured Garamsalló. With this, the German armoured fighting vehicles cleared the Kisgyarmat–Zalaba–Ipolypásztó road of the forces of the Soviet 21st Guards and the 22nd Guards Tank Brigade. In the meantime, the *Panzer-Gruppe* of *Major* Scheppelmann knocked out a total of 12 Soviet tanks, three self-propelled M17 four-barrelled anti-aircraft heavy machine guns (mounted on half-track armoured fighting vehicles), two armoured personnel carriers,

205 HM HIM *Hadtörténelmi Levéltár (Budapest), a „Szent László" hadosztály tüzérparancsnokának naplója és mellékletei. 1944. 12. 23.*

206 HM HIM *Hadtörténelmi Levéltár (Budapest), Tanulmányok és visszaemlékezések gyűjteménye* (Collection of studies and recollections), nr. 3064 Pályi Görgy: *A Szent László hadosztály repülő lövészezredének története, 1944. október – 1945. december.* (György Pályi: History of the Air Force Rifle Regiment of the Division *"Szent László"*, October 1944 – December 1945), p.19.

207 HM HIM *Hadtörténelmi Levéltár (Budapest), Tanulmányok és visszaemlékezések gyűjteménye* (Collection of studies and recollections), nr. 3138., Martin Kornél: *Néhány adat és emlék a „Szent László" felderítő osztály életéből, 1944. XI. 17.–XII. 27.* (Kornél Martin: Data and memories from the life of the Reconnaissance Battalion *"Szent László"*, 17 November – 27 December 1944) p.22. The weapons were presumably MG 151/20 heavy machine guns mounted on trucks.

208 The armoured *Kampfgruppe* consisted of parts of the *II. (Abteilung)/Panzer-Regiment 11* and the *1.* and *2. Kompanie/Panzerjäger-Abteilung 41* commanded by the commander of the *Panzerjäger-Abteilung, Major* Scheppelmann.

209 Parts of the *II. (Abteilung)/Panzer-Regiment 11*, four *StuG.* III and *StuG.* IV assault guns (from the *357. Infanterie-Division* and the *Feldausbildungs-Division 153* respectively) and an *Alarmkompanie.*

210 *Bundesarchiv–Militärarchiv* (Freiburg im Breisgau), RH 24–72, *Kriegstagebuch Ia des LXXII. Armeekorps, Anlage Nr. 1177/12 és13. 23. 12. 1944.*

one armoured car, one anti-tank gun and a number of trucks.[211]

In the course of the day, *Generalleutnant* Schmidt visited the securing forces in positions at Kéménd, Bény and Csata. Bény was defended merely by an alarm company of 70 soldiers. Csata was secured by the Hungarian 6th Company/3rd Motorized Rifle Regiment (60 men) and the German *2.* and *3. Kompanie/Panzer-Pionier-Regiment 57* of the *6. Panzer-Division* (with 60 and 80 men respectively).

According to the assessment of *LXXII. Armeekorps*, the main achievement of the day was the defensive successes of the Division *"Szent László"*. However, the division, which had fought heavily and bravely during the last two days, suffered considerable losses and its combat strength decreased significantly.

During the day, additional elements arrived at the Division *"Szent László"*: the missing elements of the Air Force Rifle Regiment and the Grenadier Regiment, as well as the cavalry company of the reconnaissance battalion. Three *Jagdpanzer* IV tank destroyers of the German *Panzerjäger-Abteilung 41* and the *1. Alarmkompanie/357. Infanterie-Division* with two 7.5cm anti-tank guns were also attached to the division. The latter company had been engaged earlier on Szentendre island.

During the day, the German *II. Bataillon/Panzergrenadier-Regiment 93* of the *13. Panzer-Division* was attached to *LXXI. Armeekorps*[212]. It was positioned at Garamkövesd as *Korps* reserve. Two *Batteries* of *Flak-Abteilung 299* were also attached, and positioned 3km northeast of Esztergom.[213] The *2. Alarmkompanie/357. Infanterie-Division* was also directed to Garamkövesd.

That day, the Hungarian 52nd Anti-Aircraft Artillery Battalion shot down two Soviet aircraft with 4cm cannon.[214]

At about 1835 hours in the evening, the Chief of Staff of the *6. Panzer-Division* informed the Chief of Staff of *LXXII. Armeekorps* that Assault Artillery Battalion "Bernolák", with its full personnel, was to relocate to the command post of *LVII. Panzerkorps* at Vámosmikola. *Generalstabs-Oberst* Möller described the relocation of the "*Hetzers*" as a "serious blow" to the units engaged in combat on the front line of *LXXII. Armeekorps* at Letkés and to its southeast.[215]

The above-mentioned extremely dangerous situation became evident when *Armeegruppe "Fretter-Pico"* attached Assault Artillery Battalion "Bernolák" to *LVII. Panzerkorps*. The previous plan, by which the part of the battalion that had been formed from the units of the 16th Assault Artillery Battalion (the Germans called this *Kompanie Nr.* 16) was to be given to *LXXII. Armeekorps*, would have been ruined by this. The part of the battalion that had been formed from elements of the 24th Assault Artillery Battalion (the Germans called this *Kompanie Nr.* 24) had already been sent toward Vámosmikola with nine *Jagdpanzer*

211 HM HIM *Hadtörténelmi Levéltár* (Budapest) microfilm archives, *Kriegstagebuch Ia der Heeresgruppe Süd, Morgenmeldung vom 24. 12. 1944* (roll no. 627. image no. 7211866).

212 Combat strength of the battalion consisted of five officers, 26 non-commissioned officers and 125 men. Their armament consisted of 11 machine guns and rifles.

213 *Bundesarchiv–Militärarchiv* (Freiburg im Breisgau), RH 24–72, *Kriegstagebuch Ia des LXXII. Armeekorps, 23. 12. 1944.*

214 *Bundesarchiv–Militärarchiv* (Freiburg im Breisgau), RH 24–72, *Kriegstagebuch Ia des LXXII. Armeekorps, Morgenmeldungen unterstellter Einheiten vom 25. 12. 1944.*

215 *Bundesarchiv–Militärarchiv* (Freiburg im Breisgau), RH 24–72, *Kriegstagebuch Ia des LXXII. Armeekorps, Anlage Nr. 1175, KTB-Notizen 23. 12. 44. Blatt 4.*

38(t) tank destroyers.[216]

In his report that was issued at 1330 hours, *Oberstleutnant* Thams thoroughly explained why he had not sent the seven Hungarian *Hetzers* to Kéménd the day before. Although the orders received were then conveyed to the battalion commander, Major Bernolák, the armoured fighting vehicles could not set off before noon on 23 December, because Thams did not have any officers he could spare to command of the *Jagdpanzers* that were to be so deployed. He had only one training officer, and that individual could not be spared because the arrival of a further 25 *Jagdpanzer* 38(t)s was anticipated. Furthermore, there were no supplies nor a supply section for the crews of the armoured fighting vehicles.[217]

It was typical of the hasty nature of German command that, according to the information provided by *LXXII. Armeekorps*, the commander of the Division *"Szent László"*, Staff Colonel Szügyi, still believed in the evening of 23 December that the two batteries of Assault Artillery Battalion "Bernolák" had been given to them. As a result, the battery created from the units of the 24th Assault Artillery Battalion (commanded by 1st Lieutenant Béla Körös) was ordered to go to Ipolyszalka and was instructed to prepare to cross the Letkés. The other battery that had been formed from elements of the 16th Assault Artillery Battalion (1st Lieutenant György Koltay) had to send its armoured fighting vehicles forward to Bajta.[218]

LVII. Panzerkorps launched an attack to recapture Pereszlény and Gyerk. The Germans thrust into Kistompa three times, but the forces of the arriving Soviet 4th Guards Mechanized Corps finally forced them back to the hills 2km from the village and engaged them in a tank battle.

On the front line of the German *3. Panzer-Division*, the soldiers of the *II. Bataillon/ Panzergrenadier-Regiment 3* (*Hauptmann* Seifert) evacuated Százd. The Soviet 22nd Guards Tank Brigade penetrated Ipolyszakállos from the west with a number of heavily firing T–34 tanks, and then retreated as quickly as they came. Some of the Soviet tanks that entered the village were destroyed by the soldiers defending the command post of the *6. Panzer-Division*.[219]

The Soviet withdrawal from Ipolyszakállos could be attributed to the fact that the *II. Bataillon/Panzergrenadier-Regiment 3*, arriving from the direction of Százd, together with the *Jagdpanzer* IV tank destroyers of the *1. Kompanie/Panzerjäger-Abteilung 543* (*Hauptmann* Benthien) launched a counterattack. However, the success was only temporary, for *Panzergrenadier-Regiment 394* was attacked in the rear by Soviet forces, whereupon it entered the area between the *3.* and *6. Panzer-Divisions*.[220]

In the morning, the Germans launched an assault against the blocking positions of the Soviet "Kochurov" anti-tank group. After the first German attempt, the Soviets claimed to have knocked out approximately 12 German armoured fighting vehicles. The Germans withdrew, then renewed their attack. This time, although the vehicles were more cautiously separated, they were, nevertheless engaged in battle with the excellently camouflaged Soviet

216 *Bundesarchiv–Militärarchiv* (Freiburg im Breisgau), RH 24–72, *Kriegstagebuch Ia des LXXII. Armeekorps, Anlage Nr. 1177., Generalkommando LXXII. A.K. Abt. Ia. Nr. 2952/44 geh. am 23. 12. 1944.*

217 *Bundesarchiv–Militärarchiv* (Freiburg im Breisgau), RH 24–72, *Kriegstagebuch Ia des LXXII. Armeekorps, Anlage Nr. 1177, 23. 12. 44.*

218 HM HIM *Hadtörténelmi Levéltár (Budapest), a „Szent László" hadosztály tüzérparancsnokának naplója és mellékletei. 62. melléklet.*

219 Paul, 1977, p.439.

220 *Geschichte der 3. Panzer-Division Berlin-Brandenburg 1935–1945*, 1967, p.452.

100mm anti-tank guns. The German attack again failed, as was the case with repeated attempts during the course of the day. The units of Major Kochurov successfully covered the rear of the 6th Guards Tank Army and its supply lines. In the meantime, the group lost two IS–2 heavy tanks and a number of 100mm guns.[221]

Heeresgruppe Süd informed *LVII. Panzerkorps* by radio, at about 2230 hours, that the establishment of contact with the right flank of the *8. Armee* and closing of the Ipolyság corridor with an offensive were of decisive importance to the battle for Hungary.[222]

On the right flank of *IV. Panzerkorps,* 10 armoured fighting vehicles and two battalions of the *24. Panzer-Division*[223], along with elements of *SS-Sturmbrigade "Dirlewanger",* attacked from the north and captured the hills southeast of Palást.

The Germans – probably soldiers of *SS-Oberführer* Dirlewanger – carried out a savage massacre that same day at Szalatnya. Soviet soldiers, the local residents and the Roma people had removed food and clothes from the German carts that had been left there earlier. The locals blamed the Roma for the act. As a retaliation, the Germans gathered all the Roma into a decrepit shack (except for those whose relatives served on the front), poured gasoline onto the shack and threw hand grenades in through the windows. A total of 56 Roma people perished in the flames; only one little girl managed to escape.[224]

Units of the arriving Soviet 6th Guards Cavalry Corps started from the direction of Középtúr, and, together with forces of the 4th Guards Motorcycle Regiment, with the support of some Mk IX Valentine tanks of the latter, recaptured Szalatnya, then Palást. This meant that the Germans again failed to cut the Soviet supply lines extending through the Ipolyság corridor.[225]

In the evening, units of the 5th Guards Tank Corps/6th Guards Tank Army were positioned as follows:

- 21st Guards Tank Brigade north of Zalaba;
- 22nd Guards Tank Brigade 2km west of Ipolyszakállos;
- 20th Guards Tank Brigade at Léva;
- 6th Guards Motorized Rifle Brigade between Nagykálna (exclusive) and Garamszentgyörgy, on the eastern bank of the Garam.

At the end of the day, the units of the 9th Guards Mechanized Corps were engaged in battle in the following positions:

- 30th Guards Mechanized Brigade west-northwest of Szete;
- 46th Guards Tank Brigade west-northwest of Szete;
- 18th Guards Mechanized Brigade in the area of Dolné Zemberovce;
- 31st Guards Mechanized Brigade was covering the main body of the Corps from

221 Lykow, 1987, p.307.

222 HM HIM *Hadtörténelmi Levéltár* (Budapest) microfilm archives, *Kriegstagebuch Ia der Heeresgruppe Süd, Kriegstagebuch vom 23. 12. 1944* (roll no. 627. image no. 7211239).

223 In the evening, the *24. Panzer-Division* had five combat-ready *Panzer* IV tanks, one *Panzer* IV/70 (A) *Jagdpanzer* and one *StuG.* III assault gun. Combat strength of the *Panzergrenadiers* was approximately 450 men.

224 Recollections of local residents as communicated to the author by Mr. Andráš Péter in writing.

225 HM HIM *Hadtörténelmi Levéltár* (Budapest) microfilm archives, *Kriegstagebuch Ia der Heeresgruppe Süd, Kriegstagebuch vom 23. 12. 1944* (roll no. 627. image no. 7211231).

the north.

The 4th Guards Mechanized Corps established defence positions between Kistompa and Gyerk.[226] In the evening, on the right flank of the 7th Guards Army, the 227th Rifle Division was regrouped so that its sector of the front was incorporated into that of the 53rd Army. In exchange for this unit, the 27th Guards Rifle Corps received the 243rd Rifle Division, which marched into the area of Középtúr–Horváti–Kistompa–Ipolyság.

Units of the 409th Rifle Division/25th Guards Rifle Corps occupied Ipolydamásd, crossed over to the western bank of the Ipoly, and were engaged in battle for the possession of the woods 1km distant from there. The 53rd Rifle Division continued its combat for Helemba.[227]

In early afternoon of that same day, the Hungarian 102nd Rapid Bomber Group launched a massive assault on the Soviet forces gathering at the northern entrance of Deménd with 500 kg AB bombs, delivered by four Me 210 aircraft per company, giving a total of 12 aircraft.[228]

On **24 December 1944**[229], in the frontal sector of *LXXII. Armeekorps*, the Soviet 3rd Guards Tank Battalion/27th Guards Tank Brigade together with the Submachine Gun Company of the Motorized Rifle Battalion of the brigade had reached the road junction 300 metres southwest of Liliom-puszta on the previous day at about 2330 hours. The Soviets reached the road leading to Letkés at 0050 hours on 24 December.

At dawn, the Air Force Rifle Battalion of Captain Pályi recaptured the hills around Liliom-puszta in a counterattack.[230] Of the six attacking T–34 tanks of the Soviet 3rd Guards Tank Battalion/27th Guards Tank Brigade, two were knocked out by *Panzerfäuste* between Lelédhidi-puszta and Liliom-puszta by the soldiers of the 1st Battalion/Air Force Rifle Regiment between 0400 and 0500 hours.[231] Captain György Pályi, commander of the battalion, recorded the event in his recollections as follows:

> One of the tanks was knocked out by a corporal. The fragments of the exploding tank injured him; he lost one eye. He shot the Soviet soldiers escaping from the blazing tank by shifting his rifle to his left shoulder. The other T–34 tank was allowed to approach too close by a soldier from the non-commissioned officer's training school

226 HM HIM *Hadtörténelmi Levéltár (Budapest), Szovjet iratmásolatok gyűjteménye a Budapest körüli harcokról. A 2. Ukrán Front hadijelentései, 1944. december 23.*

227 Daily combat reports of the Soviet 7th Guards Army to the command of the 2nd Ukrainian Front (a copy owned by the author), evening report, 23 December 1944.

228 Becze Csaba, A Magyar Királyi Honvéd Légierő harci alkalmazása a második világháborúban (1939-1945). Doktori értekezés. Pécsi Tudományegyetem Bölcsészettudományi Kar, é.n. (Csaba Becze: Combat use of the Royal Hungarian Air Force in the Second World War (1939-1945). Doctoral thesis. University of Pécs, without indication of date) (A copy owned by the author.), p.227.

229 Weather: frosty, bright, damp in certain areas, condition of the minor roads getting better due to frost.

230 HM HIM *Hadtörténelmi Levéltár (Budapest), Tanulmányok és visszaemlékezések gyűjteménye* (Collection of studies and recollections), *nr. 3064 Pályi Görgy: A Szent László hadosztály repülő lövészezredének története, 1944. október – 1945. december.* (György Pályi: History of the Air Force Rifle Regiment of the Division *"Szent László"*, October 1944 – December 1945), p.20.

231 See HM HIM *Hadtörténelmi Levéltár (Budapest), a „Szent László" hadosztály tüzérparancsnokának naplója és mellékletei. 65. sz. melléklet: Helyzetnyilvántartás, 1944. december 24.*

(some Laci, I do not know his name) [Laci is a nickname for the Hungarian first name László. The Hungarian officer did not know the full name of this soldier – the author], he knocked it out, but he then had to be carried to the dressing station because of the air pressure that struck him. The Soviet attack was halted after two tanks were knocked out.[232]

At dawn, the submachine gun units, supported by tanks, reached the edge of the wood some 700 metres from Liliom-puszta; however, their attack was halted there and the day was spent engaged in battle with the defenders.

Heavy fighting continued all day throughout the wide sector of the front. Forces of the Soviet 25th Guards Rifle Corps/7th Guards Army launched their attacks after extremely heavy artillery and mortar preparations, mainly along the railway embankment south of Helemba, around Ipolydamásd and against the Letkés bridgehead. The Soviet 1st Guards Tank Battalion/27th Guards Tank Brigade was committed again. At 0800 hours in the morning, the T–34 tanks of the unit reached the road junction 300 metres southwest of Liliom-puszta, then launched a joint attack with the 675th Rifle Regiment/409th Rifle Division toward Letkés.

The Division *"Szent László"*, with the attached German units, again blocked the Soviet thrust into the Garam valley from the west. The Grenadier Regiment recaptured Hill 204, north of Helemba. Both sides suffered heavy losses.

The 2nd Guards Tank Battalion/27th Guards Tank Brigade provided fire support for the crossing attempts of the 409th Rifle Division on the Ipoly in the Bástya area.

Heavy fighting commenced again at about 1600 hours around Letkés. Elements of the Reconnaissance Battalion (including the cavalry company) of the Division *"Szent László"* and three *Jagdpanzer* IV tank destroyers of the German *Panzerjäger-Abteilung 41* stood in reserve at Letkés.

The two arriving *Nimród* armoured self-propelled anti-aircraft guns of the Armoured Platoon/Reconnaissance Battalion were positioned by 2nd Lieutenant Martin west of the road, at the northern and southern entrances of Ipolyszalka. The *Nimród* standing in the northern entrance received a strange "shot":

Hardly had I completed my tasks in the south, when one of my men came running and reported that their vehicle had been knocked out. It turned out that the splinters of a heavy shell hitting the ground in front of the armoured vehicle destroyed the muzzle and the flash suppressor, killed one of the crew who was just about to get relieved, and wounded another. The other members of the crew were luckily dining in the nearby house. Although the *Nimród* was neither damaged nor set afire, it was rendered useless, and, as we lacked fuel, I could not even send it to the rear. As for daylight aircraft activity, not much can be said. In the following two days the other armoured

232 HM HIM *Hadtörténelmi Levéltár (Budapest), Tanulmányok és visszaemlékezések gyűjteménye* (Collection of studies and recollections), *nr. 3064 Pályi Görgy: A Szent László hadosztály repülő lövészezredének története, 1944. október – 1945. december.* (György Pályi: History of the Air Force Rifle Regiment of the Division *"Szent László"*, October 1944 – December 1945), p.14. Pályi recorded the knocking out of the two tanks as if it had happened on 22 December, but according to the 27th Independent Guards Tank Brigade's own documentation the units had not suffered any losses on that day. At the same time however, the log entry of the artillery commander of the Division *"Szent László"* confirms the knocking out of the two T–34s on 24 December.

vehicle's cannon was used only two or three times.[233]

The Soviets tried to take the bridge east of Ipolyszalka with tank support, frontal attacks and also attempts at encirclement. The T–34 tanks thrust forward to provide fire support, in line with the infantry. The 1st Battalion of the Air Force Rifle Regiment was again forced to abandon Liliom-puszta at about noon. A soldier who came back from the positions there reported to Captain Pályi that the Soviet assault, supported by tanks, had overrun the defenders. He also reported that Hungarian partisans, arriving together with the Soviet troops, were shooting the soldiers of the Air Force Rifle Regiment that were still alive, telling them "This is what you get for wanting the Division *'Szent László'*." The Soviet T–34 tanks opened fire on the foxholes, then ran over the defenders who were still alive. At about 1700 hours in the afternoon, all was silent around Liliom-puszta. 2nd Lieutenant *Vitéz* László Csörgey, commander of the heavy weapons company of the Battalion had also fallen, shot in the head. Captain Pályi recommended the officer for the gold medal for bravery award for officers (*Magyar Tiszti Arany Vitézségi Érem*).[234]

During the day, the 27th Guards Tank Brigade lost a total of five T–34 tanks knocked out during the fighting for the Letkés area (one of these was burnt out). The commander of the 1st Guards Tank Battalion/27th Guards Tank Brigade, Guards Major A. M. Pinchuk fell, and the commander of the 3rd Guards Tank Battalion/27th Guards Tank Brigade and the Machine Gun Company/Motorized Rifle Battalion was wounded.[235]

By then, the 1st Battalion/Air Force Rifle Regiment/Division *"Szent László"* had lost 80% of its officers and 70% of its enlisted men during the fighting. The commander of the Air Force Rifle Regiment ordered Liliom-puszta to be recaptured. Captain Pályi, lacking reserves and facing an enemy superior in numbers, was not able to carry out the order, which he therefore he was forced to oppose. The Cavalry Squadron/Reconnaissance Battalion of the Division *"Szent László"*[236] (Guards Captain Count Ernő Széchenyi) arrived at 1800 hours in the evening with 40 soldiers. Pályi told the commander of the regiment that he needed "tank destroyer units not cavalry".[237]

233 HM HIM *Hadtörténelmi Levéltár (Budapest), Tanulmányok és visszaemlékezések gyűjteménye* (Collection of studies and recollections), nr. 3138., Martin Kornél: *Néhány adat és emlék a „Szent László" felderítő osztály életéből, 1944. XI. 17.–XII. 27.* (Kornél Martin: Data and memories from the life of the Reconnaissance Battalion *"Szent László"*, 17 November – 27 December 1944), pp.27-28. The Hungarian armoured fighting vehicles managed to collect only enough fuel to move from Garamkövesd to Ipolyszalka. However, upon arriving, they were rendered practically immobile.

234 HM HIM *Hadtörténelmi Levéltár (Budapest), Tanulmányok és visszaemlékezések gyűjteménye* (Collection of studies and recollections), *nr. 3064* Pályi Görgy: *A Szent László hadosztály repülő lövészezredének története, 1944. október – 1945. december.* (György Pályi: History of the Air Force Rifle Regiment of the Division *"Szent László"*, October 1944 – December 1945), p.33.

235 Combat report of the 27th Independent Guards Tank Brigade to the commander of the 7th Guards Army tank and mechanized troops (a copy owned by the author), 24-25 December 1944. The operational armoured fighting vehicle strength of the unit in the evening of 24 December consisted of 19 T–34 tanks and five SU–76M self-propelled guns.

236 According to Captain Pályi, the Company had deserted and gone over to the Soviets at dawn on 27 December 1944. This can be neither confirmed nor contradicted as sources are missing. For this, see Kornél Martin – István Ugron: *Fejezetek a Szent László hadosztály történetéből. I. rész.* (Martin Kornél – Ugron István: Chapters from the history of the Division *"Szent László"*, Part I.) In: *Hadtörténelmi Közlemények* issue 1995/3, pp.133-134.

237 HM HIM *Hadtörténelmi Levéltár (Budapest), Tanulmányok és visszaemlékezések gyűjteménye* (Collection of studies and recollections), *nr. 3064* Pályi Görgy: *A Szent László hadosztály repülő lövészezredének*

The forces of the Air Force Rifle Regiment retreated to the edge of Letkés. Captain Pályi wrote in his recollections:

> The Soviets dispatched reconnaissance patrols toward Letkés. As we had no anti-tank weapons, I ordered that the attacking tanks be allowed to enter the streets among the buildings without receiving anti-tank fire. They were then to be destroyed with hand grenades thrown at the tracks. I was greatly relieved to see that the Air Force Rifles had become experienced soldiers in just a few days of ground combat. Three T–34 advanced on the road, but no close contact was made. It seemed that the great silence intimidated them; they fired a few rounds, then turned and withdrew to where they came from.[238]

The Soviet pressure forced the Hungarian units to evacuate the bridgehead by midnight. At 2400 hours the road bridge at Ipolyszalka was destroyed by a demolition section of *Pionier-Bataillon 357*[239]. Staff Major Lajtos described the battles fought for the Letkés bridgehead on that day as follows:

> Extremely strong attacks were launched against the bridgeheads. Heavy losses were caused by artillery and mortar fire, because, in fact, it was almost possible "to spit in" the positions of the Air Force Rifles from the slopes of the Börzsöny. Unluckily, it was impossible to withdraw forces during the day for it would have meant even heavier losses (the only bridge being in Letkés). The Air Force Rifles – it must be stated – fought heroically in hand-to-hand combat. At last darkness arrived. The order for withdrawal had previously been issued for the Air Force Rifle Regiment by the commander of the division. The important thing was: after darkness fell, there was to be a gradual withdrawal and assembly in Ipolyszalka, followed by a march into Bajta. At the same time we organized (in the early afternoon hours) the defence of the relieving forces. [...]
>
> Everything went according to plan, the commander of the division and the chief of staff were also present at the assembly of the Air Force Rifle Regiment, and I can only say that the troops exhibited such calmness and discipline as was almost unknown to me in this war. The role of Captain Derestey came to its end. The Air Force Rifle Battalions went away in order to be sent into reserve.

The three *Alarmkompanien* of the German *357. Infanterie-Division* (with a total of 140 soldiers) were attached to the Division *"Szent László"*. This Hungarian unit possessed 19 10.5cm light field howitzers (all attached from the Hungarian 2nd Armoured Division).

After Ipolykiskeszi fell into Soviet hands, the German *Panzer-Pionier-Bataillon 59* with

története, 1944. október – 1945. december. (György Pályi: History of the Air Force Rifle Regiment of the Division *"Szent László"*, October 1944 – December 1945), p.21.

238 HM HIM *Hadtörténelmi Levéltár (Budapest), Tanulmányok és visszaemlékezések gyűjteménye* (Collection of studies and recollections), *nr. 3064* Pályi Görgy: *A Szent László hadosztály repülő lövészezredének története, 1944. október – 1945. december.* (György Pályi: History of the Air Force Rifle Regiment of the Division *"Szent László"*, October 1944 – December 1945), p.26.

239 See Martin Kornél – Ugron István: *Fejezetek a Szent László hadosztály történetéből. I. rész.* (Kornél Martin – István Ugron: Chapters from the history of the Division *"Szent László"*, Part I.) in: *Hadtörténelmi Közlemények* issue 1995/3, p.120, footnote nr. 201.

its 24 (!) remaining soldiers in combat strength continued to hold defensive positions at the southern edge of Ipolykiskeszi and Ganádi mill.[240]

The *Divisionsgruppe "Rintelen"* was ordered to form and prepare two assault groups with which they were to cross the Garam to the east bank and attack the Soviets in the flank toward Deménd. At the same time, the left flank of *LVII. Armeekorps* advanced according to plan from the Kisölved area toward Tergenye, together with armoured *Kampfgruppe "Quentin"*[241]. The German two-direction attack was intended to secure the necessary point of departure for the planned attack toward the right flank of the German *8. Armee.* The Germans intended to close the gap between their two army formations with this movement.

The *Divisionsgruppe "Rintelen"* had to arrange for the river-crossing by its own infantry. For its armoured fighting vehicles, *Pionier-Brigade 52* prepared at least one ferry with a load capacity of 24 tons. That same day, the following units were attached to the *357. Infanterie-Division*:

- *Bataillon "Brocksch"* with 216 men;
- *Panzer-Aufklärungs-Abteilung 6* with 485 men;
- *2. Kompanie/Grenadier-Ersatz-und-Ausbildungs-Bataillon 482* with 166 men;
- *3. Kompanie/Panzer-Pionier-Bataillon 57* with 46 men;
- *3. Kompanie/Panzer-Pionier-Bataillon "Feldherrnhalle"* with 28 men;
- *Sturmgeschütz-Abteilung 1176* with 14 combat-ready *Jagdpanzer* 38(t) tank destroyers;
- *3. Batterie/Heeres-Sturmartillerie-Brigade 239* with six *StuH.* 42 assault howitzers;
- *13 10.5*cm light field howitzers in four different batteries.

The *LXXII. Armeekorps* had to take measures against the Soviet armoured fighting vehicles advancing south of the Danube toward Esztergom, which were only 12km south of the city. The *Armeekorps*, by using its last reserves, planned to establish a blocking position on the Dorog–Pilisszentkereszt line. During the afternoon, the *Regimentsstab* of *Oberstleutnant* Georg Thierfelder was ordered to Dorog, and, during the night of 24/25 December, received the *Jagdpanzer* 38(t) tank destroyers of the Hungarian Assault Artillery Battalion "Bernolák" and the *II. Bataillon/Panzergrenadier-Regiment 93* of the *13. Panzer-Division*. German *Flak* units were positioned at Dorog, the Esztergom training facility, Tát and Pilisszentkereszt. All of the supply troops of the *Armeekorps* that were stationed south of Esztergom were alerted and deployed, equipped with *Panzerfäuste*.[242]

That same day, 25 additional Hungarian *Jagdpanzer* 38 (t) tank destroyers arrived at the Esztergom training facility, presumably the armoured fighting vehicles of the 20th Assault Artillery Battalion from Kővágóőrs; following the discussion of the chief of staff of *LXXII. Armeekorps* and *Oberstleutnant* Thams at 1705 hours, one of the "companies" of the battalion was ordered to Dorog, where training was to be conducted and armoured

240 *Bundesarchiv–Militärarchiv* (Freiburg im Breisgau), RH 24–72, *Kriegstagebuch Ia des LXXII. Armeekorps, 24. 12. 1944.*

241 The *Kampfgruppe* was named after its commander, *Oberst* Friedrich Quentin, who was an officer of the *6. Panzer-Division*. The armoured fighting vehicles of the three *Panzer* divisions of *LVII. Panzerkorps* were concentrated in this unit.

242 *Bundesarchiv–Militärarchiv* (Freiburg im Breisgau), RH 24–72, *Kriegstagebuch Ia des LXXII. Armeekorps, 24. 12. 1944.*

support was to be provided at the same time. These *Jagdpanzer* (according to Major József Henkey-Hőnig, commander of the Battalion, there were 14 of them) were given to the 1st Battery of the 20th Assault Artillery Battalion (the commander of the battery was 1st Lieutenant Aladár Simák).[243]

At about 2030 hours, units of the Soviet 18th Tank Corps were engaged in battle 500 metres south of Leányvár. *Oberstleutnant* Thams had, according to a report issued at 2215 hours, set off to the area from Esztergom training facility with three *Jagdpanzer* 38 (t) tank destroyers. The crews of the armoured fighting vehicles consisted of German instructors of the training course, not Hungarians. However, the *Operationsabteilung* of *LXXII. Armeekorps* ordered the *Oberstleutnant* to commit all Hungarian *Hetzers* as soon as possible, requisitioning vehicles if necessary, and to establish communication with the commander of the forces defending Esztergom.[244]

At 2340 hours, the *Operationsabteilung* of *LXXII. Armeekorps* ordered the German liaison staff assigned to the Division *"Szent László"* to immediately track and report the exact position of the Hungarian *Hetzers*.

On the *LVII. Panzerkorps* front, the forces of the German *6. Panzer-Division* reached the Ipoly south of Gyerk, and, at last, from that position, the Soviet supply lines leading toward Kistompa could be kept under fire. On the left flank of the *Korps,* the German *II. Panzer-Abteilung/Panzer-Regiment 11* advanced with 25 combat-ready *Panzer* IV tanks[245] from the area of Garamsalló to the northern edge of Tergenye, and engaged the Soviet 22nd Guards Tank Brigade. *Panzerjäger-Abteilung 41* had 14 combat-ready *Jagdpanzer* IV tank destroyers available that day.[246] *Divisionsgruppe "Rintelen"* established a bridgehead on the eastern bank of the Garam at Szodó.[247]

On the wooded terrain reaching south of Tergenye, the German armoured fighting vehicles were attacked by 11 Il-2 ground-attack aircraft of the 451st Ground-Attack Air Regiment/264th Ground-Attack Air Division, commanded by Captain A. M. Kuchumov. The Soviet ground-attack aircraft were redirected from Vámosmikola to attack the German forces gathering in the woods – according to Soviet data, they consisted of approximately 70 armoured fighting vehicles and 50 other vehicles. Captain Kuchumov and his pilots claimed to have knocked out a total of 10 armoured fighting vehicles and 22 other vehicles with three consecutive raids. Later the Captain was awarded the Hero of the Soviet Union star.[248]

Elements of the right flank of *LVII. Panzerkorps* commenced their retreat as early as 23 December toward Garamkövesd. This traffic of the units constantly increased throughout the day. As this was remembered by 2nd Lieutenant Kornél Martin, then at Ipolyszalka:

> We noticed as early as 23 December that mechanized units – German armoured vehicles – arrived from the north in constantly increasing numbers and moved away toward Garamkövesd. The German retreat was going on even in the morning of 24

243 Written recollections of József Henkey-Hőnig about his military service (a copy owned by the author).

244 *Bundesarchiv–Militärarchiv* (Freiburg im Breisgau), RH 24–72, *Kriegstagebuch Ia des LXXII. Armeekorps, Anlage Nr. 1180, KTB-Notizen 24. 12. 44. Blatt 5.*

245 Nevenkin, Kamen, *Fire Brigades – The Panzer Divisions 1943–1945* (Winnipeg, 2008), p.198.

246 Nevenkin, 2008, p.198.

247 HM HIM *Hadtörténelmi Levéltár (Budapest) microfilm archives, Kriegstagebuch Ia der Heeresgruppe Süd, Kriegstagebuch vom 24. 12. 1944 (roll no. 627. image no. 7211242).*

248 HM HIM *Hadtörténelmi Levéltár (Budapest), Szovietunió Hőse kitüntetési javaslatok* pp.131-135.

> December. Tanks, assault guns, tank destroyers, armoured cars and personnel carriers [armoured personnel carriers – the author] followed each other in no recognizable order; some were damaged, and some were towed. We counted nearly 200 of them.[249]

We believe that these German units were those troops of *LVII. Panzerkorps* that were not directly committed and the damaged armoured fighting vehicles that needed repair and maintenance; they had been withdrawn toward the southwest to avoid possible Soviet encirclement.

In the evening, the 6th Guards Tank Army received orders from the commander of the 2nd Ukrainian Front, Marshal Malinovski, to turn over its front line between Léva and Dolné Zemberovce to the 4th Guards Cavalry Corps, and to launch an immediate assault toward Esztergom with all its forces, besides, cooperating with the right flank of the 7th Guards Army, to destroy the German—Hungarian forces in the area of Ipolyszakállos. By the end of 25 December, the 6th Guards Tank Army was to reach the Danube north of Esztergom.[250] The position of the 5th Guards Tank Corps in the evening of 24 December was as follows:

- 22nd Guards Tank Brigade north of Tergenye;
- 21st Guards Tank Brigade at Nemesoroszi;
- 20th Guards Tank Brigade turned over its front line at Léva to units of the arriving 4th Guards Cavalry Corps;
- 6th Guards Motorized Rifle Brigade also turned its front line between Nagykálna and Garamszentgyörgy over to the 4th Guards Cavalry Corps.

The 18th Guards and 31st Guards Mechanized Brigades/9th Guards Mechanized Corps were also relieved by units of the 4th Guards Cavalry Corps. The two brigades marched to Szántó. At the same time, the 46th Guards Tank Brigade was engaged west of Szete, and the 30th Guards Mechanized Brigade at Ágotamajor (4kms northwest of Szete). The 4th Guards Mechanized Corps defended the Kistompa – Gyerk sector. The 243rd Rifle Division/27th Guards Rifle Corps also marched to that location. The 303rd Rifle Division of the Rifle Corps occupied Százd and Újlak that same day. The 4th Guards Motorcycle Regiment was regrouped and sent to Dalmad.[251]

The deployment of the Hungarian *Jagdpanzers* through the Ipoly in the morning of 24 December was witnessed by 2nd Lieutenant Kornél Martin, officer of the Reconnaissance Battalion of the Division *"Szent László"*, as he wrote in his diary:

> More than thirty Skoda tracked vehicles launched the counterattack, mainly *Hetzer* type assault guns [...]. Some of the crew members were still out and singing, and they seemed a bit drunk as the vehicles rolled along the main street of Ipolyszalka and

249 HM HIM *Hadtörténelmi Levéltár (Budapest), Tanulmányok és visszaemlékezések gyűjteménye* (Collection of studies and recollections), nr. 3138., Martin Kornél: *Néhány adat és emlék a „Szent László" felderítő osztály életéből, 1944. XI. 17.–XII. 27.* (Kornél Martin: Data and memories from the life of the Reconnaissance Battalion *"Szent László"*, 17 November – 27 December 1944), p.27.

250 Zavizion & Kornyushin, 1967, p.135.

251 HM HIM *Hadtörténelmi Levéltár (Budapest), Szovjet iratmásolatok gyűjteménye a Budapest körüli harcokról. A 2. Ukrán Front hadijelentései, 1944. december 24.*

> turned toward the Letkés bridge. One of the assault guns had a huge national tricolor spread on it...
>
> A terrible massacre raged in the next few hours. Soviet anti-tank guns positioned on the wooded slopes of the Börzsöny knocked out the assault guns one by one, as they attempted to break through the Soviet infantry and reach the edge of the village [Letkés – the author]. We saw no more than five vehicles return.[252]

We believe that the eyewitness presumably saw the 21 combat-ready *Jagdpanzers* of the Assault Artillery Battalion "Bernolák" rolling over the Ipoly bridge at Letkés. The tricolour was most probably an identification signal for their own ground-attack aircraft.

The Körös battery was, according to German sources, also moved over to the east bank of the Ipoly. At 1615 hours on 24 December, *LXXII. Armeekorps* was informed by *LVII. Panzerkorps* that "*Kompanie Nr.* 24" of Assault Artillery Battalion "Bernolák" still possessed nine combat-ready *Jagdpanzer* 38(t) tank destroyers.[253] The *Operationsabteilung* of *LXXII. Armeekorps* received orders from the German *6. Armee* at 1700 hours on 24 December that these Hungarian *Hetzers* were to be directed to Zsámbék, south of the Danube, to prevent the further advance of the Soviet 18th Tank Corps to the northwest.

The forces of Assault Artillery Battalion "Bernolák" returning from the other bank of the Ipoly suffered heavy losses, according to Kornél Martin. He himself observed approximately five *Jagdpanzers* crossing the Ipoly bridge at Letkés.[254] Still extant strength reports however do not confirm such a scale of Hungarian *Jagdpanzer* loss on the east bank of the Ipoly.[255]

On **25 December 1944**[256], on the front line sector of *LXXII. Armeekorps* south of the Danube, two of the three *Jagdpanzer* 38 (t)s that had set off with German crew had already reached Leányvár by 0715 hours. The Soviet armoured fighting vehicles were only 2km southwest of village. The third *Hetzer* arrived shortly.

At 0900 hours in the morning the *Operationsabteilung* of *LXXII. Armeekorps* informed the *6. Armee* that the Hungarian *Hetzers* had not yet arrived at Dorog. *Generalmajor* Gaedcke ordered the *Armeekorps* to deploy the Hungarian *Jagdpanzers* and the German *II. Bataillon/Panzergrenadier-Regiment 93*[257] together in an assault mission from Dorog area to the south with the objective of advancing as far as possible.

252 HM HIM *Hadtörténelmi Levéltár (Budapest), Tanulmányok és visszaemlékezések gyűjteménye* (Collection of studies and recollections), nr. 3138., Martin Kornél: *Néhány adat és emlék a „Szent László" felderítő osztály életéből, 1944. XI. 17.–XII. 27.* (Kornél Martin: Data and memories from the life of the Reconnaissance Battalion *"Szent László"*, 17 November – 27 December 1944), p.29.

253 *Bundesarchiv–Militärarchiv* (Freiburg im Breisgau), RH 24–72, *Kriegstagebuch Ia des LXXII. Armeekorps, Anlage Nr. 1180, 24. 12. 1944.*

254 Martin Kornél – Ugron István: *Fejezetek a Szent László hadosztály történetéből. I. rész.* (Kornél Martin – István Ugron: Chapters from the history of the Division *"Szent László"*, Part I.) in: *Hadtörténelmi Közlemények* issue 1995/3, p.119.

255 Assault Artillery Battalion "Bernolák" counted 10 *Jagdpanzers* as total losses between 20-31 December 1944.

256 Weather: -5° Celsius, bright, sunny; the minor roads suitable to travel.

257 The battalion was part of the German *13. Panzer-Division*, and was regrouped as reinforcement from the Budapest area and attached to *LXXII. Armeekorps* on 23 December. Combat strength of the battalion was as little as 156 men, with 11 light machine guns and rifles.

At 1000 hours a report was received at *LXXII. Armeekorps* that the Soviets had broken through at Leányvár with eight T–34 tanks and cavalry. The three *Hetzers* deployed there had been knocked out by the Soviets, the *II. Bataillon/Panzergrenadier-Regiment 93* was defending at the southern edge of the village. The Hungarian *Hetzers* were still missing without a trace.

Despite the above, the Hungarian assault gun crews – as it has turned out only minutes later – crossed the Esztergom bridge with 21 *Jagdpanzers* at 0950 hours and turned toward the south.[258] Although the *LXXII. Armeekorps* war diary mentions only Assault Artillery Battalion "Bernolák", this time, according to a number of entries referring thereto, not only the *Jagdpanzers* of "*Kompanie Nr.* 24" and "*Kompanie Nr.* 16" were to be included, but also the 14 *Jagdpanzer* 38 (t) tank destroyers of the 1st Battery/20th Assault Artillery Battalion. At first, all of the *Hetzers* were attached to the Hungarian 2nd Armoured Division, then, at 1530 hours, the attachment was modified in cooperation with the *LXXII. Armeekorps* Chief of Staff.

.According to the *Korps* order of *LXXII. Armeekorps*, issued that same day, the mission of the Hungarian 2nd Armoured Division was to defend the bridgehead at Esztergom with the forces of the German *Flak-Regiment 104* and the *selbstständige Pionier-Bataillon 751*. The front line of the defence stretched along the line point no. 108 (3km southwest of the Danube-bridge)– point no. 222 (Sas Hill) – point no. 289 – point no.300 – Hill 281 – point no. 108 (2.5km west of Basaharc) line. As specified in a separate order, the bridge on the Danube at Esztergom was the responsibility of Colonel Endre Zádor.[259]

The wider defensive circle around Esztergom was to be established on the Leányvár–Ebszőny-bánya–Tát line, commanded by the headquarters of *Major* Thierfelder, reassigned from the *357. Infanterie-Division*. The most important task was to close the Dorog–Tinnye road.[260]

At 1025 hours, the *Operationsabteilung* of *LXXII. Armeekorps* ordered all of the 21 *Hetzers* to advance forward to first establish a blocking position around Dorog, then attack toward the south on a wide front line, together with the tank-riding German *II. Bataillon/Panzergrenadier-Regiment 93*. As if the said tasks would not have constituted a disproportionate weight to the scarcely trained assault gun crews, most of them having no combat experience at all, the *Armeekorps* complemented it with an additional order at 1235 hours, namely, the initiation of a reconnaissance mission toward Bajna.[261]

At 1700 hours the *LXXII. Armeekorps* Chief of Staff sent a message to the *Armeegruppe "Balck"* requesting an increased fuel allocation for the Hungarian 20th Assault Artillery Battalion and the Assault Artillery Battalion "Bernolák" in order to retain the necessary mobility. The fuel allocation of an assault artillery battalion was approximately three cubic metres of fuel.[262]

258 *Bundesarchiv–Militärarchiv* (Freiburg im Breisgau), RH 24–72, *Kriegstagebuch Ia des LXXII. Armeekorps, Anlage Nr. 1200, KTB-Notizen 25. 12. 44.*

259 *Bundesarchiv–Militärarchiv (*Freiburg im Breisgau), RH 24–72, *Kriegstagebuch Ia des LXXII. Armeekorps, Anlage Nr. 1199, Ia Nr. 2970/44 geh. am 25. 12. 1944.*

260 *Bundesarchiv–Militärarchiv* (Freiburg im Breisgau), RH 24–72, *Kriegstagebuch Ia des LXXII. Armeekorps, Anlage Nr. 1200.*

261 *Bundesarchiv–Militärarchiv* (Freiburg im Breisgau), RH 24–72, *Kriegstagebuch Ia des LXXII. Armeekorps, Anlage Nr. 1200, KTB-Notizen 25. 12. 44 Blatt 2.*

262 *Bundesarchiv–Militärarchiv* (Freiburg im Breisgau), RH 24–72, *Kriegstagebuch Ia des LXXII. Armeekorps, Anlage Nr. 1235., Fernschreiben an Armeegruppe Balck am 25. 12. 44.*

Meanwhile *6. Armee* had to admit to itself that the area of Dorog and Kesztölc could no longer be held. Therefore, at 1845 hours, *General* Balck ordered *LXXII. Armeekorps* to withdraw the Hungarian *Jagdpanzers* together with the *II. Bataillon/Panzergrenadier-Regiment 93* to the narrower Esztergom bridgehead for the direct defence of the city. This was highly necessary because the armoured fighting vehicles of the 18th Tank Corps were already entering the Esztergom training facility around 2130 hours.[263]

During the night preceding 25 December, in the *LXXII. Armeekorps* sector north of the Danube, the Division *"Szent László"* was holding on the line southwest of Helemba –Hill 204–Ipolydamásd area– point no. 279– west bank of the Ipoly.

During the day, the Soviet 27th Guards Tank Brigade concentrated its forces in the Bástya area and prepared to cross the Ipoly northeast of Helemba. The artillery of the Division *"Szent László"* successfully engaged the SU–85 self-propelled guns moving 1km southeast of the Lelédhidi-puszta.[264]

According to various reports, elements of the reconnaissance battalion of the Division *"Szent László"* were still engaged in battle in Letkés. The morning reports stated that the Hungarian units in defence along the western bank of the Ipoly had the following forces:

- 1st Battalion of the Grenadier Regiment with 500 men,
- 2nd Battalion of the Grenadier Regiment with 400 men;
- 2nd Battalion/1st Parachute Regiment with 200 men;
- Reconnaissance Battalion with 300 men;
- The Air Force Rifle Regiment did not report any combat strength ready for action[265];
- The four *Jagdpanzer* IV tank destroyers and three 7.5cm anti-tank guns of the German *Panzerjäger-Abteilung 41.*[266]

At 1200 hours Lieutenant Colonel Valér Stefán, commander of the Grenadier Regiment assumed command of the *Kampfgruppe* of Lieutenant Colonel Heinrich. This *Kampfgruppe* consisted of the 1st Battalion of the Grenadier Regiment and the main body of the reconnaissance battalion of the division. The 2nd Reconnaissance Battalion wiped out a Soviet reconnaissance party that day, which lost five dead and one of its soldiers captured. The Soviet troops gathering on the eastern end of the demolished bridge at Ipolyszalka were disrupted by the German—Hungarian artillery.

On the front line of the *"Altorjay"* group at point no. 109 (1km southeast of Lelédhidi-puszta), elements of the 409th Rifle Division tried to cross the Ipoly but were repulsed. However, another attempt succeeded at point no. 114, 500 metres northeast of Ipolydamásd,

263 *Bundesarchiv–Militärarchiv* (Freiburg im Breisgau), RH 24–72, *Kriegstagebuch Ia des LXXII. Armeekorps, Anlage Nr. 1200, KTB-Notizen 25. 12. 44. Blatt 3.*

264 Combat report of the 27th Independent Guards Tank Brigade to the commander of the 7th Guards Army tank and mechanized troops (a copy owned by the author), 25 December 1944. The Brigade on the same evening had 20 operational T–34 tanks and seven SU–85 self-propelled guns.

265 György Pályi reported to his regimental commander that there were four officers and 180 men in the 1st Battalion. See: HM HIM *Hadtörténelmi Levéltár (Budapest), Tanulmányok és visszaemlékezések gyűjteménye* (Collection of studies and recollections), nr. 3064 Pályi Görgy: *A Szent László hadosztály repülő lövészezredének története, 1944. október – 1945. december.* (György Pályi: History of the Air Force Rifle Regiment of the Division *"Szent László"*, October 1944 – December 1945), p.29.

266 *Bundesarchiv–Militärarchiv* (Freiburg im Breisgau), RH 24–72, *Kriegstagebuch Ia des LXXII. Armeekorps, Morgenmeldungen unterstellter Einheiten vom 25. 12. 1944.*

and they launched another attack from that point.

During the day the Soviet 53rd Rifle Division took point no. 204, north of Helemba, but, apart from this action, the elements of the Hungarian Division repulsed all of the attacks launched against the southern flank.

At that same time, the 2nd Battalion/1st Parachute Regiment was on river defence duty north and south of Ipolyszalka. Two companies of the Reconnaissance Battalion/Division *"Szent László"* established positions to the north, and the 1st Company/53rd Pioneer Battalion established positions south of the 2nd Battalion/1st Parachute Regiment. These positions consisted primarily of hastily built nests and foxholes with firing positions.[267]

The Soviet forces crossing north of Ipolykiskeszi were forced back to the east bank of the Ipoly by the defenders. The 1st Company/Hungarian 53rd Pioneer Battalion dispatched two reconnaissance parties led by officers. One was the size of two squads, and the other one was the size of one squad. Each of the engineers had a machine gun, four hand grenades and a *Panzerfäuste*. The parties did not meet Soviets soldiers, only retreating German and Hungarian units going toward the south.

The bridge at Ipolyszalka, which had not been properly demolished by the Germans, was blown up again by 2nd Lieutenant Ferenc Kovács, officer of the 53rd Pioneer Battalion, and a warrant officer on the night of 25/26 December, although the left side of the bridge had already been occupied by the Soviets. The 2nd Company/53rd Pioneer Battalion received orders at 2050 hours to relieve the German *Pionier-Bataillon 751* (having combat strength of only 140 men) stationed south-southeast of Leléd.[268]

In the evening, the front line of the Division *"Szent László"* stretched along the line 700 metres west of Helemba – Nagy Valley – Kabarc – point no. 279 – forester's cottage at Lelédhidi-puszta – west bank of Ipoly – Ipolyszalka – Ipolykiskeszi. There were two *Jagdpanzer* IV tank destroyers, 13 towed 7.5cm anti-tank guns and 35 artillery pieces attached to the division. 10 dead and 50 wounded were reported as battle casualties that day.[269]

The main body of the Soviet 6th Guards Tank Army moved out again at about 0900 hours in the morning south along the east bank of the Garam. The 21st Guards Tank Brigade reached Tergenye at 1300 hours. *Panzer-Aufklärungs-Abteilung 3/3. Panzer-Division* and the *Jagdpanzer* IV tank destroyers of *Panzerjäger-Abteilung 543/3. Panzer-Division* – probably as part of armoured *Kampfgruppe "Quentin"* – were also engaged in battle at Tergenye on the same day.[270]

The advance of the Soviet tanks endangered not only the rear of *LVII. Panzerkorps* but also the left flank of *LXXII. Armeekorps*. The options of the latter *Armeekorps* were extremely limited. In order to defend the rear of the Division *"Szent László"* it could only regroup elements of the Air Force Rifle Regiment and three German *Jagdpanzer* IV tank destroyers toward the north. In the course of the day, the main body of the Hungarian 53rd Pioneer Battalion also arrived; this was the engineer unit assigned to the Division *"Szent*

267 HM HIM *Hadtörténelmi Levéltár (Budapest), Tanulmányok és visszaemlékezések gyűjteménye* (Collection of studies and recollections), nr. 3138., Martin Kornél: *Néhány adat és emlék a „Szent László" felderítő osztály életéből, 1944. XI. 17.–XII. 27.* (Kornél Martin: Data and memories from the life of the Reconnaissance Battalion *"Szent László"*, 17 November – 27 December 1944), p.30.

268 HM HIM *Hadtörténelmi Levéltár (Budapest), A m. kir. 53. utászzászlóalj naplója, 1944. 12. 25.*

269 *Bundesarchiv–Militärarchiv* (Freiburg im Breisgau), RH 24–72, *Kriegstagebuch Ia des LXXII. Armeekorps, Tagesmeldungen unterstellter Einheiten vom 25. 12. 1944.*

270 *Geschichte der 3. Panzer-Division Berlin-Brandenburg 1935–1945*, 1967, p.502.

László".[271]

The forces of the German *LVII. Panzerkorps* were driven out of Gyerk by the Soviets to the bridgehead established around Ipolyvisk; the Soviets broke into the German defence. *Hauptmann* Glaubitz, commanding the German *3. Batterie/Flak-Abteilung 314* of the *3. Panzer-Division* organized a *Kampfgruppe* from his self-propelled 2cm four-barrelled anti-aircraft cannon and some of the armoured fighting vehicles of *Panzer-Aufklärungs-Abteilung 3*, and proceeded toward the point of incursion. The Germans soon ran into four Soviet self-propelled anti-tank guns, one of which was destroyed, and the other three were abandoned by their crew. However, *Kampfgruppe "Glaubitz"* was unable to advance further because Soviet artillery prevented them from doing so.[272]

The forces of the Soviet 9th Guards Mechanized Corps advanced through Lontó to Ipolyszakállos, and took the railway station at Pinczék. The Germans knocked out 20 Soviet armoured fighting vehicles during the fighting around Ipolyszakállos. At this point, elements of *Flak-Abteilung 314/3. Panzer-Division* established a blocking position. Because the Soviet tanks had destroyed the prime movers of the guns, the German crews, commanded by *Oberleutnant* Winter, had to tow the 8.8cm guns and the 2cm cannon into firing positions.

On the left flank of the German *LVII. Armeekorps*, the attack of armoured *Kampfgruppe "Quentin"* against Nagypeszek, flanking the village from the east and advancing toward the north, failed. The *Armeekorps* even had to relocate its command post from Vámosmikola to Köbölkút.[273] Despite the previous events,*General der Panzertruppe* Kirchner was ordered to regroup the main body of his forces to the western flank, prevent the Soviet units from breaking through toward Esztergom, and then launch an attack against the roads leading out of the Ipolyság corridor.[274]

On the front line of *Divisionsgruppe "Rintelen"*, *Sturmgeschütz-Abteilung 1176*, fighting in the bridgehead that had been established east of Szodó, was immediately to be withdrawn from combat and directed to the armoured headquarters at Galánta.[275] The reason for this was, presumably, the heavy losses suffered by the unit that day. That is, the unit that had been only temporarily attached to the formation had 14 *Jagdpanzer* 38(t) tank destroyers on 24 December, while they had only three on 30 December.[276]

Commanded by *Oberleutnant* Kettl, the newly reconstituted *3. Batterie/Heeres-Sturmartillerie-Brigade 239* was also engaged in battle in this area. The battery was encircled by Soviet troops, but the *StuH.* 42 assault howitzers succeeded in reaching the Garam bridge through the woods and crossed to the west bank of the river.[277]

271 *Bundesarchiv–Militärarchiv* (Freiburg im Breisgau), RH 24–72, *Kriegstagebuch Ia des LXXII. Armeekorps, 25. 12. 1944.*

272 *Geschichte der 3. Panzer-Division Berlin-Brandenburg 1935–1945*, 1967, p.452.

273 HM HIM *Hadtörténelmi Levéltár* (Budapest) microfilm archives, *Kriegstagebuch Ia der Heeresgruppe Süd, Kriegstagebuch vom 25. 12. 1944* (roll no. 627. image no. 7211258).

274 HM HIM *Hadtörténelmi Levéltár* (Budapest) microfilm archives, *Kriegstagebuch Ia der Heeresgruppe Süd, Kriegstagebuch vom 25. 12. 1944* (roll no. 627. image no. 7211261).

275 HM HIM *Hadtörténelmi Levéltár* (Budapest) microfilm archives, *Kriegstagebuch Ia der Heeresgruppe Süd, Anlage Ia Nr. 14384/44 geh. am 25. 12. 1944* (roll no. 627. image no. 7211534). The company-sized unit was planned to be transported by train to the German *8. Armee* after a short engineering checkout.

276 For the armoured fighting vehicle strength of the unit on 30 December 1944 see *Generalinspekteur der Panzertruppen, Gen. Qu./Gruppe/I/oio 243/45 g. Kdos. 22. 1. 1945* (a copy owned by the author).

277 Kurowski, Franz & Tornau, Gottfried, *Sturmgeschütze – "Die Panzer der Infanterie"* (Würzburg, 2008), p.243.

In the evening the 5th Guards Tank Corps and the 4th Guards Mechanized Corps/6th Guards Tank Army were fighting in the Tergenye area.[278]

The 303rd Rifle Division/27th Guards Rifle Corps of the 7th Guards Army occupied Ivánkamajor (near Százd) and Hill 202 (Lápos Hill). On the front line sector of the 25th Guards Rifle Corps, elements of the 6th Guards Airborne Division crossed the Ipoly to the west bank at Ipolytölgyes. The 409th Rifle Division occupied the whole area of Letkés and took point 305 northwest of Ipolydamásd.[279]

The German—Hungarian air force supported the ground forces that were engaged west and northwest of Budapest with a total of 290 sorties, during which they claimed destruction of two Soviet tanks and 80 vehicles, damage to 50 other vehicles and 21 Soviet aircraft downed. The Hungarian 102nd Rapid Bomber Group successfully attacked the railway station of Nógrádverőce.[280]

At dawn on **26 December 1944**[281], the German—Hungarian troops defending the Esztergom bridgehead had a total of 111 soldiers fighting as infantry. Of this, 63 were part of two companies of the *II. Bataillon/Panzergrenadier-Regiment 93*. Eight Hungarian *Hetzer Jagdpanzers*[282] had been committed there and three German 8.8cm anti-aircraft guns were ready for action. However, the Germans no longer saw reason for sending heavy anti-aircraft guns into the city itself; the guns covered the Esztergom bridge from the northern bridgehead of the Danube.[283]

According to a report issued by the *Operationsabteilung* of *LXXII. Armeekorps* at 0125 hours on 26 December, the tactical situation was worsening in the Esztergom bridgehead mainly because the Hungarian *Hetzers* retreated without firing a single round toward the Esztergom bridge.[284]

The Chief of Staff of *LXXII. Armeekorps* at last ordered the bridgehead to be abandoned at 0540 hours and the 'Mária Valéria' bridge to be demolished. Accordingly, the bridge was blown up at 0750 hours, following the retreat of the German—Hungarian forces.

The Soviet 181st Tank Brigade/18th Tank Corps, having occupied Dorog the evening before, continued its attack toward Esztergom and its armoured fighting vehicles entered the area of the Esztergom training facility at about 0100 hours. The Soviets destroyed three assault guns and a tank there. The brigade occupied the southern edges of Esztergom at 0920 hours, but further advance was halted by fire of the tanks and artillery of the defenders and by the mine defence.

278 HM HIM *Hadtörténelmi Levéltár (Budapest), Szovjet iratmásolatok gyűjteménye a budapesti hadművelettel kapcsolatban, a szovjet 2. Ukrán Front hadijelentései, 1944. december 25.*

279 Daily combat reports of the Soviet 7th Guards Army to the command of the 2nd Ukrainian Front (a copy owned by the author), evening report, 25 December 1944.

280 HM HIM *Hadtörténelmi Levéltár* (Budapest) microfilm archives, *Kriegstagebuch Ia der Heeresgruppe Süd, Kriegstagebuch vom 25. 12. 1944* (roll no. 627. image no. 7211259).

281 Weather: -5° Celsius, bright, sunny; minor roads suitable for travel.

282 In our opinion these *Jagdpanzer* 38 (t) tank destroyers were almost exclusively the vehicles of the Assault Artillery Battalion "Bernolák" that had previously been in action at Dorog. According to German opinions however the Hungarian assault artillery crews lacked any kind of combat experience.

283 *Bundesarchiv–Militärarchiv* (Freiburg im Breisgau), RH 24–72, *Kriegstagebuch Ia des LXXII. Armeekorps, Anlage Nr. 12503rd*

284 *Bundesarchiv–Militärarchiv* (Freiburg im Breisgau), RH 24–72, *Kriegstagebuch Ia des LXXII. Armeekorps, Anlage Nr. 1255, KTB-Notizen 26. 12. 44. Blatt 3.*

After Soviet reconnaissance confirmed that the city could be flanked from the east, the 181st Tank Brigade launched an attack to occupy Esztergom in cooperation with the 32nd Motorized Rifle Brigade and the 363rd Self-Propelled Heavy Artillery Regiment at 0600 hours in the morning from three directions (northeast, east and south). Following approximately five hours of combat within the city, Esztergom fell into Soviet hands at about 1100 hours.

The 32nd Motorized Rifle Brigade and the 181st Tank Brigade established all-around defence positions facing northeast, east and southeast. At the same time, they also established platoon-sized tank ambush positions 2.5km east of Esztergom and in the area of point no. 209. A motorized rifle battalion was concentrated 1km southeast of the quarry, 200 metres south of the Esztergom training facility in order to cover Esztergom from the south.

The 363rd Self-Propelled Heavy Artillery Regiment, the 200th Mortar and the 58th Guards Mortar Regiments prepared in Esztergom to repel German—Hungarian counterattacks launched from the northeast and the southeast.

In the evening the Soviet armoured group occupying Esztergom consisted of 37 operational T–34 and T–34/85 tanks, 19 ISU–122 self-propelled guns, 21 120mm mortars, 16 M–13 rocket launchers and 1720 motorized infantry.

The 18th Tank Corps claimed destruction of a total of eight armoured fighting vehicles, 20 assorted guns, two armoured personnel carriers, 17 machine guns and three other vehicles during the day's fighting for Esztergom, as well as a great deal of booty (among others, 15 armoured fighting vehicles, 12 small tanks[285], 200 vehicles) and 1200 (!) prisoners of war. Their own losses amounted to five dead and 21 casualties.

In the *LXXII. Armeekorps*, sector of the front, the right flank of the Division *"Szent László"* was under constant fire from Soviet heavy weapons. The Soviets crossed the Ipoly with one to two companies at Ganádmajor (3km north of Ipolytölgyes). In the morning, the *"Altorjay"* group of the Division *"Szent László"* was reported to have the following forces:

- 4th Motorized Rifle Battalion four officers, 150 enlisted men;
- 5th Motorized Rifle Battalion 12 officers, 70 enlisted men;
- 6th Motorized Rifle Battalion nine officers, 150 enlisted men;
- 1st Battalion/Grenadier Regiment three officers, 180 enlisted men;
- 2nd Battalion/Grenadier Regiment three officers, 100 enlisted men;
- *German Maschinengewehr-Bataillon "Sachsen"* three officers, 200 enlisted men;
- German *Pionier-Bataillon 751* eight officers, 181 enlisted men;
- two *Jagdpanzer* IV tank destroyers and 13 7.5cm anti-tank guns.

The "Stefán" group of the division provided no combat strength report. However, it received an order to secure the valley of the Garam from the north at Kéménd, in cooperation with one company of the reconnaissance battalion of the Division *"Szent László"* and two *Jagdpanzer* IV tank destroyers of *Panzerjäger-Abteilung 41*. The 1st Battalion/Air Force Rifle Regiment was to occupy the northern slopes of point no. 209 (the top of Baglyas).

The soldiers of the Division *"Szent László"* knocked out three Soviet armoured fighting

285 These were presumably Hungarian *Ansaldo* armoured fighting vehicles that were stationed in the Esztergom training facility for training, where the Soviet troops were able to seize them.

vehicles with *Panzerfäuste* on the reversed left flank of the division, which was also under attack from the north.[286] At least one of these was destroyed by the 2nd Company/Air Force Rifle Regiment (2nd Lieutenant Pál Góczy) while retreating from Ipolykiskeszi toward the west.[287] The vehicles destroyed were presumably the M4A2 tanks of the 46th Guards Tank Brigade engaged at Ipolypásztó, attacking toward the south.

During the day Soviet troops engaged the Párkány–Garamkövesd road with anti-tank guns and anti-aircraft guns from the northern edge of Esztergom, the city that they had earlier captured.

On the night of 25/26 December the 1st and 2nd Battalions of the 27th Independent Guards Tank Brigade crossed the Ipoly near Helemba. The Soviet armoured fighting vehicles reached the creek west of the village at about 1100 hours. The defenders established mine defences between point no. 305 and the Danube, where a T–34 tank ran over a tank mine.[288]

The forces of Division *"Szent László"* blocked the Soviet incursions in the areas west of Helemba and around Ipolydamásd in the line 3km west of Helemba – point no. 400 (Burda). In the Helemba area Soviet assaults were also supported by two T–34 tanks and two SU–85 self-propelled guns. Here the Hungarian 6th Towed Artillery Battalion knocked out a Soviet T–34 tank with a 10.5cm field artillery gun; the tank burnt out.

Heavy combat took place southwest of Leléd. The Leléd–Bajta road was cut west of Leléd by the Soviet 409th Rifle Division. The Soviets reached the northern edge of the wooded area south of Bajta, and engaged traffic on the road leading northwest from there. The Division *"Szent László"* committed the last elements of its Air Force Rifle Regiment that had been in reserve up to that point; these elements were to attack from Bajta via point no. 285 (Kövecses Hill) toward the northwest. North of Leléd the division continued to hold the Ipoly line.

After advancing 20km during the night, elements of the Soviet 21st Guards Tank Brigade/5th Guards Tank Corps, with 14 tanks and tank-rider riflemen, thrust as far as the crossing point southwest of Kéménd by morning. According to the recollections of Árpád Lajtos:

> At about 0800 hours a German staff major came to the joint room of the division commander and the chief of staff. He asked loudly for the commander of the division and wanted to be told who it was? I reprimanded him. After this he told me he was the

286 *Bundesarchiv–Militärarchiv* (Freiburg im Breisgau), RH 24–72, *Kriegstagebuch Ia des LXXII. Armeekorps, Tagesmeldungen unterstellter Einheiten vom 26. 12. 1944.*

287 The company was ordered to proceed from Ipolyszalka to Ipolykiskeszi in the evening of 25 December in order to provide reinforcement for the 2nd Battalion/1st Parachute Regiment on river-watching duty with 30-35 men, two light machine guns and two *Panzerfäuste*. The company was wiped out in the battles on 26 December. See HM HIM *Hadtörténelmi Levéltár (Budapest), Tanulmányok és visszaemlékezések gyűjteménye* (Collection of studies and recollections), nr. 3064 Pályi Görgy: *A Szent László hadosztály repülő lövészezredének története, 1944. október – 1945. december.* (György Pályi: History of the Air Force Rifle Regiment of the Division *"Szent László"*, October 1944 – December 1945), p.37 and appendices, p.22.

288 Combat report of the 27th Independent Guards Tank Brigade to the commander of the 7th Guards Army tank- and mechanized troops (a copy owned by the author), 26 December 1944. The operational armoured fighting vehicle strength of the unit in the evening consisted of 18 T–34 tanks and seven SU–85 self-propelled guns.

Chief of Operations[289] of *LXXII. Armeekorps*[290] and that he came to say that Soviet armoured fighting vehicles had reached the Bény area, Garampáld and Kicsind. And now he was to tell us what to do.

We told him that he could only issue orders if he took over command of the division. If not, he might propose recommendations, of which we might take heed. Upon hearing this he went away without offering us any proposals.[291]

At 1035 hours in the morning the German *6. Armee* ordered *LXXII. Armeekorps* that, considering the serious situation that had developed around Kéménd, they were to relocate the Hungarian *Jagdpanzer* 38(t) tank destroyers that were still capable of combat and a battalion to the area. The battalion-sized elements of the Air Force Rifle Regiment/ Division *"Szent László"* and six Hungarian 38(t) *Jagdpanzers* were to be so committed[292]

Major Pál Bernolák received the order about the relocation to Kéménd at 1055 hours. The six combat-ready *Jagdpanzers* of Assault Artillery Battalion "Bernolák" arrived at Kéménd during the day. The *Hetzers* established securing positions together with two *Jagdpanzer* IV tank destroyers of *Panzerjäger-Abteilung 41* and engaged the Soviet troops that were assembling on the east bank of the Garam in harassing fire.[293]

According to Soviet sources, 15 armoured fighting vehicles and a battalion-sized infantry unit mounted on cars, with the support of three artillery batteries, soon launched a counterattack from the northeast toward the southwest. The attack reached the road in the northern outskirts of Garampáld. This counterattack was presumably carried out by the combined armoured *Kampfgruppe* of *LVII. Panzerkorps* which attacked from the Vámosmikola area toward the southwest. With this, the Soviet 21st Guards Tank Brigade was cut off from the main forces of the 5th Guards Tank Corps.[294]

Subsequently, elements of the Air Force Rifle Regiment and the soldiers of the garrison at Kéménd secured the area against Soviet forces advancing on the east bank of the Garam toward the south and west. According to a report sent at 0940 hours, one of the German *Jagdpanzer* IV tank destroyers was knocked out by the Soviets. In the evening, Kéménd was secured by six Hungarian *Jagdpanzer* 38(t) tank destroyers and two *StuG.* IV assault guns of the *357. Infanterie-Division*. The five Hungarian *Panzer* IV tanks from the Hungarian 2nd Armoured Division were also heading for Kéménd[295] via Nána; these armoured fighting vehicles were attached to the Division *"Szent László"*. At the same time, the German *Pionier-Bataillon 751* was detached from the division and marched to Kéménd in order to carry out engineering tasks.

289 The Chief of Operations (Ia) of the *Korps* was *Stabsmajor* Jensch.

290 The original contains *Korpskommando "XVIII"* although this is an apparent error.

291 HM HIM *Hadtörténelmi Levéltár (Budapest), Tanulmányok és visszaemlékezések gyűjteménye* (Collection of studies and recollections) nr. 2598., Lajtos Árpád: *Szent László hadosztály (Visszaemlékezés).* (Árpád Lajtos: Division *"Szent László"* (Recollections)), p.62.

292 HM HIM *Hadtörténelmi Levéltár* (Budapest) microfilm archives, *Kriegstagebuch Ia der Heeresgruppe Süd, Kriegstagebuch Ia, 26. 12. 1944* (roll no. 627. image no. 7211284).

293 *Bundesarchiv–Militärarchiv* (Freiburg im Breisgau), RH 24–72, *Kriegstagebuch Ia des LXXII. Armeekorps, Anlage Nr. 1255, 26. 12. 1944.*

294 Zavizion & Kornyushin, 1967, p.135.

295 After the fall of Esztergom on 26 December, the Hungarian 2nd Armoured Division went on a river-watching mission on the Northern part of the Danube, with *levente*-units and German anti-aircraft artillery.

In the evening, in order to secure the route of the withdrawal along the Garam, the *5. Kompanie/Panzer-Regiment 11* of the *6. Panzer-Division* (*Leutnant* Theo Sander) with its *Panzer* IV tanks had been ordered from Nána to the bridge southwest of Kicsind. The officer remembered this as follows:

> I observed Soviet armoured fighting vehicles assembling on the opposite side of the bridge and securing the area against our assault. The tank destroyers positioned on our side had accomplished nothing so far and it seemed that it would be useless to commit more armoured forces because of the restricted terrain and, especially, the descending darkness. The encircled units of the division had been informed that the current situation was critical, and the area of the outbreak was cautiously moved elsewhere, toward Esztergom.
>
> I was assigned to clear the previously chosen bridge of Soviet armoured fighting vehicles on the other side for the planned counterstroke. Following this the tank destroyers were to thrust through the cleared bridge and establish a secure bridgehead with our tanks.
>
> This way, under cover of darkness, I departed with my tanks toward the Garam, entered the village [Garamkövesd – the author], via the clear road and proceeded further up along the Garam. Meanwhile it became so dark that possible contact with enemy of unknown strength became too dangerous. I was only keeping my task in mind.
>
> I stopped my tanks in a suitable place and ordered them to take securing position. In addition, full silence was ordered and sentries were set up. The planned journey was to be continued in the early morning of the next day.[296]

Thanks to the persistence of the Division *"Szent László"*, the path of the vehicles serving the supply lines and personnel transport of the *LVII. Panzerkorps* was clear southwards on the west bank of the river.[297]

At the same time, however, the commander of the Hungarian division and the chief of staff decided that "as the planned combat is over now, only one thing is to be kept in mind: retreat with the least possible losses".[298]

The attached Hungarian units received written orders via officer couriers that, in the event that communications were lost with the division staff, and that the tactical situation developed such that current positions became untenable, the units were to assemble in prescribed rear areas. This way a major hindrance could be eliminated: retreat could only be ordered by the commander of *LXXII. Armeekorps*. According to the recollections of Staff Major Lajtos:

> Lieutenant Colonel Stefán understood the order; he assured me that he would act

296 Schadewitz, Michael, *Panzerregiment 11/Panzerabteilung 65 1937–1945, Panzerersatz- und Ausbildungsabteilung 11 1939–1945* (Lünen, 1987), p.471.

297 Bundesarchiv–*Militärarchiv* (Freiburg im Breisgau), RH 24–72, *Kriegstagebuch Ia des LXXII. Armeekorps, 26. 12. 1944.*

298 HM HIM *Hadtörténelmi Levéltár* (Budapest), *Tanulmányok és visszaemlékezések gyűjteménye* (Collection of studies and recollections) nr. 2598., Lajtos Árpád: *Szent László hadosztály (Visszaemlékezés).* (Árpád Lajtos: Division *"Szent László"* (Recollections)), p.62.

> accordingly at all times. The commander of the Air Force Rifle Regiment (Lieutenant Colonel István Heinrich) stated that they all knew what the honour of the air crew and the honour of the Hungarian nation were. They were going to fight to the end. I desperately asked him to consider his responsibility for the lives of hundreds of others, not just of his own life. I asked him to retreat to the wood of the Baglyas teteje, secure the units in all directions and cross the military bridge as soon as it became ready. I warned him that the bridge was to be built at Kicsind south, and that Soviet tanks were already in Kicsind, therefore it would be advisable to cross at night. Heinrich again stated that he did not intend to retreat as a coward. At this point Colonel Szügyi took over the command and told him straight out to carry out orders immediately. Heinrich gave an elusive answer.[299]

During the night of 25/26 December the main body of the Soviet 5th Guards Tank Corps (with 50 tanks and carrying mounted infantry) advanced from the eastern outskirts of Zseliz toward the western area of Kisgyarmat. The 22nd Guards Tank Brigade and the 6th Guards Motorized Rifle Brigade were committed to relieve the 21st Guards Tank Brigade, which had, in the meantime, been cut off at Garampáld. Meanwhile the Germans noticed the movement of two motorized rifle battalions of the latter brigade east of Oroszka toward the south. The relieving mission of the 5th Guards Tank Corps was covered by the 20th Guards Tank Brigade from the east. The Soviet attack was successful. At about 1400 hours the brigades reached Garampáld and relieved the 21st Guards Tank Brigade.[300]

The Soviet 303rd Rifle Division/27th Guards Rifle Corps thrust into Ipolyvisk on the frontal sector of *LVII. Panzerkorps* and also took possession of the road leading toward the southwest. The left flank of the Soviet 141st Rifle Division was engaged in battle for Perőcsény and had broken into the village in the *8. Panzer-Division* sector of the front.

The Soviet 9th Guards Mechanized Corps with three of its Guards Mechanized Brigades – with the support of 38 armoured fighting vehicles – continued its attack from the Lontó area toward the south, and occupied Ipolyszakállos and Ipolybél. The 46th Guards Tank Brigade of the corps continued its attack on the road approaching Ipolypásztó. Those elements of the *3. Panzer-Division* that were still combat-ready, among them *Panzergrenadiers*, elements of *Panzerjäger-Abteilung 543*, and *Panzer-Pionier-Bataillon 39* had been concentrated there. During the battle, the commander of the latter unit, *Hauptmann* Sedlaczek was seriously wounded.[301]

Late in the afternoon, *Armeegruppe "Balck"* requested permission from *Heeresgruppe Süd* to have *8. Panzer-Division/LVII Panzerkorps* establish a security line between Ipolytölgyes and Oroszka, and to have the *3.* and *6. Panzer-Divisions* cross to the west bank of the Garam under cover of the securing line. The units were then to renew their attack at Saró via the Garam. Although the latter intention seemed to be impossible in the current situation, the *Armeegruppe* granted permission at 1715 hours. The forces of the *6. Panzer-Division* were disengaged from the front line.[302]

299 HM HIM *Hadtörténelmi Levéltár (Budapest), Tanulmányok és visszaemlékezések gyűjteménye* (Collection of studies and recollections) nr. 2598., Lajtos Árpád: *Szent László hadosztály (Visszaemlékezés).* (Árpád Lajtos: Division *"Szent László"* (Recollections)), p.63.

300 Zavizion & Kornyushin, 1967, p.135.

301 *Geschichte der 3. Panzer-Division Berlin-Brandenburg 1935–1945*, 1967, p.454.

302 HM HIM *Hadtörténelmi Levéltár* (Budapest) microfilm archives, *Kriegstagebuch Ia der Heeresgruppe*

During the evening the positions of the Soviet 6th Guards Tank Army were:

- The 4th Guards Mechanized Corps held Garamsalló and was in action in the western outskirts of Tergenye and Garamsalló;
- The 5th Guards Tank Corps held Kisgyarmat and Garampáld, and was in action 3km north of Kicsind with 20 German—Hungarian armoured fighting vehicles, and regiment-sized infantry;
- The 9th Guards Mechanized Corps held Ipolyszakállos and Ipolybél, and was engaged on the road approaching Ipolypásztó.[303]

On 26 December the *Me* 210 aircraft of the Hungarian 102nd Rapid Bomber Group supported the Division *"Szent László"* and were sent against targets east of the Ipoly.[304]

The German *8. Armee* originally planned that the *Kampfgruppe* of the *Armeekorps*[305] would attack toward the west and attack from the Léva area toward the south. Although forces of the *24. Panzer-Division* had captured point no. 249 south of Palást in heavy combat in the evening of 25 December, the Soviet units were constantly increasing the strength of their forces in the Palást area, which gradually reduced the possibility of a successful attack. Furthermore, the positions of *LVII. Panzerkorps* did not indicate the necessity of such an attack. Therefore it was decided that *Panzer-Aufklärungs-Abteilung/24. Panzer-Division*, 20 of its *Panzer* IV/70 (A) and (V) *Jagdpanzers*[306] and eight assault guns[307] were to attack from the Báčovce (Kisbácsfalu)–Jabloňovce (Hontalmás) area toward the south, and east of Léva.[308]

On **27 December 1944**[309], in the front line sector of *LXXII. Armeekorps*, continuous Soviet pressure had, by dawn, forced the front line of the Division *"Szent László"* back to the line foresters house 4km west of Helemba – point no. 362 – Leléd west.

The 409th Rifle Division took Bajta in the morning, and was engaged in battle for Hill 267; its elements were only 500 metres, from Garamkövesd. The 27th Independent Guards Tank Brigade, in cooperation with the 223rd and 475th Rifle Regiments/53rd Rifle Division, attacked during the night along the road leading from Helemba toward

Süd, Kriegstagebuch vom 26. 12. 1944 (roll no. 627. image no. 7211276 and next image).

303 HM HIM *Hadtörténelmi Levéltár (Budapest), Szovjet iratmásolatok gyűjteménye a budapesti hadműveletteI kapcsolatban, a szovjet 2. Ukrán Front napi jelentései, 1944. 12. 26.*

304 Kindly disclosed by military historian Csaba B. Stenge.

305 In the evening, *Sturmgeschütz-Brigade 228*, directly attached to *IV. Panzerkorps*, had seven combat-ready assault guns out of 22; *Sturmgeschütz-Brigade 286* had nine out of 20 armoured fighting vehicles in combat-ready condition. See *Bundesarchiv–Militärarchiv* (Freiburg im Breisgau), *RH 2 Ost Karte 5249.*

306 The *24. Panzer-Division* received 11 factory-new *Panzer* IV/70 (V) *Jagdpanzers* on 12 December 1944, which arrived at the units a few days later by train.

307 The *24. Panzer-Division* had on 25 December 1944 five combat-ready *Panzer* IV tanks and *Panzer* IV/70 (A) and (V) *Jagdpanzers* out of the existing 26, and only three of the existing ten assault guns. See *Bundesarchiv–Militärarchiv* (Freiburg im Breisgau), *RH 2 Ost Lagekarten 5249.* Therefore we assume that the disabled or easily repairable armoured fighting vehicles were swiftly recovered.

308 HM HIM *Hadtörténelmi Levéltár* (Budapest) microfilm archives, *Kriegstagebuch Ia der Heeresgruppe Süd, Kriegstagebuch vom 26. 12. 1944* (roll no. 627. image no. 7211287).

309 Weather: -10° Celsius, generally bright, sunny, ground-fog in certain places – the minor roads were suitable for traveling.

Garamkövesd with the mission of establishing crossing point south of the village.

At dawn of 27 December, at 0400 hours, Soviet armoured fighting vehicles reached the railway-road junction 2km southeast of Garamkövesd, and had approached to within 700 metres of the village itself from the southeast by 1730 hours. The 27th Independent Guards Tank Brigade lost two T–34 tanks knocked out (one of them burnt out).[310]

In consequence of these events new bridgeheads were to be established southeast of Kéménd at Kicsind and Garamkövesd in order to secure and cover the retreat over the Garam. *LXXII. Armeekorps* intended to reinforce the two bridgeheads primarily with German anti-aircraft artillery. At Garamkövesd four 2cm cannon were positioned on the east bank, and two 8cm gun batteries, as well as five 3.7cm and three four-barrelled 2cm cannon that were positioned on the west bank. In the bridgehead at Kicsind four 2cm cannon were positioned on the east bank of the Garam, and one 8cm gun battery, as well as two 2cm cannon, covered the crossing point on the west bank. At Kéménd one 8.8cm anti-aircraft gun battery and two 2cm anti-aircraft cannon were used to bar approach from the north.

Six *Jagdpanzer* 38(t) tank destroyers of Assault Artillery Battalion "Bernolák" that had been used at Kéménd for security tasks until then were also relocated to the bridgehead at Garamkövesd. At the same time, the anti-aircraft guns and armoured fighting vehicles had to be reinforced with infantry in order to avoid surprise attacks and ambush. For this, infantry units needed to be reassigned from the forces keeping watch on the northern bank of the Danube because the Division *"Szent László"* did not have any reserves left. Therefore observation of the Danube was taken over by "*leventes*".

At Kicsind the 53rd Pioneer Battalion finished construction of a regular military bridge with capacity of eight tons for the Division *„Szent László"*. The work called for approximately one *Pionier* company. Material was brought from the garrison at Csilizradvány.[311]

The Garam bridges themselves were to be closed against anticipated Soviet tank attacks by *Jagdpanzers*, tank destroyer units and road barriers that could swiftly be established. The commander of the newly created bridgeheads on the Garam was *Major* Georg Thierfelder, of the *357. Infanterie-Division*, who had earlier commanded the defence of the northern half of Szentendrei island and the bridgehead at Esztergom.

The 1st Company/53rd Pioneer Battalion received orders at about 0400 hours that, together with five *Panzer* IV tanks of the Hungarian 2nd Armoured Division, under command of 1st Lieutenant László Kozma, they were to block the left side of the Garam where the Baglyas teteje woods were closest to the bank of the river. At about 0700 hours in the morning, the Hungarian tanks had not yet arrived at the church in Kicsind. Therefore László Kozma moved out toward Kéménd without them. Soon the company was surprised by Soviet infantry fire. The 6th Guards Motorized Rifle Brigade/5th Guards Tank Corps, supported by a number of armoured fighting vehicles, had been fighting at Kicsind since that morning.[312]

310 Combat report of the 27th Independent Guards Tank Brigade to the commander of the 7th Guards Army tank- and mechanized troops (a copy owned by the author), 27 December 1944. The operational armoured fighting vehicle strength of the unit in the evening consisted of 13 T–34 tanks and eight SU–85 self-propelled guns.

311 HM HIM *Hadtörténelmi Levéltár (Budapest), Tanulmányok és visszaemlékezések gyűjteménye* (Collection of studies and recollections) nr. 2598., *Lajtos Árpád: Szent László hadosztály (Visszaemlékezés).* (Árpád Lajtos: Division *"Szent László"* (Recollections)), p.59.

312 Zavizion & Kornyushin, 1967, p.137.

LXXII. Armeekorps informed the Division *"Szent László"* at 1310 hour that 25 Soviet tanks had been counted at Kicsind (armoured fighting vehicles of the 21st Guards Tank Brigade).

The remains of the 1st Battalion/Grenadier Regiment, commanded by battalion commander Captain Sándor Pálfi still defended Bajta during the night of 26/27 December. According to the diary of 1st Lieutenant Szepesvári:

> We were peeping, firing and providing cover until half past three in the morning. At about half past three we were surprised by the Soviets from a close range of 10 metres (this is why they were so silent). We retreated while firing wild submachine gun fire. A German *Pionier* party blew up the road and we evacuated Bajta. We moved on unpaved roads in total darkness; Captain Pálfi led us by the map. We had to reach the military bridge at Kicsind in order to cross the Garam.
>
> It was still dark when we arrived at Kicsind. A *Pionier Hauptmann* would not let us cross. Armoured fighting vehicles, and other vehicles were jammed. There was something fishy around there! For a time we stood outside, freezing, but, as we realized that we were not going to be allowed to cross, we took up residence in the town hall. I fell asleep the moment that I sat down. At 0700 hours in the morning a man burst into a room, screaming that the Soviets had attacked the town! We sprang up and grabbed our submachine guns. Outside, a firefight was already raging. Everybody sought to escape over the bridge! Again I employed my well-tested submachine gun group to fight them off. A Soviet soldier fired from the church tower at the bridge with a machine gun – I had to knock him out. We were now alone, everybody had run away. The Soviets captured all of the heavy supplies and vehicles. With a prayer, I ran over the bridge. Luckily I succeeded in making it to the other side.[313]

Following a short firefight in the bridgehead of the military bridge at Kicsind, the 2nd Battalion of the Grenadier Regiment, consisting primarily of former guards (Captain Miklós Békássy), capitulated to the Soviet troops. With this the Soviet ring closed from the south, too, around the Air Force Rifle Regiment that was concentrated around Garamkövesdipuszta and Bajta, units of the 2nd Battalion/1st Parachute Regiment and remnants of the Reconnaissance Battalion of the Division *"Szent László"*.[314]

At Garamkövesd, in the sector of the German *Maschinengewehr-Bataillon "Sachsen"*, which was attached to the Division *"Szent László"*, seven Soviet tanks had been knocked out by 1340 hours in the afternoon, four of which were destroyed by one soldier (with *Panzerfäuste* or a *Panzerschreck).*[315]

During the day the Division *"Szent László"* was forced back in heavy fighting into the bridgehead at Garamkövesd. The Soviets forced their way into Garamkövesd from the northeast with smaller forces. The German and Hungarian defenders of the bridgehead

313 *A Hazáért mindhalálig. Vitéz Szepesvári Béla háborús naplója. Magánkiadás, é.n.* (For the Motherland, until the end. Wartime diary of *Vitéz* Béla Szepesvári, self-published, n.d.), pp.82-83.

314 HM HIM *Hadtörténelmi Levéltár (Budapest), Tanulmányok és visszaemlékezések gyűjteménye* (Collection of studies and recollections), nr. 3064 Pályi Görgy: *A Szent László hadosztály repülő lövészezredének története, 1944. október – 1945. december.* (György Pályi: History of the Air Force Rifle Regiment of the Division *"Szent László"*, October 1944 – December 1945), pp.i, 1.

315 *Bundesarchiv–Militärarchiv* (Freiburg im Breisgau), RH 24–72, *Kriegstagebuch Ia des LXXII. Armeekorps, Anlage Nr. 1280, 27. 12. 1944.*

repulsed the Soviet units attacking from the east and northeast, and knocked out eight of their tanks.[316] Hungarian elements of the division knocked out one T–34, and seriously damaged one IS–2 heavy tank with five anti-tank gun hits on the vehicles.[317]

The 1st Battalion/Air Force Rifle Regiment of the Division *"Szent László"* attacked in the morning toward the northeast in the direction of Kéménd, but the attempt was repulsed by the Soviets.

A portion of the survivors managed to fight their way back to the Garamkövesd bridgehead, where some tried to swim over to the west bank of the Garam. According to the recollections of Staff Major Lajtos:

> Later, when Captain Pályi (commander of the 1st Battalion/Air Force Rifle Regiment[318]) arrived at the division headquarters, dripping wet, he reported [319] that on 26 December the regiment was in the woods at Baglyas teteje, where it was only under artillery and mortar fire. Regimental commander Lieutenant Colonel Heinrich was killed in the mortar fire. The situation was unclear. Later they were also attacked. He did not know what happened to the others. He departed with the main body of his battalion to cross the military bridge. However they did not reach the banks of the Garam until this morning. They were not able to cross the bridge. So they waded in the water, holding each other's belts in a line through the river. Many were washed away by the current; approximately 200 soldiers made it to the other side of the river. The remnants of the units were directed by the commander of the division to Bátorkeszi, to rest.[320]

According to Captain Pályi, at the time of his report, approximately 40 of his soldiers were still on the east bank of the Garam:

> There were German armoured vehicles at Kőhídgyarmat[321]. A tank destroyer offered to take me to the bank of the Garam and provide fire support for the units crossing the river. He also gave me his fur coat, which was much appreciated. The temperature was -10°C and I had nothing on except my jacket and trousers. The crossing began. The raft carried clothes and weapons. The soldiers in underpants either swam or clung to the sides of the raft. 1st Lieutentant Ősze[322] stood in the middle of the raft, his submachine gun hanging from his neck, and he was fully dressed. The current in the water was strong, there were ice flows floating on the surface. The raft tilted, Ősze fell

316 *Bundesarchiv–Militärarchiv* (Freiburg im Breisgau), RH 24–72, *Kriegstagebuch Ia des LXXII. Armeekorps, Morgenmeldung unterstellter Einheiten vom 28. 12. 44.*

317 *Bundesarchiv–Militärarchiv* (Freiburg im Breisgau), RH 24–72, *Kriegstagebuch Ia des LXXII. Armeekorps, Tagesmeldungen an Armeegruppe Balck vom 27. 12. 1944.* The IS–2 heavy tank was presumably supporting the M4A2 tanks of the 9th Guards Mechanized Corps attacking toward Garamkövesd, as was done by the 49th Guards Heavy Tank Regiment from 5 December onwards.

318 The original contains 2nd Battalion, although this is an error.

319 According to Pályi he had reported to Lajos by telephone.

320 HM HIM *Hadtörténelmi Levéltár (Budapest), Tanulmányok és visszaemlékezések gyűjteménye* (Collection of studies and recollections) nr. 2598., Lajtos Árpád: *Szent László hadosztály (Visszaemlékezés).* (Árpád Lajtos: Division *"Szent László"* (Recollections)), p.65.

321 Presumably these were elements of *Panzerjäger-Abteilung 41* directed to Kéménd, then retreating to Kőhídgyarmat with two *Jagdpanzer* IV tank destroyers.

322 First Lieutenant Ferenc Ősze was the commander of the 1st Company/Air Force Rifle Regiment.

> into the water. He sank immediately. During the swimming another of the soldiers drowned; these constituted our casualties. The soldiers quickly picked up their clothes and weapons and ran for the village. My clothes were brought over by Corporal Lőcsér. I dressed right there at the bank of the river. [...] It seemed that the fog and the silence were on our side. The German tank destroyer was firing at the blurred hills. North of the crossing point, I thought I could see a patrol, but no enemy contact was made.[323]

2nd Lieutenant Kornél Martin spent the night of 26 December at Fenékpuszta, where the remnants of various Hungarian units and some retreating Germans gathered. In the morning, the 2nd Lieutenant departed with elements of the 2nd Battalion/1st Parachute Regiment in the wooded terrain through the hills toward Kicsind, where they expected to find the military bridge. When they got out of the woods at the vineyards of Kicsind, all hell broke loose.

> Hardly did we step out of the woods – myself, with Pista Rábay, the Földes guys and some from my platoon – right behind the paratroopers, when we came under fire from the left. On the lower edge of the sloped field – exactly where we expected the bridge would be – T–34 tanks appeared, first just one, then two more. It was as if they were waiting for us. They fired short rounds toward us as a greeting, and then the guns also joined in. The paratroopers acted like veterans, throwing themselves beside the "bonesaw"[324], feeding the belts and firing in an instant.
>
> Of course not too much damage was caused to the tanks but the infantry moving around them disappeared and the T–34s stopped; however, in a matter of minutes heavy mortar fire came our way. The tank guns continued firing. We had only small arms, and only enough ammunition for the submachine guns to fire single rounds. In any case, the range was too great. My soldiers in the rear had a few *Panzerfäuste* and hand grenades, but it would have been hopeless for them to advance toward the tanks. So we took cover, and, in the meantime, the infantry from the remnants of the platoon, encouraged by the paratroopers, themselves began to fire.[325]

2nd Lieutenant Martin continued toward Kicsind, but, at about 1400 hours, was captured as a prisoner of war. At the same time, approximately 200 soldiers from the 2nd Battalion/1st Parachute Regiment and the Grenadier Regiment swam across the Garam.[326] According to the still extant battle casualty reports the commander of the Grenadier Regiment, Lieutenant Colonel Valér Stefán also was lost in the Fenék-puszta area together with nine other soldiers of the regimental staff at about 0700 hours on 27 December.[327]

323 HM HIM *Hadtörténelmi Levéltár (Budapest), Tanulmányok és visszaemlékezések gyűjteménye* (Collection of studies and recollections), nr. 3064 Pályi Györgу: *A Szent László hadosztály repülő lövészezredének története, 1944. október – 1945. december.* (György Pályi: History of the Air Force Rifle Regiment of the Division *"Szent László"*, October 1944 – December 1945), p.43.

324 One of the popular nicknames for the German 7.92mm MG42 general machine gun.

325 HM HIM *Hadtörténelmi Levéltár* (Budapest), *Tanulmányok és visszaemlékezések gyűjteménye* (Collection of studies and recollections), nr. 3138., Martin Kornél: *Néhány adat és emlék a „Szent László" felderítő osztály életéből, 1944. XI. 17.–XII. 27.* (Kornél Martin: Data and memories from the life of the Reconnaissance Battalion *"Szent László"*, 17 November – 27 December 1944), pp.32-35.

326 HM HIM *Hadtörténelmi Levéltár* (Budapest), *m. kir. 53 utászzászlóalj naplója, 27. 12. 1944.*

327 HM HIM *Hadtörténelmi Levéltár* (Budapest), *HM 35.840/8. ny. v. –1945.*

The military bridge at Kicsind came under heavy pressure from the drifting ice, but was still usable. Because, in the meantime, Kicsind fell into Soviet hands, Lieutenant Colonel Ernő Koppányi, commander of the 53rd Pioneer Battalion, was ordered by the commander of the Division *"Szent László"* to regain the bridge at all costs and to destroy it immediately. The battalion, with its remaining forces, was ordered to the defence of Kőhídgyarmat.

However, *Major* Schleppelman asked on behalf of the Germans, that the bridge not be destroyed yet because there were considerable German and Hungarian forces on the eastern side of the river. At last, at about 1000 hours in the morning, Cadet Sergeant Ernő Barta, from the 1st Company/53rd Pioneer Battalion, approached the bridge with his four soldiers and fired *Panzerfäuste* at it, but did not succeed in destroying the bridge. Staff Major Árpád Lajtos, chief of staff of the Division *"Szent László"* issued a verbal order at 1130 hours to the Pioneer Battalion that the bridge has to be preserved as the Germans requested and was to be destroyed only if Soviet units advanced across it. At about 2000 hours in the evening, Lajtos ordered by telephone that, despite earlier requests, the bridge was to be demolished immediately. This order, too, was temporarily suspended during the evening at the request of a German *Leutnant*, because there were German vehicles crossing to the west bank of the Garam.[328]

That day's fighting wiped out the remaining strength of the Division *"Szent László"*. At that point, battle casualties for the Reconnaissance Battalion amounted to 70%, for the Grenadier Regiment 95%, for the Air Force Rifle Regiment 85%, and for the 53rd Pioneer Battalion 65% of their combat strength.[329]

The same day Lieutenant General Gyula Kovács, appointed General of the High Command, visited the joint command post of the command of *LXXII. Armeekorps* and the Division *"Szent László"* at Béla:

> The appointed General was informed of the situation and he confirmed that the Division *"Szent László"* had been nearly wiped out during the heroic fighting against manifoldly superior forces between 21-27 December.

According to statements made by the superior German *Armeekorps* and *Armee,* the division fought exceptionally well and its accomplishments were outstanding, even considering those of the German troops. The operational value and the morale of the unit were highly praised:

> Today we can not accurately estimate what remained of the division. (According to the estimate of the division commander, approximately 500 soldiers remained of the infantry.) The losses of the division were all battle casualties. None ever fled or changed sides.[330]

---

328 HM HIM *Hadtörténelmi Levéltár (Budapest), m. kir. 53. utászzászlóalj naplója 27. 12. 1944.*

329 *Bundesarchiv–Militärarchiv* (Freiburg im Breisgau), RH 24–72, *Kriegstagebuch Ia des LXXII. Armeekorps, Tagesmeldungen unterstellter Einheiten vom 27. 12. 1944.*

330 This statement is true for most of the elements of the Division, but not for all of them. Elements of the 1st Mortar Artillery Battalion, for example, refused to execute the orders directing the unit to break through toward Garamkövesd; they tore off their *Szent László* badges and rank markings and hid in the nearby houses. For this, see the combat report of the Hungarian 1st Battery/1st Mortar Artillery Battalion, HM HIM *Hadtörténelmi Levéltár (Budapest), A Szent László hadosztály tüzérparancsnokának naplója és mellékletei. 98. sz. melléklet.*

The reasons that the division was rapidly wiped out were:

a. Operational conditions were extremely harsh.
b. It was committed against superior forces.
c. Faults of the German command.
d. Exemplary resistance put up by the division.

The Division *"Szent László"* knocked out eight tanks (one with anti-tank gun, and seven by *Panzerfäuste*) and shot down two aircraft."[331]

After the *6. Panzer-Division/LVII. Panzerkorps* was informed of the destruction of the bridge at Kéménd, without orders, approval or permission, in coordination with the *3.* and *8. Panzer-Divisions*, it cancelled execution of the mission formerly assigned to it, namely, an attack toward Kéménd, and, at 0230 hours, at dawn, departed toward the south, aiming for the bridgehead at Garamkövesd and the crossing point on the Garam.

In the morning, the *5. Kompanie/Panzer-Regiment 11* ceased movement along the east bank of the Garam between Kicsind and Garamkövesd toward Kicsind, and retreated to a more advantageous position. The *Panzer* IV tanks took up positions in a line for the defence of the bridgehead at Garamkövesd.[332]

The main body of the *6. Panzer-Division* was driving toward Garamkövesd in two marching columns. The eastern group (*Divisionsstab, Divisionsbegleitkompanie, Panzer-Nachrichten-Abteilung 82, Stab/Panzer-Artillerie-Regiment 76, Stab/Panzer-Pionier-Abteilung 57, Stab* of the *I. Bataillon/Panzergrenadier-Regiment 4, III. Abteilung/Panzer-Artillerie-Regiment 76*) moved along the Ipolybél–Ipolypásztó road, crushed the weak resistance elements of the 6th Guards Airborne Division at Ipolyszalka, and, by 0700 hours in the morning, reached the Garamkövesd–Kőhídgyarmat area.

The fate of the forces of *Kampfgruppe "Stahl"* (*Stab/Panzergrenadier-Regiment 114* and regimental units, remnants of the *I.* and *II. Bataillon/Panzergrenadier-Regiment 4*, the *5. Batterie/Panzer-Artillerie-Regiment 76*, elements of the *II Abteliung/Panzer-Regiment 11* and elements of *Panzerjäger-Abteilung 41* with nine *Panzer* IV tanks and two *Jagdpanzer* IV tank destroyers) that tried to go further west turned out to be much worse.

After leaving the wooded area west of Ipolyszalka, they ran into Soviet anti-tank weapons, infantry and a number of tanks. Although they did not have sufficient infantry troops, the German *Kampfgruppe* fought intensely and, at last, succeeded in breaking through toward the German—Hungarian bridgehead. The unit lost 40 percent of its guns and anti-tank guns.

However this was not the end of its ordeal. The German armoured fighting vehicles that were approaching, while engaged in combat with the Soviets, were also engaged by three of the six Hungarian *Jagdpanzer* 38(t) tank destroyers that had been committed to secure the Garamkövesd bridgehead. The Hungarian assault artillery soldiers knocked out three *Panzer* IV tanks of the *II. Abteilung/Panzer-Regiment 11*, despite the fact that the Germans sent an officer forward to inform them of the approaching column. The reaction of the Hungarian *Jagdpanzers* may partly be explained as follows – a short while earlier a number of M4A2 tanks of the 9th Guards Mechanized Corps attacked Garamkövesd from exactly the same direction, and one was knocked out when it reached the edge of the

331 HM HIM *Hadtörténelmi Levéltár (Budapest), Fővezérség meghatalmazott tábornoka naplója* p.32.
332 Schadewitz, 1987, p.472.

village by one of the Hungarian *Jagdpanzers,* whereupon the other Soviet tanks retreated.[333]

In the meantime, the Soviets attacked the rear and flanks of *Kampfgruppe "Stahl"*. Part of the German forces were pushed to the west. They were beaten, and could only escape by destroying their vehicles and swimming across to the west bank of the Garam.

According to a short damage survey carried out that day, the *6. Panzer-Division* lost a total of six *Panzer* IV tanks, two *Jagdpanzer* IV tank destroyers, nine armoured personnel carriers, four 12cm mortars, three 2cm anti-aircraft cannon and 40-50 vehicles.[334] The remnants of the unit joined the defenders of the Garamkövesd bridgehead. While covering the retreat, *Flak-Abteilung 298/6. Panzer-Division* knocked out seven Soviet armoured fighting vehicles.

That same day, the *6. Panzer-Division* was attached to *LXXII. Armeekorps* and took over the defence of a sector on the Garam. The sector border between it and the Division *"Szent László"* extended along the line Köbölkút–Libád–Kőhídgyarmat–Bajta (all excluded to the *6. Panzer-Division*). All of the available German and Hungarian armoured fighting vehicles were to be kept concentrated in one armoured *Kampfgruppe* ready to launch counterattacks. That evening, the combat strength of *LXXII. Armeekorps* was as follows[335]:

Table 3 – Combat strength of *LXXII. Armeekorps*, 27 December 1944

Unit	Combat strength	Armament	Artillery	Armoured fighting vehicles
6. Panzer-Division				
4. Panzergrenadier-Regiment	100	3 heavy mortars 3 heavy machine guns 3 anti-aircraft cannon	4 heavy infantry guns	–
Elements of *Panzergrenadier-Regiment 114*[1]	50	2 heavy mortars 2 heavy anti-tank guns		3 self-propelled infantry guns 4 Armoured personnel carriers
II. Abteilung/ Panzer-Regiment 11	–	–	–	3 *Panzer* IVs
Panzerjäger-Abteilung 41	–	–	–	2 *Jagdpanzer* IVs
Panzer-Artillerie-Regiment 76	–	–	9 x 10.5cm 11 x 10 and 15cm	
Division *"Szent László"*				
Air Force Rifle Regiment	28	No data	–	–
Cavalry Squadron/ Reconnaissance Battalion	65	No data	–	–
53rd Pioneer Battalion	160	No data	–	–

333 Paul, 1977, p.440.

334 *Bundesarchiv–Militärarchiv* (Freiburg im Breisgau), RH 24–72, *Kriegstagebuch Ia des LXXII. Armeekorps, Tagesmeldung unterstellter Einheiten vom 27. 12. 44.*

335 *Bundesarchiv–Militärarchiv* (Freiburg im Breisgau), *RH 24–72, Kampfstärken, Anlage Nr. 1291.*

<table>
<tr><th>Unit</th><th>Combat strength</th><th>Armament</th><th>Artillery</th><th>Armoured fighting vehicles</th></tr>
<tr><td>Remnants of the 3rd Motorized Rifle Regiment</td><td>70</td><td>No data</td><td>–</td><td>–</td></tr>
<tr><td>VIII Artillery Battalion</td><td>–</td><td>–</td><td>5 x 15cm</td><td>–</td></tr>
<tr><td rowspan="2">II. Bataillon/ Panzergrenadier-Rgt. 93</td><td rowspan="2">28</td><td rowspan="3">8 machine guns</td><td>–</td><td>–</td></tr>
<tr><td rowspan="2">–</td><td rowspan="2">–</td></tr>
<tr><td>Maschinengewehr-Bataillon “Sachsen” géppuskás-zászlóalj</td><td>135</td></tr>
<tr><td>Elements of Panzergrenadier-Regiment 114</td><td>36</td><td>5 machine guns
2 medium mortars
2 heavy anti-tank guns</td><td>–</td><td>3 self-propelled infantry guns</td></tr>
<tr><td>I. Bataillon/ Panzergrenadier-Regiment 4</td><td>50</td><td>4 medium mortars
3 heavy mortars
3 anti-aircraft cannon</td><td>2 heavy infantry guns</td><td>–</td></tr>
<tr><td>II. Bataillon/ Panzergrenadier-Regiment 4</td><td>31</td><td>2 heavy mortars</td><td></td><td></td></tr>
<tr><td>1 German Marschkompanie</td><td>135</td><td>3 machine guns
50 rifles</td><td></td><td></td></tr>
<tr><td>2 German Alarmkompanien</td><td>35</td><td>No data</td><td>–</td><td>–</td></tr>
<tr><td>Other</td><td></td><td>11 heavy anti-tank guns</td><td>–</td><td>6 Jagdpanzer 38(t)s</td></tr>
<tr><td colspan="5">Hungarian 2nd Armoured Division</td></tr>
<tr><td>2nd Towed Artillery Battalion</td><td>–</td><td>–</td><td>6 x 10.5cm</td><td>–</td></tr>
<tr><td>6th Towed Artillery Battalion</td><td>–</td><td>–</td><td>8 x 10.5cm</td><td>–</td></tr>
</table>

1 Without the *II* (armoured personnel carrier) *Bataillon/Panzergrenadier-Regiment 114*.

As no other friendly units were expected from the north, the evacuation of the Garamkövesd bridgehead was ordered for *LXXII. Armeekorps* for 0400 hours the next dawn.[336]

During the night of 26/27 December the German *3. Panzer-Division* was forced to abandon its positions north of Ipolypásztó. As the division headquarters did not have communication with *LVII. Panzerkorps*, *Generalleutnant* Philipps and *Generalmajor* Fröhlich, commanding the *8. Panzer-Division*, acted on their initiative.

The *3.* and *8. Panzer-Division* moved toward Bény. The *8. Panzer-Division* proceeded around to the south, the *3. Panzer-Division* broke through Vilmos farm.

336 *Bundesarchiv–Militärarchiv* (Freiburg im Breisgau), RH 24–72, *Kriegstagebuch Ia des LXXII. Armeekorps, 27. 12. 1944.*

The forces of the two divisions reached the Garam late in the afternoon. The *Panzergrenadiers* and *Panzer-Aufklärungs-Abteilungen 3* and *8* established a bridgehead in the evening east of Bény. The soldiers of *Panzer-Pionier-Bataillon 39* built a 16-ton military bridge over the river which was ready at 0900 hours the next day. The work of the *Pioniers* was secured by *Flak-Abteilung 314*.[337]

After the forces of *LVII. Panzerkorps* reached the Garam, *LXXII. Armeekorps* was temporarily attached to the command of *General der Panzertruppe* Kirchner. With this, *Armeekorps-Gruppe "Kirchner"* was activated.[338]

In the evening, at 2035 hours, the German *6. Armee* informed *LXXII. Armeekorps* that a *Sperrverband* from the Protectorate of Bohemia and Moravia was attached to it. The hastily organized unit consisted of an assault gun company, a tank destroyer company and a bicycle infantry company. According to plans it was to be deployed on the southern section of the Garam line.[339]

At Garamdamásd on the front line of *Divisionsgruppe "Rintelen"*, the Soviets crossed with a battalion-sized unit to the west bank of the river. The Germans launched a counterattack. Soviet forces assembled in front of the German Garam bridgehead east of Szodó.[340]

The 5th Guards Tank Corps/6th Guards Tank Army was engaged during the evening at Garamkövesd (against 15-20 German and Hungarian armoured fighting vehicles and a regiment-sized infantry unit, according to its report). The 4th Guards Mechanized Corps was in action in the area of Zalaba against 10-12 armoured fighting vehicles and infantry units amounting to the size of two battalions. The 46th Guards Tank Brigade/9th Guards Mechanized Corps was fighting to capture Ipolypásztó.[341] The position of the units on the right flank of the 7th Guards Army were:

- 27th Guards Rifle Corps
    - 303rd Rifle Division on the east bank of the Garam at Zseliz and the Ároki forest;
    - 243rd Rifle Division marched to Garamsalló and Rozmaringmajor;
    - 36th Guards Rifle Division marched to Ipolybél and Bélipuszta;
    - 141st Rifle Division on the road leading from Nagybörzsöny to Vámosmikola;
- 25th Guards Rifle Corps
    - 6th Guards Airborne Division occupied Baglyasszőlő 3km west of Ipolyszalka;
    - 409th Rifle Division engaged in battle for Hill 285 (Kövecses Hill) and Garamkövesd;
    - 53rd Rifle Division with its units crossed to the west bank of the Garam.[342]

337 *Geschichte der 3. Panzer-Division Berlin-Brandenburg 1935–1945*, 1967, p.454.

338 The command post of *General der Panzertruppe* Kirchner was at Bátorkeszi that day.

339 *Bundesarchiv–Militärarchiv* (Freiburg im Breisgau), RH 24–72, *Kriegstagebuch Ia des LXXII. Armeekorps, Anlage Nr. 1280, 27. 12. 1944.*

340 HM HIM *Hadtörténelmi Levéltár* (Budapest) microfilm archives, *Kriegstagebuch Ia der Heeresgruppe Süd, Kriegstagebuch vom 27. 12. 1944* (roll no. 627. image no. 7211291).

341 HM HIM *Hadtörténelmi Levéltár (Budapest), Szovjet iratmásolatok gyűjteménye a budapesti hadművelettel kapcsolatban, a szovjet 2. Ukrán Front hadijelentései, 1944. december 27.*

342 Daily combat reports of the Soviet 7th Guards Army to the command of the 2nd Ukrainian Front (a copy owned by the author), evening report, 27 December 1944.

On **28 December 1944**[343], on the *LXXII. Armeekorps* sector of the front, the German—Hungarian units attached to the Division *"Szent László"* evacuated the Garamkövesd bridgehead. The Company Commander of the German *5. Kompanie/Panzer-Regiment 11, Leutnant* Sander, still remained in the bridgehead with his *Panzer* IV tanks. He remembered the events as such:

> The evacuation of the bridgehead was planned to take place after the breakout. My tanks were to secure as rearguard. The engineers prepared to destroy the bridge.
>
> Then I, too, received orders to evacuate the bridgehead. In the meantime, the Soviets reached the banks of the Garam, and fired from below at our troops on the bridge.
>
> A small armoured unit of our allied Hungarian comrades was also stationed in the bridgehead[344]. Because the enemy fire gradually became heavier and heavier, the crews of the armoured fighting vehicles abandoned their vehicles and left them, moving freely in the area of the bridgehead, thereby eliminating the possibility for the still arriving German armoured troops to escape via the bridge.
>
> Thus, I and my tanks were again in grave danger because the assaulting Soviet tanks could run me down at any minute. I received an order by radio from my last vehicle that the head of the column was to clear the road in front of the bridge of any vehicles. This almost became a failure because the Soviet fire increased and created an extremely dangerous situation, when, in the last seconds, some of my brave men succeeded in clearing the road.[345]

Garamkövesd was first entered by elements of the 53rd Rifle Division and the armoured fighting vehicles of the 27th Independent Guards Tank Brigade at about 0500, at dawn, followed by the arrival of elements of the 9th Guards Mechanized Corps from the northeast. Before the Soviet troops could drive onto the Garamkövesd road bridge, which had a capacity of 24 tons, it was blown at 0440 hours by the German *Pioniers*, after the retreat of the German—Hungarian defenders.[346]

At about 0800 hours one company of the Motorized Rifle Battalion/27th Independent Guards Tank Brigade successfully crossed to the west bank of the Garam 200 metres east of the Garamkövesd road bridge. Elements of the Soviet Motorized Rifle Battalion that crossed the Garam reached the eastern part of Nána at about 1200 hours and occupied the village by 1700 hours. The tank battalions of the brigade spent the day in Garamkövesd and prepared to cross the river.[347]

The Garam bridge at Kicsind was blown up by Cadet Sergeant Ernő Barta and his group at 0305 hours. The 24-ton capacity Garamkövesd road bridge on the front line sector of the German *6. Panzer-Division* was blown at 0440 hours. This left the *3. Kompanie/I.*

343 Weather: -8· Celsius, visibility impaired, light snow at times, minor roads suitable for travel.

344 This was presumably the Assault Artillery Battalion "Bernolák" with six *Jagdpanzer* 38(t) tank destroyers.

345 Schadewitz, 1987, p.472.

346 *Bundesarchiv–Militärarchiv* (Freiburg im Breisgau), RH 24–72, *Kriegstagebuch Ia des LXXII. Armeekorps, Morgenmeldung unterstellter Einheiten vom 28. 12. 44.*

347 Combat report of the 27th Independent Guards Tank Brigade to the commander of the 7th Guards Army tank- and mechanized troops (a copy owned by the author), 28 December 1944. The operational armoured fighting vehicle strength of the unit in the evening consisted of 18 T–34 tanks and seven SU–85 self-propelled guns.

Bataillon of the *Panzergrenadier-Regiment 4*, which had been assigned to secure the eastern outskirts of the bridge, stuck on the east bank of the Garam. Its soldiers had to swim across to the west bank.[348]

In the morning, the combat-ready armoured fighting vehicle strength of *LXXII. Armeekorps* was:

- Division "*Szent László*": three *Panzer* IV tanks and six *Jagdpanzer* 38(t) tank destroyers;
- *6. Panzer-Division*: four *Panzer* IV tanks and three *Jagdpanzer* IV tank destroyers.[349]

During the day, Soviet troops attempted to cross the river in the sectors of both divisions, especially near the demolished bridges, exploiting the drifting ice in the river. The Division *"Szent László"* and its attached German and Hungarian troops that had been fully exhausted in the battles of the previous days could not prevent the Soviet infantry from entering Párkány and Nána with a force the size of two battalions.

The commander of the German *Maschinengewehr-Bataillon "Sachsen"*, *Hauptmann* Müller, was wounded in these battles. The remnants of the battalion, (approximately 50-60 soldiers) under command of a *Feldwebel*, were forced back to the railway station of Párkány. According to Staff Major Lajtos, who had seen them, "they did not walk, but staggered". However, *Stabsmajor* Jensch, *erster* (Operations) *Generalstabsoffizier* of the *LXXII. Armeekorps*, forced them back to the front line at pistol point.[350]

Further westward advance of the Soviet forces was prevented by elements of the *6. Panzer-Division*, a battalion of the Division *"Szent László"* and the *Jagdpanzer* 38(t) tank destroyers of Assault Artillery Battalion "Bernolák".[351]

640 unarmed and untrained enlisted men and 20 officers had been waiting at Pápa as reinforcements for the Division *"Szent László"* to finally get buses with which they were to be transported to Köbölkút. However the buses did not arrive that day nor on the next. Arming these untrained fresh soldiers was the responsibility of the *6. Armee*. 500 soldiers of the 1st Battalion/1st Parachute Regiment were also stuck *en route*. Until then, they had been fighting south of the Balaton. The paratroopers tarried long at Celldömölk for want of a locomotive to pull their train. Their supplement units at Pápa assumed they had been employed in the defence of Mór or Tata.[352]

Soviet pressure forced the German—Hungarian defence out of two thirds of Kőhídgyarmat and back to the Nána–Kőhídgyarmat road.

The eastern edge of Kőhídgyarmat was still unoccupied; therefore elements of the Soviet 409th Rifle Division that crossed the Garam occupied the area from the south and east. The Hungarian 53rd Pioneer Battalion, with its reserve of 40 soldiers, launched

348 Paul, 1977, p.440.

349 *Bundesarchiv–Militärarchiv* (Freiburg im Breisgau), RH 24–72, *Kriegstagebuch Ia des LXXII. Armeekorps, Morgenmeldung unterstellter Einheiten vom 28. 12. 44.*

350 HM HIM *Hadtörténelmi Levéltár (Budapest), Tanulmányok és visszaemlékezések gyűjteménye* (Collection of studies and recollections) nr. 2598., Lajtos Árpád: *Szent László hadosztály (Visszaemlékezés).* (Árpád Lajtos: Division *"Szent László"* (Recollections)), p.66.

351 HM HIM *Hadtörténelmi Levéltár* (Budapest) microfilm archives, *Kriegstagebuch Ia der Heeresgruppe Süd, Kriegstagebuch vom 28. 12. 1944* (roll no. 627. image no. 7211306).

352 *Bundesarchiv–Militärarchiv* (Freiburg im Breisgau), RH 24–72, *Tätigkeitsbericht über Fahrt nach Pápa am 30. 12. 1944, Anlage Nr. 1350.*

a counterattack which got to the cemetery. However, the Hungarian engineers were met there by heavy machine gun and submachine gun fire. The assault bogged down. The Hungarians lost 10 soldiers. Lieutenant Colonel Koppányi ordered the 20 German soldiers found in the village to close the road leading from the church to the eastern edge of the village. These German—Hungarian forces held the village until 1600 hours.

At this time, four assault guns and *Jagdpanzers* arrived from Kéménd to Kőhídgyarmat. One of these went into reserve. 30 Hungarian engineers mounted two of the remaining three vehicles and 20 German soldiers mounted one. In the meantime, the German artillery started to lay down heavy fire on area of the church of the village. The German armoured fighting vehicle with the mounted German soldiers thrust forward on the main street to the southern edge of the village. The other two reached the southeastern and eastern edges and established defence positions there. At about 2300 hours in the night, *Hauptmann* Göttke's *I. Bataillon/Panzergrenadier-Regiment 114* arrived, reinforced by five *Panzer* IV tanks. These soldiers then defended Kőhídgyarmat together with 43 soldiers of the 53rd Pioneer Battalion.[353]

This village, as mentioned above, was recaptured from the Soviets by the German—Hungarian units, but Nána, Párkány and the southern bank of the Garam remained in Soviet hands. The Soviet 7th Guards Army thereby also gained a foothold on the west bank of the Garam.

In the evening of 28 December the armoured strength of the *LXXII. Armeekorps* comprised[354]:

Table 4 – Armoured fighting vehicle strength of *LXXII. Armeekorps*, 28 December 1944

Armoured fighting vehicles	Combat-ready	Repairable within a short time	Repairable within a longer time	Total	Total losses from 22 Dec 1944
6. Panzer-Division					
Panzer IV	3	15	5	23	11
Command *Panzer* IV	–	1	1	2	–
Jagdpanzer IV	4	3	3	10	4
Hungarian 2nd Armoured Division					
Panzer IV	10	–	–	10	–
Panther	–	1	–	1	–
Turán–40	–	–	4	4	–
Turán–75	–	–	5	5	–
Nimród	1	–	–	1	–
Assault Artillery Battalion "Bernolák"					
Jagdpanzer 38(t)	4	3	7	14	No data[1]

1 Although the documentation does not provide data concerning total loss, the unit originally had 24 armoured fighting vehicles. Based on this, the Battalion had lost 10

353 HM HIM *Hadtörténelmi Levéltár (Budapest), A m. kir. 53. utászzászlóalj naplója, 1944. 12. 28.*

354 *Bundesarchiv–Militärarchiv* (Freiburg im Breisgau), RH 24–72, *Generalkommando LXXII. A.K. Ia Nr. 2992/44 geh., Anlage Nr. 1295.*

Jagdpanzer 38(t)s.

Together with the 10 new *Panzer* IV tanks that arrived for the Hungarian 2nd Armoured Division, the extremely weak forces of the Division *"Szent László"* and the German *Kampfgruppe "Reimar"*[355] launched a counterattack at midnight, and, during a two-hour night battle, recaptured Párkány and Nána by 0200 hours of the following morning.[356] Private 1st Class Ödön Bese, one of the drivers of the Hungarian *Panzer* IV tanks remembered as follows:

> [...] in the afternoon, the company was ordered to form up; the tank strength consisted of ten panzerfours [*Panzer* IVs – the author]. At the same time this was the tank strength of the whole battalion [1st Battalion/3rd Tank Regiment]. As we formed up, a platoon of black clad SS commando soldiers with skull insignia on their clothes arrived[357] with thirty *leventes*. We introduced ourselves to them. I saw the so-called assault rifle [*Sturmgewehr 44* – the author] for the first time with the Germans. This weapon was larger than a submachine gun but smaller than the infantry rifles. This had a slightly bent magazine and could fire single shot and burst fire. Its ammunition was larger and more powerful than that of the submachine gun. [The Germans] told us that they were going to fight with us, together with the *leventes*. From here we went to the Párkánynána station [Párkány railway station – the author], all of us, although we were on combat alert so we could not even enter the houses. During the waiting we found the cellar of the railway station buffet and two hectolitres of rum. We also found five-litre empty bottles on the shelves. That was an opportunity! We filled bottles for each tank – the railway station was not functioning and no one was in the building except for us. Alarm at 2200 hours! We headed for Párkánynána. We were to attempt to drive the Soviets out of Nána because they did not have any tanks on this front line section. So, if that was the order, we had to try to carry it out.
>
> We departed with ten tanks, a platoon of German soldiers, thirty *leventes* and,of course, ten times five litres of rum. I don't know for sure, but I assume the Germans also took their share of rum. The weather became extremely cold; it was below -20° C[358]. The full moon provided almost daylight visibility. During the march we occasionally sipped the rum, so we did not feel the dread of cold so much. It is true that the engines also gave out some heat but we became a bit bolder and more adventurous. As we arrived to Párkánynána [to Párkány – the author], we fired a burst from the machine guns wherever and whenever we saw the tiniest movements, even if it was only a dog or a cat. We have also swept each street with the guns. As all of our ammunition was tracer ammo, they drew ghastly light streaks in the air. It is no wonder that the Soviet infantry withdrew from us; we made as much clatter as if we were a division, or at

355 The remnants of the German *Panzergrenadier-Regiment 4* under command of *Major* Gustav Reimar, commander of the *II* (armoured personnel carrier) *Bataillon/Panzergrenadier-Regiment 114*. Reimar had earlier received the Knight's Cross of the Iron Cross with Oak Leaves.

356 *Bundesarchiv–Militärarchiv* (Freiburg im Breisgau), RH 24–72, *Kriegstagebuch Ia des LXXII. Armeekorps, 28. 12. 1944.*

357 In all probability these were not SS soldiers, but the crew of the armoured fighting vehicles of the *6. Panzer-Division* without their vehicles; they were assigned to the Hungarian tanks as supporting *Grenadiers*.

358 This is an exaggeration. The temperature at night could not have fallen below –10° Celsius. Of course this is still very low considering the situation while sitting in a tank.

least a full regiment. Of course they did not know how many of us were coming, and if we are Germans or Hungarians. The Soviets had enough of our clattering noise, and withdrew from Nána.

We found a wounded Hungarian private 1st class lying on the ground in the main street. He was stone drunk, and, although his injuries were minor, he was unable to speak because of his drunkenness. He might not have been Hungarian at all, because changing clothes[359] was not uncommon in those times.[360]

On the *LVII. Panzerkorps*[361] front line, at Bény, the *3.* and *8. Panzer-Division*, although in extremely difficult circumstances, crossed the river during the day. The crossing was seriously impeded by the fire of Soviet artillery and rocket launchers, drifting ice and the inadequate capacity of the military bridge. The T–34/85 tanks of the 4th Guards Mechanized Corps also tried to disrupt the operation, but the *Jagdpanzer* IV tank destroyers of *Panzerjäger-Abteilung 543* and elements of *Panzer-Aufklärungs-Abteilung 3* prevented them from carrying out their plans in the area of Kisgyarmat.

In the evening, *Panzer-Aufklärungs-Abteilungen 3.* and *8.* held a bridgehead at Kisgyarmat on the east bank of the Garam in order to receive the last arriving units. The main bodies of the two divisions however, including 1400 vehicles, all of the armoured fighting vehicles and their towed guns (among them two 21cm howitzers) were already on the western bank of the Garam.[362]

The battalion-sized Soviet formation that had crossed the day before at Garamdamásd was repulsed by the counterattack of *Panzer-Aufklärungs-Abteilung 6*.[363]

On the right flank of the German *8. Armee,* the *24. Panzer-Division* made a desperate attempt to close the gap between the two German army groups. The army unit attacked from the southern outskirts of Kisbácska at 1000 hours together with two *Kampfgruppen*, among them elements of *Panzer-Aufklärungs-Abteilung 24*, 20 *Panzer* IV/70 (V) *Jagdpanzers* of the the newly arrived *Panzerjäger-Abteilung 40*, besides, four *StuG. III* assault guns and four *StuH* 42 assault howitzers of the *III. Abteilung/Panzer-Regiment 24*. The Germans broke the considerable resistance of the 6th Guards Cavalry Corps and advanced to Egyházmarót, causing heavy losses to the Soviets. However, part of the group was soon to be committed against Soviet forces that were advancing from the Egeg area toward the northeast and that had entered Teszér.[364] The *Kampfgruppen* of the *24. Panzer-Division* had constantly increasing problems with the shortage of fuel.[365]

In the evening, the 9th Guards Mechanized Corps/6th Guards Tank Army was stationed in Garamkövesd, the 5th Guards Tank Corps was *en route* toward there, and the

359 The Soviet reconnaissance units often used German and Hungarian clothes during their missions.

360 HM HIM *Hadtörténelmi Levéltár (Budapest), Tanulmányok és visszaemlékezések gyűjteménye* (Collection of studies and recollections) nr. 3799. sz., Bese Ödön: *Ahogy történt.* (Ödön Bese: As it has happened.), p.85.

361 Command post of the *Armeekorps* was at Udvard.

362 *Geschichte der 3. Panzer-Division Berlin-Brandenburg 1935–1945*, 1967, p.454.

363 HM HIM *Hadtörténelmi Levéltár* (Budapest) microfilm archives, *Kriegstagebuch Ia der Heeresgruppe Süd, Kriegstagebuch vom 28. 12. 1944* (roll no. 627. image no. 7211306).

364 HM HIM *Hadtörténelmi Levéltár* (Budapest) microfilm archives, *Kriegstagebuch Ia der Heeresgruppe Süd, Kriegstagebuch vom 28. 12. 1944* (roll no. 627. image no. 7211307).

365 HM HIM *Hadtörténelmi Levéltár* (Budapest) microfilm archives, *Kriegstagebuch Ia der Heeresgruppe Süd, Kriegstagebuch vom 28. 12. 1944* (roll no. 627. image no. 7211319).

4th Guards Mechanized Corps was concentrating its forces at Kisgyarmat and in its area.[366] The units on the right flank of the 7th Guards Army occupied the following positions:

- 27th Guards Rifle Corps on the east bank of the Garam
  - 303rd Rifle Division on the sector extending 3km northeast of Újmajor Árok farm;
  - 243rd Rifle Division on the Garamvezekény Lekér sector;
  - 36th Guards Rifle Division on the Lekér Csata (both excluded) sector;
  - 141st Rifle Division committed for the occupation of Csata and Kisgyarmat;
- 25th Guards Rifle Corps
  - 6th Guards Airborne Division on the east bank of the Garam between Garampáld and Kicsind (excluded);
  - 409th Rifle Division between Kicsind Garamkövesd, with its elements on the west bank of the Garam;
  - 53rd Rifle Division crossed the Garam and occupied Nána and Párkány.[367]

On **29 December 1944**[368], at dawn, on the front line sector of *Armeekorps-Gruppe "Kirchner"* the German—Hungarian *Kampfgruppe* that had been entering Párkány was still there. As Private 1st Class Ödön Bese remembered:

> It was already past midnight, about 0200 hours. A baker came out to see what all this noise was; when he was informed that we were Hungarians, he said 'Why did you come here? The situation was almost settled, now you come and disrupt everything again.' We found six Soviet soldiers in one of the cellars. They were left there because they had fallen asleep. We escorted them to the tanks, offered them cigarettes, and talked. Strangely, though, there was no sign of enmity, either in us or in them. Truth was, we thought that the majority of the ordinary Soviet soldiers had to go in the army regardless of their opinion on the issue. [...]
>
> [...] As daylight drew near, one of our soldiers, I do not remember his name, found a dysfunctional old bicycle without its rubber tyres, and started to ride it to and fro on the main street's clinkers. As the rubber tyres were missing he was clattering like a machine gun letting off bursts. Meanwhile dawn was breaking and we noticed that the 5-litre bottle was empty. By morning the five of us who had been together in the tank, drank all five litres and we were not drunk at all! The extreme cold weather and the excitement drew it all out of us.
>
> Three T–34 tanks were in firing positions by a building on the hill of the Esztergom cathedral[369]. They were unable to come over because the bridge over the Danube had earlier been destroyed, but they were able to observe the Nána [Párkány –

366 HM HIM *Hadtörténelmi Levéltár* (Budapest), *Szovjet iratmásolatok gyűjteménye a budapesti hadművelettel kapcsolatban, a szovjet 2. Ukrán Front hadijelentései, 1944. december 28.*

367 Daily combat reports of the Soviet 7th Guards Army to the command of the 2nd Ukrainian Front (a copy owned by the author), evening report, 28 December 1944.

368 Weather: frost melting, sky overcast, bright in other areas, lightly snowing at certain places, the minor roads were suitable for travel.

369 These were the armoured fighting vehicles of the Soviet 18th Tank Corps that had occupied Esztergom.

> the author] main road in its entirety and could engage it from one end to another. One of the T–34s got irritated by the bicycle clatter and our walking on the main street and sent a burst of machine gun fire. Suddenly we had five wounded soldiers. Pista Habony was shot in the knee and Private 2nd Class Kasuba[370] was shot through the ankle etc. Luckily no one died.[371]

At about 0300 hours, at dawn, five tanks of the 3rd Battalion/27th Guards Tank Brigade crossed to the west bank of the Garam and went to help the Motorized Rifle Battalion of the Tank Brigade. Two T–34s occupied firing positions on the north-western edge of Nána and three joined the counterattack of the motorized rifle infantry at Párkány.

At 0400 hours the Soviets launched a new assault with units having the strength of two regiments from the 53rd and the 409th Rifle Divisions and forced the German—Hungarian forces that had advanced during the night back to their starting positions. By 0700 hours Nána was again in Soviet hands.

We turn now again to Corporal Ödön Bese who served in the crew of one of the *Panzer* IV tanks fighting in Párkány:

> We heard strange noises from the alleys and I went to see what was going on. I saw nothing so I went across the road intersection. The moment I came out of the street, machine guns and an anti-tank [gun – the author] fired across the street. The Soviets were already streaming from the alleys. They realized we are only few in number. I thought I had to get back to the tank at all costs; I waited at the corner to see when they fired with the anti-tank gun. Following a shot I ran across the street to the other corner. As I reached the other corner, the house that I was hiding behind just seconds earlier was blasted away. I returned to our tank. My soldiers were securing one of the Germans to one of the doors from the pharmacy. He was seriously wounded and we had no stretchers. He was swiftly pulled up to the tank behind the turret, where he was held fast by two soldiers who prevented him from falling off. All the others, Germans and *leventes*, quickly mounted the vehicles and off we went! It was high time, because the T–34s at the cathedral also began to engage the road. And Soviets were running out of the alleys positioning anti-tank weapons. I accelerated, and swept by as fast as we could. I was driving in a zigzag line in order to prevent them from firing accurately. The others were further forward, because when we arrived there, I was the first with the 1st Lieutenant[372] and now I was the last, at the rear. At last I reached the road bend that turned toward the station. There I was out of their weapons' range.
>
> We actually accomplished our mission. We drove the Soviets out of Párkánynána. In order, however, to occupy and hold the village, the thirty *leventes* and the platoon of German soldiers was ridiculously inadequate. [...] But, if this assault had taken place without surprise and in daylight, rather than by night, I think we would not have gotten away so well, and would have paid a high price for our little excursion.

---

370 Privates First Class István Habony and Pál Kasuba – both in the Hungarian 1st Battalion/3rd Tank Regiment – were wounded at Párkány on 29 December 1944.

371 HM HIM Military History *Tanulmányok és visszaemlékezések gyűjteménye* (Collection of studies and recollections) nr. 3799. sz., Bese Ödön: *Ahogy történt.* (Ödön Bese: As it has happened.), p.86.

372 1st Lieutenant *Vitéz* Dezső Korponay was the commander of the company-sized Hungarian armoured group.

> We did not stop at the station because we received orders by radio to proceed to Muzsla. We were relieved by infantry equipped with anti-tank weapons. As we proceeded toward Muzsla, the railway ran along on the embankment parallel to the road. We have saw at least a kilometre of open railway cars loaded with *Turán* and *Nimród* Hungarian armoured fighting vehicles and cars. They were to be transported to the repair station but were stranded there.[373]

The German—Hungarian forces in Párkány were forced back to the road junction in the middle of the village. Their infantry suffered serious losses. The Soviet motorized infantry, supported by tanks, reoccupied Párkány by 1200 hours.

In the morning, the Division *"Szent László"* had nine *Panzer* IV tanks of the Hungarian 2nd Armoured Division attached, as well as four other *Panzer* IVs of the *6. Panzer-Division*, two *Jagdpanzer* 38(t) tank destroyers of Assault Artillery Battalion "Bernolák", one *Nimród* armoured self-propelled anti-aircraft gun and two 7.5cm anti-tank guns.

By 1100 hours, all 18 operational T–34 tanks of the Soviet 27th Independent Guards Tank Brigade had crossed to the west bank of the Garam.

The Motorized Rifle Battalion of the Soviet Brigade launched an assault at 1300 hours from the western edge of Nána which soon reached point no. 119, 1km northeast of the Párkány railway station. The reconnaissance patrol of the Hungarian 6th Towed Artillery Battalion soon reported Soviet tanks approaching from the direction of Párkány, and then became involved in close combat with infantry.[374]

The 27th Independent Guards Tank Brigade fought for the Párkány railway station between 1200 and 1600 hours. The first T–34 appeared near the railway station at about 1330 hours. A Soviet tank circled the station at 1415 hours and, while going in reverse, attacked the German—Hungarian defenders from the rear.

During the afternoon, combat activity fluctuated, in which the continually renewed counterattacks of the German and Hungarian armoured fighting vehicles (according to Soviet sources, approximately 20 vehicles) helped to hold the positions. During this fighting, the German—Hungarian troops recaptured Káptalanpuszta, 2.5km southwest of Nána, and knocked out two of the five T–34 tanks of the 3rd Battalion/27th Independent Guards Tank Brigade.[375] Following this, forces of the 27th Independent Guards Tank Brigade established defence positions:

- 2nd Battalion/27th Independent Guards Tank Brigade at the north-west edge of Nána;
- 1st Battalion/27th Independent Guards Tank Brigade at the south edge of Nána;
- 3rd Battalion/27th Independent Guards Tank Brigade at the west edge of Párkány;
- The Motorized Rifle Battalion at the railway passage at point no. 119, 1km northeast

373 HM HIM *Hadtörténelmi Levéltár* (Budapest), *Tanulmányok és visszaemlékezések gyűjteménye* (Collection of studies and recollections) nr. 3799. sz., Bese Ödön: *Ahogy történt.* (Ödön Bese: As it has happened.), pp.86-87.

374 HM HIM *Hadtörténelmi Levéltár (Budapest), a „Szent László" hadosztály tüzérparancsnokának naplója és mellékletei. 1944. 12. 29.*

375 HM HIM *Hadtörténelmi Levéltár* (Budapest) microfilm archives, *Kriegstagebuch Ia der Heeresgruppe Süd, Kriegstagebuch vom 29. 12. 1944* (roll no. 627. image no. 7211323).

of the Párkány railway station.

The Soviet tank brigade lost another T–34 that day, which went to the bottom of the Garam during the crossing. At the same time, the 3rd Battalion/27th Independent Guards Tank Brigade, commanded by Guards Captain L. A. Zhdanovskiy, seized, among others, 33 Hungarian tanks, three *Nimród* armoured self-propelled anti-aircraft guns, one light tank and four anti-aircraft guns[376], presumably those that were mentioned by Private 1st Class Ödön Bese that were sitting on the open railway cars west of the railway station. Guards Captain L. A. Zhdanovskiy was later awarded the Hero of the Soviet Union star for this deed.[377]

In the morning, the German *6. Panzer-Division* reported that it had three combat-ready *Panzer* IV tanks, three *Jagdpanzer* IV tank destroyers and two 7.5cm anti-tank guns.[378] The division defended Kőhídgyarmat throughout the entire day. The Soviet 6th Guards Airborne Division entered the village again with a battalion-sized unit and, by morning, occupied its southeastern parts. The Germans slowly retreated to the church in Kőhídgyarmat.

At 1425 hours in the afternoon, five armoured fighting vehicles arrived at Kőhídgyarmat. At 1535 hours, the observer of the Hungarian 2nd Towed Artillery Battalion reported to the artillery commander of the Division *"Szent László"* that a unit of approximately 1000 soldiers was gathering in the village, reinforced by heavy infantry weapons.[379]

At about 2000 hours, after twilight fell, the Germans launched a counterattack to regain the village with an armoured *Kampfgruppe* of the *6. Panzer-Division* (five armoured fighting vehicles and approximately 80 soldiers). The *Panzergrenadiers* of the *Kampfgruppe* of *Hauptmann* Göttke again advanced to the edge of the village. but it proved impossible to clear the houses because of the shortage of appropriate forces. At 2210 hours the Germans reported that they had cleared Kőhídgyarmat. The village came under heavy Soviet artillery and mortar fire and air raids.[380]

LXXII. Armeekorps estimated accurately that its excessively weary infantry (a total of 900 men) would be unable to hold the area that had been recaptured by the armoured fighting vehicles.

Armoured *Kampfgruppe "Medicus"/3. Panzer-Division* (according to Soviet data, a total of 50 tanks, *Jagdpanzers* and armoured personnel carriers[381]) launched an attack at 2000 hours from the area of Kistata-puszta to the southeast toward Párkány and Nána in order to clear the west bank of the Garam. From 2025 hours onwards the attack was also

376 Combat report of the 27th Independent Guards Tank Brigade to the commander of the 7th Guards Army tank and mechanized troops (a copy owned by the author), 29 December 1944. The operational armoured fighting vehicle strength of the unit in the evening consisted of 17 T–34 tanks and seven SU–85 self-propelled guns.

377 *Hősök. A Sovietunió Hősei a magyarországi felszabadító harcokban 1944-1945.* (Heroes. Heroes of the Soviet Union during the liberation battles in Hungary) (Budapest, 1981), p.188.

378 *Bundesarchiv–Militärarchiv* (Freiburg im Breisgau), *RH 24–72, Kriegstagebuch Ia des LXXII. Armeekorps, Morgenmeldung unterstellter Einheiten vom 29. 12. 44.*

379 HM HIM *Hadtörténelmi Levéltár (Budapest), a „Szent László" hadosztály tüzérparancsnokának naplója és mellékletei. 1944. 12. 29.*

380 HM HIM *Hadtörténelmi Levéltár (Budapest), A m. kir. 53. utászzászlóalj naplója, 29 December 1944.*

381 Daily combat reports of the Soviet 7th Guards Army to the command of the 2nd Ukrainian Front) (a copy owned by the author), report issued at 0540 hours in the morning of 30 December 1944

supported by German artillery fire.

The armoured units attained the Kőhídgyarmat–Nána road at 2105 hours, and, at 2230 hours, reached the area 500 metres southwest of the Garamkövesd bridge that was the actual objective of the attack.[382]

The *Panzergrenadiers* of the *3. Panzer-Division* – according to Soviet data, with a regiment-sized force and the support of eight armoured fighting vehicles – moved out at 2200 hours toward Nána.

German—Hungarian aircraft units of *Luftflotte 4* flew 170 sorties that day, with a *Schwerpunkt* [point of main emphasis or concentration] placed on targets southwest of Bánhida, and with lesser forces to support the troops in combat north of Esztergom. The Hungarian 102nd Rapid Bomber Group attacked the railway station at Hont.[383]

On the left flank of the German *6. Armee, Divisionsgruppe "Rintelen"* could only maintain contact between Nagykálna and Nová Baňa in Slovakia (Újbánya, in German, Königsberg) with recurring reconnaissance patrols advancing with armoured personnel carriers. Nová Baňa was the village where the units of the *18. SS-Freiwilligen Panzergrenadier-Division "Horst Wessel"* were stationed that were fighting on the right flank of the *IV. Panzerkorps/8. Armee.*[384]

The *24. Panzer-Division/IV. Panzerkorps* of the *8. Armee* reoccupied Gyűgy and Alsóterény that same day and repulsed the Soviet units attacking Palást.[385] As the front line of the *4. SS-Panzergrenadier-Division*, centered at Csáb, was assaulted by three Soviet Rifle Divisions, the reinforced units of *Panzer-Aufklärungs-Abteilung 24* had to be relocated to Csall.[386] Because of this and the acute shortage of fuel that affected the *24. Panzer-Division*, closure of the gap between the *6.* and *8. Armee* failed permanently.

On **30 December 1944**[387], according to German reconnaissance, there were two Soviet Rifle Divisions supported by armoured fighting vehicles in combat at the Nána bridgehead on the front line of *Gruppe "Kirchner"*.[388]

At 0330 hours, at dawn, the *Panzergrenadiers* of the German *3. Panzer-Division*[389], supported by 15 armoured fighting vehicles, reached the railway-road junction 1km east of Nána, but their attack was halted at the west and north edge and in front of the military quarters of Párkány. The Germans knocked out two more of the six T–34 tanks of the

382 *Bundesarchiv–Militärarchiv* (Freiburg im Breisgau), *RH 24–72, Kriegstagebuch Ia des LXXII. Armeekorps, 29. 12. 1944.*

383 HM HIM *Hadtörténelmi Levéltár* (Budapest) microfilm archives, *Kriegstagebuch Ia der Heeresgruppe Süd, Kriegstagebuch vom 29. 12. 1944* (roll no. 627. image no. 7211325).

384 HM HIM *Hadtörténelmi Levéltár* (Budapest) microfilm archives, *Kriegstagebuch Ia der Heeresgruppe Süd, Kriegstagebuch vom 29. 12. 1944* (roll no. 627. image no. 7211338).

385 HM HIM *Hadtörténelmi Levéltár* (Budapest) microfilm archives, *Kriegstagebuch Ia der Heeresgruppe Süd, Kriegstagebuch vom 29. 12. 1944* (roll no. 627. image no. 7211324).

386 HM HIM *Hadtörténelmi Levéltár* (Budapest) microfilm archives, *Kriegstagebuch Ia der Heeresgruppe Süd, Kriegstagebuch vom 29. 12. 1944* (roll no. 627. image no. 7211337).

387 Weather: -2° Celsius, cloudy in certain areas, otherwise bright, the minor roads were suitable for travel.

388 HM HIM *Hadtörténelmi Levéltár* (Budapest) microfilm archives, *Kriegstagebuch Ia der Heeresgruppe Süd, Kriegstagebuch vom 30. 12. 1944* (roll no. 627. image no. 7211350).

389 Combat strength of the *Panzergrenadiers* of the *3. Panzer-Division* fighting north of the Danube was approximately 300 men.

3rd Guards Tank Battalion/27th Guards Tank Brigade that were employed there.[390] The Soviets positioned their tanks in extremely well chosen firing positions, among barns and civilian houses.[391]

Elements of the Soviet 6th Guards Airborne Division again entered Kőhídgyarmat. *Kampfgruppe "Göttke"* of the *6. Panzer-Division*[392], reinforced with three *Panzer* IV tanks and 15 soldiers of the relocated *Kampfgruppe "Reimar"* launched a counterattack at 1715 hours, in which they successfully recaptured the southeast part of the village. However, further German advance was halted at the creek bed east of Kőhídgyarmat.

Reconnaissance patrols observed a Soviet landing stage being built at the wooded area on the riverbank, 1km east of point no. 113, north of their location. At about 0300 hours the *6. Panzer-Division* launched an attack to prevent construction of the stage. The battalion-sized Soviet unit was forced back to the east side of the river. The Germans took two prisoners and seized one machine gun, two light automatic rifles and two anti-tank rifles.

During the day, the 2nd Battalion/27th Independent Guards Tank Brigade and the Motorized Rifle Battalion, with the Anti-tank Artillery Battery and the Mortar Company defended the west and north-west edges of Nána against the German—Hungarian infantry and armoured fighting vehicles that were attacking from the direction of Kőhídgyarmat and the railway station of Párkány. The 1st Battalion/27th Independent Guards Tank Brigade defended the west edge of Párkány, and repulsed the smaller armoured and infantry attacks launched from the Párkány railway station and Ebedipuszta. The 3rd Battalion of the brigade, with the main body of the Motorized Rifle Battalion were in reserve of the brigade commander 500 metres southwest of Garamkövesd. The tank brigade claimed to have knocked out a total of 10 enemy armoured fighting vehicles while losing three (two of them were burnt out) of their own T–34 tanks.[393]

At 1010 hours the *Kampfgruppe* of the *3. Panzer-Division* was ordered back from Nána, where 18 Soviet tanks assembled shortly thereafter. By that time, armoured *Kampfgruppe "Medicus"* had only one combat-ready *Jagdpanzer* IV tank destroyer and five armoured personnel carriers left. The Division *"Szent László"* had six combat-ready *Panzer* IVs, three *Jagdpanzer* 38(t) tank destroyers, and nine German armoured personnel carriers on alert. Some of the armoured fighting vehicles were stationed in Káptalanpuszta, others at the Párkány railway station.

The *Kampfgruppe* of the *357. Infanterie-Division* had two combat-ready *StuG.* IV assault guns that day, and the elements of the *8. Panzer-Division* tht were fighting north of the Danube had two combat-ready *Marder* tank destroyers and a combat strength of

390 HM HIM *Hadtörténelmi Levéltár* (Budapest) microfilm archives, *Kriegstagebuch Ia der Heeresgruppe Süd, Kriegstagebuch vom 30. 12. 1944* (roll no. 627. image no. 7211342).

391 *Geschichte der 3. Panzer-Division Berlin-Brandenburg 1935–1945*, 1967, p.455.

392 Elements of the *6. Panzer-Division* north of the Danube had five combat-ready *Panzer* IV tanks and five *Jagdpanzer* IV tank destroyers. Combat strength of its *Panzergrenadiers* was approximately 350 men. In the evening, the unit had four combat-ready *Panzer* IV tanks and 11 *Jagdpanzer* IV tank destroyers.

393 Combat report of the 27th Independent Guards Tank Brigade to the commander of the 7th Guards Army tank- and mechanized troops (a copy owned by the author), 30 December 1944. The operational armoured fighting vehicle strength of the unit in the evening consisted of 25 T–34 tanks, eight SU–85 and one SU–76M self-propelled guns. Of this, 12 T–34 tanks and six SU–85 self-propelled guns were operational.

approximately 900 infantry.[394]

LXXII. Armeekorps turned over command and control over its former front line and all troops to *LVII. Panzerkorps* at midnight and departed for Nyitra in Slovakia.[395]

On **31 December 1944**[396], Soviet units continually attacked Kőhídgyarmat in the sector of the *6. Panzer-Division* of the German—Hungarian *Gruppe "Kirchner"*. Following failed attempts by company-sized units, they managed to enter the eastern part of the village at 0315 hours.

On the front line of the *8. Panzer-Division* the Germans engaged the presumed Soviet attack positions with harassing artillery fire.

Forces of the arriving *211. Volksgrenadier-Division* were to relieve the forces of the *3.* and *6. Panzer-Division*. After taking over the front line, these were relocated to the Dunántúl (Transdanubia).[397]

Forces of the Soviet 6th Guards Tank Army were withdrawn from combat as early as 28 December and assembled behind the front line as reserve for the 2nd Ukrainian Front:

- 5th Guards Tank Corps in the area of Szántó, Csánk and Hontfüzesgyarmat with 84 operational tanks;
- 9th Guards Mechanized Corps in the area of Deménd, Alsószemeréd and Hévmagyarád, with 54 operational tanks;
- 4th Guards Mechanized Corps in the area of Tergenye, Nagypeszek, with 28 operational tanks;
- 4th Guards Motorcycle Regiment had 10 operational tanks.[398]

According to Soviet data, in the fighting along the Ipoly and Garam during the period of 20-30 December 1944, the German—Hungarian forces lost:

- 7000 battle casualties (dead and wounded);
- 7551 prisoners;
- 150 armoured fighting vehicles;
- 84 armoured personnel carriers;
- 23 reconnaissance armoured cars;
- 87 various guns.[399]

The right flank units of the 6th Guards Tank Army and the 7th Guards Army seized a

394 HM HIM *Hadtörténelmi Levéltár* (Budapest) microfilm archives, *Kriegstagebuch Ia der Heeresgruppe Süd, Wochenmeldung Stand vom 30. 12. 1944* (roll no. 628. image no. 7212192).

395 *Bundesarchiv–Militärarchiv* (Freiburg im Breisgau), *RH 24–72, Kriegstagebuch Ia des LXXII. Armeekorps, 30. 12. 1944.*

396 Weather: -2° Celsius, occasional snow falling, visibility impaired; the minor roads were suitable for travel although partly covered in ice.

397 HM HIM *Hadtörténelmi Levéltár* (Budapest) microfilm archives, *Kriegstagebuch Ia der Heeresgruppe Süd, Kriegstagebuch vom 31. 12. 1944* (roll no. 627. image no. 7211359).

398 *Budapestskaya Operaciya*. Contemporary summary of the 2nd Ukrainian Front about the operations around Budapest. (A copy owned by the author), p.127.

399 Zaharov, 1973, p.227.

further 54 armoured fighting vehicles, 17 armoured personnel carriers, 62 guns, 40 mortars, 219 railway wagons and eight locomotives.[400]

The following table summarizes the total armoured losses of the German and Hungarian units according to their own sources:

Table 5 – German and Hungarian armoured fighting vehicle losses, 20-30 December 1944

Units	Tanks	*Jagdpanzers*	Assault guns	Armoured SP anti-aircraft gun (*Nimród*)	Totals
Hungarian 2nd Armoured Division[1]	31 *Turán* 40s 3 *Turán* 75s 16 *Toldis* (20mm) 1 *Panzer* III 21 *Panzer* IVs 3 *Panthers*[2]	–	1 *StuG.* III	25	101
8. Panzer-Division	14 *Panzer* IVs	6 *Jagdpanzer* IVs	–	–	20
3. Panzer-Division	–	5 *Jagdpanzer* IVs	–	–	5
6. Panzer-Division	11 Panzer IVs	4 *Jagdpanzer* IVs	–	–	15
Assault Artillery Battalion "Bernolák"[3]	–	10 *Jagdpanzer* 38(t)s	–	–	10
Sturmgeschütz-Abteilung 1176	–	11 *Jagdpanzer* 38(t)s	–	–	11
Total	100	36	1	25	162

1 In the case of the Hungarian 2nd Armoured Division the data indicate the losses suffered in the period between 7 and 28 December 1944.

2 The majority of these tanks were under repair during the period in question. In the case of most of them, the losses more often meant Soviet seizure than combat loss.

3 Unfortunately the losses of the Assault Artillery Battalion "Bernolák" cannot be distinguished geographically as yet. The greater part of the 10 lost *Jagdpanzers* were, in our opinion, lost south of the Danube and not during the combat activity along the Ipoly and the Garam.

The scale of the German armoured personnel carrier and armoured car losses given by the Soviets is not supported by data found in archives. In our opinion, the actual losses could be rather closer to the number of seized armoured personnel carriers.

On the other hand, the Hungarian 2nd Armoured Division suffered considerable fighting vehicle losses during the combat activity in December 1944. Approximately one-third of these were vehicles on the trains stranded west of Párkány which were later seized by the Soviets. In this way the armoured losses of the German and Hungarian units reached

400 Zaharov, 1973, p.227.

or even surpassed the Soviet data.

Of the losses of the Division *"Szent László"* between 20-27 December 1944 we only have approximate data regarding the Grenadier Regiment. The regiment lost a total of 1134 men (most of them missing in action).[401]

The following table summarizes Soviet tank and self-propelled gun total losses suffered between 20-30 December 1944, according to data deduced from the sources already mentioned:

Table 6 – Soviet tank and self-propelled gun losses, 20-30 December 1944

Date	Location	Number of knocked out vehicles	Type	Unit	Unit scoring the hit
20 Dec.	Ipolyság northwest	1	Presumably M4A2	9th Guards Motorized Corps	*8. Panzer-Division*
20 Dec.	Hévmagyarád	2	T–34	5th Guards Tank Corps	*Divisionsgruppe "Rintelen"*
20 Dec.	Gyűgy south	10	presumably M4A2	9th Guards Mechanized Corps	securing forces of the *IV. Panzerkorps*
21 Dec.	Szob – Ipolydamásd	2	T–34	27th Guards Tank Brigade	*Maschinengewehr-Bataillon "Sachsen"*
22 Dec.	Nagykálna	14	T–34	5th Guards Tank Corps	*Divisionsgruppe "Rintelen"/ Panzer-Aufklärungs-Abteilung 6*
22 Dec.	Lontó	3	T–34	5th Guards Tank Corps	*Panzer-Nachrichten-Abteilung 39*
23 Dec.	Zseliz	3	T–34	5th Guards Tank Corps	*1. Panzerjäger-Kompanie/ Panzerjäger-Abteilung 43.*
23 Dec	Lelédhidipuszta	2	T–34	27th Guards Tank Brigade	Div. *"Szent László"* Tank Destr. Battalion and Artillery
23 Dec	Kéménd – Garamsalló	12	T–34	5th Guards Tank Corps	*Panzergruppe "Scheppelmann"*
23 Dec	Between the Ipoly and the Börzsöny	2	IS–2	49th Guards Heavy Tank Regiment	*LVII. Panzerkorps*
24 Dec	Letkés southeast	5	T–34	27th Guards Tank Brigade	Division *"Szent László"*
24 Dec.	Ipolyvisk	4[1]	Self-propelled gun	Unknown	*Kampfgruppe "Glaubitz"*

401 HM HIM *Hadtörténelmi Levéltár (Budapest), HM 35.840/8. ny. v. –1945.*

Date	Location	Number of knocked out vehicles	Type	Unit	Unit scoring the hit
25 Dec.	Ipolyszakállos	20	M4A2	9th Guards Motorized Corps	*LVII. Panzerkorps*
26 Dec	Helemba	1	T-34	27th Guards Tank Brigade	6th Towed Artillery Battalion
26 Dec	Ipolykiskeszi	3	Presumably M4A2	9th Guards Motorized Corps	Division *"Szent László"*
27 Dec	Garamkövesd north	1	M4A2	9th Guards Motorized Corps	Assault Artillery Battalion "Bernolák"
27 Dec	Garamkövesd	7	2 T-34 s, the other: M4A2s	27th Guards Tank Brigade 9th Guards Motorized Corps	*Maschinengewehr-Bataillon "Sachsen"* Division *"Szent László"*
27 Dec	Ipolyszalka	7	Presumably M4A2	9th Guards Motorized Corps	*Flak-Abteilung 298*
29 Dec	Párkány west	2	T-34	27th Guards Tank Brigade	Assault Artillery Battalion "Bernolák" Hungarian 2nd Armoured Division
30 Dec	Nána northwest	3	T-34	27th Guards Tank Brigade	*3. Panzer-Division*
Total		104	Tanks and self-propelled guns		

1 Three of these were seized by the Germans, and one was knocked out.

According to the data above, the approximate armoured losses of the Soviet tank and motorized units may have been as follows:

- 5th Guards Tank Corps: 34 T-34 and T-34/85 tanks;
- 9th Guards Mechanized Corps: 53 M4A2 and Mk IX Valentine tanks;
- 6th Guards Tank Army's independent units: two IS-2 heavy tanks and four self-propelled guns;
- 27th Independent Guards Tank Brigade: 17 T-34 and T-34/85 tanks[402].

402 These are total losses of the 27th Independent Guards Tank Brigade, suffered in combat, which were deleted from the Tables of Organization and Equipment. We have not counted here the tank of the unit that fell into the Ipoly. Furthermore, four SU-85 and three SU-76M self-propelled guns have also been deleted from the strength of the Brigade, however, these vehicles had been damaged during earlier combat activities, and their general repair was considered to be impossible in the field. These were either melted down or sent to the rear for general factory repairs.

According to Soviet data, the 5th Guards Tank Corps went into reserve on 28 December with 84 operational tanks. This means that this large military unit received repaired or new armoured fighting vehicles as replacements (approximately 30 tanks considering its losses).

The condition of the 9th Guards Mechanized Corps on 28 December (54 operational tanks) supports the losses suffered, the disabling of approximately 53 armoured fighting vehicles. Of this, the table above helps to determine the place and date of the destruction of 47 tanks.

In the case of these two Soviet corps the exact number of total armoured losses cannot be determined due to lack of sources. However, in the case of the 27th Independent Guards Tank Brigade the number of vehicles knocked out exactly matches reports provided by the German—Hungarian units and the Soviet unit's own battle casualty reports. Therefore we assume that, in the case of the two corps of the 6th Guards Tank Army, similar rates can be expected, and most of the knocked out Soviet armoured fighting vehicles can be considered as total losses.

Among the German units, the 6. *Panzer-Division* knocked out the largest number of Soviet armoured fighting vehicles, a total of 70 during a period of six days in combat, according to their claims (26 of them by anti-tank weapons – including *Panzerfäuste*, *Panzerschrecks*, magnetic mines with hollow charge, anti-tank rifle grenades – in close combat).[403]

On the German side, the elements of the *3., 6.* and *8. Panzer-Divisions* committed north of the Danube had primarily *Panzer* IV tanks and *Jagdpanzer* IV tank destroyers. These German armoured fighting vehicles had minor disadvantages as opposed to the Soviet T–34/85 tanks – considering only the military technical data. However these tanks were equal to the T–34, M4A2 and Mk IX Valentine tanks in combat.

The German *Panzer-Aufklärungs-Abteilungen* played a decisive role in the armoured combat between the Ipoly and the Garam. Not only did they have to supplement the armoured *Panzergrenadier* battalions within the armoured *Kampfgruppen*, but they also had important individual tasks assigned to them, and they showed their considerable combat value during these missions.

Panzer-Aufklärungs-Abteilung 6 performed excellently at Nagykálna. The *Panzer-Aufklärungs-Abteilungen 3* and *8* also did their job superbly. The latter unit, for example, claimed to have caused the following losses to the Soviets in the second half of December 1944: 11 destroyed tanks, four self-propelled guns, two Universal Carrier armoured personnel carriers[404], 46 trucks, 19 trophy anti-tank guns (12 of these blown up), the demolition of a crash-landed Il-2 ground attack aircraft and the capture of its crew; 223 counted and 577 estimated Soviet soldiers killed, and 55 prisoners.[405]

From an operational point of view, the German—Hungarian forces suffered almost total defeat. They failed to close the Ipolyság corridor and they failed to destroy the Soviet 6th Guards Tank Army that passed through the corridor, even with the help of the forces of the *LVII. Panzerkorps*.

The large Soviet armoured formation, however, was unable to hold the bridgehead it had established on the western bank of the Garam and, consequently, was unable to attain

403 Paul, 1977, p.440.

404 These were, presumably, fighting as part of the 9th Guards Mechanized Corps.

405 For this, see Kindel, Richard, *Die 8. Panzer-Division der Deutschen Wehrmacht 1939-1945*, Band 2 (Wuppertal, 2007), p.561.

its combat objective. It therefore became necessary to turn the 6th Guards Tank Army southward, especially after two additional German armoured units joined the attack of the *8. Panzer-Division*.

However, we shall not forget that the 5th Guards Tank Corps, comprising the right flank of the 6th Guards Tank Army, which was advancing southward on the east bank of the Garam, was actually stopped by German armoured units on 22 December and forced back substantially to the north on 23 December.

The Division *"Szent László"* proved its excellence against the three rifle divisions of the Soviet 25th Guards Rifle Corps that attacked with tank support and considerable artillery reinforcement. Various elements of the division even had to fight with units of the 6th Guards Tank Army between the Ipoly and the Garam. However, it must be stressed that they secured the supply lines of the German armoured units until the evening of 24 December, rather than their retreat, with the defence the Letkés bridgehead. The majority of the units of the *LVII. Panzerkorps* did not retreat via the Ipolyszalka bridge, but from the north, along the west bank of the Ipoly.

The excellent achievements of the Hungarian units received considerable support from such lesser German units as were, for a period of time, attached to the division within the time frame in question (except for the bridgehead at Letkés).

However hard they tried, the Soviet units failed to cut off the German and Hungarian units between the Ipoly and the Garam, although they did inflict heavy losses (mainly in personnel) to them. The forces of the 7th Guards Army closed up to the eastern part of the Garam and occupied a bridgehead on the western bank of the river during the last days of December, between Párkány and Kőhídgyarmat. The bridgehead also served as a departure point for an assault operation.

2

Averting the counterattack: the tank battle at Komárom (6-22 January 1945)

Several Hungarian and international publications have dealt with the relief campaigns launched by the German troops in January 1945 toward Budapest. None of those, however, has discussed in detail[1] the attack by the left-flank troops of the Soviet 2nd Ukrainian Front that was meant to prevent the Germans from continuing their previously bogged down "Operation *Konrad*", north of the Danube.

It was the above-mentioned Soviet attempt that resulted in a fierce tank battle between 6 and 22 January 1945, which indirectly influenced the situation of both the German and Hungarian defenders of Budapest and the Soviet troops that kept the Hungarian capital under siege. Consequently we are convinced that this battle is an organic part of the battle for Budapest.

Operational situation of *Armeegruppe "Balck"* on the northern flank at the beginning of January 1945

Between 20-27 December 1944, as General-Colonel M. V. Zaharov, chief of staff of the 2nd Ukrainian Front put it, "The battle between the German and Soviet tanks continued for eight days on a line of no great length between the Ipoly and the Garam".[2]

A gap yawned between *Armeegruppe "Balck"*[3] and the flank of the German *8. Armee* in the line at Léva. A Soviets attack through this gap with significant forces would expose the entire left flank of *Heeresgruppe Süd*. Therefore it was quickly decided that the Germans would try to close the gap by directing a division there. The formation chosen for this was *20. Panzer-Division*, but before it could reach Hungarian soil, the situation had fundamentally changed.

On 30 December the weary and exhausted elements of *LVII. Armeekorps* of *Korpsgruppe "Kirchner"*[4] abandoned further pointless attempts to eliminate the Soviet

---

1 One of the reasons for this could be that this particular part of the *Felvidék* (Upper Hungary) was reattached to Czechoslovakia after the Second World War. Therefore Hungarian military historians did not consider the combat activities in this area to be integral parts of the Hungarian operations.

2 Zaharov, M. V, *A 2. és a 3. Ukrán Front felszabadító hadműveletei Délkelet-és Közép-Európában, 1944–1945.* (Liberating operations of the 2nd and 3rd Ukrainian Fronts in Southeastern and Central Europe, 1944-1945) (Budapest, 1973), p.227.

3 This operational formation was activated on 24 December 1944 after the change of command of the German *6. Armee*, by renaming the *Armeegruppe* of *General der Artillerie* General Maximilian Fretter-Pico. *General der Panzertruppe* Hermann Balck assumed command of the Hungarian 3rd Army (removed from the chain of command and control) and the German *6. Armee* that same day at 1330 hours.

4 The *Korpsgruppe* under command of *General der Panzertruppe* Kirchner was activated on 29 December, comprising *LVII. Panzerkorps, LXXII. Armeekorps, Divisionsgruppe "Rintelen"*, formed from the

bridgehead between Nána and Párkány, and, instead, went over to the defence.

The exhausted remnants of the Division "*Szent László*", including a *Kampfgruppe* reinforced by *Panzer* IV tanks that was attached to the Hungarian 2nd Armoured Division, were attached to the German *LXXII. Armeekorps*, and, for the two days after 31 December, were in defence positions on the line between the Danube and the Párkány-Nána railway station. On 2 January 1945 the Hungarian forces were relieved by their neighbours to the north, the German *3. Panzer-Division*.

As it soon turned out, this was only temporary. On 1 January, *Armeegruppe "Balck"* initiated the counteroffensive "*Konrad*", south from the Danube toward Budapest. In order to keep this offensive in motion the *Armeegruppe* wanted to concentrate the forces of the two *Panzer* divisions that had been split, reuniting them again in Kelet-Dunántúl (eastern part of Transdanubia), and wanted to hold the third in readiness behind the northern flank of *LVII. Panzerkorps*.

The Division "*Szent László*", which was still extraordinarily weak, and which, at that time, was without its own artillery or the Hungarian *Jagdpanzers,* was resting in the area of Bátorkeszi, Köbölkút and (in part) Ógyalla. Accordingly, it received orders, at about 1200 hours on 4 January, stating that, on the night of 4/5 December, it was to take over the front line sector of the *3. Panzer-Division* facing the Soviet 7th Guards Army in the Párkány bridgehead.

The southern boundary of the Hungarian formation was the Danube. On the north the boundary followed the line Köbölkút south – Libád south – Kőhídgyarmat south – Bajta south. The main line of defense was, in part, the same one which the division had defended a few days earlier (the Danube-Párkány-Nána railway station area), but it was now extended to Kőhídgyarmat along the railway leading toward the village, including points no. 119, 120 and 124.[5]

The Hungarian defensive zone was divided into a southern and a northern defensive region. In the south the two German battalions that were attached to the Division "*Szent László*", the exhausted *II. Bataillon/Panzergrenadier-Regiment 93*[6] and the *Maschinengewehr-Bataillon "Sachsen"*, held the position, reinforced by four Hungarian 7.5cm anti-tank guns. In the north, under the command of Captain Edömér Tassonyi, the 1st Battalion/1st Parachute Regiment with 368 men and the remnants of the 2nd Battalion/1st Parachute Regiment[4172], established three all-round strongpoints at Káptalanpuszta, at the Párkány-Nána railway station and Ebedipuszta, each with a strength of half of a company and each supported by three or four 7.5cm anti-tank guns[8]. The combined headquarters of the two consolidated battalions, with two companies and the regimental sub-battalions, were positioned north of Káptalanpuszta, on the eastern

remains of the *357. Infanterie-Division*, *Panzer-Pionier-Bataillon 6* and anti-aircraft artillery units. On 31 December *LVII. Panzerkorps* took over control of the front line sector earlier held by *LXXII. Armeekorps*.

5 HM HIM *Hadtörténelmi Levéltár (Budapest), a "Szent László" hadosztály tüzérparancsnokának naplója és mellékletei. 95. melléklet.*

6 This battalion, with a combat strength of just 50 men, was one of the units that were stuck outside the siege lines when its original parent formation, the *13. Panzer-Division,* was encircled in Budapest.

7 After the fighting between the Garam and Ipoly the combat strength of the battalion was down to 113 men. Captain Tassonyi assumed command of this Battalion as well, and sent the previous commander, Captain Zoltán Kiss to Pápa.

8 The crews of these anti-tank guns were German in most cases, presumably from the (independent) *Panzerjäger-Abteilung 721*.

slopes of the so-called "Hegyfarok". A parachute company secured the right flank of this gap-filled defensive line (1st Lieutenant Ferenc Godó).

The artillery support of the northern defensive zone was provided by 1st and 2nd Batteries/VIII Towed Medium Artillery Battalion, equipped with 15cm field howitzers, commanded by Lieutenant Colonel László Bobiss-Selmeczy, from their firing position west of Káptalanpuszta. The 120mm mortars of the 1st Battery/1st Medium Mortar Battalion were also expected to arrive here. The southern defensive region was supported by the German *1.* and *2. Batterie/leichte Artillerie-Abteilung 52*, as well as the Hungarian 3rd horse-drawn Medium Howitzer Battery/76th Artillery Battalion with 10.5cm light field howitzers.

The divisional reserve was the Air Force Rifle Battalion[9] at Béla, fleshed out with new recruits, a combined company formed from the 53rd Pioneer Battalion (91 men), as well as a bicycle platoon of the Reconnaissance Battalion and a tank destroyer platoon at Muzsla. Units of the Hungarian 20th Assault Artillery Battalion[10] (1st Lieutenant György Koltay) were similarly in readiness at Muzsla, as well as the armoured vehicles of the Hungarian armoured group[11] serving as reserve for the corps. On 5 January, the German *Panzerjäger-Abteilung 13* was also attached to the Division *"Szent László"*.[12]

Northeast of Muzsla the *LVII. Panzerkorps* established a barrier sufficient to impede any armoured attack, southwest of the eastern point of "Hegyfarok", along the road leading to Ebed, approximately in line with points no. 125 and 135. The barrier consisted of 20 8.8cm anti-aircraft guns and 8.8cm anti-tank guns[13].

---

9 The majority of the 630 men of the Battalion received only two weeks of training. Their commander was Captain Sándor Pálfi, who commanded the 1st Battalion of the destroyed Grenadier Regiment of the division. The remaining combat strength from the former Grenadier Regiment and the Air Force Rifle Regiment totalled 24 officers and 172 soldiers.

10 The 2nd Battery and parts of the 1st Battery/Assault Artillery Battalion were attached to the Division at the end of December 1944. On 1 January 1945 seven out of their total of 11 *Jagdpanzer* 38(t) tank destroyers were in combat-ready condition. For this, see *Bundesarchiv–Militärarchiv* (Freiburg im Breisgau), *RH 2 Ost Karte 5263 (Panzer-Lage am 1. Jan. 1945).*

11 According to the log of the artillery commander of the Division *"Szent László"* the armoured group consisted of four combat-ready *Panzer* IV tanks of the 1st Battalion/3rd Tank Regiment of the Hungarian 2nd Armoured Division and four combat-ready *Jagdpanzer* 38(t) tank destroyers of the elements of the Assault Artillery Battalion 16 constituting part of Assault Artillery Battalion "Bernolák". According to other sources the 1st Battalion/3rd Tank Regiment had, in reality, 10 combat-ready *Panzer* IV tanks on 5 January commanded by 1st Lieutenant of armoured troops Dezső Korponay. The armoured fighting vehicles had been painted white by their crews at Muzsla as winter camouflage. See HM HIM *Hadtörténelmi Levéltár (Budapest), Tanulmányok és visszaemlékezések gyűjtemény(ede* (Collection of studies and recollections) nr. 3799. sz., Bese Ödön: *Ahogy történt.* (Ödön Bese: As it has happened), p.87. On 1 January 1945 six out of 14 armoured fighting vehicles of the Assault Artillery Battalion were in combat-ready condition. For this, see *Bundesarchiv–Militärarchiv* (Freiburg im Breisgau), *RH 2 Ost Karte 5263 (Panzer-Lage am 1. Jan. 1945*). However, the fact that neither the Assault Artillery Battalion "Bernolák", nor the 20th Assault Artillery Battalion had any maintenance repair service of their own significantly decreased the operational value of the Hungarian *Jagdpanzers*.

12 This unit was part of the *13. Panzer Division*, but, because it was being reconstituted in Germany at that time, it escaped the Budapest cauldron. On 1 January 1945 the A*bteilung* had 12 towed 7.5cm anti-tank guns (of which 10 were combat-ready) and 21 *Panzer* IV/70 (V) *Jagdpanzers* (of which 20 were in combat-ready condition).

13 These were presumably the guns of the *schwere Heeres-Panzerjäger-Abteilung 662*. This unit had 14 such guns, of which seven were in combat-ready condition on 1 January. The *Panzerjäger-Abteilung* was subordinated to the *LVII. Panzerkorps* together with *Armee-Panzerjäger-Abteilung 721* on 4 January.

By the morning of 5 January, the Division *"Szent László"* completed its task of relieving the *3. Panzer-Division*. The movement of the elements was speeded up by the fact that German transport vehicles were been used to transport some of them. The command post of the Hungarian unit was established in the mansion at Béla, the rest of the staff remained in Bátorkeszi.

Adjoining the Hungarian unit on its left was the German *211. Volksgrenadier-Division* (*Generalleutnant* Johann Heinrich Eckhardt), which arrived there in the first days of January 1945, and relieved the forces of the *6.* and *8. Panzer-Division*s on the front line along the Garam. Most of the officers and soldiers of the division were recent replacements that were not completely trained[14] and were extraordinarily young. On the other hand the commander of the division, who had previously been awarded the Knight's Cross of the Iron Cross and the Oak Leaves, was, according to his superiors, one of the best German generals. On 6 January the six battalions of the division mustered a combat strength of about 2400 men and eight 7.5cm anti-tank guns. The *Panzerjäger-Abteilung* was, at that time, equipped only with anti-aircraft guns.[15]

On the northern flank of *LVII. Panzerkorps* was the weak *Kampfgruppe* of the *357. Infanterie-Division* (*Generalleutnant* Josef Rintelen). The group consisted of two *Alarm* battalions, the *2. Kompanie/Ersatz-und Ausbildungs-Abteilung 482* and *Panzer-Aufklärungs-Abteilung/6. Panzer-Division*, reinforced with 13 combat-ready 7.5cm anti-tank guns and four *StuG.* III assault guns (two of them combat-ready).[16]

After the partially accomplished regrouping of the 6. *Panzer-Division* and the regrouping of the *3. Panzer-Division* that was planned to be exacuted on 5 January, the real key to the *LVII. Panzerkorps*' defence was the German *8. Panzer-Division* (*Generalmajor* Gottfried Fröhlich) positioned behind the Division *"Szent László"*. In case of Soviet attacks this unit was to carry out counterattacks and stop the attacking forces.

In the evening of 4 January, the armoured *Kampfgruppe* of the division[17] was ordered to the north bank of the Danube. However, because of traffic problems, it did not arrive in time, nor did *Panzerjäger-Abteilung 13*. According to data from 1 January the unit had 42 (two of these combat-ready) *Panther* and 18 (0 combat-ready) *Panzer* IV tanks, 12 (eight combat-ready) *Jagdpanzer* IV tank destroyers, nine (three combat-ready) *Marder* tank destroyers and 10 (four combat-ready) 7.5cm anti-tank guns. Around 5 January, apart from the *Jagdpanzers*, there were six *Panthers*, four *Panzer* IVs and four *Marder* tank destroyers in combat-ready condition.[18] The combat strength of the three *Panzergrenadier* battalions

---

This latter had 19 towed 7.5cm anti-tank guns on 1 January, of which 11 were in combat-ready condition.

14 The units had not yet been trained in operating as a formation.

15 The *Jagdpanzer-Kompanie* and the towed *Flak-Kompanie* were still in the process of being organized back in the Reich.

16 HM HIM *Hadtörténelmi Levéltár* (Budapest) microfilm archives, *Kriegstagebuch Ia der Heeresgruppe Süd, Wochenmeldung vom 6. 1. 1945* (roll no. 628. image no. 7212271).

17 This concentrated the following units: the *Kompanien* of the *I. (Abteilung)/Panzer-Regiment 10* equipped with *Panther* and *Panzer* IV tanks, the *I. Bataillon/Panzergrenadier-Regiment 98* equipped with armoured personnel carriers, the *I. Abteilung/Panzer-Artillerie-Regiment 80* equipped with self-propelled howitzers and the 3. *(gepanzerte) Kompanie/Panzer-Pionier-Bataillon 59*. One *Kompanie* of the *I. (Abteilung)/Panzer-Regiment 10* equipped with *Panzer* IV tanks, furthermore, the *Panzerjäger-Abteilung 43* equipped with *Jagdpanzer* IV tank destroyers and *Marder* tank destroyers had already been fighting in attachment to the division north of the Danube.

18 *Bundesarchiv–Militärarchiv* (Freiburg im Breisgau), *RH 2 Ost Karte 5263 (Panzer-Lage am 1. Jan. 1945)*, and Haupt, 1987, p.382.

to push on to the Nyitra and secure the area of Kozmalovce-Érsekújvár.

On 4 January 1945 the 6th Guards Tank Army (Colonel General Andrej Grigorjevich Kravchenko) was ordered to concentrate its units in the area of Ipolyszalka-Letkés by the evening of 5 January, then, at dawn on 6 January, to launch an assault in the direction of the main strike of the 7th Guards Army. The Tank Army was to seize the Komárom crossing points on the Danube by the evening of 7 January. Then it was to drive into the rear of the *IV. SS-Panzerkorps*. At the same time, units of the force were to occupy and secure Érsekújvár and wait for the infantry troops of 7th Guards Army.

Accordingly, the 9th Guards Mechanized Corps (Lieutenant General Mihail Vasilevich Volkhov) was ordered to cooperate with the 53rd Rifle Division/25th Guards Rifle Corps in a night ambush to break through the German—Hungarian defences north of Nána, then to advance and break through Muzsla, Bátorkeszi and Madar and to occupy the railway bridge at Komárom. In order to be able to secure the attack of the Tank Army from the north, the Corps had to turn its 46th Guards Tank Brigade toward Érsekújvár after reaching Bátorkeszi. The strength of the 9th Guards Mechanized Corps on 5 January consisted of the following:

Table 7 – Strength of 9th Guards Mechanized Corps, 5 January 1945

9th Guards Mechanized Corps †			
Unit	**Armoured fighting vehicles**	**Infantry combat strength**	**Artillery**
18th Guards Mechanized Brigade (including the 83rd Guards Tank Regiment)	3 M4A2 tanks 6 Mk IX Valentine tanks 3 SU–76 self-propelled guns	620 men[1]	No data
30th Guards Mechanized Brigade (including the 84th Guards Tank Regiment)	2 M4A2 tanks 2 Mk IX Valentine tanks	45(!) men[2]	No data
31st Guards Mechanized Brigade (including the 85th Guards Tank Regiment)	14 M4A2 tanks 4 Mk IX Valentine tanks 2 SU–76 self-propelled guns	420 men	No data
46th Guards Tank Brigade	29 M4A2 tanks	91 men[3]	No data
14th Guards Motorcycle Battalion	3 M4A2 tanks 1 SU–76 self-propelled guns	118 men	–
31st Guards Engineer Battalion	–	260 men	–
15th Guards Signals Battalion	2 M4A2 tanks	–	–
Corps Artillery	–	–	No data
Total	**71 armoured fighting vehicles**	**1554 men**	–

† After-action report of the 9th Guards Mechanized Corps on the operations in the direction of Komárom–Érsekújvár in January 1945 (copy owned by the author), pp.3-4.

The 389th Guards Self-Propelled Heavy Artillery Regiment is not included in the tables because it did not have any operational vehicles at that time.

1 As a comparison: a fully reinforced and equipped mechanized brigade had 3781 men in its combat strength, three motorized rifle battalions (with 649 men in each) besides its own tank regiment, one mortar battalion, an artillery battalion, an anti-aircraft machine gun company, a submachine gun company (with 94 men), one reconnaissance company, an anti-tank rifle company, an engineer company and its own logistics units. Equipment and armament thereof consists of 177 submachine guns, 45 machine guns, nine anti-aircraft heavy machine guns, 30 82mm and six 120mm mortars, 12 76.2mm guns, 12 45mm anti-tank guns, 99 14.5mm anti-tank rifles, 41 tanks, 10 armoured fighting vehicles, 10 armoured cars 360 trucks and 94 radio devices.

2 The tank and personnel strength were integrated into the 18th Guards Mechanized Brigade by 5 January 1945.

3 There was a Motorized Rifle Battalion in the line of battle for each Soviet Tank Brigade, with theoretically 507 soldiers in its Tables of Organization and Equipment.

Colonel General Kravchenko reinforced the Corps with an anti-tank artillery brigade, a light artillery regiment, an anti-aircraft artillery regiment and an engineer battalion.

The units of the 5th Guards Tank Corps (Major General Mihail Ivanovich Savelyev) were to break the German—Hungarian defences with a night assault south of Nána, then after capturing Búcs, Marcelkeszi[43273] and Hetény, they were to occupy the road bridge at Komárom. The strength of the Corps on 5 January consisted of the following:

Table 8 – Strength of 5th Guards Tank Corps, 5 January 1945

5th Guards Tank Corps†			
Unit	**Armoured fighting vehicles**	**Infantry combat strength**	**Artillery[1]**
20th Guards Tank Brigade[2]	–	No data	No data
21st Guards Tank Brigade	43 T–34/85 tanks	146 men	No data
22nd Guards Tank Brigade	42 T–34 tanks	86 men	No data
6th Guards Motorized Rifle Brigade	–	500 men 5 heavy machine guns 13 machine guns 35 light machine guns 26 anti-tank rifles	7 76mm guns 6 45mm anti-tank guns 4 120mm mortars 25 82mm mortars
15th Guards Motorcycle Battalion	4 tanks	No data	No data
4th Guards Signal Battalion	2 tanks	–	–
391st Guards Anti-Tank Artillery Regiment	–	–	12 76mm mortars
454th Guards Mortar Regiment	–	–	17 120mm mortars

27 Marcelháza and Kurtakeszi conjoined in 1942 as Marcelkeszi.

5th Guards Tank Corps†			
Unit	**Armoured fighting vehicles**	**Infantry combat strength**	**Artillery**[1]
127th Guards Mortar Artillery Battalion	–	–	4 M–13 rocket launchers
392nd Anti-Tank Artillery Battalion	–	–	6 37mm cannon 10 12.7mm machine guns
Total	**91 armoured fighting vehicles**	**732 men**	–

† After-action report of the 5th Guards Tank Corps, 1-31 January 1945 (copy owned by the author), p.3. Two units are missing from the table: the 390th Guards Heavy Self-Propelled Artillery Regiment did not have any operational armoured fighting vehicles; the 301st Light Artillery Regiment had 24 76mm guns.

1 Data from 1 January 1945

2 Of this, eight assault guns were part of the strength of the *Sturmgeschütz-Brigade 286.*

The commander of the 6th Guards Tank Army reinforced the 5th Guards Tank Corps with a light artillery brigade, an artillery regiment and an engineer battalion.

The 4th Independent Guards Motorcycle Regiment was to attack with 10 tanks along the north bank of the Danube toward Komárom, and thereby cover the left flank of 6th Guards Tank Army from the south.

As mentioned earlier, the other army units – the 202nd Light Artillery Brigade and the 34th Anti-Tank Artillery Brigade (with a total of 107 guns), as well as the 22nd Motorized Engineer Brigade and 57th Guards Mortar (rocket launcher) Artillery Regiment – supported the two fast moving corps.

The assigned units of the 2nd Ukrainian Front had a combined strength of 202 operational tanks and self-propelled guns[28], 719 artillery guns and mortars. The formations of the two air armies of the 2nd and 3rd Ukrainian Fronts also prepared for cooperation with the land troops.

The Soviet forces were far from being at full strength. The 5th Guards Tank Corps, for example, had been replenished to no more than 33 percent of its authorized complement, and the 9th Guards Mechanized Corps was lacking more than two-thirds of its authorized number of armoured fighting vehicles.[29] The combat strength of the two corps in the

28 In the two corps of the 6th Guards Tank Army there were altogether 156 combat-ready tanks and six self-propelled guns. The army-level units (51st Guards Self-Propelled Artillery Brigade, the 49th Guards Heavy Tank Regiment, 364th Guards Heavy Self-Propelled Artillery Regiment, the 697th and 1458th Self-Propelled Artillery Regiment, and the 4th Guards Motorcycle Regiment) possessed a total(!) of 16 further combat-ready tanks and two self-propelled guns. So, these formations were facing the attack with even less strength than the corps. Apart from the 178 tanks and 113 motorcycles of the 6th Guards Tank Army the operational group consisted also of 16 operational tanks and eight self-propelled guns of the 27th Independent Guards Tank Brigade.

29 According to the Tables of Organization and Equipment in effect as of 1 January 1945 a tank corps in full strength had 207 medium (T–34 or T–34/85) tanks, 21 light (SU–76), 21 medium (SU–85/100) and 21 heavy (ISU–122/152) self-propelled guns (total: 270 armoured fighting vehicles exclusive of armoured cars and armoured personnel carriers). At the same time, the combat strength of the mechanized corps

evening of 5 January was closer to that of an average German *Panzer-Division* than that of a proper corps.[30]

In such circumstances, the success of the operational plan depended essentially on operational and tactical surprise, on continuous combat (including combat actions carried out by night as well), and, above all, on the swift action of the units.

The Soviet forces, equipped with armoured fighting vehicles, moved mainly at night toward their new concentration areas in order to deceive enemy reconnaissance. During the night of 4/5 January the 5th Guards Tank Corps arrived in the area of Nána and Párkány after a 45km night march. In the meantime, that same night, the 46th Guards Tank Brigade/9th Guards Mechanized Corps moved 80km to reach its new attack position, but, in order to camouflage its movements, the unit was located 20km from the German—Hungarian front line.[31]

One of the most fundamental prerequisites for an effective tank attack by night was accurate orientation. The Soviet forces were given the exact azimuths for the direction of the attack, and had to stick to these at any cost: "These azimuths had to be written on the inside of the tanks' turrets, on the gun-shields of the field and anti-aircraft guns, and, for the tank-rider riflemen, on the stocks of their submachine guns".[32]

The British and American-built tanks of the 9th Guards Mechanized Corps were equipped with compasses, but the T–34 and T–34/85 tanks of the 5th Guards Tank Corps were not. Therefore the former corps was ordered that all of the compasses, except for those that were in the tanks of the battalion and company commanders, were to be taken out and handed over to the Tank Corps.[33]

There were other differences between the two corps: while the 9th Guards Mechanized Corps painted its vehicles white[34], the 5th Guards Tank Corps did not do this, resulting in rather disadvantageous consequences later.

For the sake of maximum psychological effect, the Soviet command even sacrificed the artillery preparation for the attack. In this situation one of the most fundamental questions was this: what were the expectations of the German—Hungarian forces?

On 1 January, *Armeegruppe "Balck"* still assumed that the 6th Guards Tank Army had been withdrawn from the front line, presumably for replenishing its strength. Three days later, however, on 4 January, German reconnaissance aircraft identified 300 vehicles moving southwards on the east bank of the Garam. They were immediately identified as

consisted of 183 medium tanks, 21 light (SU–76), 21 medium (SU–85/100) and 21 heavy (ISU–122/152) self-propelled guns (total: 246 armoured fighting vehicles exclusive of armoured cars and armoured personnel carriers). For detailed description, see: Zaloga, Steven J. & Ness, Leland S., *Red Army Handbook 1939–45* (Stroud, 1998), pp.61-99.

30 The notable British military historian, Michael Reynolds, often compares the Soviet tank and mechanized corps organized between 1943–1945 to German *Panzer* divisions, and likewise, the Soviet tank armies to German *Panzerkorps*. Although generally we cannot agree with these comparisons – in the case of a Soviet tank army for example or considering tank or mechanized corps in full strength – the combat values of the 6th Guards Tank Army at the beginning of January 1945 still match this kind of comparison.

31 Loza, 1996, p.66. The author commanded a Battalion of the 46th Guards Tank Brigade in the Second World War, three of his M4A2 tanks were knocked out, and he was awarded the "Hero of the Soviet Union" star.

32 Loza, 1996, p.66.

33 Loza, 1996, p.65.

34 Loza, 1996, p.67.

vehicles of the 6th Guards Tank Army in two marching columns.[35]

The Germans still thought that these forces might cross the Danube at Szob and rush to reinforce the right flank of 3rd Ukrainian Front. However, the situation aroused doubts in *General der Panzertruppe* Balck, and, that same day, two *Panzerjäger-Abteilungen* were attached to *LVII. Panzerkorps* to strengthen its right flank. At the same time, he requested all of the combat-ready aircraft of the *4. Luftflotte* to attack the regrouping 6th Guards Tank Army.[36]

On 5 January the Germans concluded from reconnaissance reports that a new offensive was imminent, which would be launched from the Soviet bridgehead at Párkány westwards toward Komárom, in order to relieve pressure on the Soviet forces that were defending south of the Danube. This was discussed openly for the first time by the Chief of Staff of *Heeresgruppe Süd, Generalleutnant* Helmuth von Grolman, with *Generalmajor* Heinz Gaedcke, Chief of Staff of *Armeegruppe "Balck"*, at 1650 hours on 5 January[37]. Thus – even if that was at he last moment – the Germans, nevertheless, discovered the Soviets intentions to attack, and this significantly reduced the operational surprise.

On 5 January the Division *"Szent László"* relieved the German forces on the front line of the *LVII. Panzerkorps*. As Reserve Warrant Officer Géza Marosújvári, one of the platoon commanders of 2nd Company/1st Battalion of the 1st Parachute Regiment positioned in the central defensive sector, recalled:

> The German unit which my company relieved was dug in along the Érsekújvár-Párkány railway line, directly next to the railway embankment. It was a miserably chosen defensive line. My company commander, 1st Lieutenant Szakács [József – the author], told me where the defensive sector of my platoon was, and I went forward to the German unit holding the position. It was already late afternoon, and I could barely see the dome of the Esztergom basilica. Nevertheless the sky was clear and it was -7-8 °Celsius. It was really unusually quiet, and you could feel that something was in the air. In the far distance I could hear sounds resembling that of tanks roaring.
>
> I looked for the commander of the German unit in my sector, and told him that we were to relieve them. It turned out that this sector was being defended by a German company, and I was supposed to hold it with a platoon. The command post of the German company commander was set up in a railway culvert.
>
> In front of us I saw an expanse of flat terrain, covered with snow and dotted with dungheaps. Behind us it was the same with cornfields; further away were the slopes of the Köbölkút-Muzsla vineyards, with their little press-houses here and there. According to the German *Oberleutnant*, it was all peaceful and there was no serious combat activity. We were very happy to hear this, as all of us were very tired and ready to sleep wherever we could.
>
> Considering our strength, we received an extremely broad sector to defend.

35 HM HIM *Hadtörténelmi Levéltár* (Budapest) microfilm archives, *Kriegstagebuch Ia der Heeresgruppe Süd, Kriegstagebuch vom 4. 1. 1945* (roll no. 627. image no. 7211980).

36 The following day, despite adverse weather conditions, the German *Luftwaffe* flew 140 sorties targeting vehicle traffic and the towns east of the Garam that were occupied by the Soviets, but, unfortunately, the war diary of *Heeresgruppe Süd* did not record the results.

37 HM HIM *Hadtörténelmi Levéltár* (Budapest) microfilm archives, *Kriegstagebuch Ia der Heeresgruppe Süd, Kriegstagebuch vom 5. 1. 1945* (roll no. 627. image no. 7211993).

> Therefore I organized the defence around strongpoints. During the relieving process I noticed that the Germans acted very suspiciously, and vacated the position with feverish haste. While I was talking to the German *Oberleutnant* I asked him if he heard the noises coming from the direction of Párkány and if these sounded like tanks to him. He reassured me that the noise was being made by German tanks. I accepted this in good faith, since I thought that our senior commanders had suitably checked out what was in front of us before we were brought here. With my squad leaders I positioned the bonesaws [German-made MG 42 machine guns – the author] and determined the sectors of the squads.[38]

According to the recollections of Captain Edömér Tassonyi, the Soviet tanks and self-propelled guns started to concentrate at about 2200 hours in the evening of 5 January, directly in front of the German—Hungarian front line. The commander of the concentrated Parachute Battalion immediately reported to the chief of staff of the Division *"Szent László"* – Staff Major Árpád Lajtos – that 60-80 tanks had already arrived, and that the concentration was in progress.

Lajtos – who, by his own admission, received a number of warnings in the course of that evening from the front line regarding the imminent tank attack – slightly doubted the accuracy of Tassonyi's report, although, according to his own recollections, he also ordered that, in the event of any major Soviet pressure, all Hungarian defensive areas and strongpoints could be evacuated. However, no directions of retreat were specified. Only one thing was determined, that all retreating units were to try to reach Köbölkút.[39]

After this Tassonyi told 1st Lieutenant Godó, commander of the company on the right flank, that, if a Soviet attack was launched, the nearby haystacks were to be set afire; he then went to sleep around midnight.[40] At that time he did not know that it would be a very short snooze.

The first phase of the battle: the Soviet breakthrough (6 January 1945)

On **6 January 1945**[41], at 0300 hours, at dawn, the Soviet attack formations received the signal *"ТРОЗА"* (Thunderstorm), and the assault started without suitable artillery preparation, as previously planned.

The 21st Guards Tank Brigade/5th Guards Tank Corps – reinforced by the 391st Guards Anti-Tank Artillery Regiment and one battalion of the 22nd Motorized Engineer Brigade – launched its attack from Nána toward the Párkány-Nána railway station. At

38 HM HIM *Hadtörténelmi Levéltár (Budapest), Tanulmányok és visszaemlékezések gyűjteménye* (Collection of studies and recollections) nr. 2904. Marosújvári Géza: *Ejtőernyős katonai szolgálatom emlékei, 1941–1945.* (Géza Marosújvári: My recollections of my paratrooper service, 1941-1945), pp.6-7.

39 HM HIM *Hadtörténelmi Levéltár (Budapest), Tanulmányok és visszaemlékezések gyűjteménye* (Collection of studies and recollections) nr. 2598, Lajtos Árpád: *Szent László hadosztály (Visszaemlékezés).* (Árpád Lajtos: Division *"Szent László"* (Recollections)), p.69.

40 Tassonyi Edömér 1982. *január 12-én kelt levele Pályi Györgyhöz*, pp.1-2. In: HM HIM *Hadtörténelmi Levéltár (Budapest), Tanulmányok és visszaemlékezések gyűjteménye* (Collection of studies and recollections), nr. 3063 Pályi Görgy: *A Szent László hadosztály repülő lövészezredének története, 1944. október–1945. december.* (György Pályi: History of the Air Force Rifle Regiment of the Division *"Szent László"*, October 1944–December 1945).

41 The weather in the morning was damp, foggy and visibility was impaired. Temperature was around -2° Celsius and it was lightly snowing. The snow continued during the day, visibility did not improve and the temperature dropped by 1° Celsius.

about 0500 hours the tanks ran into a minefield 200 metres east of the railway station. Barely had they crossed this, than, after another 300 metres, the engineers had to clear a corridor in another mine field.

At the same time, the 22nd Guards Tank Brigade (with the 3rd Battalion/22nd Motorized Engineer Brigade) was thrusting forward from the outskirts of Párkány toward Ebed, which was occupied at 1000 hours.[42]

Not long before the Soviet attack started, at about 0100 hours, at night, the armoured group of *Panzer* IVs stationed in Muzsla, commanded by 1st Lieutenant Korponay, was also alerted; it immediately set off toward the Párkány-Nána railway station. The Hungarian armoured fighting vehicles didn't travel on the road, but were spread out in combat formation on both sides of it. The call-sign was "Dezső" after the given name of their commander. Corporal Ödön Bese, driver of the company commander's tank, recalls:

> We departed with 10 tanks, but one of our vehicles stopped at the entrance of the village [Muzsla – the author] because of engine trouble. Its radio was tuned to the same frequency as the other radios of the company. As we set off into the darkness, because the moon was hidden behind the snowclouds and there was no light, we couldn't see much until our eyes got used to the darkness, which the snow made a little lighter. In the half-light I noticed that, here and there, small groups or individual infantrymen were retreating. I didn't talk to them, only observed what was going on. Suddenly the tank on the right reported: 'Attention Dezső! Attention Dezső! There's a dark mass coming toward us from Nána. Probably a tank. That is why I ask: is it ours?' He was asking because it could have been German. The 1st Lieutenant replied 'I don't know'. A couple of minutes later there was an explosion, and the oncoming tank suddenly burned like a torch. Then we could see it was a T–34. Our flank tank reported: 'He almost ran into me, I had to fire'.
>
> The T–34 presumably found it more difficult to see our tanks, because they had been whitewashed and thus blended into the snow-covered terrain. By contrast the Russian tanks were obvious, seen as dark shapes against the snow.
>
> Well, as the T–34 was burning bright, we saw lots and lots of T–34s and T-43s[43] all over the place. There was nothing else to do, so we opened fire as usual. It was all we could do. Meanwhile we moved from position to position. A T–34 suddenly turned round and mindlessly drove backwards. A metre-high plume of sparks gushed out of its exhaust behind it. Further off a tree caught fire from the flames from the burning tank. Because we were familiar with the road, we knew that here it curved off to the left. Marci [the gunner of the tank of the company commander – the author] aimed at the burning tree and, when the exhaust flame reached the area, he knocked out the fleeing tank.
>
> Next moment we heard on the radio: 'Dezső's! Dezső's! Look out, T–34 behind you!' At that we quickly turned our turret round, and – boom! – knocked out the T–34 that was some 60 metres behind us, showing his side to us. The crew jumped out, tore off their burning clothes and rolled in the snow, because they were all on fire.
>
> Here the skirmish lasted 15-20 minutes. The Russians retreated. They didn't know

42 After-action report of the 5th Guards Tank Corps, 1-31 January 1945 (copy owned by the author), p.5.

43 The Hungarian armoured crews, likewise the Germans, referred to the T–34 version with commander cupola and the T–34/85 tank like that. In this case the designation marks the latter.

> who we were, what forces we had, or how many of us were there. We had knocked out some 15 Soviet tanks, and three were abandoned in operational condition, with their engines still running.[44]

The company of the *I. Bataillon /Panzer-Regiment 3* that was there lost two *Panzer* IV tanks knocked out in this clash. As the Soviets were significantly superior in numbers, and the ammunition shortage became apparent, the Hungarian tanks took advantage of the Soviet wavering and retreated. They moved directly along the northern bank of the Danube in order to avoid the forces of 5th Guards Tank Corps.

Meanwhile, dawn was breaking. The Hungarian tank that had earlier become stuck at the eastern entrance of Muzsla informed the armoured group by radio that the Soviet tanks had already moved in behind them and cut the road into the village. After the Hungarian tank knocked out two approaching T–34s, the Soviet tanks knocked it out as well.

After this, 1st Lieutenant Korponay ordered that the tanks should avoid Muzsla and should try individually, one by one, to get to the village of Búcs. Two tanks – out of sight of each other – headed for Karva, with a T–34 in pursuit. Both Hungarian tanks occupied ambush positions behind the houses – still unaware of each other. The Soviet tank entered the village not suspecting anything; the nearest Hungarian *Panzer* IV destroyed the T–34 from 4-5 metres. Then the Hungarian tanks tried to reach Búcs across the fields. As Ödön Bese saw these events:

> It was already afternoon, when a Soviet tank turned up out of nowhere. It noticed us, and as we didn't open fire, it began to chase us, though from a fair distance. I caught up with a small modified Czech tank which the Germans had taken the turret off so they could fit it with a bigger gun. That is how it was turned into an 11 ton light tank.[45] [...] It had reached here from somewhere. We came to a stretch of water; it was so large it could have easily been a lake. All the autumn rain and the snowfall at the beginning of December had collected there in a dip. Of course it was frozen. This light tank ran onto it, and crossed it without problem. I considered it was cold enough for me to try the same with mine [with the *Panzer* IV tank – the author]. I drove onto it, got a little ahead, then, about 20-25 metres from the bank, the ice broke under me. The water was not very deep, maybe 70-80 centimetres, but the bottom was silt. I went forward another 3-4 metres. The tank was breaking the ice ahead when I felt the tracks losing their grip. [...] I stopped and then began moving backwards, slowly, carefully, because, if the tracks slipped, we would really be stuck there. The guys in the tank were shouting: 'not backwards, let's go forwards!' – I didn't listen to them, and slowly we succeeded in driving out. [...]
>
> 300-400 metres beyond the lake a wide drainage ditch crossed our path. It was about 3-3.5 metres deep and approximately four metres wide. The light tank stopped, it could not go any further. It was searching for a place to cross because the sides of the ditch were extremely steep. The T–34 arrived behind it and did not even bother to fire,

44 HM HIM *Hadtörténelmi Levéltár (Budapest), Tanulmányok és visszaemlékezések gyűjteménye* (Collection of studies and recollections) nr. 3799. sz., Bese Ödön: *Ahogy történt*. (Ödön Bese: As it has happened), pp.88-89.

45 The Hungarian company command tank presumably caught up with one of the *Marder* tank destroyers of the German *Panzerjäger-Abteilung 43*.

> but simply pushed it into the ditch. Then it also began to look for a possible area to cross. The crew of the small tank climbed out [they were Germans – the author]; their platoon leader was an artillery *Unteroffizier*. He knocked out the T–34 from behind with a "*Faustpatrone*" (*páncélököl* in Hungarian, that is, *Panzerfäuste*). It immediately blew up. It folded open like a horse-drawn sleigh because the fuel and ammunition in the tank were set off by the '*faust*', which destroyed the tank. After this incident we went on our way undisturbed.[46]

At 0130, at dawn, elements of the Hungarian 20th Assault Artillery Battalion were also alerted. Two *Jagdpanzer* 38(t) tank destroyers had already left Muzsla at 1600 hours the previous day, in order to take positions on the road leading to Ebed. Thus, only the three *Jagdpanzers* of warrant officer Győző Óvári set off from the village to join the two armoured fighting vehicles that had departed earlier. *En route* one of the vehicles broke down in the middle of Muzsla because of mechanical problems.[47] The other two *Jagdpanzers* reached their fellow tanks in the outskirts area north of Ebed.

The tank guns were turned to the south. Warrant Officer Óvári was not expecting a tank attack, so they loaded with high-explosive rounds. Shortly thereafter, the commander of one of the *Jagdpanzer* 38(t) tank destroyers reported that his vehicle had been knocked out, and the crew abandoned it. The Warrant Officer turned his *Jagdpanzer* to the east, and spotted two or three approaching Soviet tanks. Then a round penetrated the glacis plate of the Hungarian armoured fighting vehicle, and another round tore off the track. The Soviet tanks then retreated. The Hungarian crew quickly returned to Muzsla on foot. The remaining two Hungarian *Jagdpanzers* retreated into the village on their own, where 1st Lieutenant Koltay soon ordered them to continue the retreat toward Ógyalla.[48]

At about 1000 hours the Soviet 22nd Guards Tank Brigade occupied Ebed, then its units provided support for the 21st Guards Tank Brigade that was attacking Muzsla.

In Muzsla, two platoons of the combined engineer company that had been formed from the Hungarian 53rd Pioneer Battalion occupied defensive positions on the east side of the village and one half-platoon was positioned on the north side. At 0600 hours in the morning, Soviet tanks began to fire on the village, and the engineer platoons, while returning the fire, retreated.

While this was happening, two T–34 tanks broke into the village from the east. One of them knocked out a *Jagdpanzer* 38(t) tank destroyer of the Hungarian 16th Assault Artillery Battalion, which had backed into a deep drainage ditch in the middle of the village while moving into a firing position, and thus become immobilized. The Soviet armoured fighting vehicle was then knocked out by 2nd Lieutenant György Székely, commander of the 1st Platoon/Pioneer Company, with his one remaining *Panzerfäuste*. He then finished the task by shooting the crew down at close range with his submachine gun as they were climbing out of the tank.

46 HM HIM *Hadtörténelmi Levéltár (Budapest), Tanulmányok és visszaemlékezések gyűjteménye* (Collection of studies and recollections) nr. 3799. sz., Bese Ödön: *Ahogy történt*. (Ödön Bese: As it has happened), pp.90-91.

47 In all probability they managed to repair the vehicle later, because the 20th Assault did not leave any *Jagdpanzers* at Muzsla.

48 From the interview of Győző Óvári by András Palásthy on 28 June 2005. The author wishes to thank Mr. Palásthy for his kind cooperation.

General key for all maps

Red	Soviet
Blue	German
XXXX	Army
XXX	Corps
XX	Division
X	Brigade
II	Regiment/Battalion
I	Company
	Infantry
	Armoured
	Reconnaissance
	Motorcycle unit
	Motorized infantry
	Tank destroyer
	Armoured personnel carrier
	Artillery
	Engineers
	Airborne
Pz	Panzer
Gr	Grenadier
Gds	Guards

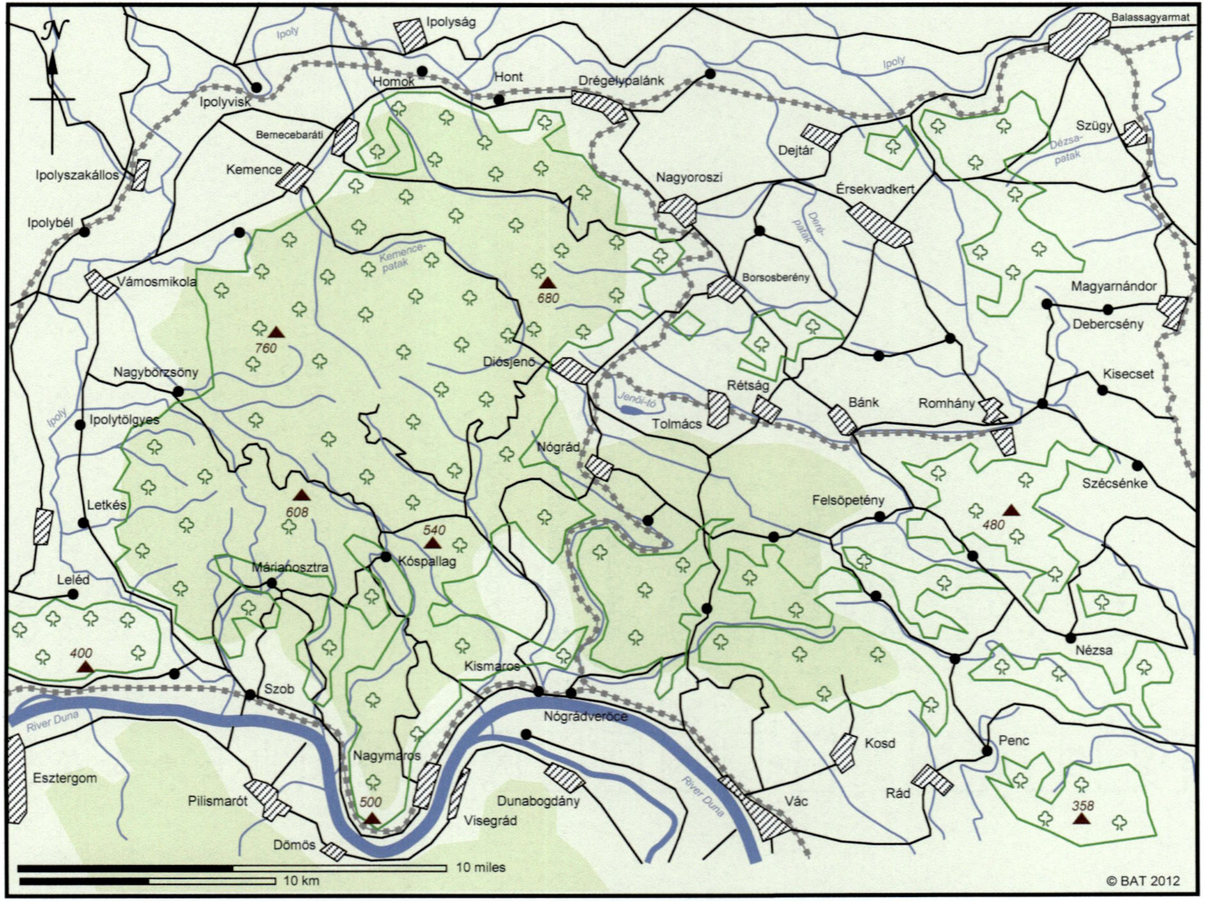

The region of Ipolyság, area of combat actions 11-17 December 1944.

The region of the Garam and Ipoly rivers, area of combat actions 18-31 December 1944.

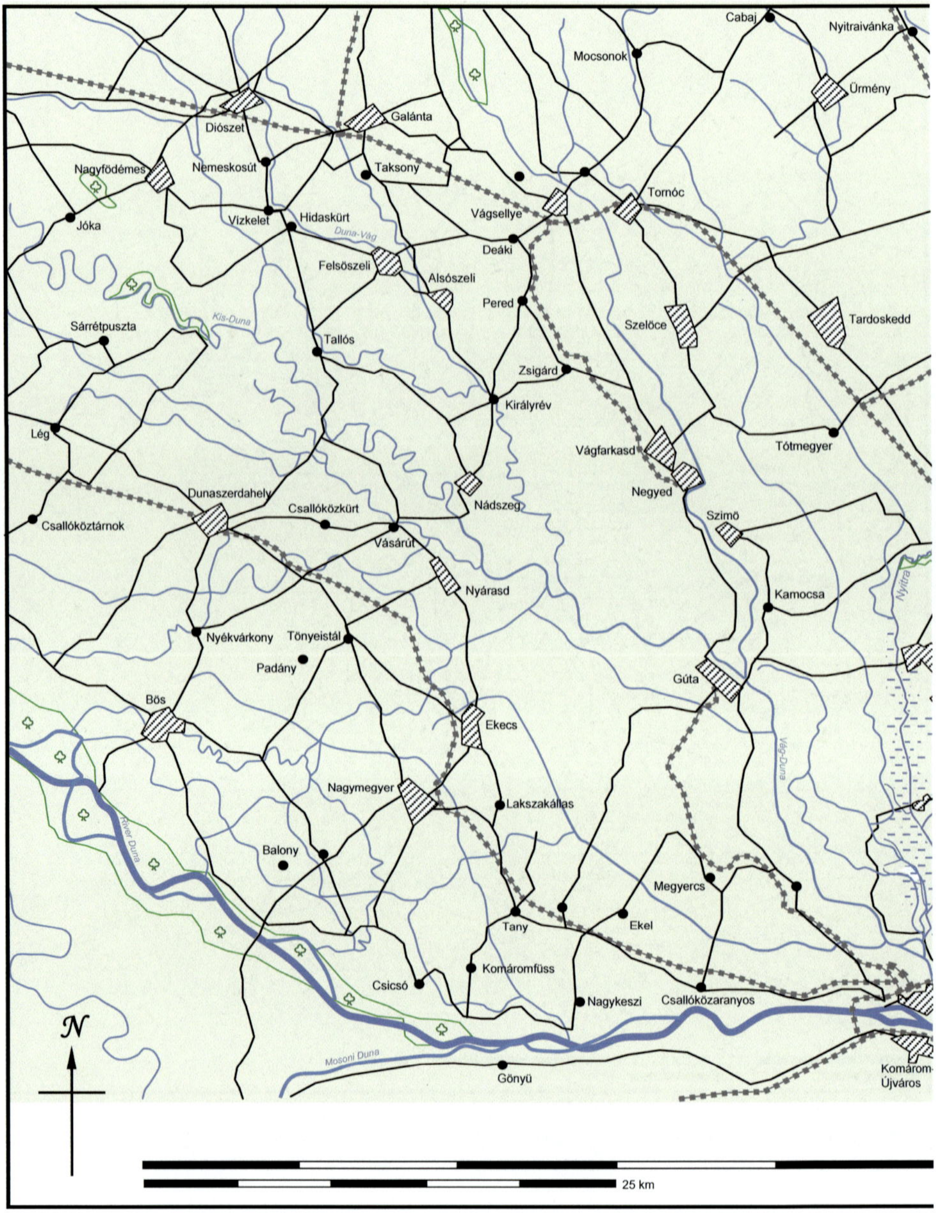

Overview map for combat actions 6 January-31 March 1945.

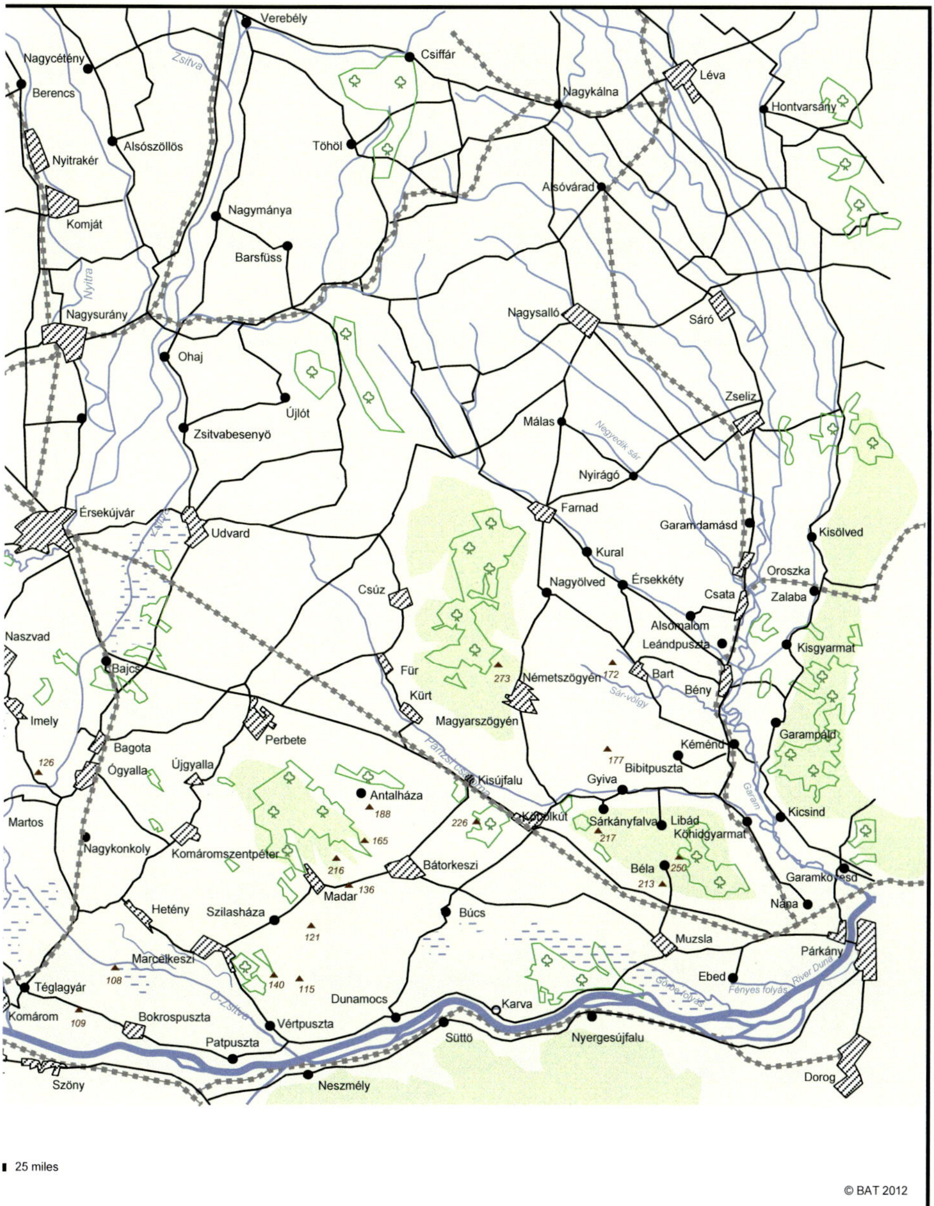
Verebély
Csiffár
Léva
Nagycétény
Zsitva
Berencs
Nagykálna
Hontvarsány
Alsószöllös
Töhöl
Nyitrakér
Alsóvárad
Nagymánya
Komját
Barsfüss
Nyitra
Nagysalló
Sáró
Nagysurány
Ohaj
Zseliz
Újlót
Málas
Zsitvabesenyö
Negyedik sár
Nyirágó
Érsekújvár
Farnad
Udvard
Garamdamásd
Kisölved
Kural
Oroszka
Csúz
Nagyölved
Érsekkéty
Csata
Zalaba
Naszvad
Alsómalom
Leándpuszta
Kisgyarmat
Bajcs
Für
273
Németszögyén
172
Bart
Imely
Kürt
Sár-völgy
Bény
Magyarszögyén
Perbete
Bagota
Garampáld
126
Ógyalla
Újgyalla
177
Kéménd
Bibitpuszta
Kisújfalu
Gyiva
Garam
Antalháza
188
Martos
226
Kőhídgyarmat
Sárkányfalva
Libád
217
Kicsind
Nagykonkoly
Komáromszentpéter
165
216
Bátorkeszi
Béla
250
213
Garamkövesd
Madar
136
Nána
Hetény
Szilasháza
Búcs
121
Muzsla
Marcelkeszi
Párkány
108
Ebed
Téglagyár
140
115
Dunamocs
River Duna
Fényes folyás
Karva
Komárom
109
Bokrospuszta
Vértpuszta
Süttö
Nyergesújfalu
Patpuszta
Szöny
Neszmély
Dorog
25 miles
© BAT 2012

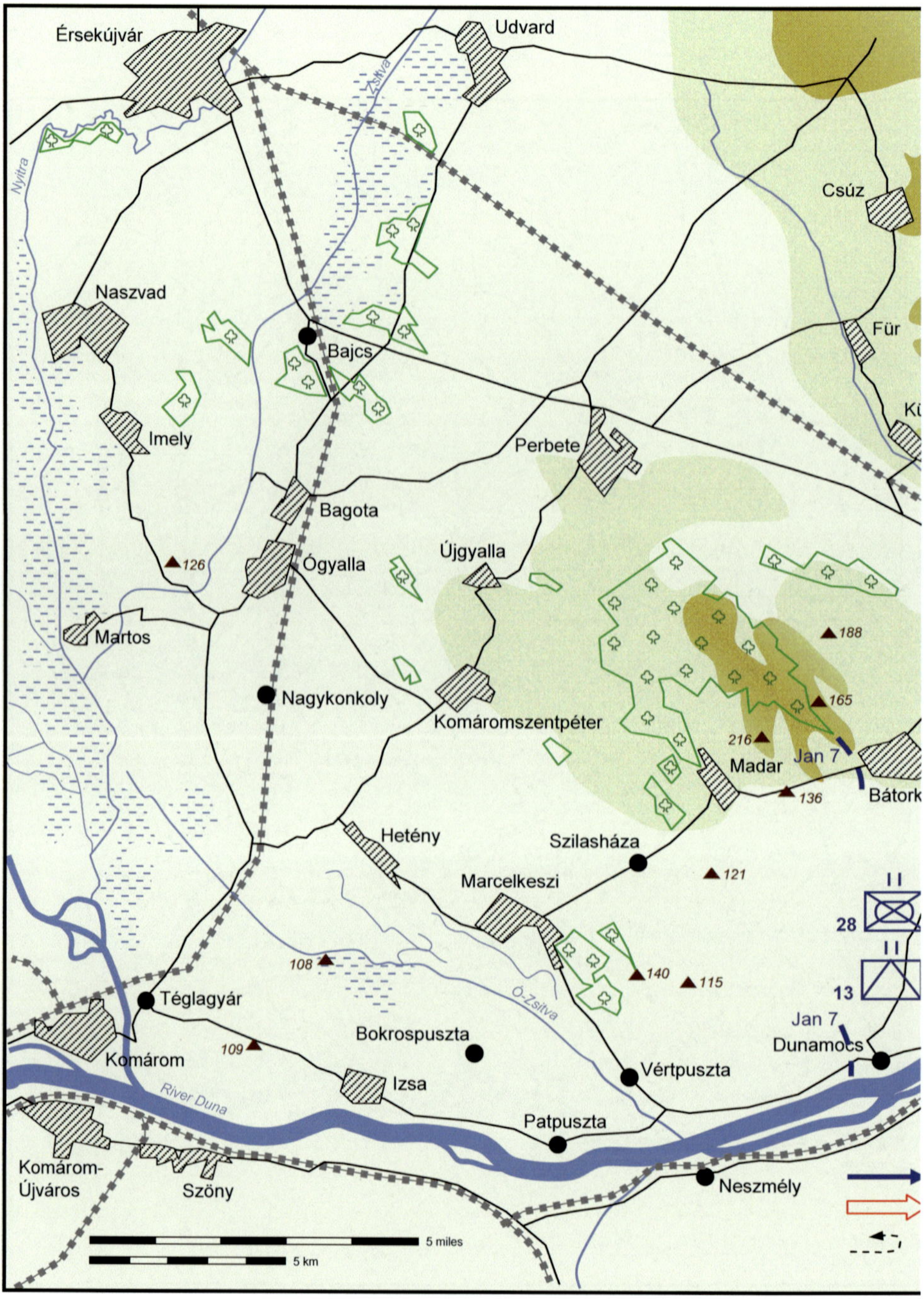

The battle of Komárom 6 January to the dawn of 7 January 1945.

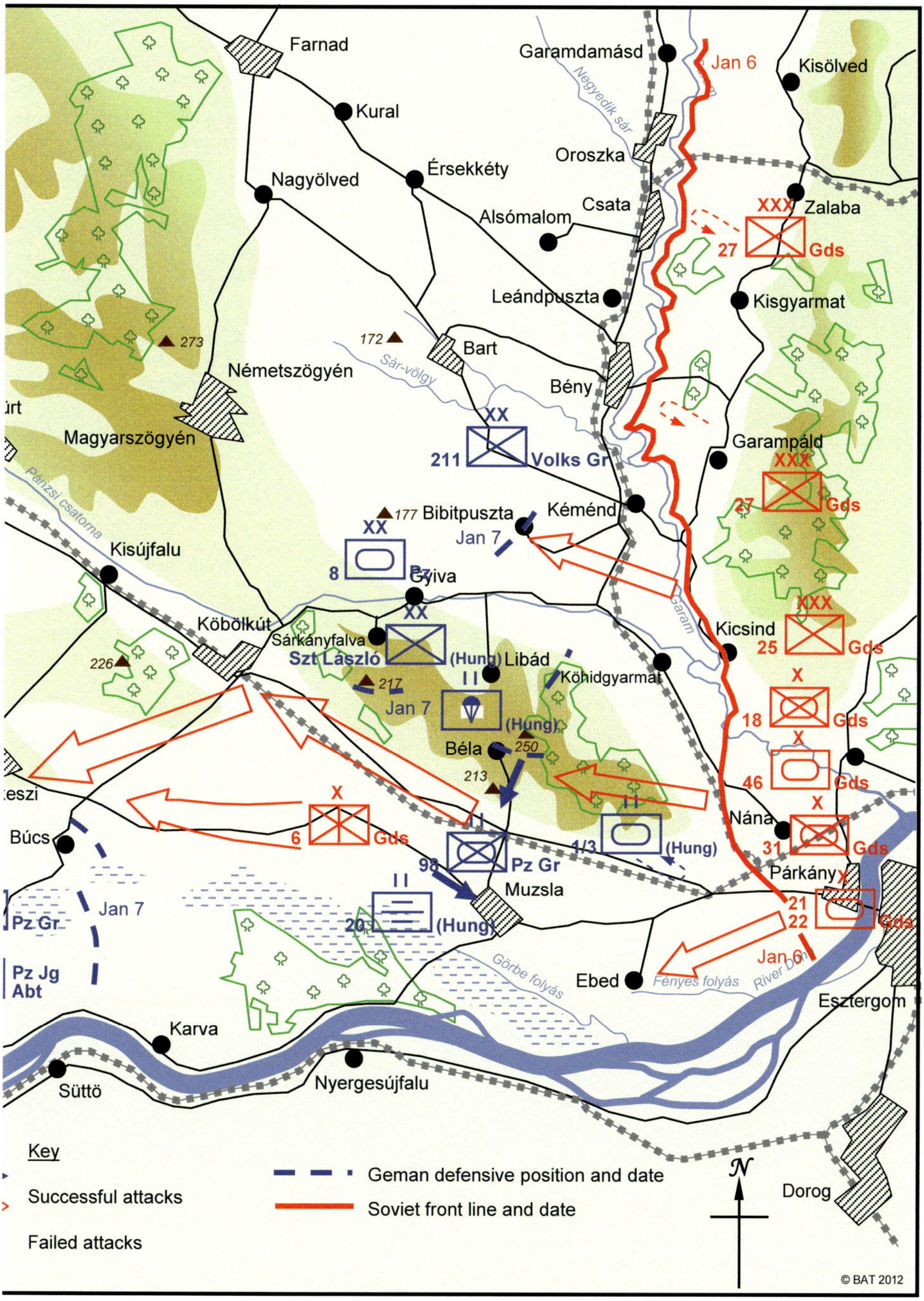

Farnad
Garamdamásd
Jan 6
Kisölved
Kural
Negyedik sár
Oroszka
Érsekkéty
Nagyölved
Zalaba
Csata
Alsómalom
XXX
27
Gds
Leándpuszta
Kisgyarmat
172
273
Bart
Németszögyén
Sár-völgy
Bény
XX
211
Volks Gr
Magyarszögyén
Garampáld
XXX
27
Gds
Párizsi csatorna
177
Bibitpuszta
Kéménd
XX
Jan 7
8
Pz
Gyiva
Kisújfalu
XX
Garam
Kicsind
Köbölkút
Sárkányfalva
Szt László
XXX
25
Gds
(Hung)
Libád
226
Köhidgyarmat
217
X
18
Gds
Jan 7
(Hung)
250
Béla
X
46
Gds
213
teszi
X
II
Nána
X
31
Gds
6
Gds
1/3
(Hung)
Búcs
98
Pz Gr
Párkány
X
21
22
Gds
Muzsla
Jan 7
II
Pz Gr
20
(Hung)
Pz Jg
Abt
Görbe folyás
Jan 6
Ebed
Fényes folyás
River Dn
Esztergom
Karva
Süttö
Nyergesújfalu
Key
Successful attacks
Failed attacks
Geman defensive position and date
Soviet front line and date
N
Dorog
© BAT 2012

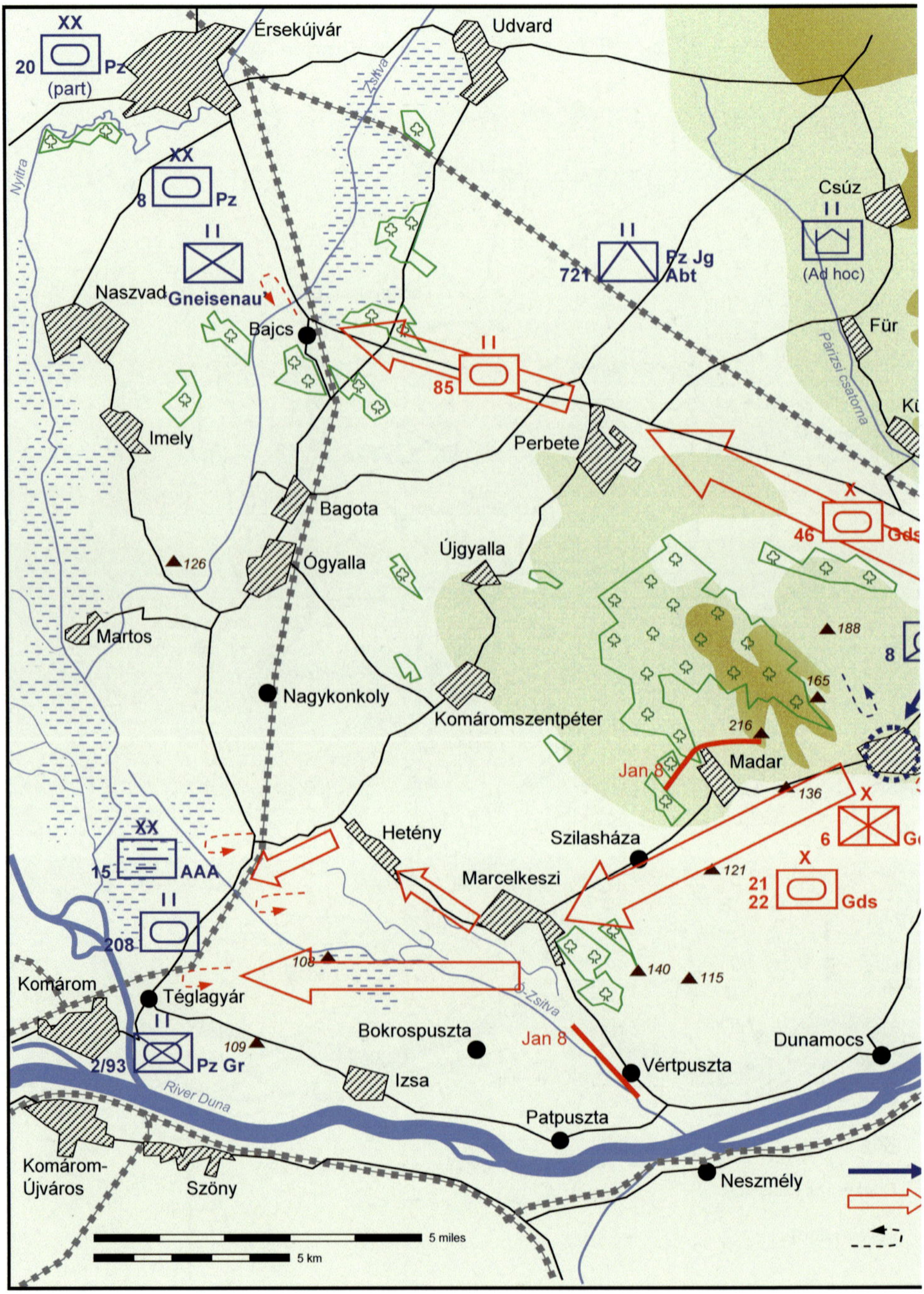

The battle of Komárom 7 January 1945.

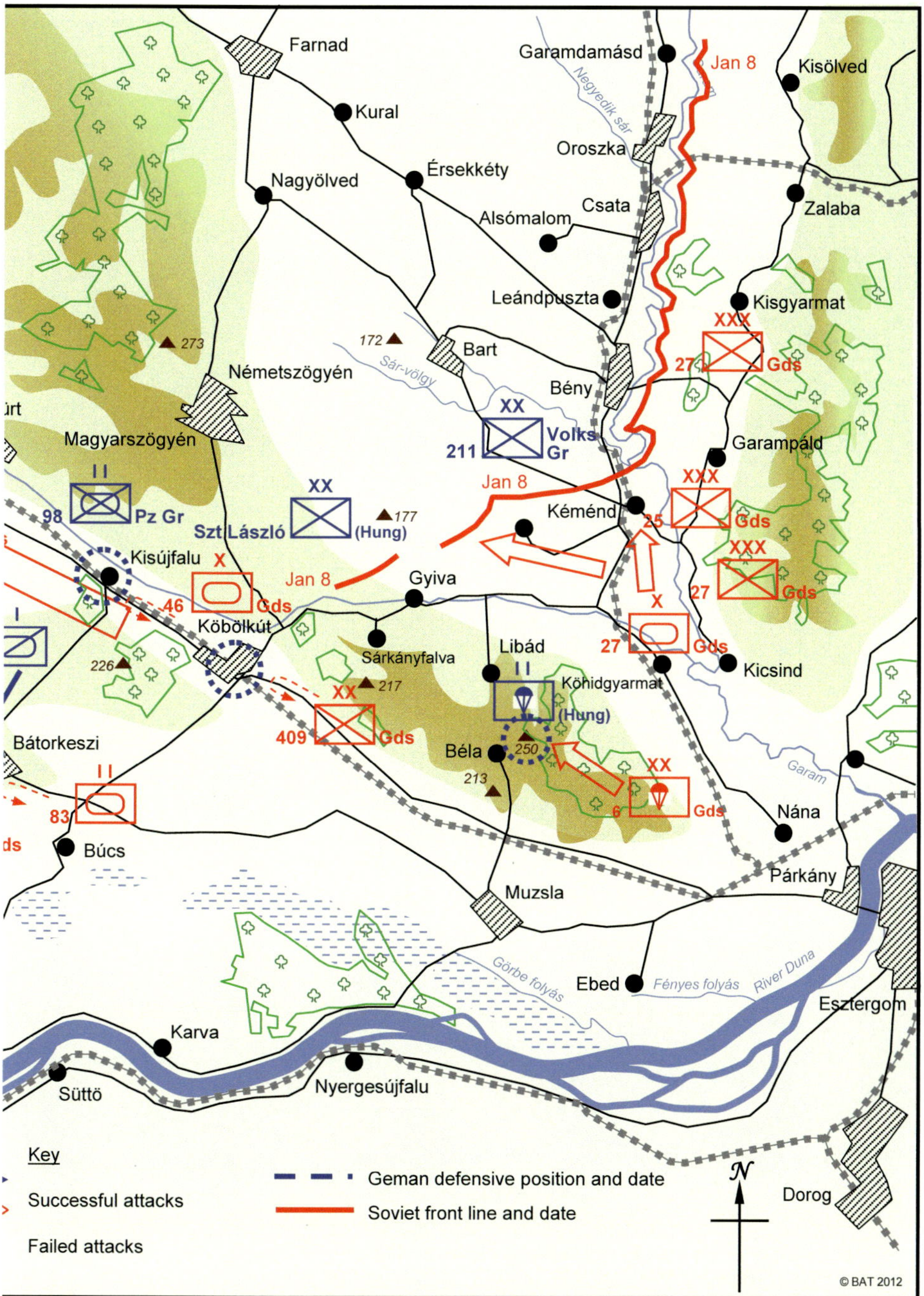
Farnad
Garamdamásd
Jan 8
Kisölved
Kural
Negyedik sár
Oroszka
Nagyölved
Érsekkéty
Zalaba
Csata
Alsómalom
Leándpuszta
Kisgyarmat
172
273
Bart
27
Gds
Németszögyén
Sár-völgy
Bény
Magyarszögyén
211
Volks Gr
Garampáld
Jan 8
98
Pz Gr
Szt László
177
(Hung)
Kéménd
25
Gds
27
Gds
Kisújfalu
Jan 8
Gyiva
46
Gds
Köbölkút
Libád
27
Gds
226
Sárkányfalva
Kicsind
217
Köhidgyarmat
(Hung)
409
Gds
Bátorkeszi
Béla
250
213
6
Gds
Garam
83
Nána
Búcs
Párkány
Muzsla
Görbe folyás
Ebed
Fényes folyás
River Duna
Esztergom
Karva
Süttö
Nyergesújfalu
Key
Successful attacks
Failed attacks
Geman defensive position and date
Soviet front line and date
Dorog
© BAT 2012

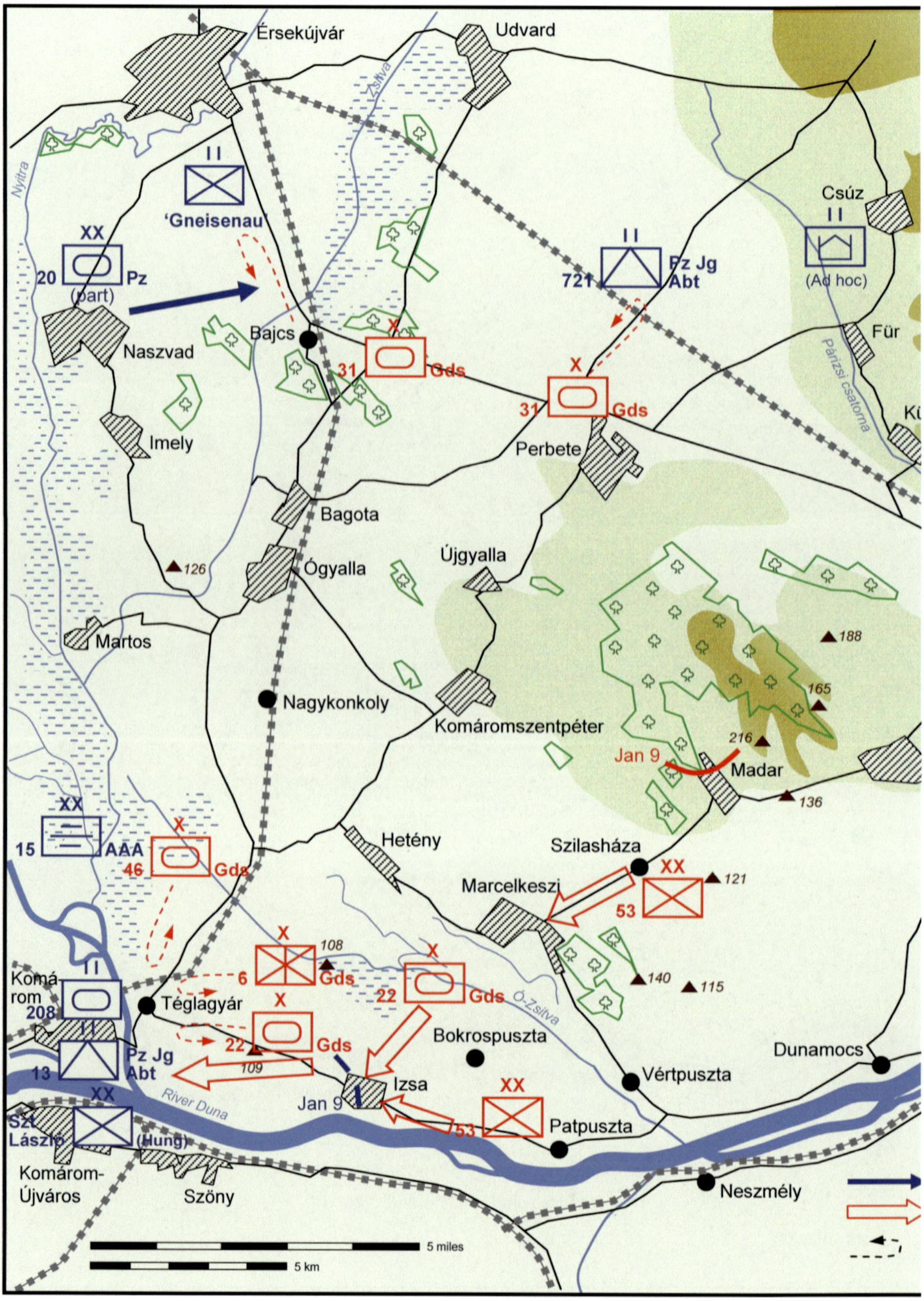

The battle of Komárom 8-9 January 1945.

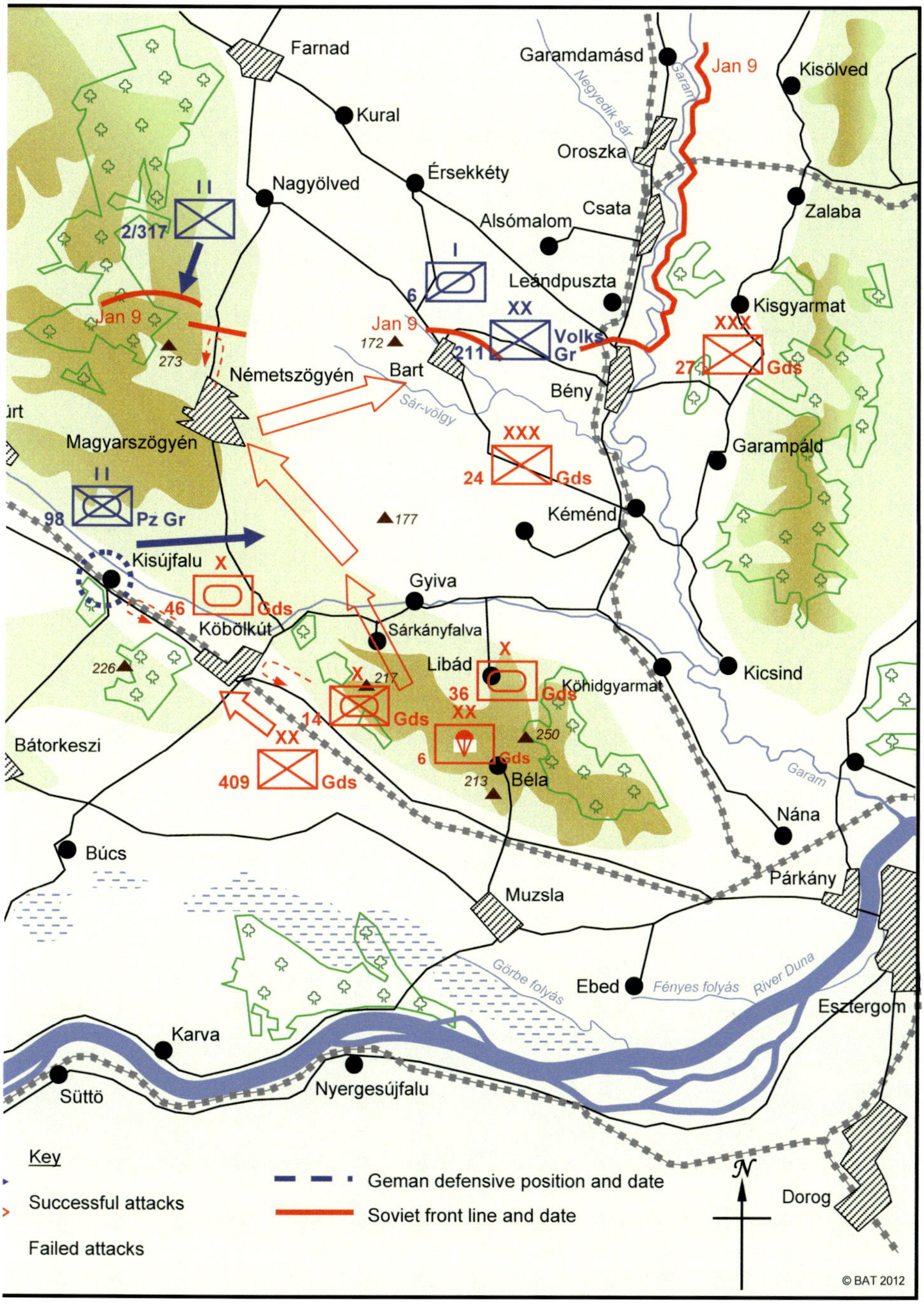
Farnad
Garamdamásd
Jan 9
Kisölved
Kural
Negyedik sár
Garam
Oroszka
Érsekkéty
Nagyölved
Csata
Alsómalom
Zalaba
2/317
I
6
Leándpuszta
Jan 9
Kisgyarmat
XX
Volks Gr
211
Jan 9
172
273
Bart
XXX
27
Gds
Németszögyén
Bény
Sár-völgy
Magyarszögyén
XXX
24
Gds
Garampáld
98
Pz Gr
177
Kéménd
Kisújfalu
X
46
Gds
Gyiva
Köbölkút
Sárkányfalva
226
X
217
14
Gds
Libád
X
36
Gds
Köhidgyarmat
Kicsind
XX
6
Gds
250
XX
409
Gds
213
Béla
Bátorkeszi
Garam
Nána
Búcs
Párkány
Muzsla
Görbe folyás
Ebed
Fényes folyás
River Duna
Esztergom
Karva
Süttö
Nyergesújfalu
Key
Successful attacks
Failed attacks
Geman defensive position and date
Soviet front line and date
N
Dorog
© BAT 2012

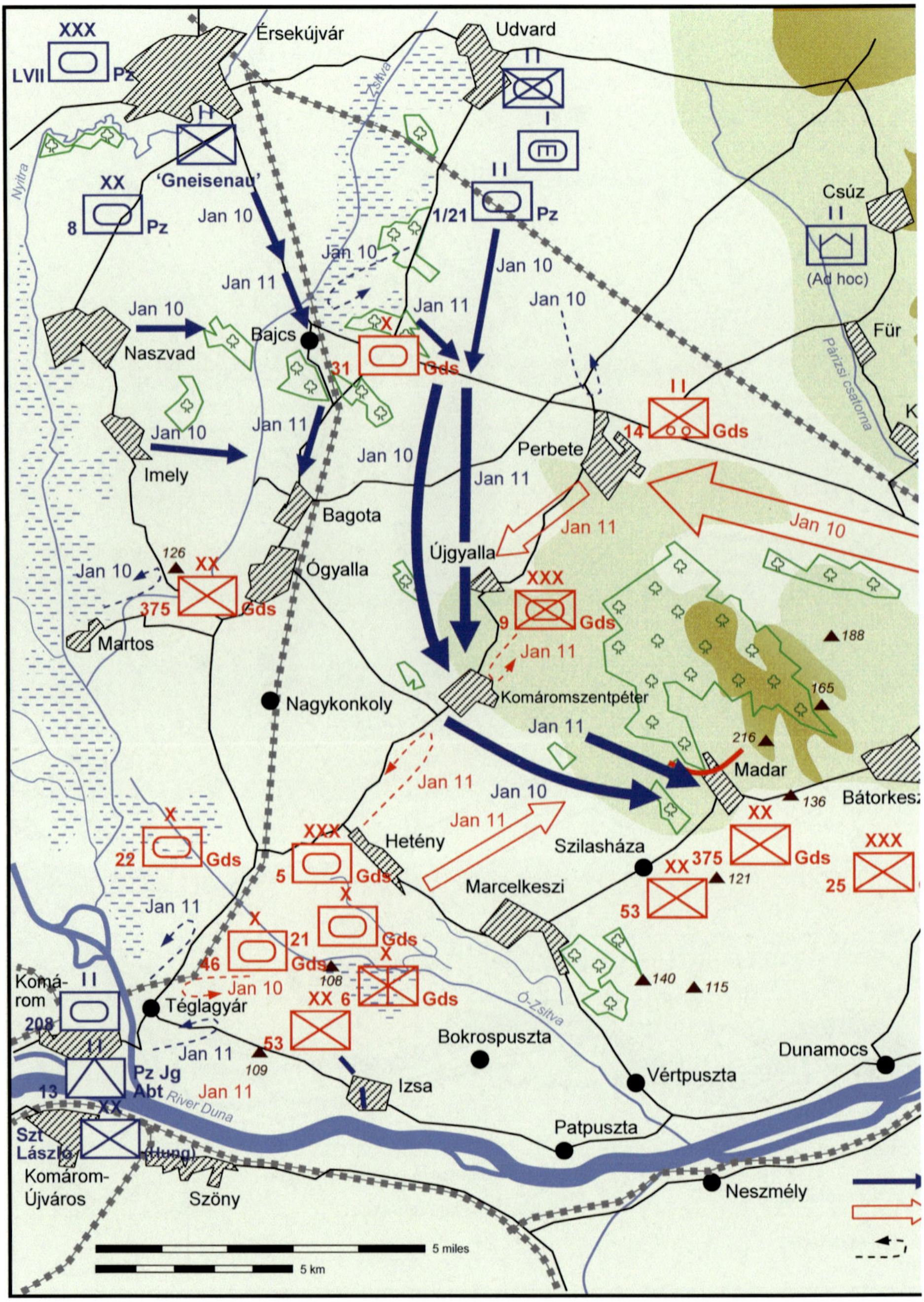

The battle of Komárom 10-11 January 1945.

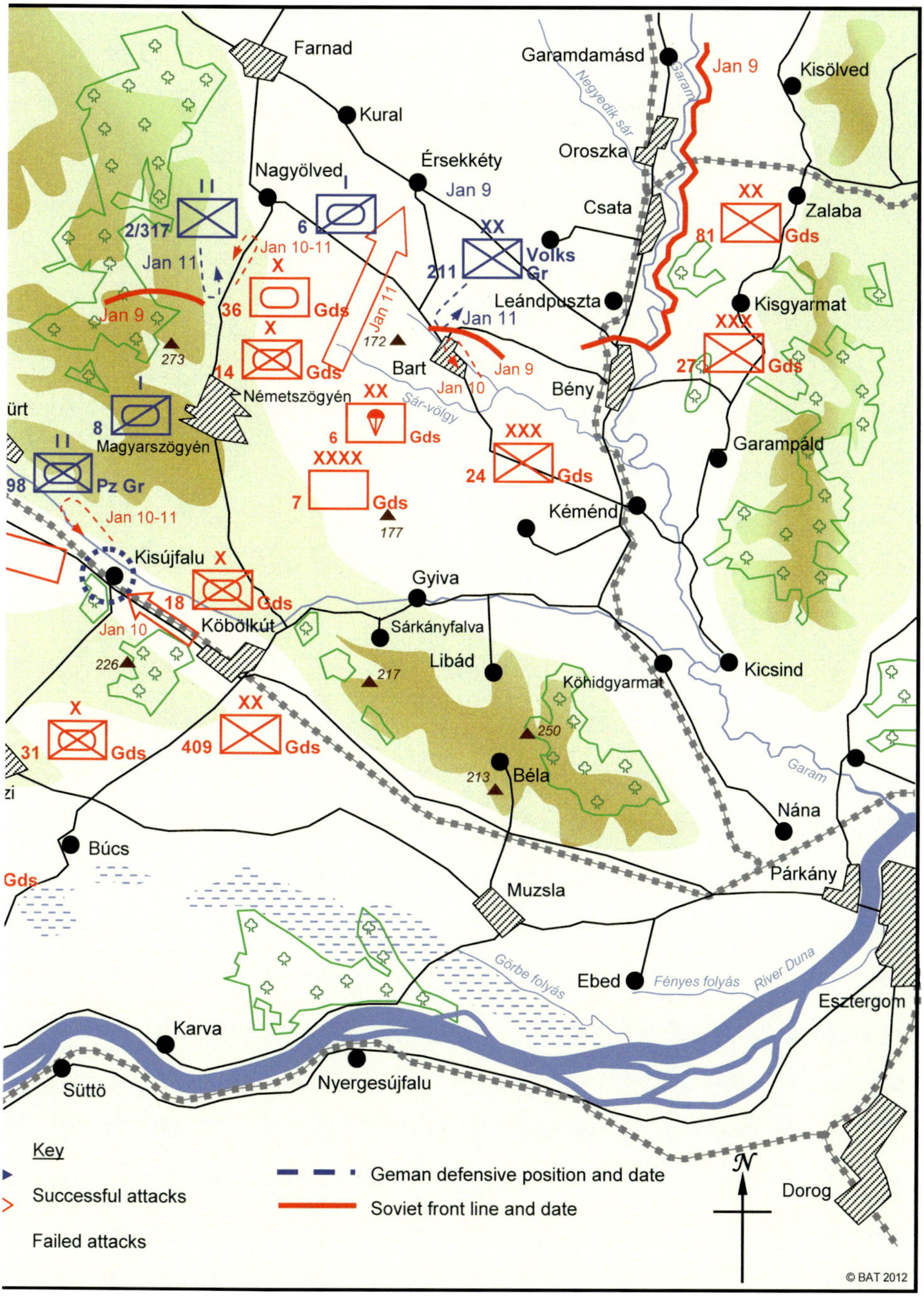
Farnad
Kural
Garamdamásd
Negyedik sár
Garam
Jan 9
Kisölved
Oroszka
Nagyölved
Érsekkéty
Jan 9
Csata
Zalaba
XX
81
Gds
2/317
6
XX
211
Volks Gr
Jan 10-11
Jan 11
X
36
Gds
Jan 11
Leándpuszta
Jan 11
Kisgyarmat
XXX
27
Gds
Jan 9
172
273
X
14
Gds
Bart
Jan 9
Jan 10
Bény
Németszögyén
XX
Sár-völgy
8
Magyarszögyén
6
Gds
XXX
24
Gds
Garampáld
98
Pz Gr
XXXX
7
Gds
177
Kéménd
Jan 10-11
Kisújfalu
X
18
Gds
Gyiva
Jan 10
Köbölkút
Sárkányfalva
Libád
226
217
Kicsind
Köhidgyarmat
X
31
Gds
XX
409
Gds
250
Béla
213
Garam
Nána
Búcs
Gds
Párkány
Muzsla
Görbe folyás
Ebed
Fényes folyás
River Duna
Esztergom
Karva
Süttö
Nyergesújfalu
Key
Successful attacks
Failed attacks
Geman defensive position and date
Soviet front line and date
N
Dorog
© BAT 2012

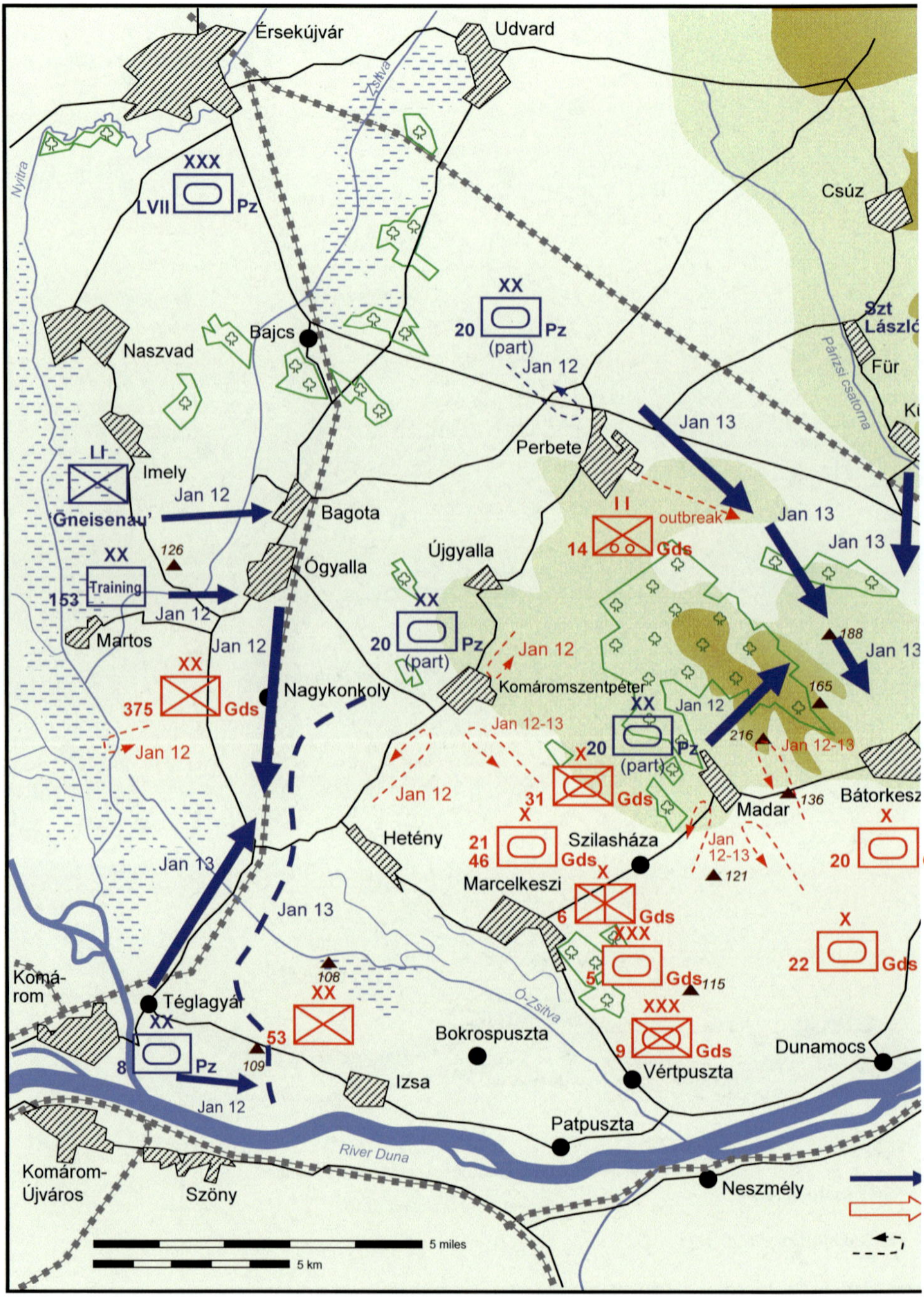

The battle of Komárom 12-13 January 1945.

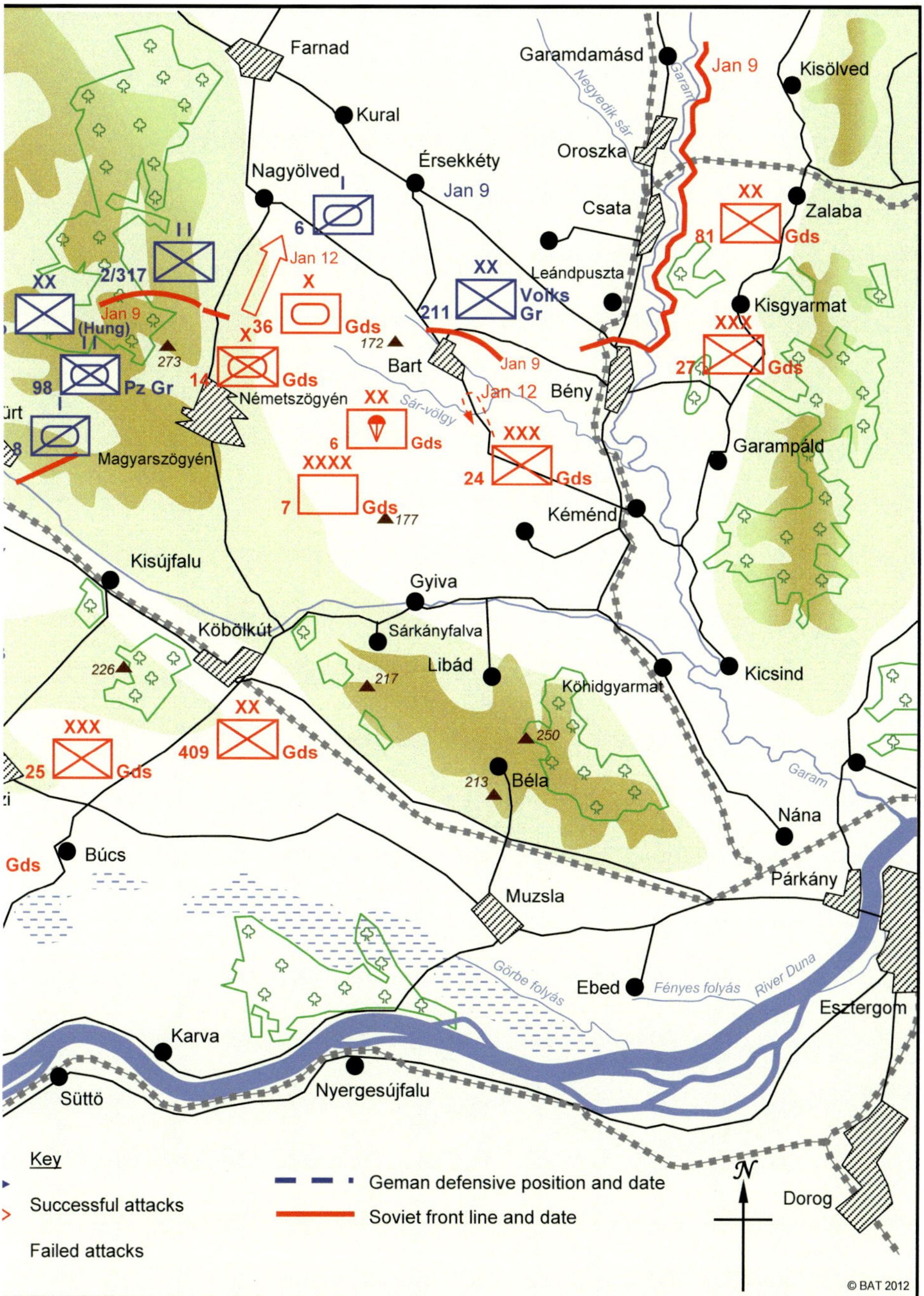

Farnad
Kural
Garamdamásd
Jan 9
Kisölved
Negyedik sár
Garam
Oroszka
Nagyölved
Érsekkéty
Jan 9
Csata
Zalaba
XX
81
Gds
2/317
Jan 12
Leándpuszta
XX
Volks
Gr
211
Kisgyarmat
XXX
27
Gds
XX
(Hung)
Jan 9
36
Gds
172
Bart
Jan 9
Jan 12
Bény
98
Pz Gr
14
Gds
Németszögyén
XX
6
Gds
Sár-völgy
XXX
24
Gds
Garampáld
Magyarszögyén
XXXX
7
Gds
177
Kéménd
Kisújfalu
Gyiva
Köbölkút
Sárkányfalva
Libád
226
217
Köhidgyarmat
Kicsind
XXX
25
Gds
XX
409
Gds
250
213
Béla
Garam
Nána
Búcs
Gds
Muzsla
Párkány
Görbe folyás
Ebed
Fényes folyás
River Duna
Esztergom
Karva
Süttö
Nyergesújfalu
Key
Successful attacks
Failed attacks
Geman defensive position and date
Soviet front line and date
N
Dorog
© BAT 2012

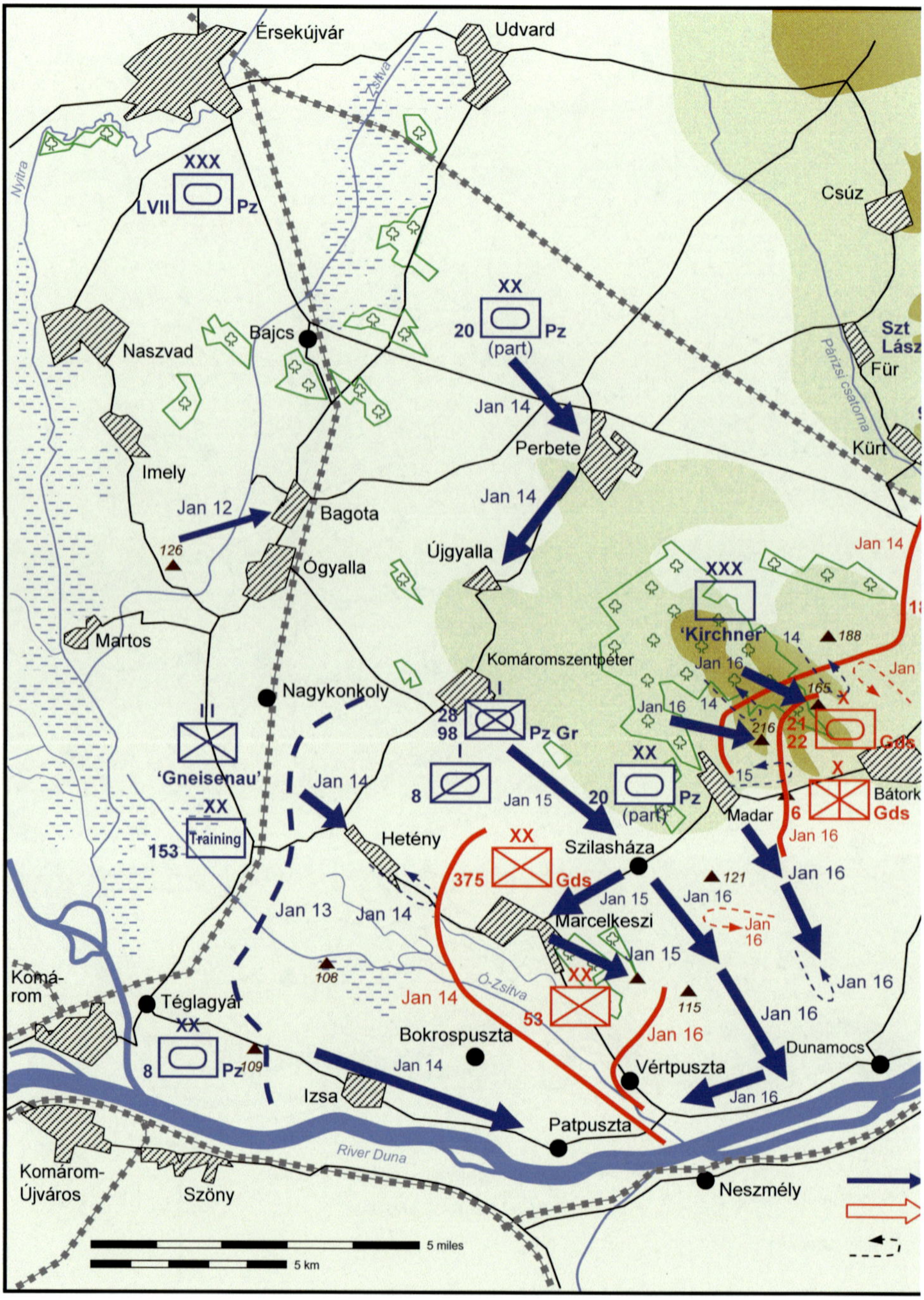

The battle of Komárom 14-16 January 1945.

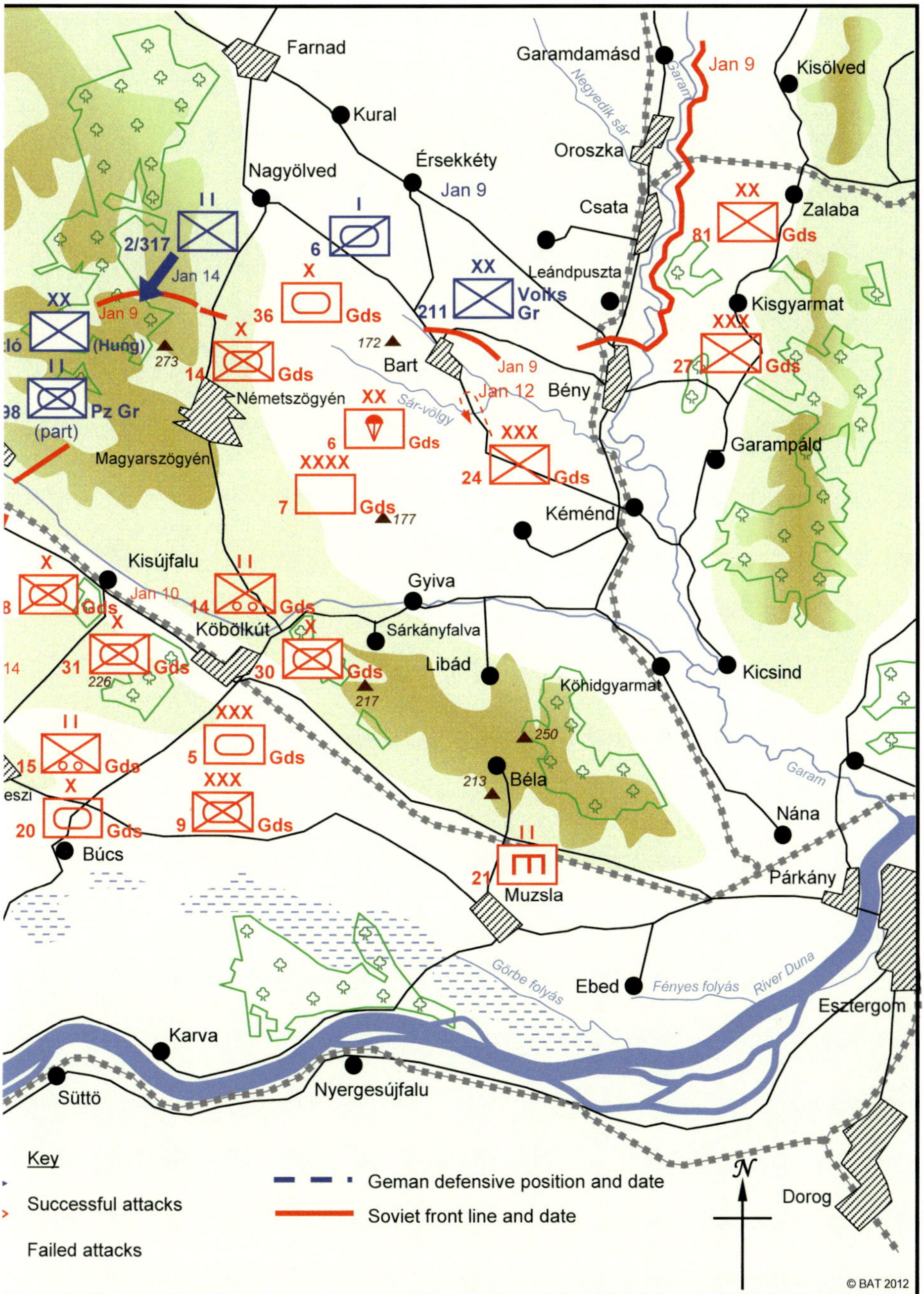
Farnad
Kural
Garamdamásd
Jan 9
Kisölved
Negyedik sár
Garam
Oroszka
Érsekkéty
Nagyölved
Jan 9
Csata
Zalaba
XX
81
Gds
2/317
Jan 14
I
6
X
36
Gds
XX
Volks Gr
211
Leándpuszta
Kisgyarmat
XXX
27
Gds
XX
Jan 9
(Hung)
273
II
98
Pz Gr
(part)
X
14
Gds
Németszögyén
172
Bart
Jan 9
Jan 12
Bény
XX
6
Gds
Sár-völgy
XXX
24
Gds
Garampáld
Magyarszögyén
XXXX
7
Gds
177
Kéménd
X
Kisújfalu
Jan 10
II
14
Gds
Gyiva
Köbölkút
X
31
Gds
226
X
30
Gds
Sárkányfalva
Libád
217
Köhidgyarmat
Kicsind
II
15
Gds
XXX
5
Gds
250
213
Béla
Garam
X
20
Gds
XXX
9
Gds
Búcs
II
21
Muzsla
Náná
Párkány
Görbe folyás
Ebed
Fényes folyás
River Duna
Esztergom
Karva
Süttö
Nyergesújfalu
Key
Successful attacks
Failed attacks
Geman defensive position and date
Soviet front line and date
N
Dorog
© BAT 2012

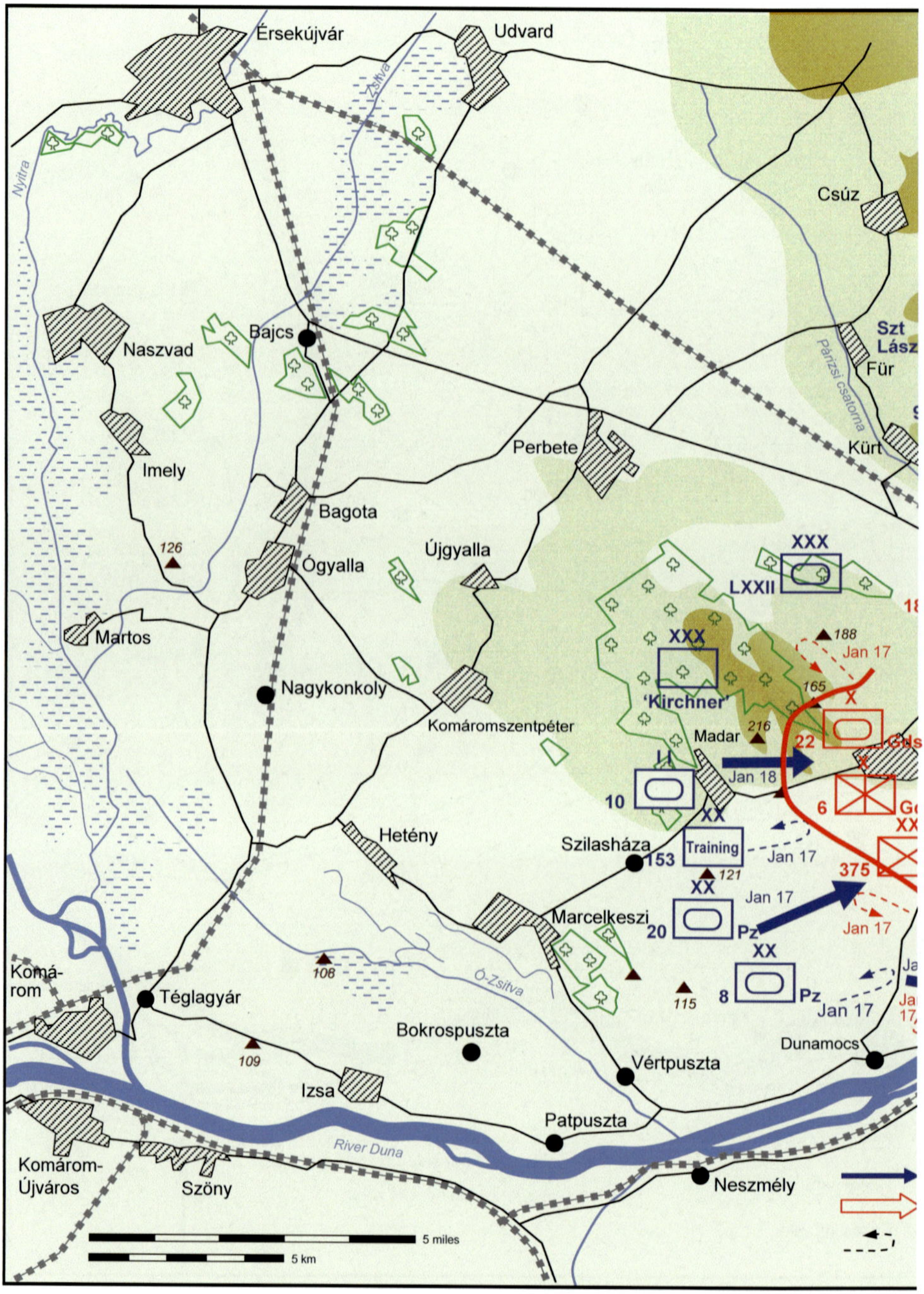

The battle of Komárom 17-22 January 1945.

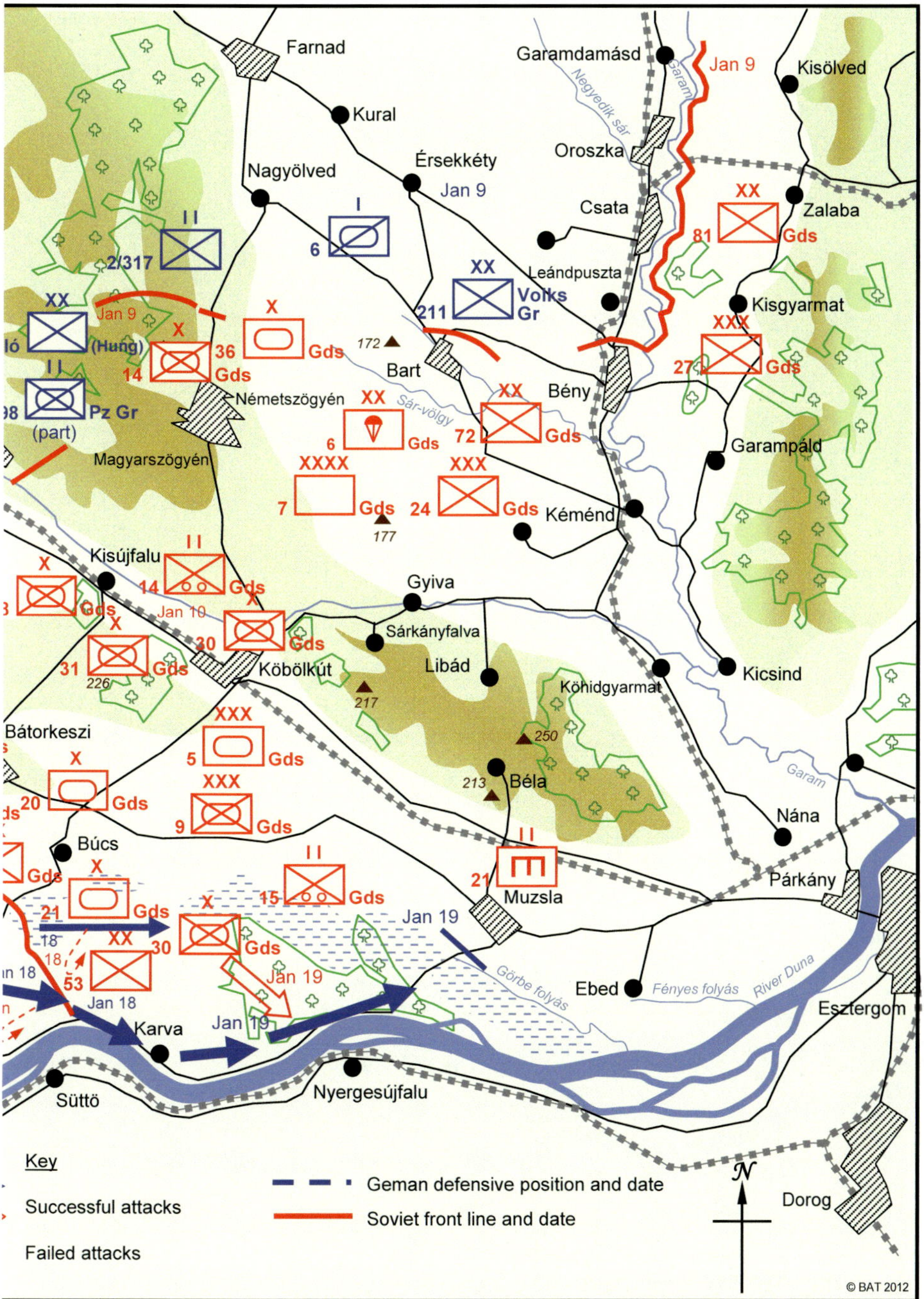

Farnad
Kural
Garamdamásd
Jan 9
Kisölved
Negyedik sár
Garam
Oroszka
Érsekkéty
Nagyölved
Jan 9
Csata
XX
Zalaba
81
Gds
I
6
II
2/317
Leándpuszta
XX
211
Volks
Gr
Kisgyarmat
XX
Jan 9
(Hung)
X
36
Gds
14
X
Gds
172
Bart
XXX
27
Gds
II
98
Pz Gr
(part)
Németszögyén
XX
Sár-völgy
6
Gds
XX
72
Gds
Bény
Magyarszögyén
XXXX
7
Gds
XXX
24
Gds
Garampáld
Kéménd
177
Kisújfalu
X
II
14
Gds
Jan 10
X
30
Gds
X
31
Gds
226
Gyiva
Sárkányfalva
Libád
Köbölkút
217
Kőhidgyarmat
Kicsind
Bátorkeszi
XXX
5
Gds
X
20
Gds
XXX
9
Gds
250
213
Béla
Garam
Nána
Búcs
Gds
X
21
Gds
II
15
Gds
II
21
Muzsla
Párkány
X
30
Gds
Jan 19
XX
53
Jan 18
Jan 19
Görbe folyás
Ebed
Fényes folyás
River Duna
Esztergom
Karva
Jan 19
Süttö
Nyergesújfalu
Key
Successful attacks
Failed attacks
Geman defensive position and date
Soviet front line and date
N
Dorog
© BAT 2012

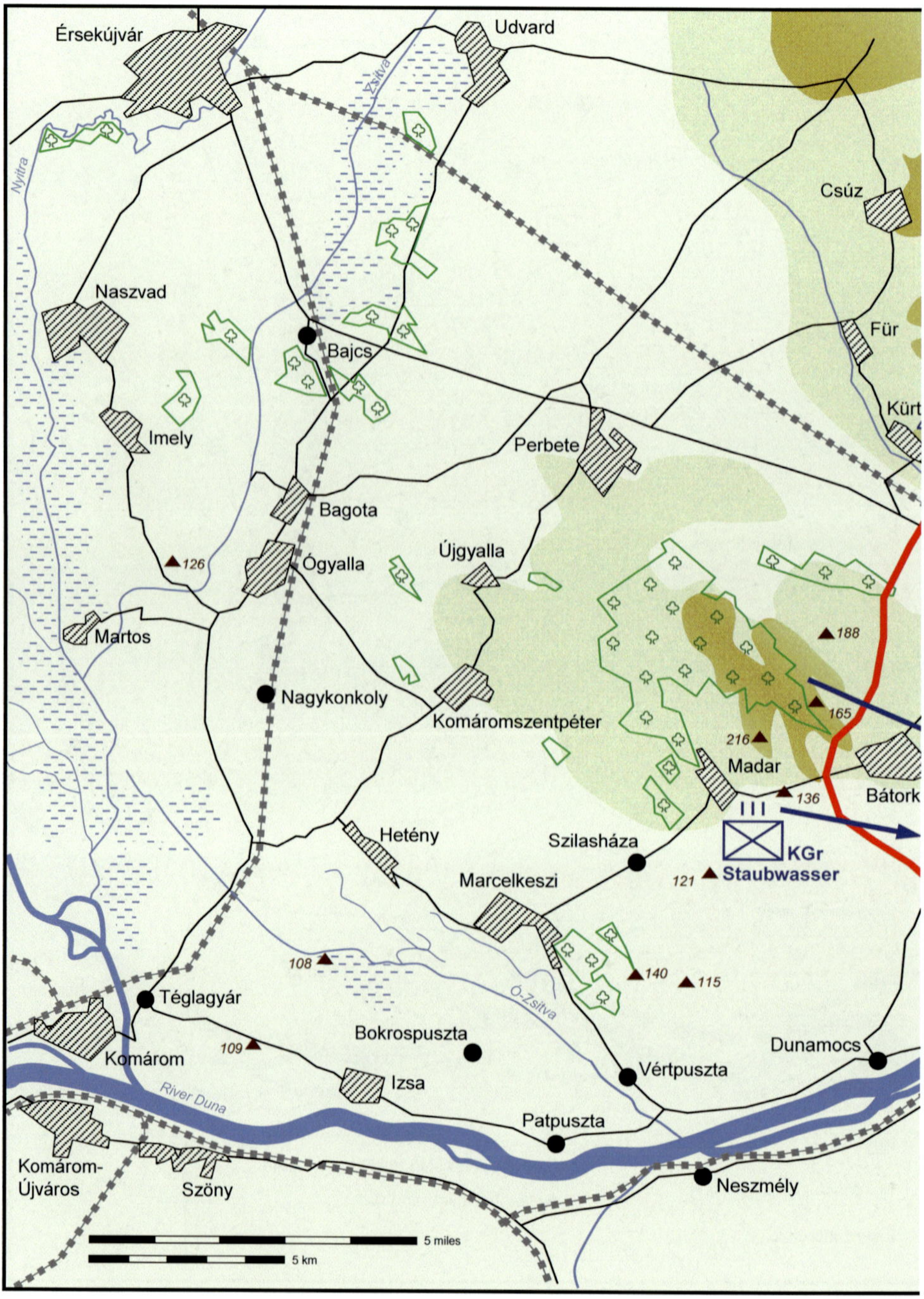

Operation "*Südwind*" 17-24 February 1945.

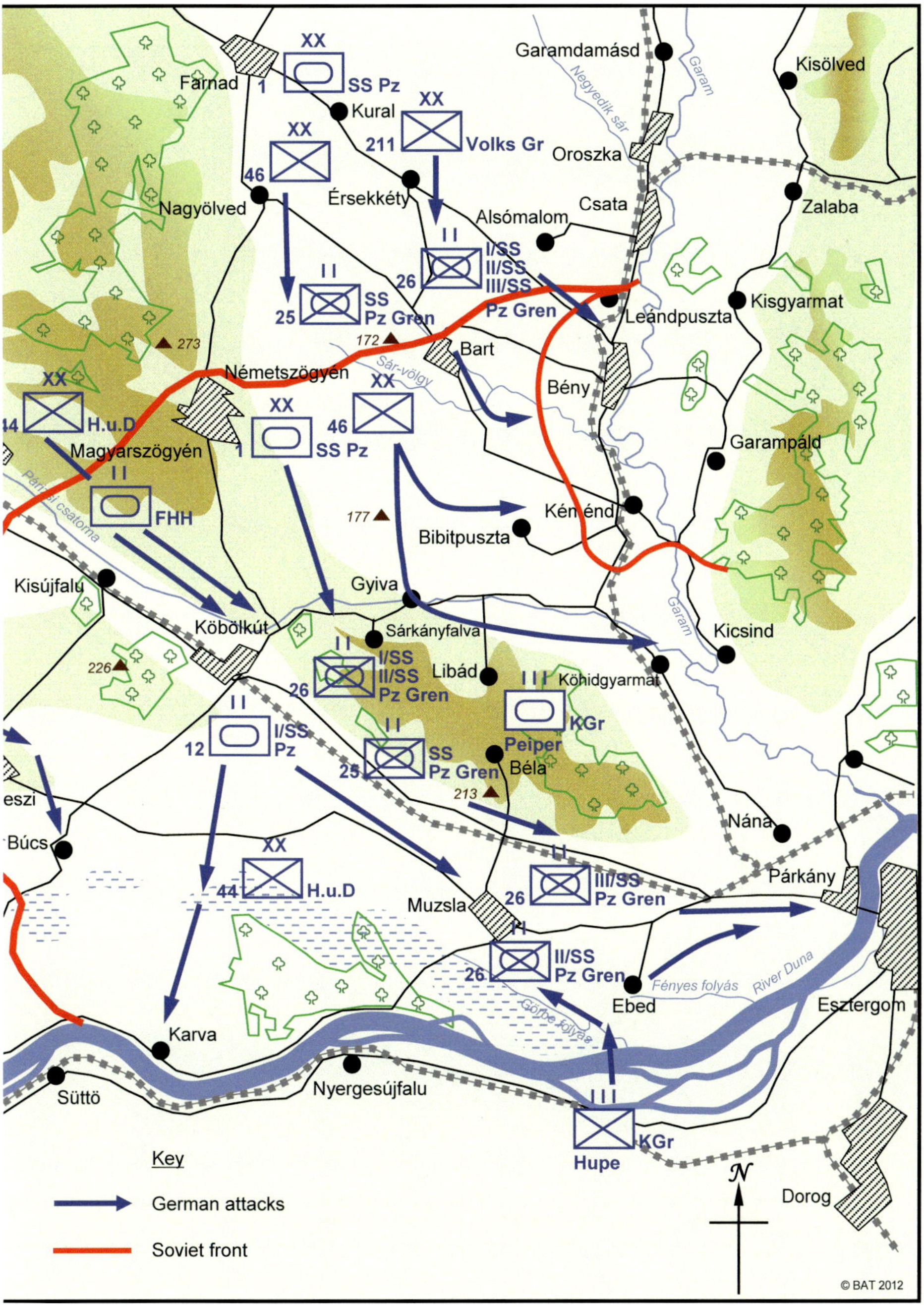
Garamdamásd
Kisölved
Farnad
SS Pz
Kural
211 Volks Gr
46
Oroszka
Érsekkéty
Nagyölved
Csata
Zalaba
Alsómalom
I/SS
II/SS
III/SS
Pz Gren
26
25
SS
Pz Gren
Leándpuszta
Kisgyarmat
273
172
Bart
Németszögyén
Sár-völgy
H.u.D
Bény
Magyarszögyén
SS Pz
Garampáld
FHH
177
Kéménd
Bibitpuszta
Kisújfalu
Gyiva
Köbölkút
Sárkányfalva
Kicsind
226
Libád
Köhidgyarmat
KGr
Peiper
12
I/SS
Pz
Béla
213
Náná
Búcs
44 H.u.D
Párkány
Muzsla
III/SS
Pz Gren
II/SS
Pz Gren
Ebed
Fényes folyás
River Duna
Esztergom
Karva
Garam
Negyedik sár
Süttö
Nyergesújfalu
KGr
Hupe
Key
German attacks
Soviet front
Dorog
N
© BAT 2012

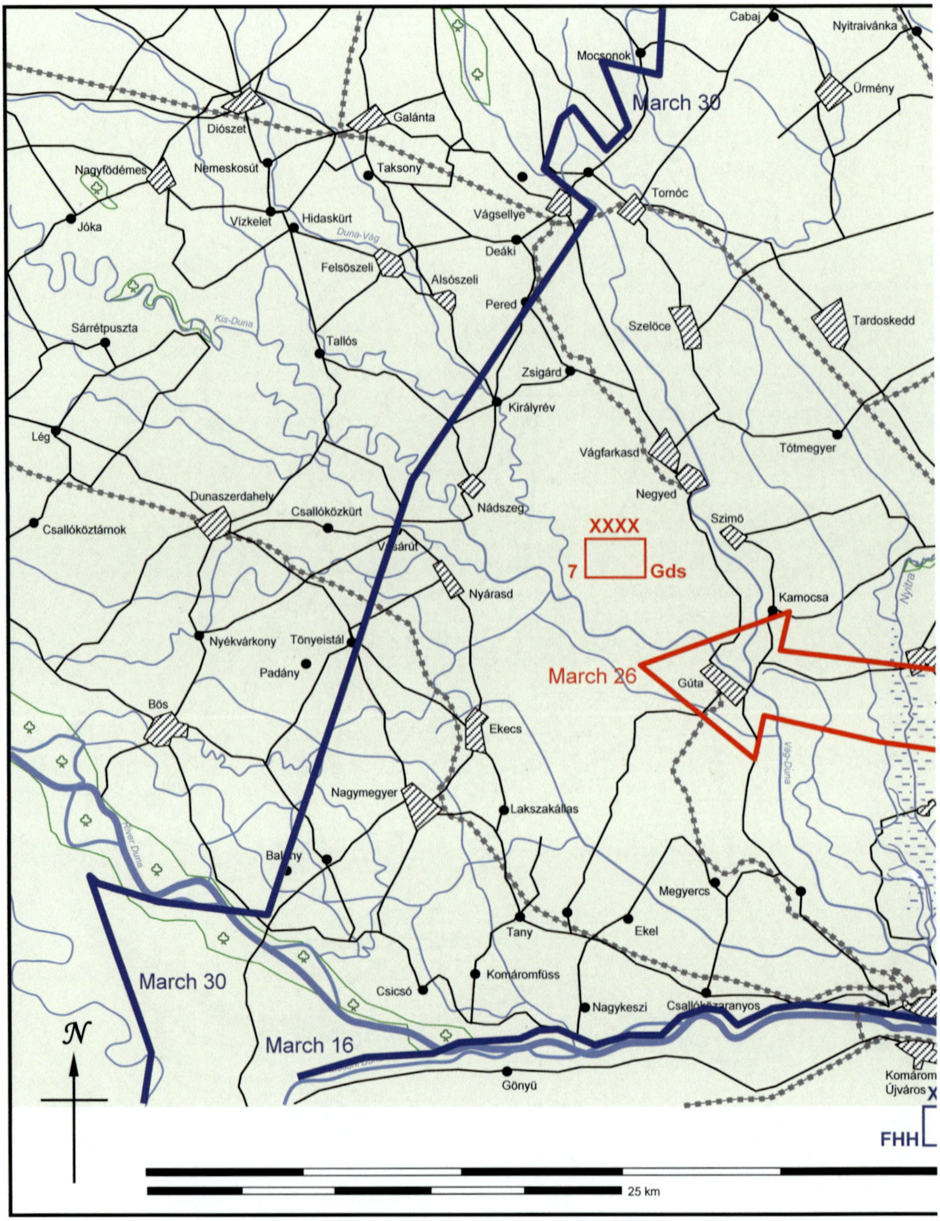

The Soviet advance towards Brno and Bratislava 25-31 March 1945.

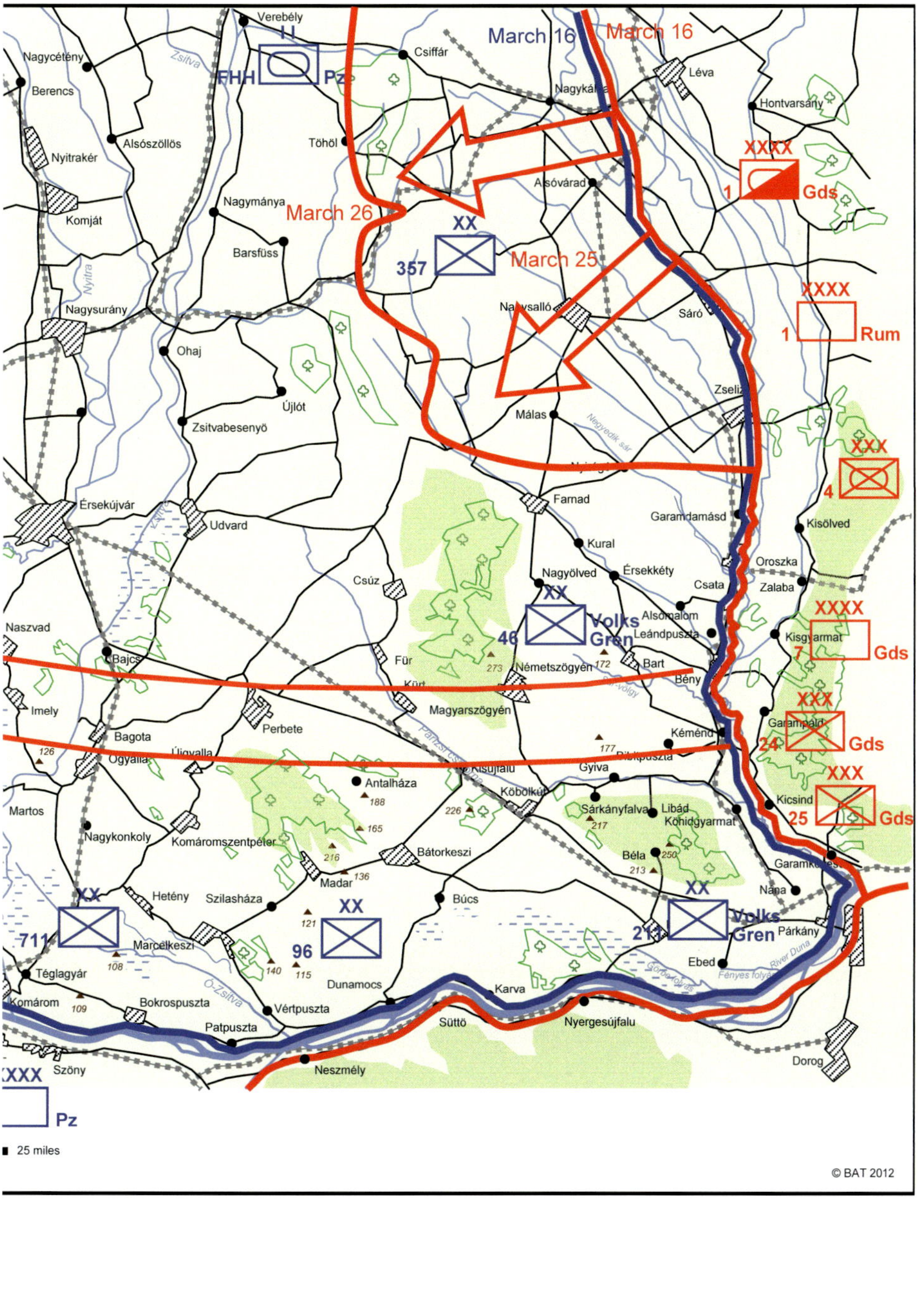

March 16
March 16
March 26
March 25
FHH
Pz
357
1 Gds
1 Rum
4
Volks Gren
46
7 Gds
24 Gds
25 Gds
711
96
211 Volks Gren
Pz
25 miles
© BAT 2012
Verebély
Csiffár
Léva
Nagycétény
Berencs
Nagykálna
Hontvarsány
Nyitrakér
Alsószöllös
Töhöl
Alsóvárad
Komját
Nagymánya
Barsfüss
Nagysurány
Nagysalló
Sáró
Ohaj
Újlót
Zseliz
Zsitvabesenyö
Málas
Érsekújvár
Farnad
Udvard
Garamdamásd
Kisölved
Kural
Oroszka
Csúz
Nagyölved
Érsekkéty
Csata
Zalaba
Naszvad
Alsónalom
Leándpuszta
Kisgyarmat
Bajcs
Für
Németszögyén
Bart
Bény
Imely
Magyarszögyén
Perbete
Kéménd
Bagota
Ógyalla
Újgyalla
Gyiva
Antalháza
Kisújfalu
Köbölkút
Martos
Sárkányfalva
Libád
Kohidgyarmat
Kicsind
Nagykonkoly
Komáromszentpéter
Bátorkeszi
Béla
Madar
Hetény
Szilasháza
Búcs
Nána
Marcelkeszi
Párkány
Téglagyár
Ebed
Komárom
Dunamocs
Karva
Bokrospuszta
Vértpuszta
Nyergesújfalu
Patpuszta
Süttö
Szöny
Neszmély
Dorog
River Duna
Zsitva
Nyitra
Ó-Zsitva

It is very probable that, during the fighting in Muzsla, the Soviets also knocked out at least one *Jagdpanzer* 38(t) tank destroyer from Assault Artillery Battalion "Bernolák".[49]

The anti-tank gun positioned at the western entrance of Muzsla destroyed two more T–34s. The machine gun of the Hungarian Pioneer Company inflicted heavy losses on the Soviet infantry that was pushing into the village.[50]

The 1st Battalion/6th Guards Motorized Rifle Brigade circled Muzsla from the north, and the 2nd Battalion attacked the village from the south. Muzsla fell into Soviet hands at about 1030 hours, but it was at about 1200 hours that the defending positions were completely wiped out.[51] According to Soviet sources the German—Hungarian forces lost a total of three tanks, nine "self-propelled guns" (presumably *Jagdpanzers*), 100 dead and wounded.

The retreating 8. *Panzer-Division* fought a delaying action with its *Kampfgruppe* of *Jagdpanzers*, tank destroyers, armoured personnel carriers and self-propelled howitzers. Therefore, the 21st Guards Tank Brigade could not break into Bátorkeszi, which originally lay in the sector of the 9th Guards Mechanized Corps, until about 1800 hours[52], and occupied the village after a five-hours battle.

At about 1730 hours, the 1st and 2nd Battalions/6th Guards Motorized Rifle Brigade, meeting no organised resistance, reached Hill 127, 2km northeast of Búcs; they then advanced toward Bátorkeszi, which was under attack by the Tank Brigade.[53]

Meanwhile, the Soviet 22nd Guards Tank Brigade continued its assault, but was halted by heavy German gunfire 1km east of Madar. Thus the brigade stopped, and in cooperation with the 21st Guards Tank Brigade prepared for the occupation of the village.[54]

Presumably this was the area where the tank duel took place which a soldier of the 3. *Kompanie/Panzer-Regimen*t 10, Kurt Bergau, remembered as such:

> The *I. Zug*/3. *Kompanie* (a *Leutnant*, two other crews and me, with my crew, all equipped with *Panthers*) was ordered to stop and contain the advance of the Soviets at all costs. We established our outpost positions 3km in front of a village, to the left and right of the large road leading toward Komárom. [...] We were in an advance position; communication was established and was continuous with the *3. Kompanie*, and we frequently reported the situation.
>
> After approximately two hours, we began to hear a powerful, deep roar. This was unmistakably the sound of the Soviet heavy tanks. Soon we identified 10 enemy tanks: four *Stalin* heavy tanks and six T–34s. This was going to be a hard task. The T–34s were not considered to be any problem for our *Panthers*. Apparently we were in

49 The battle casualties report given by the 1st Battery/24th Assault Artillery Battalion states the same (see HM HIM *Hadtörténelmi Levéltár (Budapest), HM 22. veszteségi osztály anyaga* (documentation of the battle casualties and material losses department), 14912/8. ny. v.–1945). According to this, three soldiers of the battery were killed at Muzsla in their knocked out armoured fighting vehicle, and three others went missing.

50 HM HIM *Hadtörténelmi Levéltár (Budapest), A m. kir. 53. utászzászlóalj naplója, 06.01.1945. 01.*

51 According to the diary of the Hungarian 53rd Pioneer Battalion, the soldiers of the combined pioneer company retreated from the area of the village only upon the "sound of the bells [being] heard through the Danube".

52 There were 752 houses in the village.

53 After-action report of the 5th Guards Tank Corps, 1-31 January 1945 (copy owned by the author), p.5.

54 After-action report of the 5th Guards Tank Corps, 1-31 January 1945 (copy owned by the author), p.5.

an advantageous position regarding them now; but the *Stalins*, equipped as they were with 12cm main guns and with their new, improved ultra thick armour, were going to be difficult opponents. [...]

We immediately report to the company by radio. According to orders, we were to occupy firing positions, let the Soviets come closer, and try to catch them one by one. It may sound simple, but executing it was much harder. We did not have time to think. During battle we acted as simple mechanisms – even if somebody was killed, that remained unnoticed, everything was so swift. We had some nerves left, of course, but during the engagements they simply switched themselves off. Only well after the fighting was over did our normal consciousness return, so we concentrate on checking if each of our organs were in their right places. During the battles the real self was switched off. We reacted to anything with automatic responses and movements that had been exercised a hundred or thousand times. We did what had to be done in order to defeat the enemy and thus to survive.

The Soviet tanks slowly drew closer. A *Stalin* came right toward our *Panther*. The *Stalins* must have noticed us because they start firing at our *Panther*. I, the tank commander, decided to switch firing positions. The situation became increasingly critical. We were positioned at the edge of a wooded area and the woods to our rear were thickly overgrown. Moreover, there was not much light left to aid targeting – the sun had already set. My gunner, Walter Korell, was also my best comrade. We had gone through four campaigns together and we had survived all dangers standing next to each other. He was from Eastern Prussia, just as I was, and was an excellent, able-minded and extremely steady-handed gunner; here and now he was the only one of the crew who did not lose his mind.

The others were shocked at the sight of the extremely huge guns of the *Stalins* from such a close distance.[55] Their natural instincts demanded immediate flight from the area. However, because of my position of observation, only I could acquire a full overview of our position. Our fates depended on the swift and unconditional execution of my orders. I ordered our gunner to fire at the *Stalins*. At that moment it was totally unimportant whether we hit them or not; our fire unsettled them and their self-control was shattered; and that is what we had to exploit. Aim at the hull – that was my order. The tank is like a U-boat. Apart from the commander, the crew see little or even nothing of the situation outside of the fighting compartment of the vehicle. This situation puts a maximum burden on the nerves of the tank crew members.

My tank driver, Moritz Fister, from Upper Silesia, had already started the engine arbitrarily, and wanted to retreat. The radio operator and the loader were completely overwhelmed with fear and slowly slipped into panic. The running engine let off huge, piercing flames and that could easily call attention to our situation. Although I was also excited, I did not lose my mind. The responsibility was mine. We had to act, and, in order for this, I had to provide exact and definite orders, which could be executed by my best friend.

The Soviets also stopped their engines; they, too, were watching the surroundings, just as we were. We could not see anymore in the darkening twilight, but both sides knew that the other was on the alert. My gunner, Walter, aimed at the *Stalin* as closely

55 The German and Soviet tanks approached each other less than 50-100 metres at certain times.

> and accurately as possible. 'Fire!' – I shouted to Walter. A flash, a roaring explosion, the round left the barrel. The round hit the *Stalin* directly. At the same moment, the *Panther* positioned to our right also fired. What a horror! Although the other *Panther* also hit the *Stalin*, both rounds glanced off its thick armour – and as the tracers showed, they disappeared into the night sky. We had never experienced anything like this with our 7.5cm tank gun with its huge penetration power. I provided a more exact firing direction and again I ordered 'fire'! The tank on our right also fired, but to no avail. Unfortunately, we could not see anything extraordinary. The distance between us and the *Stalin* was simply too short. The velocity and penetration ability of our round could not take effect. If we had been 400-600 metres away from the *Stalin*, we would definitely have destroyed the tank. However, now it only stood there. It was not bothered too much, but it did not fire anymore. We could not hit the hull of the *Stalin* because it stood on a slope and was therefore covered on the side which would otherwise have been vulnerable [hull down]. The *Panther* on our right somehow reversed to the side, got a better firing position and hit the *Stalin* in the rear on a less armoured spot, thus giving it the fatal blow. The *Stalin* almost burst open when the ammunition exploded inside it.
>
> But then the second *Stalin* approached. It must have noticed our muzzle flash and now opened fire at us. I immediately got the gunner orientated and ordered him to fire, with the same effect as against the first, now destroyed, *Stalin*.
>
> Meanwhile our advance guard was in combat, and our four *Panthers* had knocked out five T–34s and two of the attacking four 'giant *Stalins*'. It was getting dark, and we had to retreat. But before that, I managed to send a shot at the *Stalin* rolling in front of me: I hit it between the hull and the turret, when it heedlessly got into a sloped position in front of my *Panther* for a short time. At first nothing happened except for smoke puffing out of the escape hatches. Then, at the moment the cover of the escape hatch opened and the Soviet tank commander tried to get out, my gunner hit the *Stalin* once again, in almost exactly the same spot as before, and the turret of the *Stalin* was blown off the hull with a huge piercing flame. None of the Soviet crew got out of the wreck alive. Not too long after this, the Soviets stopped their advance. We managed to get back to the company and this day in the last year of the Second World War finally ended for us. [56]

In the meantime, the *Panzer* IV tank of 1st Lieutenant Dezső Korponay arrived at Búcs, where the Germans were fleeing in panic at the news of the rapidly approaching Soviet forces. They assigned the task of securing the entrance toward Komárom to the Hungarian tank; however, its gunsight was damaged and it was also short of ammunition. Therefore it could not take up the battle against the T–34 tanks circling the village and attacking from the west. After a short exchange of fire the Hungarian *Panzer* IV was knocked out. Private 2 János Kapusi, the loader, was killed and he burned in the tank, but the rest were able to escape. As Corporal Bese recalled:

> After all this we went through the whole village from yard to yard and over the fences, because Soviet tanks were already rumbling down the street. When we were about

56 Kregel, Heiko, *Geschichte des Panzer-Regiments 10, 1938–1945* (Berlin, 2010), pp.208-210.

> halfway through, three German soldiers on a side-car motorcycle charged out of a yard and tried to get out of the village at high speed in the same direction as we were also trying to go. As they got to a bridge over a small stream, they were hit by a fragmentation round. The motorcycle and all the Germans were blown to pieces. [...] When we got out of Búcs, we found a truck waiting for us in which we got to Érsekújvár. Then we made it further, avoiding Komárom, and crossed the Danube at Medve bridge.[57]

Thus the "Korponay" Company of the 1st Battalion/3rd Tank Brigade knocked out at least 18 Soviet armoured fighting vehicles and lost five of its own *Panzer* IVs on the first – and for it the last – day of the tank battle at Komárom. The remaining five tanks crossed the Danube and joined the Hungarian 2nd Armoured Division.[58]

The 9th Guards Mechanized Corps occupied its starting positions just one hour before the launch of the general attack.

The 18th Guards Mechanized Brigade was awaiting orders on the right flank of the corps, the 31st Guards Mechanized Brigade in the middle, on the north-south front line between Nána and the Garam river. The 46th Guards Tank Brigade – in cooperation with the 301st Independent Anti-Tank Artillery Regiment – launched an attack on the northern end of Nána, and advanced toward the railway station of Muzsla.

The M4A2 tanks advancing at the point ran into a minefield at Káptalanpuszta, then were engaged by a sudden concentration of artillery fire. Two tanks were hit.[59] The commander of the advance troop of the brigade[60], Guards Captain Dimitriy Loza, remembered the start of the night battle:

> At 0300, Nikolay Mikhno [Guards Lieutenant Colonel, commander of the 46th Guards Tank Brigade – the author] issued the detachment the order: '200' (commence the attack). With muffled engines, the tanks moved to the forward edge. The sappers guided us through the passage lines in our own minefields. They directed us precisely through the narrow lane prepared in the enemy's explosive obstacle belt. Our artillery was silent, prepared at any moment (upon signal) to open fire. Because of the weather conditions, the use of close air support was totally out of question. We were counting on surprise.
>
> The column of the forward detachment crushed the enemy in his first position on a narrow sector of the front. The brigade's main body crashed into the enemy's position behind us while still in march formation. The distance between tanks was

57 HM HIM *Hadtörténelmi Levéltár (Budapest), Tanulmányok és visszaemlékezések gyűjteménye* (Collection of studies and recollections) nr. 3799. sz., Bese Ödön: *Ahogy történt.* (Ödön Bese: As it has happened), pp.92-93.

58 HM HIM *Hadtörténelmi Levéltár (Budapest), Tanulmányok és visszaemlékezések gyűjteménye* (Collection of studies and recollections) nr. 3799. sz., Bese Ödön: *Ahogy történt.* (Ödön Bese: As it has happened), p.93.

59 Loza, 1996, pp.69-70. In our opinion, the 8.8cm anti-aircraft and/or anti-tank guns opened fire from the German anti-tank blocking position and engaged the Soviet tanks.

60 The advance troop consisted of the following: a tank company of the 1st Battalion /46th Guards Tank Brigade (Guards Captain Ivan Ignatyevich Yakushkin), two tank-rider infantry platoons, and some M–17 self-propelled anti-aircraft heavy machine guns (12.7cm four-barrelled heavy machine guns mounted on American M5 half-track transport vehicles). See Loza, 1996, p.67.

> for frontal fire. The space between the tanks was twenty to twenty-five metres. In such a column formation, each Sherman [M4A2 tank– the author] could only fire in one direction, with hardly a deflection to the left or right. Only the lead tank had a full sector of frontal fire. The Emchas'[61] machine gun fire was supplemented by submachine gun bursts from the tank riders. When necessary, the motorized riflemen also hurled their grenades.[62]

The Soviets distracted the six towed anti-tank guns positioned along the road leading to the Muzsla railway station by engaging them with fire. Following this, the 46th Guards Tank Brigade occupied the railway station without significant resistance, and its tanks crushed a column of vehicles.

According to Staff Major Lajtos, the twin-line anti-tank blocking position between Káptalanpuszta and Ebed, and along the road connecting Béla and Muzsla, retreated without putting up any resistance.[63] According to a later inquiry carried out by the *Heeresgruppe Süd*, the cause of this was that, while the Soviet troops illuminated the way for their armoured fighting vehicles with phosphorus rounds, the German anti-tank and anti-aircraft gun crews had no illumination at all.[64]

Thus by launching their tank attack in the dark, during bad weather conditions, the Soviets achieved tactical surprise over the defenders. Because of this they encountered practically no initial resistance.

The Soviet tank and mechanized corps took advantage of this. In order to carry out a rapid advance, they advanced without fanning out and attempted to break through the defence of the German—Hungarian troops. The attack was initially concentrated on the front line of the Division "*Szent László*" and the sector where the former unit was attached to its neighbour, the *211. Volksgrenadier-Division*. By dawn, the Soviet forces penetrated deeply into the front line, had pushed as far as Muzsla and the eastern edge of Ebed, and had occupied the southern parts of the "Hegyfarok", rising east of Béla. The Division "*Szent László*" was scattered. Only the Parachute Battalion was still fighting as a coherent formation.

The parachute battalion of Captain Tassonyi held out in its original strongpoints until 0600 hours in the morning, despite the fact that only 48 men remained in the company of 1st Lieutenant Godó that was assaulted on the right flank (the rest were killed, wounded, dispersed or captured). The Parachute Battalion withdrew 1km to the nearby valley and blocked it to approaches from the south. After 0700 hours the Air Force Rifle Battalion, filled out with new recruits and commanded by Captain Pálfi, joined the paratroopers, fighting in a pocket of approximately 400 x 400 metres on the vineyard hills at Béla; in the meantime a mortar crew with 42 mortar shells somehow also got there.[65]

61 Russian nickname for the M4A2 tanks derived from the letter "m" and the Russian word "four".

62 Loza, 1996, pp.67-68.

63 HM HIM *Hadtörténelmi Levéltár (Budapest), Tanulmányok és visszaemlékezések gyűjteménye* (Collection of studies and recollections) nr. 2598, Lajtos Árpád: *Szent László hadosztály (Visszaemlékezés).* (Árpád Lajtos: Division *"Szent László"* (Recollections)), p.70.

64 HM HIM *Hadtörténelmi Levéltár* (Budapest) microfilm archives, *Kriegstagebuch Ia der Heeresgruppe Süd, Fernschreiben an Armeegruppe Balck Ia Nr. 660/45 geh.* (roll no. 628. image no. 7212356).

65 *Tassonyi Edömér 1982. január 12-én kelt levele Pályi Györgyhöz*, pp.2-3. In: HM HIM *Hadtörténelmi Levéltár (Budapest), Tanulmányok és visszaemlékezések gyűjteménye* (Collection of studies and recollections), nr. 3063 Pályi György: *A Szent László hadosztály repülő lövészezredének története, 1944.*

1st Lieutenant Béla Szepesvári, commander of the 2nd Company/Air Force Rifle Battalion, wrote in his recollections based on his diary:

> At half past five the most hideous day of my life began. I led the company to the meeting point in low spirits, surrounded by total darkness. The front was raging, tanks roaring, guns thundering, tracer bullets flashing past over our heads. The paras were defending the hills in front of Béla, and we had to go and help them. Captain Pálfi entrusted me and the 2nd Company with the advance guard task. I was given a tank-destroyer squad as well.
>
> In the pitch darkness the map was of no use to me, I just followed my instincts. Hardly had we set off when a tank gun projectile hit among us. The company lay down to seek cover; I could barely kick them back onto their feet. This was the first sign that the unit was untrained and had no combat experience. But somehow we managed to move on. When we reached the hill a fearful sight awaited us – to the right of the main road, as far as we could see, a flood of tanks was moving. Occasionally they were illuminated by the knocked out and burning tanks and the light of their own tanks. Hungarian artillerymen were heading for the rear positions. The uncertainty was almost unbearable. The Soviet tanks were already roaring behind us, but we had to go forward. At maximum alert we carried on. Dawn was already breaking when I meet the commander of the paratroopers [Captain Tassonyi – the author]. Meanwhile I learned that two of my platoons had been left behind. I reported to a captain, to the commander of the paratroopers. Their losses were horrible; they knocked out eight armoured fighting vehicles with *Panzerfäuste*[66], but this was only a drop of water in the ocean. They were retreating.
>
> Finally the rest of the battalion arrived. The two battalion commanders talked briefly, then the paras withdrew, while we prepared to counterattack. Luckily my two missing platoons arrived. I had to advance on the ridge.
>
> I had barely organized the company, when we came under wild submachine gun fire at short range. My company turned and began to run. Only personal example could help here. In the hail of bullets, I did not even lie down to take cover, but pretended to be completely calm and ordered my men to take cover.
>
> The 1st Company attacked and drove off the Russkies. I got my men onto the hill [67]. [...] But the 1st Company continued its attack, and the Russkies fled. I also opened fire with seven light machine guns. And, well, this brought its consequences. The mortars engaged us and there came fire from a *Ratsch-bum*[68]. Four of us were lying in a hole when a mortar shell hit us, killing one and wounding another. It is a

október–1945. december. (György Pályi: History of the Air Force Rifle Regiment of the Division *"Szent László"*, October 1944–December 1945).

66 We know by name the destroyers of three armoured fighting vehicles out of the eight. Private First Class József Domonkos, soldier of the staff company of the Hungarian 1st Parachute Regiment waited for the attacking Soviet tanks at 0400 hours at dawn by the Párkány–Nána road junction, and he knocked out one with a *Panzerfäuste*. Sergeant Imre Kocsis, another soldier from the staff company, also waited for the attacking Soviet tanks and knocked out two with a *Panzerschreck* from a distance of 80 metres.

67 In all probability this was point no. 250 (Béla Hill).

68 The widely known nickname of the Soviet infantry-support anti-tank gun among the German—Hungarian soldiers. The high muzzle velocity of the projectile caused the impact to be heard in the target area before the sound of the gun's discharge.

> miracle that I was unharmed, I was not even struck by the air pressure (That was when the company started to believe I was bullet-proof). I treated the wounded soldier by myself, since he was asking so much for it. My adjutant was struck by the air pressure, I sent him back. Behind me, soldiers were sneaking away, no matter how hard I tried to watch them through my binoculars, I could not see who they were. I did not dare to order fire. Suddenly the battalion adjutant ran over to me: 'Retreat immediately, we're being surrounded!' Feigning calmness I ordered withdrawal. I stayed until the last moment, but one of my platoons was not able to escape the encirclement. Almost the whole 1st Company remained there. I waited in the rear for some time but nobody showed up. I led the rest of the company toward the village of Libád.
>
> Captain Pálfi was waiting in the woods in front of Libád. There I found the rest of the battalion, some 500 men. The captain ordered that we hold out there. I heard that all those who remained behind me were captured. A warrant officer shot himself in the head when he was captured (I might have done that myself).[69]

The staff of the Division "*Szent László*" left the command post that had been established in the mansion of Béla in the morning, already in daylight, in the crossfire of Soviet tanks and through the open terrain. First they went to Köbölkút; then they retreated to Magyarszőgyén.

The staff of the *8. Panzer-Division* also relocated from Sárkányfalva to Magyarszőgyén. At about noon, the staff of the Hungarian division received orders from *LVII. Panzerkorps* to retreat to Ógyalla. At the same time, Captain Tassonyi and his soldiers were attached to the *8. Panzer-Division*.[70]

In the course of the morning, a battalion of *Panzergrenadier-Regiment 98/8. Panzer-Division*, which was encircled by the forces of the 5th Guards Tank Corps at Muzsla, was relieved by soldiers of the *Panzergrenadier* regiment (Oberstleutnant von Knoop) in a counterattack launched from Köbölkút, but Muzsla – as we have mentioned before – fell into Soviet hands.

Béla was, for a time, held by the recruits of the Air Force Rifle Battalion/Division "*Szent László*", but the Soviet assaults soon destroyed the defence. In Béla Szepesvári's words:

> Soviet planes circled over us all day. There were only a couple of us in the deep ditches, together with 2nd Lieutenant Karácsony. We did not have any entrenching tools, so the men could not dig themselves in. Surprisingly and luckily, the Soviets did not fire at us. Evening slowly set in. As I saw the left flank retreating, Germans came to bring the left flank forward, but they, too, were forced back. I reported to Captain Pálfi that there was no left flank left. He said that if I could not hold my positions I was to retreat.
>
> I should hold out! And thus began the most difficult night of my life. Our engineers constantly fired at the Soviets from some 10 metres behind me. I could hear the talking and shouting of the Soviets on the road nearby. There was a snow-capped edge running around the steep ditch. I ordered sentries with submachine guns to

69 *A Hazáért mindhalálig. Vitéz Szepesvári Béla háborús naplója. Magánkiadás, é.n.* (For the Motherland, until the end. Wartime diary of *Vitéz* Béla Szepesvári, self-published, n.d.), pp.86-90.

70 HM HIM *Hadtörténelmi Levéltár (Budapest), Tanulmányok és visszaemlékezések gyűjteménye* (Collection of studies and recollections) nr. 2598, Lajtos Árpád: *Szent László hadosztály (Visszaemlékezés)*. (Árpád Lajtos: Division *"Szent László"* (Recollections)), pp.70-71.

watch the edges in shifts. I started the shifts, staring at the edge. As a Russkie head popped up, I fired. The head disappeared. And this went on for the whole night.[71]

Although the paratroopers of Captain Edömér recaptured Béla in a counterattack, they could not hold the place against the assaults launched from the south and southwest. Following this the parachute battalion was forced back to the north; the unit recaptured Libád during its retreat – in the meantime the Soviets had entered the village.

At about 1100 hours in the morning, the Soviets launched a new attack against the positions of the paratroopers, but, as this attack also collapsed, they made no further attempts that day. A *Radfahr-Zug* [bicycle platoon]/*Füsilier-Bataillon* of the *211. Volksgrenadier-Division* reported to the commander of the Parachute Battalion in the outskirts of Libád, which was sent to seal off the edges of the woods, 400 metres west of Libád.[72]

Soviet artillery had already set fire to the houses of Libád with rocket launchers, so that the attacking infantry could see in the darkness that was setting in. The Hungarian paratroopers tried to put out the fires that were destroying the houses.[73]

In the morning of 6 January, Soviet reconnaissance reported that the Germans had concentrated infantry, tanks, *Jagdpanzers* and anti-tank guns in Köbölkút. The commander of the 46th Guards Tank Brigade ordered his advance troop to move forward on the road toward Köbölkút, so that it could contain the Germans until the rest of the brigade arrived. Guards Lieutenant Colonel Mikhno sent the following report to the Corps Staff: "I go to Köbölkút. The infantry of the 31st Guards Mechanized Brigade is to hurry."[74]

The armoured fighting vehicles of the 46th Guards Tank Brigade, *en route* to Köbölkút. were clearly seen by 2nd Lieutenant Zoltán Balnay, commander of the 2nd Battery/ Hungarian 1st Medium Mortar Artillery Battalion, and he reported as follows:

> The Russian tanks noticed the German—Hungarian forces which were already in panic-stricken retreat, and kept the road under fire with explosive illumination rounds. The vehicles [wagons – the author] rushed forward, four abreast, and tried to get ahead of each other, even in the ditch; thus traffic was seriously impeded. When they reached Köbölkút, the German vehicles that were driving out from among the houses blocked the road and pushed a wagon into the ditch, smashing it.[75]

At about 0800 hours the Soviet tanks reached the village that was defended by elements of the *8. Panzer-Division* with, among others, artillery and four armoured fighting vehicles

71 *A Hazáért mindhalálig. Vitéz Szepesvári Béla háborús naplója. Magánkiadás, é.n.* (For the Motherland, until the end. Wartime diary of *Vitéz* Béla Szepesvári, self-published, n.d.), p.91.

72 *Tassonyi Edömér 1982. január 12-én kelt levele Pályi Györgyhöz*, p.3. In: HM HIM *Hadtörténelmi Levéltár (Budapest), Tanulmányok és visszaemlékezések gyűjteménye* (Collection of studies and recollections), nr. 3063 Pályi Görgy: *A Szent László hadosztály repülő lövészezredének története, 1944. október–1945. december.* (György Pályi: History of the Air Force Rifle Regiment of the Division *"Szent László"*, October 1944–December 1945).

73 *A Hazáért mindhalálig. Vitéz Szepesvári Béla háborús naplója. Magánkiadás, é.n.* (For the Motherland, until the end. Wartime diary of *Vitéz* Béla Szepesvári, self-published, n.d.), p.91.

74 After-action report of the 9th Guards Mechanized Corps on the operations in the direction of Komárom–Érsekújvár in January 1945 (copy owned by the author), p.7.

75 See HM HIM *Hadtörténelmi Levéltár (Budapest), a "Szent László" hadosztály tüzérparancsnokának naplója és mellékletei. 99. melléklet.*

(presumably *Panzer* IV tanks of the *I. Abteilung/Panzer-Regiment 10*).

According to Hungarian sources, not long before 0800 hours, German armoured fighting vehicles launched an attack northeast of Köbölkút, against the woods stretching along the bend in the road. The Germans knocked out three armoured fighting vehicles of the advance troop of 46th Guards Tank Brigade (one of which was completely destroyed), thus temporarily holding up the Soviet advance. Another Hungarian officer also witnessed these events:

> When I arrived at the Köbölkút-Bátorkeszi-Kisújfalu road junction the enemy fire intensified, so I got off the car and tried to free up the completely jammed road after ordering the cars into cover [sic.]. The lead vehicle was already on the stretch of road leading to Bátorkeszi. After about a quarter of an hour, at about 0800 hours, Russian T–34 tanks[76] charged into the town, firing heavily. I was out on the street during this and saw that the first tank was knocked out [sic.], the other one ran over the Steyer car of the artillery commander[77] and completely crushed it. The T–34 blew away the ambulance car beside me, though, a few seconds later, the tank itself was knocked out by a German soldier with a *Panzerschreck*. I myself helped a wounded ambulance soldier down to the cellar of one of the nearby houses. In the meantime, Karácsony took a German officer to the aid-station. Six Soviet tanks passed through the village. After their disappearance I gathered the vehicles and the men.[78]

When the main body of the 46th Guards Tank Brigade followed the Soviet advance troops along the road leading toward Párkány and broke into the southern and eastern parts of Köbölkút with 20 M4A2s, followed by the 301st Independent Anti-Tank Artillery Regiment that had also arrived and occupied firing positions, the Germans defending Köbölkút started to panic again. The defenders fled toward Bátorkeszi and Kisújfalu. The Soviets took possession of the village at about 1000 hours in the morning.[79]

The 46th Guards Tank Brigade and the 301st Independent Anti-Tank Artillery Regiment stopped in the south-western part of Köbölkút, in the area of the railway station, and waited for the arrival of the 31st Guards Mechanized Brigade, so that they could hand over the captured areas and be able to advance further westwards.

However, the Guards Mechanized Brigade did not push forward to Köbölkút as was planned. That is because the right flank of 9th Guards Mechanized Corps (and at the same time, the 6th Guards Tank Army) was unprotected. The withdrawing German–Hungarian forces cut the Nána-Köbölkút road, which the corps had designated as its main supply line, at several points. The brigade's infantry was ordered by the corps to clear the road.

Meanwhile, the units of the *8. Panzer-Division* brought their panic under control and launched a counterattack against the positions of the 46th Guards Tank Brigade and the 301st Independent Anti-Tank Artillery Regiment that was defending north and northwest

76 The artillery officer writing the report had mistaken the M4A2 tanks of the 46th Guards Tank Brigade for T–34s.

77 The car of Artillery Colonel Vilmos Dárday, artillery commander of the Division *"Szent László"*.

78 HM HIM *Hadtörténelmi Levéltár* (Budapest), *A "Szent László" hadosztály tüzérparancsnokának naplója, 100. sz. melléklet.*

79 *Sbornik materialov po izucheniiu opyta voiny* Nr. 21 (Moscow, 1946), p.122.

of Köbölkút. The German armoured fighting vehicles thrust into the village and the battle raged on the streets. At about 1600 hours the armoured fighting vehicles and the motorized rifle infantry of the 31st Guards Mechanized Brigade at last arrived. In cooperation with these units the Soviets pushed the Germans out of Köbölkút.

Toward evening, the 18th Guards Mechanized Brigade also arrived and took over the defence of the village. Thus when darkness fell, the 46th Guards Tank Brigade and the 31st Guards Mechanized Brigade could continue their westward-facing attack.[80]

At dawn on 7 January, two M4A2 armoured fighting vehicles of the 1st Tank Battalion/46th Guards Tank Brigade returned to Ipolyszalka to escort the trucks bringing fuel and ammunition supplies to the brigade.[81]

Meanwhile the 4th Guards Motorcycle Regiment took Karva, on the left flank of the 6th Guards Tank Army, and continued its attack toward Dunamocs[82] which the soldiers of the regiment first entered at about 2300 hours on 6 January.[83]

On 6th January, the 6th Guards Tank Army penetrated 23km into the defences of *LVII. Panzerkorps/Armeegruppe "Balck"*. In the course of the battle, the Soviets claimed to have knocked out 29 enemy armoured fighting vehicles and captured another 54 (the great majority of these on a train standing at the Párkány-Nána railway station).[84]

The Soviets, on the other hand, lost approximately 60 tanks in the sector of the Division "*Szent László*".[85] It is clear from the data mentioned above that at least 27 of these were knocked out by Hungarian units.

In the morning, behind and on the right flank of the 6th Guards Tank Army, two rifle corps of the 7th Guards Army also launched their attack. The forces of 25th Guards Rifle Corps, supported by the 27th Guards Tank Brigade, broke through the German—Hungarian defences along the west bank of the Garam between Keménd and the Danube on a 15km wide sector, and, by the end of the day, had pushed forward 18km in some directions.

The Soviet infantry advanced behind the Tank Brigades. The 6th Guards Airborne Division occupied Keméndipuszta, the 409th Rifle Division occupied Kőhídgyarmat and the woods east of Libád. The 375th Rifle Division was fighting for Béla, and the 53rd Rifle Division gained possession of Káptalanpuszta, Párkány-Nána railway station, Ebed, Muzsla, Kismuzsla, Kengyeles farm, Csenke and Szentgyörgyhalma.[86]

At the end of the day, the 25th Guards Rifle Corps/7th Guards Army was fighting on the Libád – Béla – Sárkányfalva railway station – Karva front line, and the 27th Guards

80 After-action report of the 9th Guards Mechanized Corps on the operations in the direction of Komárom–Érsekújvár in January 1945 (copy owned by the author), pp.9-10.

81 Loza, 1996, p.70.

82 There were 220 houses in Karva and 392 in Dunamocs.

83 *Sbornik materialov po izucheniiu opyta voiny* Nr. 21. Moscow, 1946, p.123.

84 HM HIM *Hadtörténelmi Levéltár (Budapest), Szovjet iratmásolatok gyűjteménye a Budapest körüli harcokról. A 2. Ukrán Front hadijelentései.1945/24.* The majority of the immobile armoured fighting vehicles waiting for transport had Hungarian insignia on when the Soviet troops captured the railway station. However, the 2nd Ukrainian Front did not transport them away either, and, therefore, the German troops attacking within the framework of Operation *"Südwind"*, on 19 February 1945, were able recover them without any losses.

85 See HM HIM *Hadtörténelmi Levéltár (Budapest), a "Szent László" hadosztály tüzérparancsnokának naplója és mellékletei. 101. melléklet.*

86 Combat reports of the Soviet 7th Guards Army to the 2nd Ukrainian Front, 1-31 January 1945 (copy owned by the author) Report issued at 1950 hours on 6 January 1945.

Tank Brigade was deployed on the south side of Kéménd. On this day, German guns knocked out two T–34s and one SU–85 self-propelled gun of the brigade supporting the rifle troops (the tanks burned out), two additional T–34s were blown up on a minefield, and one tank and one self-propelled gun became unfit for combat out due to mechanical problems.[87]

However, it was impossible to carry out the assigned task on the front line of the 27th Guards Rifle Corps. One rifle regiment of 243rd Rifle Division crossed the Garam, occupied Garamvezekény, and was engaged in battle to occupy Garamdamásd. On the other hand, the 303rd Rifle Division evacuated a bridgehead around Tőre, which – according to Soviet sources – was attacked by two infantry battalions and 22 tanks.[88]

The 5th Air Army of the 2nd Ukrainian Front supported the ground forces with a total of 221 sorties on the first day of the Komárom tank battle.[89] For the first half of the day dense fog hindered employment of the aircraft. In the afternoon the bombers and ground attack aircraft were committed against Bátorkeszi, Magyarszőgyén and Kisújfalu. Soviet fighter aircraft claimed to have shot down 10 enemy aircraft in nine combats.[90]

Heeresgruppe Süd first received news of the Soviet attack at 0620 hours. Ten minutes later the *Heeresgruppe* ordered *Armeegruppe "Balck"* that all elements of the *3. Panzer-Division* that were still north of the Danube were to be turned immediately and employed in sealing off the Soviet penetration.

Füsilier-Bataillon 211/211. Volksgrenadier-Division and units of *Panzer-Aufklärungs-Abteilung 8* launched a counterattack southward from Sárkányfalva. These forces occupied Hill 217, situated east of Köbölkút, and held onto it, despite several Soviet assaults from the south and southwest.

The main body of *Panzer-Aufklärungs-Abteilung 8* was brought forward via Antalháza toward Bátorkeszi. As this event was remembered by *Oberfeldwebel* Walter Böhm:

> I was the commander of an armoured reconnaissance unit and led a light armoured reconnaissance unit, which consisted of three light (half-track) armoured reconnaissance vehicles, [91], two medium armoured fighting vehicles[92], each with one 2cm gun and machine guns, and an armoured fighting vehicle with built-in radio [...]
>
> Once alarmed, the company was directed to the mouth of the Garam. [The Garam is a tributary of the Danube]. During the march, I and my reconnaissance unit were at the spearhead, in front of even the lead vehicles, in order to take control of a certain village (named A)[93], and secure it until the *Abteilung* arrived.
>
> The enemy succeeded in breaking through, and the *Abteilung* and its *Kampfgruppe*

87 Battle casualties for the brigades counted to one dead and 17 wounded. See: Reports of the commander of the tank and mechanized units of the 7th Guards Army from January 1945 (copy owned by the author) Issue nr. 006, 6 January 1945.

88 HM HIM *Hadtörténelmi Levéltár (Budapest), Szovjet iratmásolatok gyűjteménye a Budapest körüli harcokról. A 2. Ukrán Front hadijelentései. 1945/22-23.*

89 HM HIM *Hadtörténelmi Levéltár (Budapest), Szovjet iratmásolatok gyűjteménye a Budapest körüli harcokról. A 2. Ukrán Front hadijelentései.1945/24.*

90 Malakhov, 1960, p.82.

91 These were *Sd.Kfz.* 250/1 light armoured personnel carriers.

92 These were *Sd.Kfz.* 250/9 light armoured personnel carriers.

93 The data provider does not mention the full name of the village. Based on the circumstances and the first letter we assume it may be Antalháza.

were to repel this breakthrough. I managed to reach (A) under cover of darkness and managed to secure it. The *Abteilung* arrived during the night and established quarters.[94]

Meanwhile, *Armeegruppe "Balck"* ordered the Hungarian armoured group that was fighting in the sector of the Division *"Szent László"* to attack northward from Ebed with its 11 combat-ready *Panzer* IV s and *Jagdpanzer* 38(t) tank destroyers. At the same time, the Hungarian parachute battalion was to launch an attack from the direction of Béla. However, this was rendered impossible by the encircling manoeuvres of the Soviet troops.

Some minutes later, *Armeegruppe "Balck"* requested that the Hungarian battalions that had been named after *"Gneisenau"* and ordered to secure the oil refineries at Komárom should be relocated to the outskirts of Komárom north of the Danube. The *Armeegruppe* granted this request.

Not long after this, *Generaloberst* Guderian, who had been appointed Chief of the General Staff of the *Heer* [*OKH*], and who was, at that time, at the command post of *IV. SS-Panzerkorps* and was informed of the situation north of the Danube, made an extraordinarily important decision that fundamentally influenced the further course of the campaign. He decided that the *20. Panzer-Division*, then *en route*[95], should not unload at Léva, as previously agreed, but at Érsekújvár, and that it should be attached to *LVII. Panzerkorps*. At the same time, Guderian arranged for the *3. Panzer-Division* to continue its regrouping to the areas south of the Danube.

At 1225 hours, *Generalleutnant* Grolman explained to *Generalmajor* Gaedcke that, in his opinion, the Soviet offensive had the limited objective of interdicting the roads running along the south bank of the Danube in order to harass the supply lines of the troops deployed in Operation *"Konrad"*. According to the chief of staff of the *Armeegruppe*, the Soviets had not even committed the full strength of the 6th Guards Tank Army, as the 4th Guards Mechanized Corps was held back further north. The Germans did not know that Marshal Malinovski had already ordered this corps into reserve.

In the afternoon, Soviet forces broke through the improvised line of defence which the Germans had established extending northward from the eastern edges of the woods north of Nyergesújfalu. The assault wedge (40 armoured fighting vehicles, according to German aerial reconnaissance) had approached Búcs and was only 4km away from the village; it was heading for Bátorkeszi.

Because they were unable to carry out any effective countermeasures, the elements of *Panzergrenadier-Regiment 28/8. Panzer-Division* that had been forced back to the west

94 Cited by Kindel, 2007, pp.640-641.

95 The *20. Panzer-Division* set off from East Prussia. At 1700 hours, on 6 January, *Heeresgruppe Süd* informed the division that, according to the new order, they were to assemble in the Bajcs–Udvard–Komját–Tardoskedd–Érsekújvár area, and, for the time being, they were to remain directly attached to *Armeegruppe "Balck"*. Commanding the *20. Panzer-Division* was *Oberst* Hermann von Oppeln-Bronikowski, who had won Gold Medal in the Olympic Games in 1936 as a member of the dressage team. He had also fought in the battles in Normandy.

On 1 January 1945 the division had 48 *Panzer* IV tanks (of which 45 were combat-ready), 31 (29) *Panthers*, four (three) *Panzer* IIIs and two T–34 tanks, 19 (16) *Jagdpanzer* IV tank destroyers, and 16 (16) armoured cars (13 of which were *Pumas*) and 278 (255) armoured personnel carriers. Of the latter, there were 16 *Sd. Kfz.* 251/16 flamethrower versions, and 19 *Sd.Kfz.* 251/17 equipped with 2cm automatic cannon. For this, see *Bundesarchiv–Militärarchiv (Freiburg im Breisgau)*, RH 10/157.

established new defence positions under command of *Major* von Hochberg, in cooperation with the *Maschinengewehr-Bataillon "Sachsen"* and the newly arrived *Panzerjäger-Abteilung*[96] on the line Süttő north – eastern edge of Búcs.

The Germans established another blocking position consisting of heavy anti-tank guns and anti-aircraft guns in the depths of the gap between Búcs and Köbölkút on the German—Hungarian front line. However, this did not help much, as, at about 1700 hours, the Soviet 5th Guards Tank Corps – without any apparent trouble or resistance from the German—Hungarian side – advanced into into Búcs with 10 armoured fighting vehicles, and to Bátorkeszi with another 14.[97]

On the right flank of the *211. Volksgrenadier-Division*, the Soviet 684th Rifle Regiment/409th Rifle Division launched an attack from the east, and the 675th Rifle Regiment/409th Rifle Division attacked from the southeast; as a result of these assaults, the units occupied Kőhídgyarmat in the course of the day. There was heavy fighting for the crossroads northwest from the village.

The 6th Guards Airborne Division found a gap in the *Volksgrenadiers'* line, and, in cooperation with nine armoured fighting vehicles of the 27th Guards Tank Brigade and about 500 men, attacked toward the north-west and took Kéméndipuszta. However, the units of the German division forced the Soviet company- and battalion-sized units[98] that were crossing from Bény and north of Csata back to the eastern bank[99].

General der Panzertruppe Balck placed all of the blame for the defeat on the *8. Panzer-Division* and blamed its division commander, *Generalmajor* Fröhlich, for failing to carry out the counterattack as ordered. Balck initiated his replacement at the *Korpsgruppe*, through *Generalmajor* Gaedcke. In Balck's view, the commander of the *8. Panzer-Division* was completely indolent and positioned his forces too far west of the assembly positions.[100]

In the late night hours *General der Infanterie* Otto Wöhler, *Oberbefehlshaber* [Commander in Chief] of *Heeresgruppe Süd*, decided to reinforce the Komárom bridgehead with the independent *Panzer-Abteilung 208*.[101] According to various sources, certain parts

96 The *Panzerjäger-Abteilung* and the armoured *Kampfgruppe* of the *8. Panzer-Division* did not arrive in time at Köbölkút, where they were supposed to launch a counterattack, because their armoured fighting vehicles got stuck on the Komárom road bridge.

97 See *Sbornik materialov po izucheniiu opyta voiny Nr. 21* (Moscow, 1946), p.123.

98 In order to better understand the combat activities to be described later, we would like to note that the German Supreme High Command of the Land Forces (*Oberkommando des Heeres, OKH*) ordered each unit, staff and commander, even before 1942 to communicate the strength of the enemy attack according to the following:

1-50 men → exact number (for example "34 men"),
51-100 men → "company size force",
101-200 men → "force sized one to two companies",
201-300 men → "battalion size force",
301-500 men → "force of approximately two battalions",
501-1000 men → "regiment-sized force".

99 HM HIM *Hadtörténelmi Levéltár* (Budapest) microfilm archives, *Kriegstagebuch Ia der Heeresgruppe Süd, Kriegstagebuch vom 6. 1. 1945* (roll no. 627. image no. 7211999-7212000).

100 HM HIM *Hadtörténelmi Levéltár (Budapest), Tanulmányok és visszaemlékezések gyűjteménye* (Collection of studies and recollections) nr. 3085, Hermann Balck *német tábornok visszaemlékezése és naplója a magyarországi harcokról és a fegyverszünetről.* (Recollections and diary of *General* Hermann Balck of the battles in Hungary and of the armistice), p.4.

101 On 1 January 1945 *Panzer-Abteilung 208* (Commander: *Hauptmann* Mentor Loytved) had 25 *Panzer* IV tanks (of which 21 were in combat-ready condition) and 10 *Panzer* IV/70 (A) *Jagdpanzers* (of which seven

of the *2. Kompanie/Panzer-Abteilung* (Company Commander, *Hauptmann* Karl-Friedrich Bohn) was already committed with *Panzer* IV tanks north of Komárom as early as 6 January.[102]

At the same time, at the suggestion of *Generalleutnant* Grolman, *Armeegruppe* "*Balck*" assigned the command of the remains of the *8. Panzer-Division* and the defence of the bridgehead at Komárom to *Generalmajor* Emmo von Roden, who was the special-tasks-General of the *Armeegruppe*.[103]

The second phase of the battle: developing the Soviet successes (7 January 1945)

The units of the 6th Guards Tank Army and the 7th Guards Army continued their attack on the night of **6/7 January 1945**.[104]

The 21st Guards and 22nd Guards Tank Brigades/5th Guards Tank Corps captured Madar at 0200 hours, then continued their advance and took Szilasháza without facing any considerable resistance, then approached Marcelkeszi.

At about 0600 hours, forces of the corps broke into Hetény, taking the town at about 1000 hours; the tanks claimed the destruction of three *Jagdpanzers*, two guns set for direct fire, and one prime mover. Advancing further, the 21st Guards Tank Brigade reached the area of Gyula farm at 1040 hours.[105]

Captain Ferenc Gereben, commander of the 3rd Battery/76th Artillery Battalion, spent the night with his sub-battalion in Hetény. The battery was ready to march at 0530 hours. The captain wrote of the Soviet inrush at dawn in his combat report:

> Immediately after we moved out, a tank opened fire on the battery. Then we received enemy infantry fire from both sides of the narrow village (from right and left). Then Cadet Dr. Gyula Pőcze came forward to the battery commander, who was with the combat echelon, and reported that the Soviet tanks had completely closed up to the rear of the battery in the complete darkness and many horses had been killed; furthermore, as the fire was coming from all sides, the men dispersed among the houses and ditches. At the same time, the leading element of the battery was stuck at the western edge of the village among some German tanks[106], one of which pushed

were in combat-ready condition) available. This was the only major armoured force which was definitely detached from their formation and that was fighting south of the Danube during the tank battle at Komárom.

102 See Di Giusto, Stefano, *Panzer-Sicherungs-Kompanien and Panzer-Abteilung 208–I./Panzer-Regiment Feldherrnhalle. Italy 1943–1944. Hungary –Slovakia–Moravia 1944–1945* (Erlangen, 2010), p.148.

103 HM HIM *Hadtörténelmi Levéltár* (Budapest) microfilm archives, *Kriegstagebuch Ia der Heeresgruppe Süd, Kriegstagebuch vom 6. 1. 1945* (roll no. 627. image no. 7212013). *Generalmajor* von Roden was promoted to this rank in July 1943, and took part, among others, in the battles in Transylvania. Following the tank battle at Komárom, in February 1945, he was commanding a German—Hungarian *Kampfgruppe* in the Dunántúl (Transdanubia). He went missing near Berlin around 3 May 1945 (he was presumably killed).

104 In the morning it snowed heavily and the temperature reached 0° Celsius. In the course of the day the temperature was -2° Celsius, with a low cloud base and it continued snowing. Because of the snow and ice the roads were only usable with considerable difficulties.

105 After-action report of the 5th Guards Tank Corps, 1-31 January 1945) (copy owned by the author), p.6.

106 Although the Hungarian artillery officer mentions German tanks, we read of "self-propelled" in the contemporary Soviet document of the Corps. Regarding the type of armoured fighting vehicle, we deem

> the second gun into the roadside ditch. Meanwhile two of our horse-drawn wagons and the lead half-platoon managed to get through between the German tanks [...]. As the battery was in crossfire between German and Soviet tanks, there were only 4-5 men that appeared out of the darkness. This strength was insufficient to pull out the gun, no matter how long we tried. Now a German tank caught fire near the gun in the ditch, and the German tanks started to withdraw; the German infantry soldiers began to sneak away toward the west. The situation was completely confusing. [...].[107]

The 6th Guards Motorized Rifle Brigade reorganized its forces, and, at 0200 hours, left Bátorkeszi. At 0400 hours it passed through the north-eastern part of Madar, at 0500 hours reached Szilasháza, where it dispersed a few enemy infantry, then, at 0730 hours, entered combat in the northeast part of Marcelkeszi. By 1040 hours the brigade had occupied the whole village. At 1400 hours it then approached the railway-road crossing northeast of Komárom from the northeast. It was halted there by the resistance of German *Jagdpanzers* and armoured personnel carriers. A battalion of the 6th Guards Motorized Rifle Brigade approached to within 300 metres of Gyula farm from the southwest at about 1600 hours.

At the same time, the two tank brigades launched an assault toward Komárom, but the attack against the bridgehead – with 20 tanks according to German sources – proved to be a complete failure; the Soviets lost nine armoured fighting vehicles. The 21st Guards Tank Brigade was counterattacked by 12 German *Jagdpanzers* and an infantry battalion. Therefore, it was forced to retreat 1.5km west from Gyula farm to the area of point no. 108.

The 22nd Guards Tank Brigade fought a four-hour battle with another German armoured *Kampfgruppe*, which consisted of 10 *Jagdpanzers*,seven tanks, four armoured personnel carriers and an infantry battalion. In the course of this battle two tanks of the brigade reached the banks of the Vág-Danube immediately east of Komárom. However, at 1500 hours, the renewed counterattack of the German *Kampfgruppe* forced the Soviet tanks to retreat to the area 200 metres north of the Téglagyár (brick factory).[108]

The German armoured unit that was conducting the counterattack was most probably *Panzer-Abteilung 208*, arriving with its 12 armoured fighting vehicles from attachment to *IV. SS-Panzerkorps* to reinforce the *8. Panzer-Division/LVII. Panzerkorps*; the unit reached the railway – road crossing northeast of Komárom.

Nevertheless, the 6th Guards Tank Army advanced 25km further. Komárom was surprised by the Soviet advance; as Zoltán Szénássy told later:

> On 7 January, in the early hours of the morning, a series of deafening explosions startled the city's populace. There were no planes anywhere, but it was thundering as if the gates of hell had opened. The bombardment, coming from the direction of the Vág-Danube, caught most residents of Komárom still in bed. The Reformed College was also hit. Generally, the riverfront parts of the city were seriously damaged, like Tó Street, where a prominent citizen of the town, Pál Banai Tóth, headmaster of the higher elementary school, was killed when a round struck his house.[109]

the Soviet source to be more accurate and reliable.

107 HM HIM *Hadtörténelmi Levéltár (Budapest), a "Szent László" hadosztály tüzérparancsnokának naplója és mellékletei. 98. melléklet.*

108 After-action report of the 5th Guards Tank Corps, 1-31 January 1945 (copy owned by the author), p.6.

109 Szénássy Zoltán, *Komáromi m. kir. 22. gyalogezred.* (Hungarian 22nd Infantry Regiment at Komárom)

The key to the defence of the Komárom bridgehead, in the event of an attack from the east, was control of the Vág-Danube railway and highway bridges. East of the city the river, with its irregular riverbed, provided a 90-200 metre wide natural, anti-tank ditch in the path of the attacking forces. Bridging it would require three to seven military bridging columns.[110]

In case of emergency, the defenders could utilize the fortifications erected around the city in the 19th century, as well as the ramparts still visible on the east bank of the mouth of the Vág-Danube. The eastern outskirts of the railway bridge were also protected by a flood-control embankment. If the Soviets managed to capture the two bridges, then, to get to the real objective of the offensive, that is, the bridges on the Danube at Komárom, they would have to get through the city of more than 4,200 buildings. The railway bridge on the Danube was about 2km southwest of Komárom, the highway bridge crossed the river south of the city.

In addition to German tanks and *Jagdpanzers*, 10 anti-tank guns and the 8.8cm guns of a German *Flak-Abteilung* could be used by the defenders of the bridgehead to contain and repulse the Soviet armoured fighting vehicles. Infantry support consisted of the *II. Bataillon/Panzergrenadier-Regiment 98/8. Panzer-Division*, the *Maschinengewehr-Bataillon "Sachsen"* and remnants of the *II. Bataillon/Panzergrenadier-Regiment 93* (altogether about 200-300 soldiers). According to *General* Balck, on this day one of the German "*Gneisenau*" battalions was also committed in defence of the bridgehead, and the unit served well.

Generalmajor Emmo von Roden commanded the German defence. That day the Germans claimed to have knocked out a total of nine Soviet armoured fighting vehicles in front of the bridgehead.

However not only German forces were defending the city. An alarm battalion was organized from convalescent[111] Hungarian soldiers recovering from their wounds in Komárom and its vicinity, and from reserves that had not yet been committed; one of the companies consisted of 250 men. The battalion must have had at least two companies. Some sources also state that a battalion of the newly reorganized 1st Cavalry Division was also committed in the bridgehead.[112]

The Hungarian infantry mainly defended the eastern outskirts of the highway and the railway bridges, first around the Téglagyár, then entrenched on the embankment of the Vág-Danube flood defences. The commander of the Hungarian defenders – naturally subordinated to *Generalmajor* von Roden – was 45-year-old Lieutenant Colonel Antal Ujváry-Menhárt.[113]

At this time, a battery of the Hungarian 7th Assault Artillery Battalion[114], under

---

(Komárom, 2000), p.166.

110 A standard Hungarian military bridging column in service was able to bridge a 53m wide water obstacle. See *Hazánk katonai földrajza. Összeállította: dr. vitéz Bokori Ignác szaksz. alezredes.* (Military geography of Hungary, compiled by Lieutenant Colonel (on specialized duty) Dr. *vitéz* Ignác Bokori) (Budapest, 1943), pp.39-40.

111 Many of the soldiers of the unit had earlier been looked after in the Hungarian 520th Military Hospital in the city.

112 Szénássy, 2000, p.170. The after-action report of the Soviet 5th Guards Tank Corps mentions on 11 January parts of the of the "Hungarian 3rd Hussars Regiment/1st Cavalry Division" in the bridgehead.

113 Szénássy, 2000, p.170.

114 The majority of the 7th Assault Artillery Battalion (two batteries) was fighting in encircled Budapest.

Reserve 1st Lieutenant Endre Szőke, was also stationed in Komárom. The 1st Lieutenant had left for two days to go to Dunaszerdahely, where he was to survey new accommodations for the battery. In the absence of Reserve 1st Lieutenant Endre Szőke, command passed to Reserve Warrant Officer László Végh. At that time, the Hungarian Assault Gun Battery had seven or eight combat-ready *StuG.* III assault guns. As requested by the Germans, this battery also took part in the defence of the Komárom bridgehead, and knocked out several Soviet tanks without suffering losses. Later the Germans awarded decorations to several Hungarian assault gun crew members for this deed.[115]

The artillery support of the defence was primarily provided by the German *II. Abteilung/Panzer-Artillerie-Regiment 80*, with two batteries, each consisting of four towed 10.5cm light field howitzers. The firing positions of the batteries were around Széna-tér, the region of Kis-Ér, and in the Vargha Gardens.[116] Komárom also came under mortar and rocket-launcher fire in the evening.

Still under cover of darkness, the forces of the 46th Guards Tank Brigade/9th Guards Mechanized Corps – according to the German reconnaissance, the Soviets had 15-20 armoured fighting vehicles and armoured personnel carriers – reached the southeastern outskirts of Perbete. En route – according to Soviet sources – they met German armoured personnel carriers and tank destroyers and inflicted heavy damage to them.[117]

The 46th Guards Tank Brigade then continued its advance toward Komáromszentpéter. Within the village, the German *Panzergrenadiers* positioned tank destroyer units – equipped mostly with *Panzerfäuste* – in ambush positions. However the Soviet tanks scattered the defenders and, by dawn, took Komáromszentpéter. The 46th Guards Tank Brigade continued its attack toward Komárom, and, at the western edge of Hetény, reached the line of march of the 5th Guards Tank Corps, and joined that corps' assault on Komárom. The tank brigade established positions in the Hetény train station – Pintér-tanya area. In the evening the brigade was attached to the 5th Guards Tank Corps.[118]

The 31st Guards Mechanized Brigade/9th Guards Mechanized Corps took Perbete by 1300 hours.[119] The Soviet 85th Guards Tank Regiment/31st Guards Mechanized Brigade and two Motorized Rifle Battalions/ 31st Guards Mechanized Brigade entered Bajcs at about 1145 hours, then launched an attack toward Érsekújvár from the area of the occupied village[120]. However, their assaults against the defenders of the bridgehead – essentially two German *"Gneisenau"* battalions – were repelled, and the Germans knocked out two of their tanks.

115 *Szőke Endre 1981. április 12-én kelt levele a rohamtüzérosztály korábbi parancsnokához, vitéz harasztosi Török Pál századoshoz.* (copy owned by the author), pp.2-3.

116 HM HIM *Hadtörténelmi Levéltár (Budapest), a "Szent László" hadosztály tüzérparancsnokának naplója és mellékletei. 98. melléklet,* and Szénássy, 2000, p.166. The remaining gun of the Hungarian 3rd horse-drawn medium howitzer battery of the 76th Artillery Battalion had been incorporated into the German *5. Batterie/Artillerie-Regiment 80* but was withdrawn from there one day later.

117 After-action report of the 9th Guards Mechanized Corps of the operations in the direction of Komárom–Érsekújvár in January 1945 (copy owned by the author), pp.10-11.

118 After-action report of the 9th Guards Mechanized Corps of the attack toward Komárom–Érsekújvár in January 1945 (copy owned by the author), p.11.

119 *Sbornik materialov po izucheniiu opyta voiny* Nr. 21. Moscow, 1946, p.123. The 31st Guards Mechanized Brigade seized a considerable amount of equipment in Perbete (besides six guns), 200 – mainly Hungarian – soldiers were also captured.

120 The 31st Guards Mechanized Brigade seized a considerable amount of war material and captured 200 soldiers at Bajcs.

The *Panzer-Aufklärungs-Abteilung/8. Panzer-Division* spent the night on Antalháza. As seen by *Oberfeldwebel* Böhm:

> At dawn I was ordered by the commander (*Hauptmann* Sell) to reconnoiter a farmstead that was some 5km distant, and to see if the enemy had occupied it or not. If yes, I was to observe their strength and composition. The terrain was overgrown and it was dark, therefore I could approach to within 150 metres of it. I was very close to the enemy, so I could see the whole area and observe everything. I marked the exact positions of anti-tank artillery, mortars and tank positions on my map.
>
> During the morning, the order came: 'Back to the *Abteilung*!'
>
> Following my oral report to the commander, a discussion of the situation took place, and the assault was launched at 1230 hours. Objective: attack the breakthrough point and eliminate it; if possible, destroy the enemy.
>
> I was ordered to cover the right flank of the *Kampfgruppe* with my reconnaissance party. Based on what I observed in the morning, we expected to find heavy resistance. Our *Kampfgruppe* was reinforced by three *Königstigers*[121], the task of which was to combat the enemy armoured fighting vehicles. During the assault we received the anticipated heavy defensive fire. Therefore our attack threatened to collapse. As my vehicle was almost hit twice, I decided to take a 300 metre turn to my right, then turn toward the enemy to attack it in the flank. I was going well until I reached a gravel pit which was occupied by considerable amounts anti-tank guns, artillery, mortars and riflemen, who were just leaving. I instantly recognized my advantage in this situation, and ordered my crew to shoot first at the prime movers and the horses with all available weapons in order to inflict chaos and panic. The confusion caused by the wounded and balking horses was perfect. Those infantrymen who were still able to run left everything behind and fled. Of course I followed them with my reconnaissance party and engaged them as best as we could. When the enemy at the farmstead noticed what was happening on its flank and in the rear, this group fled also. Thus *Kampfgruppe "Sell"* gathered new energy and the task was successfully accomplished.
>
> On this day, *Kampfgruppe "Sell"* seized 74 anti-tank guns, artillery weapons and mortars, as well as lots of small arms, ammunition and prime movers, and knocked out four tanks, besides capturing a few hundred enemy soldiers. Of these quantities, my unit alone obtained 30 guns from the gravel pit, together with the prime movers.[122]

Following all this, *Panzer-Aufklärungs-Abteilung 8* – according to Soviet data, approximately 200 soldiers mounted on armoured personnel carriers and with four "self-propelled guns" – launched an attack and recaptured Bátorkeszi. The Germans held the village against the renewed assaults of the armoured fighting vehicles and tank-rider

121 The experienced sergeant first class mentions "Königstigers" specifically. There is little chance that he was mistaken in determining the type of the tank. His statements are made even more credible by the fact that one *Werkstatt-Zug* of the *schwere Panzer-Abteilung "Feldherrnhalle"* (formerly known as *503*) was stationed in Vágsellye, where a number of *Tiger* B heavy tanks were going under repair. In our opinion it is possible that, on 6 January 1945, the Germans alerted any and all German armoured forces in the area of Komárom and Érsekújvár. This way the *Tiger* Bs could have been sent to reinforce the *Panzer-Aufklärungs-Abteilung 8*. The one and a half days that were available were enough to catch up with the unit in the area of Antalháza.

122 Cited by Kindel, 2007, p.641.

infantry of the Soviet 83rd Guards Tank Regiment/18th Guards Mechanized Brigade. Meanwhile, the motorized rifle battalions of the Soviet brigade attacked Kisújfalu, which was defended by elements of *Panzergrenadier-Regiment*[123], but they were unable to take the village. However, the 375th Rifle Division/25th Guards Rifle Corps arrived shortly after, significantly reinforcing the strength of the Soviet assault.

By the end of the day, the 14th Guards Motorcycle Battalion/9th Guards Mechanized Corps reached Szentistvánpuszta, situated east of Perbete.[124]

The still combat-ready units of the Parachute and Air Force Rifle Battalions of the Division *"Szent László"* that had held out all night in the eastern outskirts of Libád and Béla around point no. 250 (Béla Hill) were assaulted by the Soviet 6th Guards Airborne Division/25th Guards Rifle Corps (Major General Mikhail Nikolayevich Smirnov) at 0730 hours on 7 January.

Captain Tassonyi covered the retreat with a handful of paratroopers in Libád. When the assaulting Soviet rifle infantry approached within 400 metres of their positions, the Hungarian paratrooper rearguard engaged them with surprise fire, then began to sneak away in small groups, avoiding the roads that were also used by the armoured fighting vehicles. The German *Fahrrad-Zug/Füsilierbataillon 211* had already carried out this movement at about 0700 hours.[125]

The retreating Hungarian soldiers, covered by two heavy armoured reconnaissance vehicles of the German *Panzer-Aufklärungs-Abteilung 8*, were heading northwest from Libád, but soon came under Soviet fire:

> When we in the first wave emerged from the village, we came under hellish mortar fire. We tumbled down on the cobblestone road, sticking closely in the diluted mud, while a stream of explosive and incendiary shells prevented us even from moving into the roadside ditches. Corporal Sipos from the machine gun unit was killed here. He was crawling on his belly when we heard shots whistling over. A phosphorus round hit him, blowing off both his legs at the thigh.[126]

Most of the remaining soldiers of the Air Force Rifle Battalion attempted to retreat toward Magyarszőgyén, detouring to the northwest. Some days later, the remnants of these two battalions of the Division *"Szent László"* joined their parent formation, in the area of Komárom and Guta, whence it was directed toward the Dunántúl (Transdanubia) for reconstitution and replenishment.[127]

The German defenders of Köbölkút repelled several attacks by the Soviet 409th Rifle

---

123 Commander of the *I. (gepanzerte) Bataillon/Panzergrenadier-Regiment 98* equipped with armoured personnel carriers, *Hauptmann* Otto Paul was killed during the day in the area of Komáromszentpéter.

124 After-action report of the 9th Guards Mechanized Corps of the operations in the direction of Komárom–Érsekújvár in January 1945 (copy owned by the author), p.13.

125 *Tassonyi Edömér 1982. január 12-én kelt levele Pályi Györgyhöz*, p.3. In: HM HIM *Hadtörténelmi Levéltár (Budapest), Tanulmányok és visszaemlékezések gyűjteménye* (Collection of studies and recollections), nr. 3063 Pályi Görgy: *A Szent László hadosztály repülő lövészezredének története, 1944. október–1945. december.* (György Pályi: History of the Air Force Rifle Regiment of the Division *"Szent László"*, October 1944–December 1945).

126 János Bárczy, *Zuhanóugrás* (Sky-diving) (Budapest, 1981), pp.534-535.

127 *A Hazáért mindhalálig. Vitéz Szepesvári Béla háborús naplója. Magánkiadás, é.n.* (For the Motherland, until the end. Wartime diary of *Vitéz* Béla Szepesvári, self-published, n.d.), pp.91-94.

Division. It appeared that even though there were gaps between the blocking positions in the line of Bátorkeszi, Köbölkút and Kéménd, the positions were able to resist the Soviet assaults.

However, later in the afternoon, the situation significantly deteriorated. The Soviet 6th Guards Airborne Division forced back the right flank of the *211. Volksgrenadier-Division* to the line between the group of farms 2km west of Kéméndipuszta and the northern outskirts of Kéménd. Kéménd was attacked by the14th Guards Rifle Regiment, supported by the 27th Guards Tank Brigade, and consequently fell into Soviet hands. In the evening the tank brigade was fighting 2km north of Libád with nine operational T–34s and two SU–85s, where it repulsed the counterattacks of the German armoured fighting vehicles and infantry. On the same day, the large military unit permanently lost one of its tanks and one of its self-propelled guns.[128]

Soviet forces also broke through the blocking positions northeast of Köbölkút. The gap between Érsekújvár and the strongpoint still holding out at Bátorkeszi was controlled in part by an improvised armoured personnel carrier battalion of the *211. Volksgrenadier-Division,* based at Csúz; the towed 7.5cm anti-aircraft guns of the independent *Panzerjäger-Abteilung 721* were securing from north of Perbete, between Szentmiklóspuszta and the crossroads near the Perbete railway station.

In his diary, *General* Balck mentions that *General* Otto-Wilhelm von Renz, commanding the German *Armee-Flakkorps V,* wanted to withdraw his troops, dismantle the anti-tank block positions established with elements of the *15. Flak-Division* along the Nyitra, and withdraw his forces. The general cited tactical regulations that forbade the use of anti-aircraft guns in the MLR. Balck intervened at the last moment, making it possible for the power of the anti-aircraft gun fire to play a significant role in slowing down the breakthrough of the Soviet tanks.[129] However, after the war, *Luftwaffe Hauptmann* Dr. Schaeben, the first general staff officer of the *Flak-Division*, vehemently repudiated the charge of withdrawing the guns.[130]

On the right flank of 7th Guards Army, the 25th Guards Rifle Corps continued the attack, and its units pressed forward 10-15km. The 6th Guards Airborne Division occupied Kéménd, the 409th Rifle Division captured Sárkányfalva and Köbölkút. The 375th Rifle Division took Bátorkeszi and Madar. Their left flank moved 3km south. The 53rd Rifle Division occupied Virth-puszta.[131] In the meantime, the corps repulsed several German counterattacks, one in the northern outskirts of Kéménd, and another launched from the direction of Antalháza northwest of Bátorkeszi – the assault force consisted of a total strength of two infantry battalions supported by 30 tanks. The 27th Guards Rifle Corps crossed the Garam with the 303rd Rifle Division, built a bridgehead 1.5km east of Tőre, and fought to widen it.[132]

---

128 See Reports of the commander of the 7th Guards Army tank and mechanized troops in January 1945. Report nr. 007, 7 January 1945.

129 HM HIM *Hadtörténelmi Levéltár (Budapest), Tanulmányok és visszaemlékezések gyűjteménye* (Collection of studies and recollections) nr. 3085, Hermann Balck *német tábornok visszaemlékezése és naplója a magyarországi harcokról és a fegyverszünetről.* (Recollections and diary of *General* Hermann Balck of the battles in Hungary and of the armistice), p.5.

130 See Maier, Georg, *Drama zwischen Budapest und Wien* (Osnabrück, 1985), p.430, note 126.

131 Combat reports of the Soviet 7th Guards Army to the 2nd Ukrainian Front, 1-31 January 1945 (copy owned by the author) Report issued at 1950 hours on 7 January 1945.

132 HM HIM *Hadtörténelmi Levéltár (Budapest), Szovjet iratmásolatok gyűjteménye a Budapest körüli*

The Germans established a line of outposts between Érsekújvár and Komárom – for the time being with only one *"Gneisenau"* battalion – 2km east of the Nyitra. Scattered elements of the *8. Panzer-Division* were also incorporated into the defense of the two towns because the various fragments and elements had not yet be restored to their parent formations.

The Germans counterattacked Soviet elements that had crossed northeast of Tőre. South of Nagykálna the Soviets crossed the Garam with a force the size of two battalions. Their incursion was cut off by the Germans.

For Marshal Malinovski, commander of the 2nd Ukrainian Front, it was clear that without reinforcements the forces assaulting Komárom would be prematurely exhausted. Therefore he attached the staff of the 24th Guards Rifle Corps and the 72nd Guards Rifle Division to the 7th Guards Army from his own reserves, while the 6th Guards Tank Army received the units of the 4th Guards Mechanized Corps (General Lieutenant Vladimir Ivanovich Zhdanov), whose combat value had been seriously reduced, which were already marching toward Nána from the area of Deménd at 2030 hours on 7 January.[133]

The Guards Mechanized Corps was ordered to concentrate its 14th Guards Mechanized Brigade in the part of Köbölkút that was already in Soviet hands, and, in addition, to concentrate the 36th Guards Tank Brigade northwest of Muzsla, then launch an assault at 0200 on 8 January toward Magyarszőgyén and Farnad, eliminate the defences of *211. Volksgrenadier-Division* along the Garam, and, by the end of the day, seize the area between Kolta and Málas.[134]

As we can see, the Soviets did not plan to use the 4th Guards Mechanized Corps toward the west – toward Komárom or Érsekújvár – rather, they wanted it to break through the German blocking position between Köbölkút and the Garam.

Thus, the 6th Guards Tank Corps received reinforcements but, at the same time, did not receive anything, although these reinforcements were badly needed. German sources reveal that on 6 and 7 January Kravchenko's army lost 101 of its armoured fighting vehicles, mostly to *Panzerfäuste* and *Panzerschrecks*. German records show that in a single day the *Panzergrenadiers* of the *8. Panzer-Division* destroyed 58 tanks and self-propelled guns in close combat.[135]

This was mainly possible because the rapidly advancing Soviet armoured fighting vehicles had only a small number of tank-rider riflemen to protect them, but they were, nevertheless, forced to fight at night. Because of the foggy weather, visibility was limited during the day, and, besides, they often attacked through densely built-up areas, where it was easier to approach the armoured fighting vehicles under cover and to destroy them with close combat devices. Even on the second day, the infantry of the 7th Guards Army could

harcokról. A 2. Ukrán Front hadijelentései. 1945/26-27.

133 HM HIM Hadtörténelmi Levéltár (Budapest), *Szovjet iratmásolatok gyűjteménye a Budapest körüli harcokról. A 2. Ukrán Front hadijelentései. 1945/27.* The Corps had altogether two operational brigades (one mechanized and one tank brigade), in which there were only 28 operational tanks according to data from 30 December 1944. Other sources (see Erickson, John, *The Road to Berlin* (London, 1983), p.743) state that the Corps had 5600 men, 96 guns and mortars, but only 15 armoured fighting vehicles. Soviet sources however contain data according to which the Corps went into reserve on 28 December 1944 with 28 operational armoured fighting vehicles.

134 Malakhov, 1960, p.84.

135 Wegmann, Günter (Mitarb.), "*Das Oberkommando der Wehrmacht gibt bekannt ...* " (Osnabrück, 1982); further referred to as: Wegmann; p.394.

not keep up with the tank and mechanized forces.

That same day the first of three trains carrying the *20. Panzer-Division* arrived, bringing the division staff and elements of *Panzer-Nachrichten-Abteilung 92*, *Panzer-Aufklärungs-Abteilung 20* and *Panzergrenadier-Regiment 59*. Because of the heavy fighting going on in the outskirts of Érsekújvár, the new assembly area for the Division was designated in the area of Bánkeszi – Nagysurány – Nyitra – Mocsonok – Tornócz. The formation's transport was delayed by small arm fire from partisans in Polish territory, and by railway sabotage near Žilina (Zsolna, Sillein) in Slovakia.

The elements of *Panzer-Aufklärungs-Abteilung 20* that had already arrived were committed that evening to secure the Érsekújvár bridgehead and, in so doing, the detraining area of the *20. Panzer-Division*, with three combat-ready *Jagdpanzer* 38(t) tank destroyers[136] of the Hungarian 20th Assault Artillery Battalion.

There were also changes in command. *LXXII. Armeekorps* was again attached to the *LVII. Panzerkorps* (command post at Nagysurány), the two units forming *Panzergruppe "Kirchner"*. The *LXXII. Armeekorps* (command post at Guta) commanded the *153. Feldausbildings-Division*, the securing forces of the *Rückwartiges Armeegebiets 593*, and the following: *Bataillon 2 "Gneisenau"/XVIII*, *Bataillon 16 "Gneisenau"/XVII*, *Bataillon 14 "Gneisenau"/XVII* and the *Bataillon 7 "Gneisenau"/XVIII*. The latter were ordered to defend the "*Susanne*" (*Zsuzsanna*) positions along the Nyitra.

Because of the Soviet offensive north of the Danube, that same day *Heeresgruppe Süd* considered the possibilities of either calling off the attempt to relieve Budapest and Operation "*Konrad*", or carrying on with reduced forces. However, this option was not realized. *General* Wöhler and his Chief of Staff, *Generalleutnant* Grolman, decided that the serious situation that was developing north of the Danube was to be stabilized without weakening the forces attacking Budapest, employing only the troops that were already there until the arrival of the *20. Panzer-Division*, which would eliminate the Soviet wedges with its counterattack.

At 1030 hours in the morning *General der Panzertruppe* Balck informed the *Armeegruppe* that, considering the serious situation that had developed between Komárom and Érsekújvár, his formation was to form an attack that concentrated *Panzer-Abteilung 208*, anti-aircraft guns and other anti-tank weapons with the aim of crushing the Soviet forces attacking the bridgehead. This plan also contained the idea that the *20. Panzer-Division* was to be committed along the Érsekújvár railway in the direction of Esztergom. *General* Balck also suggested an assault to be carried out west of Esztergom, from the south over the Danube toward the north, which would cut the Soviet supply lines leading to Komárom.

Upon hearing this, *General* Wöhler reasserted his decision that the situation that had developed north of the Danube was to be stabilized without weakening the forces attacking south of the river. He proposed that the Soviet supply lines should be harassed by fire from German artillery positioned around Esztergom, after it was retaken by *711. Infanterie-Division* on 6 January; thus the *Artillerie* could also engage the crossing points established

136 Commanded by 1st Lieutenant György Koltay, these Hungarian *Jagdpanzers* were fighting on 7 January south of Bajcs, at Pálpuszta. They had been covering the retreat of the Germans to Udvard. By 9 January all three armoured fighting vehicles had become disabled; one stood at Pálpuszta, and two had been left at Udvard. For this, see HM HIM *Hadtörténelmi Levéltár (Budapest), a "Szent László" hadosztály tüzérparancsnokának naplója és mellékletei. 101. melléklet.*

on the Garam at Nána.

At 1520 hours *Generaloberst* Guderian, on behalf of *Oberkommando des Heeres* (*OKH*), proposed that the *6. Panzer-Division* be regrouped to Komárom. The *Heeresgruppe* argued that the division was needed to protect the Felsőgalla manufacturing district. At 1920 hours *Generalleutnant* von Grolman returned the same answer to Guderian's repeated question.

At 2325 hours *Generalleutnant* Walther Wenck, commanding *OKH's Operationsabteilung*, also joined the planning when he called Grolman. According to him, the whole *Korpsgruppe "Breith"* should have been immediately transferred to Komárom, because, in his opinion, the *20. Panzer-Division* alone could not achieve the prescribed results, and he feared that the Soviets would advance toward the west, north of Komárom. However, Wenck did not have any suggestions as to which units were to relieve the troops currently engaged in heavy armoured combat at Zámoly. The Chief of Staff of *Heeresgruppe Süd* reassured him that the Komárom bridgehead position was well secured, and, for the time being, there was absolutely no sign of Soviet intentions to advance beyond Komárom.

A few minutes before 1900 hours in the evening, *General* Balck shared his plan with the Commander in Chief of *Heeresgruppe Süd* that he was going to attack with the *20. Panzer-Division* from the direction of Bátorkeszi toward the south and reach the Danube, thereby cutting the Soviet line of retreat. This attack was scheduled for 9 January. It was almost midnight when *General* Wöhler finally managed to convince Guderian that it was unnecessary to transfer *Korpsgruppe "Breith"*.

At 0100 hours on 8 January *General* Wöhler again discussed the situation with *Generalmajor* Gaedcke. Gaedcke thought that, for the time being, they would still be able to hold Komárom and Érsekújvár. The Commander in Chief of *Armeegruppe "Balck"*, however, predicted that the Soviets were soon going to commit the 4th Guards Mechanized Corps, not toward the west, but toward the north in order to break through the German blocking positions. Nevertheless, if this shaky defence still held out, it would improve the prospects for successful attacks by *20. Panzer-Division* in the future. Gaedcke now also shared the opinion of *OKH* that, if *Korpsgruppe "Breith"* did not break through at Zámoly, it was to be transferred with its 100 combat-ready armoured fighting vehicles to Komárom. On the other hand, he proposed that this decision should be postponed until noon on 8 January.

On the evening of 7 January the deadline given for the Soviet forces expired. The forces of the 5th Guards Tank Army approached close to the road and railway crossing points at Komárom, but were unable to capture the area. Further north, the 9th Guards Mechanized Corps assaulted the German bridgeheads with one single mechanized brigade, without significant success. The 25th Guards Rifle Corps/7th Guards Army was marching far behind these tank and mechanized units, while the other corps was engaged in heavy fighting in a 5km deep bridgehead around Tőre. However, the Germans had only gained a momentary pause, because the reserves that had been handed over by the commander of the 2nd Ukrainian Front were now committed.

The third phase of the battle: the Soviet offensive bogs down (8-9 January 1945)

On **8 January**[137], at 0800 hours in the morning, the Soviet 5th Guards Tank Corps renewed its assault on the bridgehead at Komárom.

The 6th Guards Motorized Rifle Brigade, in cooperation with 21st Guards Tank Brigade, advanced toward the southwest, with the task of seizing the highway bridge spanning over the Vág-Danube, occupying the eastern part of Komárom and securing the crossing for the tanks. The 1st Guards Motorized Rifle Battalion of the brigade advanced along the highway and reached the railway crossing, which lay 1.5km from the Vág-Danube railway bridge. There, however, the Soviet infantry encountered resistance from German *Jagdpanzers* and armoured personnel carriers. The battalion suffered significant losses, and its advance was halted.

The 2nd Battalion/6th Guards Motorized Rifle Brigade attacked on the left side of the 1st Battalion, reached the embankment southeast of the railway-highway crossing, but could not get any further due to the German counterattacks. The 3rd Battalion/6th Guards Motorized Rifle Brigade attacked in support of the other two, ready to exploit their success. On that day, however, there was not much for them to do.

The 22nd Guards Tank Brigade attacked toward of Izsa with the objective of joining forces with the 53rd Rifle Division (Colonel David Veniaminovich Vasilyevskiy). Advancing further westward, at about 1900 hours, they reached point no. 109; their advance troop got as far as the Komárom rifle range.

According to Soviet reconnaissance, the 5th Guards Tank Army was facing the *Panzer-Abteilung* of the German *13. Panzer-Division* (*Panzer-Abteilung 208*), elements of one "Hungarian Brigade" (actually the Division "*Szent László*"), 15 "self-propelled guns" (in fact the *Jagdpanzers* of *Panzerjäger-Abteilung 13*), six armoured personnel carriers, three artillery batteries and two *Mörser* batteries. The Soviet forces met counterattacks around the Komárom bridgehead carried out by 25-30 German armoured fighting vehicles[138] and regiment-sized infantry units.

In order to strengthen the assaults against Komárom, during the day, Colonel General Kravchenko attached the 46th Guards Tank Brigade/9th Guards Mechanized Corps

---

137 The sky was cloudy in the morning, the temperature was around freezing point. During the day there was occasional snow, with low cloud base and mild frost.

138 According to Soviet sources (among others, Malakhov, 1960, p.85 and *Sbornik materialov po izucheniiu opyta voiny* Nr. 21. Moscow, 1946, p.63) one-third of these (that is, eight armoured fighting vehicles) were *Tiger* heavy tanks. There is no direct evidence of this in German sources. However, in Szénássy, 2000, p.171, we read: "However, this was only the first phase of the counterattack. The second, by the *Tigers*, which were unloading at the [Komárom] southern railway station, followed soon after. This was the '*Totenkopf*' [*3. SS-Panzerdivision "Totenkopf"*], one of the infamous elite *SS* divisions. The huge steel monsters rolled along the Rákóczi street; their whitewashed hulls hardly fitting into the narrow street."

It is a fact that there is no such record still extant of the combat activity of the *Tiger E* heavy tanks of the *3. SS-Panzer-Division "Totenkopf"* from the period between 7 and 17 January that would indisputably exclude the possibility of their employment in the Komárom bridgehead. For this, see Schneider, Wolfgang, *Tiger im Kampf. Band II* (Uelzen, 2001), p.227, and Vopersal, Wolfgang, *Soldaten, Kämpfer, Kameraden. Marsch und Kämpfe der SS-Totenkopfdivision. Band Vb* (Bielefeld, 1991), pp.547-568) At the same time, the after-action report of the 5th Guards Tank Corps mentions three *Tiger* tanks on 12 January in the area of Madar and Komáromszentpéter. However, no such evidence can be found later, and this might be in connection with the regrouping of the *Tigers* for Operation "*Konrad 3*".

(with 17 M4A2 tanks[139]) and 57th Guards Mortar (rocket launcher) Artillery Regiment to the 5th Guards Tank Corps. The tank brigade concentrated in the area of Várföldpuszta, immediately east of the Vág-Danube.[140] However, the attack of the 46th Guards Tank Brigade against the road junction near the Téglegyár railway station east of Komárom also failed on that day. Five of the brigade's tanks were knocked out (of which three burned out). The 46th Guards Tank Brigade reported that the Soviets lost seven tanks and tank destroyers.[141]

Throughout that entire day, the two tank brigades of the 5th Guards Tank Corps launched heavy tank attacks against the Komárom bridgehead. The Germans claimed to have knocked out 32 of the 60-80 armoured fighting vehicles attacking from the east and northeast.[142]

In the course of the fighting along the road leading to Izsa and the Téglagyár railway station, the German *Panzer-Abteilung 208* knocked out a total of 24 Soviet tanks, seven by the *Jagdpanzers* of the *1. Kompanie*. The German unit, itself, lost three *Panzer* IV tanks and one *Panzer* IV/70 (A) *Jagdpanzer*, and a number of dead and wounded men.[143]

The 31st Guards Mechanized Brigade/9th Guards Mechanized Corps attacked from Bajcs toward Érsekújvár with 20 armoured fighting vehicles. The defenders, however, carried out a counterattack from the area of Naszvad with 15 armoured fighting vehicles and two battalions – these were presumably elements of the *20. Panzer-Division* that had already arrived – and forced the Soviets back, besides destroying 10 armoured fighting vehicles.

The Soviet 2nd Battalion/31st Guards Mechanized Brigade fought 3km south of Érsekújvár. Meanwhile, the 18th Guards Mechanized Brigade continued attacking Kisújfalu, without, however, achieving any results.

In order to seal the gap in the front line between Udvard and Bátorkeszi, the Germans committed *Panzer-Aufklärungs-Abteilung/20. Panzer-Division*, which had, among others, 13 *Puma schwere Panzerspähwagen*[144]. After heavy street fighting, Bátorkeszi fell into Soviet hands. Two kilometres northeast of the village, Miklósházapuszta was still defended by *Panzer-Aufklärungs-Abteilung 8*, which had retreated there.

At 0230 hours, the 2nd Motorized Rifle Battalion/14th Guards Mechanized Brigade of the 4th Guards Mechanized Corps occupied its jump-off points. At 0630 hours, after artillery preparation, the attack was launched from the southern part of Köbölkút against the northern side of the village and the railway station; the attack also aimed at occupying

139 This means that the tank brigade lost 12 of its original 29 armoured fighting vehicles, that is, 41% of its operational armoured fighting vehicle-strength as early as in the period between 6-8 January.

140 After-action report of the 5th Guards Tank Corps, 1-31 January 1945) (copy owned by the author), p.7, HM HIM *Hadtörténelmi Levéltár (Budapest), Szovjet iratmásolatok gyűjteménye a Budapest körüli harcokról. A 2. Ukrán Front hadijelentései. 1945/31-32.*

141 After-action report of the 9th Guards Mechanized Corps on the attack in the direction of Komárom–Érsekújvár in January 1945) (copy owned by the author), p.14.

142 According to the report of *Armeegruppe "Balck"* that was issued at 1740 hours, the bridgehead was attacked during the day by 40 Soviet armoured fighting vehicles, 14 of which were knocked out by the defenders. The loss of 32 vehicles is to be counted together with the losses suffered when the units repulsed the attack of the 46th Guards Tank Brigade and losses caused by the German—Hungarian air formations.

143 Di Giusto, 2010, pp.148, 206.

144 The main armament of the eight-wheeled, diesel-fuelled *Puma* heavy reconnaissance armoured car was a long-barrelled 5cm heavy tank gun which made it possible to carry out missions against any sort of light tanks. The gun penetrated 57-76mm armour at a range of 500 metres at an angle of impact of 30 degrees – depending on the type of the projectile.

point no. 144. The 3rd Battalion/14th Guards Mechanized Brigade advanced toward the Párizs Canal. The Soviet assaults against the northern part of Köbölkút were unsuccessful; therefore the main body of the 14th Guards Mechanized Brigade turned toward the western part of Sárkányfalva.

At 0900 hours in the morning, the 36th Guards Tank Brigade joined the battle, captured Hill 212 after a half-hour struggle, then pursued the elements of the *211. Volksgrenadier-Division* and took Sárkányfalva. The brigade crossed the Párizs Canal, then – according to the German reconnaissance, with 30 armoured fighting vehicles – broke through the German MLR at Alsómacskás and occupied Hill 177 with a supporting company of the 2nd Battalion/14th Guards Mechanized Brigade.

The Soviet group then continued its attack, and, between 1700 and 1800 hours, occupied Magyarszőgyén with 25 armoured fighting vehicles[145], in cooperation with two battalions of the 6th Guards Airborne Division. It then stormed Hill 213, north of the village. According to Soviet records, the German *Bau-Pionier-Bataillon 144* was completely destroyed.

In these battles, the *211. Volksgrenadier-Division* knocked out four tanks of the 36th Guards Tank Brigade, and set up new blocking positions 1.5km north-northwest of the village. In the evening, battalion-sized Soviet infantry units marched south of Magyarszőgyén toward the west (probably from the 14th Guards Mechanized Brigade), reinforced by a number of tanks.

A tank company of the 36th Guards Tank Brigade, with its own tank-rider riflemen, captured point no. 172, northeast of Németszőgyén, and then, at about 1630 hours, cleared the northern part of Bart of German defenders. In the course of the fighting for the village, Guards Lieutenant Yadikin's tank destroyed two anti-tank guns, and caused 60 casualties.[146]

On 8 January the combat formations of the Soviet 6th Guards Tank Army were attacked by the German *2. Schlachtgeschwäder "Immelmann"* (*Oberstleutnant* Hans-Ulrich Rudel) with *Fw* 190 F8, *Ju* 87D5 and G2 aircraft, the *14. Staffel/9. Schlachtgeschwäder* (*Oberleutnant* Hans-Hermann Steinkamp) with *Hs* 129B[147] aircraft, as well as the Hungarian 1st Squadron/102nd Fighter Group (Captain Győző Lévay) with *Fw* 190 F8 ground-attack aircraft, and the Hungarian 102nd Rapid Bomber Group[148] (Major Albert

145 Eight tanks and four self-propelled guns of the 27th Guards Tank Brigade had also been in combat here. One SU–85 suffered irrecoverable damage. The Brigade claimed to have destroyed three enemy guns, two mortars and 120 men. See: Reports of the commander of the 7th Guards Army tank and mechanized troops in January 1945 (copy owned by the author) Report nr. 008, 8 January 1945.

146 Summarized report of the 4th Guards Mechanized Corps of the combat activity fought between 31 December 1944.–16 January 1945 (copy owned by the author), pp.4-5.

147 The Soviet ground forces reported spotting not only *Fw* 190s and Ju 87s but also Bf 110 aircraft, but most probably the twin-engined *Hs* 129 and Hungarian *Me* 210 aircraft were mistaken for these. The *Fw* 190 F8 and the *Ju* 87 D5 versions were ground-attack aircraft, while the *Ju* 87 G2 and the *Hs* 129 B2 were tank destroyers.

148 The battle of the nine ground-attack aircraft of the Squadron was led by the Squadron leader who had also taken off. See HM HIM *Hadtörténelmi Levéltár (Budapest), Tanulmányok és visszaemlékezések gyűjteménye* (Collection of studies and recollections) nr. 3070, Lévay Győző: *A m. kir. 101/I. csatarepülő osztály működése, 1944. okt.–1945. ápr.* 81. fólió. (Győző Lévay: Operations of the Hungarian 101/I. csatarepülő osztály between October 1944–April 1945, foolscap nr. 81).

Martini) with *Me* 210 aircraft[149] (altogether approximately 100 sorties flown).[150] That day the Soviet Air Force was not present in the area[151], so the German—Hungarian ground-attack aircraft were unopposed in carrying out their missions.

In the hours around noon, 18 dive bomber *Ju* 87 aircraft attacked the Soviet positions east of Komárom:

> The aircraft cruised above the designated target in a circle, and only one attacked at a time, diving down on the Soviet tanks and positions along the Vág. At about 100 metres above the target they dropped their bombs, and immediately pulled up steeply to make way for the next one. The *Stukas* made about four turns like this. Once they got rid of their bombs, they did a lap of honour and machine-gunned the area. Then the circle broke up, the aircraft resumed their formations and then flew off to the west. The Soviet anti-aircraft artillery – evidently there was none – did not fire a single shot.[152]

However, the cooperation between the German air and ground forces was not perfect, and on one occasion the ground attack aircraft attacked their own positions by mistake. In consequence of this, signal rounds were also fired, besides ultra short wave radio connection to identify the targets for the aircraft.[153]

On this day 7th Guards Army continued to attack with units of the 25th Guards Rifle Corps, and was engaged in heavy fighting against the infantry and armoured units carrying out German counterattacks.[154]

By the end of the day the 53rd Rifle Division of the corps occupied Marcelkeszi and Bokrospuszta. The 6th Guards Airborne Division, in cooperation with the 4th Guards

149 The Hungarian 102nd Rapid Bomber Group had been attacking mainly the Köbölkút–Párkány road which was the main supply line of the Soviet troops. Kindly disclosed by military historian Csaba Becze; the author wishes to thank Mr Becze for the information.

150 After-action report of the 5th Guards Tank Corps, 1-31 January 1945 (copy owned by the author), p.7, and after-action report of the 9th Guards Mechanized Corps of the operations in the direction of Komárom–Érsekújvár in January 1945 (copy owned by the author), p.14. The German *I Fliegerkorps/Luftflotte 4* flew a total of 450 sorties, and claimed destruction of 27 armoured fighting vehicles, as well as a number of other vehicles, and to have shot down seven Soviet aircraft. For this, see HM HIM *Hadtörténelmi Levéltár* (Budapest) microfilm archives, *Kriegstagebuch Ia der Heeresgruppe Süd, Kriegstagebuch vom 8. 1. 1945* (roll no. 627. image no. 7212039). Taking into consideration the number of armoured fighting vehicles reported to have been knocked out by the German ground forces, we estimate the number of Soviet armoured fighting vehicles knocked out by German ground-attack aircraft north of the Danube to be 13.

151 HM HIM *Hadtörténelmi Levéltár (Budapest), Szovjet iratmásolatok gyűjteménye a Budapest körüli harcokról. A 2. Ukrán Front hadijelentései. 1945/32.*

152 Szénássy, 2000, p.171. According to this work, the air raid took place on 14 January. However, by that time the Soviet positions had been moved from the Vág-Duna, and there weren't any operational Soviet tanks nearby.

153 See Hinze, Rolf, *Hitze, Frost und Pulverdampf – Der Schicksalweg der 20. Panzer-Division* (Meerbusch, 1991), p.330. The German air assault targeted at their own forces appears in other sources too. This happened in spite of the fact that the liaison officer of the aircraft units, who was equipped with a radio, accompanied the ground forces and directed the targeting of the aircraft in the area.

154 According to Soviet sources, the 25th Guards Rifle Corps was engaged in the area of Magyarszőgyén with infantry regiment-sized units and 15-20 armoured fighting vehicles, and with a force larger than regiment-sized and 25-30 armoured fighting vehicles around Kisújfalu. Most probably, the number of German armoured fighting vehicles is exaggerated.

Mechanized Corps, took Magyarszőgyén. At nightfall the corps continued fighting for control of Bart, point no. 213 and Kisújfalu, as well as clearing Madar and the northeastern part of Izsa.[155]

The Germans pulled the *Kampfgruppe* of *Grenadier-Regiment 317* out of *211. Volksgrenadier-Division*'s line along the Garam in order to seal off the Soviet breakthrough. At the same time, *Panzer-Aufklärungs-Abteilung 6* (*Hauptmann* Bock) was attached to the division and transferred to the right flank of the formation.[156]

On 8 January twenty-one trains arrived carrying the supplies and equipment of the *20. Panzer-Division*. These brought the *Divisionsstab*, *Panzer-Aufklärungs-Abteilung 20*, *Panzerjäger-Abteilung 92*, *Panzergrenadier-Regiment 112*, *Panzer-Regiment 21*, *Panzer-Artillerie-Regiment 92* and elements of the supply columns, as well as most of *Panzergrenadier-Regiment 59*.

Although, during the day, *Heeresgruppe Süd* again raised the possibility of suspending the operation aimed at relieving Budapest and transferring forces into the Komárom bridgehead, this was eventually dropped because it would have meant abandoning the units fighting in the capital.

In the end, the decision was made that a counterattack was to be launched against the Soviet forces carrying out the breakthrough north of the Danube using the newly arrived *20. Panzer-Division*, together with the somewhat reorganized remnants of *8. Panzer-Division* and a regimental *Kampfgruppe* of the *211. Volksgrenadier-Division*. Since the Soviet positions directly west of the Garam had been significantly reinforced with tanks, anti-tank guns and rifle infantry troops, the Germans were compelled to find a "lesser solution" than the total elimination of the bridgehead. According to this version of the plan, the first objective was to cut off the Soviet wedges advancing toward the bridgeheads at Komárom and Érsekújvár from their supply lines and then to annihilate them. Thereby the direct danger threatening the oil refineries near Komárom would be removed.[157]

The commitment of the 4th Guards Mechanized Corps did not come as a surprise to the Germans, nor did the fact that it was directed northward. *Generalmajor* Gaedcke thought that, in case of emergency, it would be possible to transfer *3. Panzer-Division* and a cavalry brigade to Komárom in order to make the three units attack jointly. However, the point of departure for the *20. Panzer-Division* was designated in the northeastern outskirts of Perbete, because the original sector at Bátorkeszi was already held by the Soviets, who had established a strong tank defence area there. From Perbete the division was to thrust toward the southwest, then later turn eastwards.

On **9 January** [158], the Soviet troops continued their attack from the northeast against the bridgehead at Komárom with large numbers of armoured fighting vehicles and two battalions of infantry.

It is uncertain which large military unit carried out this operation, since the after-

155 HM HIM *Hadtörténelmi Levéltár (Budapest), Szovjet iratmásolatok gyűjteménye a Budapest körüli harcokról. A 2. Ukrán Front hadijelentései. 1945/30.*

156 For this, see 1986 Art of War Symposium – From the Vistula to the Oder: Soviet Offensive Operations–October 1944–March 1945. A Transcript of Proceedings, US Army War College, 1986. (Further referred to as: 1986 Art of War Symposium), drafts on pp.685, 687.

157 HM HIM *Hadtörténelmi Levéltár* (Budapest) microfilm archives, *Kriegstagebuch Ia der Heeresgruppe Süd, Kriegstagebuch vom 8. 1. 1945* (roll no. 627. image no. 7212042).

158 There was light frost in the morning, it snowed from time to time, and it was foggy. During the day temperature hovered at about 0° Celsius. The sky was cloudy.

action report of the 5th Guards Tank Corps for the day in question only reports that the units organized their ranks, drew ammunition, regrouped their strength and prepared themselves to renew the attack.[159] At the same time, according to the report of the 9th Guards Mechanized Corps, the 46th Guards Tank Brigade supported the failed attack of the 5th Guards Tank Corps only by directed fire.[160]

Whatever happened, one of the larger Soviet military formations, nevertheless, attempted a new assault, because the positions of the German *Panzer-Abteilung 208* initially came under mortar, anti-tank gun and tank gun fire, then the tanks themselves were sent in. The German *Panzer-Abteilung*, without any losses on its own side, knocked out four of the attackers and repelled their attempt.[161]

The Germans again blocked all assaults by Soviet forces against Komárom. They even launched counterattacks (according to the Soviets, with approximately 45 tanks and *Jagdpanzers*), and claimed to have knocked out a total of seven enemy tanks. Of these, five were knocked out by the *Panzer* IV/70 (A) *Jagdpanzers* of the *1. Kompanie/Panzer-Abteilung 208*.[162]

On an average, the front line of the Érsekújvár bridgehead was extended outward by approximately 1km. In the course of this, seven Soviet tanks were captured (one in undamaged condition), which their crews had abandoned because of lack of fuel. Thus the Soviet supply lines were already impeded.

The forces of the Soviet 31st Guards Mechanized Brigade and their strong armoured support had moved out of Perbete toward the railway-highway crossing north of the village. When they then ran into a unit of the *Panzer-Aufklärungs-Abteilung 20*, which was also supported by a *Panzer* company of *Panzer-Regiment 21* (15 armoured fighting vehicles as recorded by Soviet reports), the Soviets abandoned their plan, and immediately retreated. In the meantime, they blew up the highway bridge 3km north of Perbete. The engineer company of the Soviet brigade then mined the road in front of the Germans.

According to certain sources[163], the 9th Guards Mechanized Corps took Naszvad that day, although neither Soviet nor German sources support this.

The 409th Rifle Division attacked Bátorkeszi and Köbölkút, supported by 25 armoured fighting vehicles. The Germans desperately defended the places and knocked out four tanks. However, the attackers captured both villages. The Germans still held the road running southward from Kürt and Kisújfalu against attacks by the Soviet 18th Guards Mechanized Brigade (however, Soviet sources[164] relate that the brigade captured the southern part of Kisújfalu by nightfall).

Elements of *Panzergrenadier-Regiment 98* launched an attack from Kisújfalu against Soviet infantry coming from the southern outskirts of Németszőgyén and advancing to

159 After-action reports of the 5th Guards Tank Corps, 1-31 January 1945 (copy owned by the author), p.7.

160 After-action report of the 9th Guards Mechanized Corps of the operations in the direction of Komárom–Érsekújvár in January 1945 (copy owned by the author), p.14.

161 See Volleth, Karl, "Die Kompanie Honstetter. Der Weg der alten 3./Pz. Rgt. 35 nach dem Ausscheiden aus dem Regiment" in: *Panzernachrichten. Kameradschaft ehem. Panzer-Regiment 35 e.V. Nr. 45,* April 1975.

162 Di Giusto, 2010, p.206.

163 HM HIM *Hadtörténelmi Levéltár (Budapest), Szovjet iratmásolatok gyűjteménye a Budapest körüli harcokról. A 2. Ukrán Front hadijelentései. 1945/35.*

164 After-action report of the 9th Guards Mechanized Corps of the operations in the direction of Komárom–Érsekújvár in January 1945 (copy owned by the author), p.14.

the west; the attack was further supported by armoured fighting vehicles. Strong Soviet infantry forces also advanced toward the northwest and reached Hill 273, dominating the area, and also the edges of the woods stretching 3km north-northwest of the village. The German *II. Bataillon/Grenadier-Regiment 317* that was relocated from the bank of the Garam was committed to recapture Hill 273.

The Soviet 6th Guards Airborne Division attacked along the road connecting Németszőgyén and Nagyölved with support of 10 armoured fighting vehicles of the 4th Guards Mechanized Corps, but was stopped by troops of the *211. Volksgrenadier Division* 1.5km north of Németszőgyén, after the German unit knocked out four tanks. Soviet accounts mention a counterattack carried out by 10-12 German armoured fighting vehicles – presumably the vehicles of *Sturmgeschütz-Brigade 286*, reassigned from the *8. Armee* as reinforcement.[165]

Colonel General Sumilov, commander of the 7th Guards Army, thought – correctly – that the staff of the 25th Guards Rifle Corps spread its forces on too wide a front line. Therefore, in the morning of 9 January, he attached the 6th Guards Airborne Division, the 27th Independent Guards Tank Brigade and the newly deployed 72nd Guards Rifle Division to the 24th Guards Rifle Corps (Major General Appolon Yakovlevich Kruze).

The mission of the corps was to attack from the area of Keménd through Bart and Nagyölved toward Érsekújvár, and to reach the Kolta-Perbete area by nightfall. However Kruze's forces were barely able to move forward on 9 January, and were still fighting for Nagyölved and Érsekkéty at the end of the day.[166]

Forces of 24th Guards Rifle Corps advanced from the Keméndipuszta area with support of 30 armoured fighting vehicles[167] and broke through the German defences. At about 1800 hours, units of the 72nd Guards Rifle Division occupied the whole area around Bart. *1st Battalion/Grenadier-Regiment 317*, despite a successful counterattack, only managed to contain the attack 1km north of the village. During the evening, the Soviet 243rd Rifle Division, driving along the Garam, also penetrated Bény.

In the above-mentioned battles, the 25th Guards Rifle Corps/7th Guards Army advanced 10km in some directions. The 409th Rifle Division took Antalháza, and was fighting for Kisújfalu. The 375th Rifle Division captured Újgyalla and Komáromszentpéter, and the 53rd Rifle Division took Hetény, Kurtakeszi (part of Marcelkeszi) and Izsa. Elements of the latter two divisions reached the Nyitra between the Vág-Danube estuary and Martos, 3km to the north. The forces of the corps finished clearing the railway stations at Kisújfalu and Ógyalla and the railway line running south from them.[168]

165 Of the deployment of *Sturmgeschütz-Brigade 286* in the Garam bridgehead – first around Keméndipuszta – see Kurowski, Franz & Gottfried Tornau, *Sturmartillerie 1939-1945: Die dramatische Geschichte eine Waffengattung* (Stuttgart, 1978), p.257. The assault guns knocked out more than 30 Soviet armoured fighting vehicles during the defensive fighting of the next few days. Of these, three were heavy self-propelled guns. According to data from 11 January 1945 the *Sturmgeschütz-Brigade* had 25 available armoured fighting vehicles, however, only eight of them were in combat-ready condition.

166 Malakhov, 1960, pp.85-86.

167 These armoured fighting vehicles were presumably employed together by units of the 4th Guards Mechanized Corps and the 27th Independent Guards Tank Brigade. That same day, the latter unit lost one burnt out T–34 tank and two dead soldiers, but claimed to have destroyed four machine guns and 80 enemy soldiers.

168 HM HIM *Hadtörténelmi Levéltár (Budapest), Szovjet iratmásolatok gyűjteménye a Budapest körüli harcokról. A 2. Ukrán Front hadijelentései. 1945/34.*

The *Schwerpunkt* of the Soviet attacks had clearly been transferred to the blocking position of the *211. Volksgrenadier-Division*. Apart from that little territorial gain, the Soviets had not achieved a successful penetration.

During the day, another 15 trainloads of equipment belonging to the German *20. Panzer-Division* arrived, bringing the *Divisionsstab*, *Panzer-Aufklärungs-Abteilung 20*, units of *Panzer-Nachrichten-Abteilung 92*, two-thirds of *Panzer-Regiment 21*, units of *Panzergrenadier-Regiment 59.* and *112.*, units of *Panzer-Artillerie-Regiment 92*, *Panzer-Pionier-Abteilung 92* and logistic elements.

On this day, *General der Panzertruppe* Balck changed the plans prepared for the attack of the *20. Panzer-Division*. According to the new version, the division was to attack southward from the Udvard area toward Komáromszentpéter. Parallel with this, the defenders of the Komárom bridgehead were to attack northeastward, the forces holding the Nyitra securing line were to attack toward the east, the units in the Érsekújvár bridgehead toward the southeast, and the troops of the *211. Volksgrenadier-Division* toward the south.

At a few minutes before 1900 hours in the evening, *Generaloberst* Guderian conveyed Hitler's concept to Wöhler, according to which the *20. Panzer-Division* should be committed further toward the east, along the Garam, in order to eliminate the whole of the Soviet bridgehead west of the river. Wöhler finally managed to dissuade Guderian from that idea by arguing that, in the case of an east-facing attack, the *Panzer*-division would have to march by a longer route, exposed to the Soviet flanking fire.

The fourth section of the battle: the German forces' counterattack (10-19 January 1945)

Armeegruppe "Balck" did not wait until all combat units of the *20. Panzer-Division* had arrived[169], but immediately launched a counterattack with the forces already available against the left flank of the 2nd Ukrainian Front. Thus commenced the last, and, at the same time, the longest part of the Komárom tank battle.

On **10 January**[170], at 0700 hours in the morning, three *Kampfgruppen* of the German *20. Panzer-Division* attacked with 30 *Panzer* IV tanks[171] from the area of the railway-highway crossing south of Udvard toward the south. The centre *Kampfgruppe* struck the main blow. The main body of the *I. Abteilung/Panzer-Regiment 21*, a *Panzergrenadier* battalion and a *Panzer-Pionier*-company, penetrated the Soviet front line with a vigorous attack, and, flanking from the west, recaptured Komáromszentpéter at about 1200 hours.

After the German *Kampfgruppe* regrouped its forces, it continued its advance toward the southeast in the afternoon and reached the area 2km northwest of Madar. On this day, this armoured *Kampfgruppe* claimed to have knocked out 22 tanks and self-propelled guns of the 9th Guards Mechanized Corps. According to an ambiguous report, however, eight armoured fighting vehicles of the same unit thrust into Madar at about 1500 hours, but the

169 During the day on 10 January a further 18 (bringing the total to 57) trains arrived to the station. With this, all combat elements of the division had arrived.

170 The weather was cloudy in the morning, the temperature was around 0° Celsius, it snowed lightly. During the day the temperature was around freezing point, it snowed continuously, visibility was limited. Roads were hardly passable because of the snow and ice.

171 At this time, only the *I. (Abteilung)/Panzer-Regiment 21* had been committed.

snow prevented them from further manoeuvres.

Nobody was able to confirm or deny the news, however, because the reports were late. Exact situation analysis was also hindered by the fact that the officer commanding the *20. Panzer-Division*, *Oberst* von Oppeln-Bronikowski, was not with the attacking armoured *Kampfgruppe*, but at the division command post that had been established behind the front line. Thus, he could not see the situation with his own eyes, and could not command his troops when they turned southeast from Komáromszentpéter. Because of this strange behaviour for a commander of armoured forces, *General* Kirchner, commanding *LVII. Panzerkorps,* had to gather information for himself on site.

During the day, the *Kampfgruppen* attacking on the left and right flank of the *20. Panzer-Division* were unable to draw up to the armoured *Kampfgruppe* advancing in the centre. The Soviets held up the right flank *Kampfgruppe* at Bajcs and the left flank unit at Perbete. Perbete was defended at the time by the 14th Guards Motorcycle Battalion, and Bajcs by the 31st Guards Mechanized Brigade. Taking these facts into consideration, the German forces were ordered to bypass these built-up areas and thus continue to attack south.

According to contemporary Soviet documents that are considered to be exact and accurate, six German armoured personnel carriers and approximately 400 *Panzergrenadiers* advanced from Szentmiklóspuszta and the Perbete railway station toward Hill 124 and Perbete. From the Udvard railway station an armoured *Kampfgruppe* consisting of 20 tanks, 10 armoured personnel carriers and a *Panzergrenadier* battalion attacked toward Komáromszentpéter. At the same time, according to the Soviets, the German *Kampfgruppe* attacking Bajcs from the north with five or six tanks and two companies of infantry.[172]

The German defenders of the bridgeheads along the Nyitra (Érsekújvár, Naszvad, Imely and Martos) also launched attacks toward the east and southeast. They reached the Zsitva, building bridgeheads on its east bank at Bagota and Bajcs. Fourkm northeast of Martos, forces of the Soviet 375th Rifle Division/25th Guards Rifle Corps still held Hill 126. During the day *Generalmajor* Hermann Winkler, commanding *Feldausbildungs-Bataillon 153*, assumed command over the German units fighting in the bridgehead at Érsekújvár.

The advance of the German units along the road leading to Ógyalla was halted after gaining 4km by the counterattack launched by the Soviet 22nd Guards Tank Brigade at about 1540 hours. The Soviet tanks attacked the German right flank.

In the meantime, at about 0730 hours in the morning, following an artillery preparation, forces of the 5th Guards Tank Corps launched new assaults against the Komárom bridgehead. The 1st Battalion/6th Guards Motorized Rifle Brigade, in cooperation with a battalion of the 12th Rifle Regiment/53rd Rifle Division, supported by M4A2 tanks of the 46th Guards Tank Brigade, pushed toward the railway bridge. However, the attack failed, as did assaults by the other two battalions of the brigade, because of a counterattack carried out around 1230 hours by 30 German tanks, *Jagdpanzers* and armoured personnel carriers.

The German armoured fighting vehicles made three attempts by 1600 hours to recapture Gyula farm and the railway signal house 200 metres to its east, but, each time, the Soviets forced them back to their starting positions.[173]

Elements of the Soviet 18th Guards Mechanized Brigade captured Kisújfalu, in

172 After-action report of the 9th Guards Mechanized Corps of the operations in the direction of Komárom–Érsekújvár in January 1945) (copy owned by the author), pp.16-17.

173 After-action report of the 5th Guards Tank Corps, 1-31 January 1945 (copy owned by the author), pp.7-8.

the front line sector of the *211. Volksgrenadier-Division*, at about 0500 hours. Then, the brigade turned over its front line sector to the 25th Guards Rifle Corps, as ordered by the commander of the 9th Guards Mechanized Corps, and went in a forced march to Perbete in order to reinforce the defence of the village by establishing defensive positions to the north, east and west. After this, the 18th Guards Mechanized Brigade was to attack west toward Nagyharasztpuszta, and clear the road toward Bajcs.[174] This manoeuvre would cut the supply lines of the *Kampfgruppe* of the *20. Panzer-Division* which had reached Komáromszentpéter in the interim.

In the meantime, the German armoured *Kampfgruppen* suffered painful losses. Thirty armoured personnel carriers had either been knocked out by the Soviets or disabled by mechanical problems. Many German soldiers had been wounded by mortar fire, but the armoured personnel carriers were able to carry them to the rear. However, they were not able to replenish their ever-dwindling fuel supplies in this process. Therefore, some soldiers of *Panzer-Regiment 21* slipped through the Soviet lines north, in a captured Soviet transport vehicle, in Soviet winter uniforms. Only after they returned did it turn out that the great majority of the barrels transported on the truck were full of diesel fuel, which the German tanks could not use, rather than gasoline.[175]

Panzergrenadier Regiment 98/8. Panzer-Division, attached to the *211. Volksgrenadier-Division*, repulsed a strong attack against Kürt by elements of the Soviet 409th Rifle Division, then pursued the retreating attackers with armoured personnel carriers,[176] causing heavy losses to the Soviet infantry. Meanwhile, the armoured personnel carriers reached the woods north of Antalháza.

One of the motorcycle couriers of the *Stab/Panzergrenadier-Regiment 98, Obergefreiter* Kurt Schwarm, in less than an hour, on only one of his rides during the day's fighting, destroyed three Soviet tanks and one anti-tank gun in close combat (presumably using *Panzerfäuste).*[177] For this deed, he was awarded with the Knight's Cross of the Iron Cross on 19 January 1945.[178]

Two km north of Németszőgyén, the 14th Guards Mechanized Brigade and 36th Guards Tank Brigade/4th Guards Mechanized Corps, as well as the 6th Guards Airborne Division/24th Guards Rifle Corps, moving out from the Bart area, launched a number of violent attacks against the blocking positions of the *211. Volksgrenadier-Division* and its attached *Panzer-Aufklärungs-Abteilung 6*. The defenders repulsed these attacks with, for example, a counterattack south from Nagyölved by two infantry battalions and 10 armoured fighting vehicles[179]. According to German sources, their units knocked out 16 Soviet armoured fighting vehicles. The commander of *Pionier-Bataillon 211* of the German division, *Hauptmann* Rippe, was also killed in this action.

174 After-action report of the 9th Guards Mechanized Corps of the operations in the direction of Komárom–Érsekújvár in January 1945 (copy owned by the author), p.17.

175 Hinze, 1991, p.330.

176 According to Soviet sources the counterattack had been launched with four to six armoured personnel carriers and a company-sized infantry unit.

177 HM HIM *Hadtörténelmi Levéltár* (Budapest) microfilm archives, *Kriegstagebuch Ia der Heeresgruppe Süd, Tagesmeldung vom 10. 1. 1945* (roll no. 628. image no. 7212955)

178 Haupt, 1987, p.386.

179 Presumably assault guns of *Sturmgeschütz-Brigade 286* and *Jagdpanzer* IV tank destroyers of *Panzerjäger-Abteilung 92/20. Panzer-Division*, attached to reinforce the anti-tank capabilities of the *211. Volksgrenadier-Division*.

That same day, the 81st Guards Rifle Division also appeared in the front line sector of the 24th Guards Rifle Corps west of the Garam, and, in coordination with the 72nd Guards Rifle Division, supported by nine T–34s and four SU–85 self-propelled guns of the 27th Guards Tank Brigade, advanced toward Érsekkéty. By 1700 hours the Soviets had approached the village from the south and were within 1km of the village to the south, but four of their tanks and one self-propelled gun were destroyed in the combat. By the evening, the 27th Guards Tank Brigade had just three operational armoured fighting vehicles left.[180]

In the afternoon, *General der Infanterie* Wöhler travelled to *Armeegruppe "Balck"* and discussed the developing operational situation with its commander in chief. In the meantime, the question arose that, in the case of the success of the German counteroffensive north of the Danube, that is, in the case of the annihilation of Soviet forces engaged west of the Garam, would it be necessary to commit not only the German *Kavallerie-Brigade 3* but also the newly arriving *schwere Panzer-Abteilung 509* with its *Tiger* II heavy tanks?[181]

According to *General* Balck, on this day the attack was to be pushed to the Karva-Köbölkút line, and then continued, with the Garam River as a further objective. *General der Panzertruppe* Balck calculated that the Soviets between Dunamocs and Bátorkeszi would hold up the German advance, but he considered that this could be avoided by regrouping. *Generalleutnant* Grolman called attention to the fact that Soviet fire, which was reaching the oil refineries east of Komárom, needed to be stopped immediately.

On **11 January**[182], the counteroffensive continued, although the attacks launched from Komárom toward the east and the northeast on the Várföldpuszta – Gyula farm sector were repulsed by the 5th Guards Tank Corps, and, east of Komárom, by the 53rd Rifle Division. The tank corps had only 23 tanks left. During the day, Major General Savelyev arranged for the regrouping of his forces. In the evening, the 21st Guards Tank Brigade was already engaged in the southwestern outskirts of Madar with eight tanks and four armoured personnel carriers of the *20. Panzer-Division*. The 22nd Guards Tank Brigade and the 6th Guards Motorized Rifle Brigade also turned over their front line sections to the 53rd Rifle Division, and, at about 2000 hours, marched toward Marcelkeszi.[183]

Following the withdrawal of the tank brigades, approximately 50-55 burnt out or knocked out Soviet tanks remained in front of the Komárom bridgehead in the triangle formed by the two bridges and the Téglagyár railway station.[184]

The relocation of the Soviet armoured fighting vehicles from the immediate vicinity of Komárom was the result of an order issued by the commander of the 2nd Ukrainian

180 See Reports of the commander of the 7th Guards Army tank and mechanized troops in January 1945 (copy owned by the author) Report nr. 010, 10 January 1945.

181 HM HIM *Hadtörténelmi Levéltár* (Budapest) microfilm archives, *Kriegstagebuch Ia der Heeresgruppe Süd, Kriegstagebuch vom 10. 1. 1945* (roll no. 627. image no. 7212078). However this was not carried out later. *Kavallerie-Brigade 3* was employed to provide relief to the *IV. SS-Panzerkorps*, and *schwere Panzer-Abteilung 509* was committed to Operation *"Konrad 3"*.

182 In the morning, the temperature was –3° Celsius and it snowed. It was hard to travel on the roads because of the fresh snow. During the day, the temperature rose to about 0° Celsius, the frost was melting, but snow and rain both fell. The passability of the roads remained the same.

183 HM HIM *Hadtörténelmi Levéltár (Budapest), Szovjet iratmásolatok gyűjteménye a Budapest körüli harcokról. A 2. Ukrán Front hadijelentései. 1945/43.*

184 Szénássy, 2000, p.170.

Front at about 1300 hours. Marshal Malinovski ordered that the forces of the 6th Guards Tank Army and the 7th Guards Army were initially to eliminate the German armoured formation attacking in the region of Madar and Komáromszentpéter. In order to achieve this, the 2nd and 11th Anti-Tank Artillery Brigades were also committed in the sector of the 25th Guards Rifle Corps/7th Guards Army.

On this day, the forces of the German *8. Panzer-Division* that were fighting around Komárom with 42 combat-ready tanks[185] were attached to *LXXII. Armeekorps*.

The Germans captured the commanding Hill 126, northeast of Martos, thus eliminating the last Soviet positions west of the Zsitva.

LXXII. Armeekorps, together with units of the *20. Panzer-Division*[186], recaptured Bajcs, the road junction east of Pálpuszta, and Bagota, from 31st Guards Mechanized Brigade. According to its own account, the Soviet brigade fell back in a fighting retreat to the east, toward Perbete, but found its way blocked by a German *Kampfgruppe* consisting of 20 tanks and 12 armoured personnel carriers. The 31st Guards Mechanized Brigade was engaged in combat with 12 German tanks and six armoured personnel carriers north of Bagota.

From Perbete, the Soviets, with infantry the size of two regiments and 40 armoured fighting vehicles, as stated in apparently exaggerated German reports[187], launched an attack toward the southwest and the west and occupied Nagyharasztpuszta and Újgyalla. That was followed by 30 Soviet tanks breaking into Ógyalla.

At Komáromszentpéter, elements of the *20. Panzer-Division* repulsed assaults launched from the southwest and northeast and reinforced with tank support. Later, however, the Soviets penetrated into the town, where street fighting commenced.

According to Soviet sources, Perbete, defended by the 18th Guards Mechanized Brigade, was attacked by a *Kampfgruppe* of 10 tanks, 20 armoured personnel carriers and a regiment-sized infantry force.[188]

One *Panzergrenadier* battalion of the *20. Panzer-Division*, reinforced by the tanks of a newly arrived *Panzer* company of the German *Panzer-Regiment 21*, advanced from the north, and after knocking out two Soviet tanks, recaptured Nagyharasztpuszta from the Soviet 18th Guards Mechanized Brigade. It then bypassed Újgyalla, which was strongly held by Soviet troops, and reached Komáromszentpéter. In the afternoon, the *Kampfgruppe* was reinforced with *Panzer-Aufklärungs-Abteilung 20* and two artillery *Abteilungen*. These units combined forces to try to clear the supply lines of the *Kampfgruppe* of the *20. Panzer-Division*. *Hauptmann* von Hannecken, commander of the *Panzer-Abteilung*, was also

185 The *I./Panzer-Regiment 10* of the formation had no more than two combat-ready *Panzer* IVs and five *Panther* tanks that day. *Panzer-Abteilung 208*, attached to the division, however, had 24 *Panzer* IV tanks (of which 23 were in combat-ready condition) and 11 (seven) *Panzer* IV/70 (A) *Jagdpanzers*. Only five of the 21 *Panzer* IV/70 (V) *Jagdpanzers* of *Panzerjäger-Abteilung 13* were in combat-ready condition. See *Bundesarchiv–Militärarchiv* (Freiburg im Breisgau), *RH 2 Ost Karte 5280 (Panzer-Lage am 11. Jan. 1945)*.

186 Of the 39 *Panzer* IV tanks of the *20. Panzer-Division*, 24 were in combat-ready condition that day, as were 12 of the 32 *Panther* tanks and 17 of the 19 *Jagdpanzer* IV tank destroyers. A portion of the latter (five armoured fighting vehicles) was attached to the *211. Volksgrenadier-Division*. See *Bundesarchiv–Militärarchiv* (Freiburg im Breisgau), *RH 2 Ost Karte 5280 (Panzer-Lage am 11. Jan. 1945)*.

187 That day the 9th Guards Mechanized Corps did not even have 40 operational tanks. Therefore, this was even less likely in the case of the 18th Guards Mechanized Brigade attacking from Perbete.

188 After-action report of the 9th Guards Mechanized Corps of the operations in the direction of Komárom–Érsekújvár in January 1945 (copy owned by the author), p.19.

wounded in this fighting.

At about 0200 hours, at dawn, the German armoured *Kampfgruppe* – with 20 tanks and 60 armoured personnel carriers, according to Soviet sources, ran into a strong Soviet anti-tank position west of Madar. At about 0900 hours, after an artillery preparation, the *Kampfgruppe* launched an attack toward Madar and then engaged in heavy fighting with the forces of 375th Rifle Division that were defending the sector; the latter was supported by anti-tank guns and M4A2 tanks of the 46th Guards Tank Brigade.

Early in the afternoon, at about 1300 hours, the Germans – according to the Soviet sources[189], 20 tanks, 15 armoured personnel carriers and a *Panzergrenadier* battalion– entered Madar and occupied the village. The German *Kampfgruppe* claimed to have knocked out one Soviet tank and three anti-tank guns. The commander of the 375th Rifle Division, Major General Vasili Dmitriyevich Karpukhin underestimated the strength of the attack, nor did he heed the report of the 46th Guards Tank Brigade about the rapidly advancing German tanks. He fled from Madar to Bátorkeszi and asked for help at the command post of the 9th Guards Mechanized Corps.

That same day, the 46th Guards Tank Brigade, in combat south of Komáromszentpéter, claimed to have destroyed 12 German armoured fighting vehicles. Two of these were knocked out by the M4A2 tank of the commander of the brigade, Guards Lieutenant Colonel Mikhno. At the same time, Guards Captain Yakushkin, commander of the 1st Battalion/46th Guards Tank Brigade,[190] was mortally wounded in this action. That afternoon, the brigade attacked Komáromszentpéter.

The 14th Guards Motorcycle Battalion cleared the woods around Antalháza of the elements of the German *Panzergrenadier-Regiment 98* which had reached the area during the course of a counterattack on the previous day. The Soviet battalion claimed destruction of three German tanks and four armoured personnel carriers.

The commander of the 9th Guards Mechanized Corps, Lieutenant General Volkhov, ordered the exhausted forces of the 30th Guards Mechanized Brigade (totalling only 78 men, four guns, three 120mm and 10 82mm mortars) from reserve at Muzsla to Bátorkeszi. At the same time he also ordered that his troops were to carry out a regrouping manoeuvre during the night of 11/12 January. The 31st Guards Mechanized Brigade was to assemble in the Marcelkeszi area while the 46th Guards Tank Brigade was to be regrouped around Szilasháza with the aim of preparing an attack against Komáromszentpéter.[191] By 11 January, the corps had only 26 operational tanks to carry out this mission.[192]

The units of the 25th Guards Rifle Corps/7th Guards Army were engaged in heavy battle that day, and, in cooperation with the 6th Guards Tank Army, destroyed – according to their own reports – the German armoured *Kampfgruppe* that had broken into the lines between Komáromszentpéter and Madar.[193] This, as we have mentioned above, was only partially true.

As the tanks and mechanized troops assembled during the day behind the front line

189 After-action report of the 5th Guards Tank Corps, 1-31 January 1945 (copy owned by the author), p.8.

190 Yakushkin received the Hero of the Soviet Union award following his death.

191 After-action report of the 9th Guards Mechanized Corps of the operations in the direction of Komárom–Érsekújvár in January 1945 (copy owned by the author), pp.19-21.

192 *Sbornik materialov po izucheniiu opyta voiny* Nr. 21. Moscow, 1946, p.124.

193 HM HIM *Hadtörténelmi Levéltár (Budapest), Szovjet iratmásolatok gyűjteménye a Budapest körüli harcokról. A 2. Ukrán Front hadijelentései. 1945/42.*

of the rifle divisions in order to form a unit able to carry out a counterattack, the Soviet infantry faced intensified enemy pressure.

That same day, the Soviets found the documents of a fallen soldier from *Panzergrenadier-Regiment 112,* north of Újgyalla. Only then did the staff of the 2nd Ukrainian Front realize that the counterattack was primarily being carried out by the *20. Panzer-Division.*

According to *Generalmajor* Gaedcke, Chief of Staff of *Armeegruppe "Balck"*, communications and cooperation did not go smoothly among the recently reconstituted elements of the *20. Panzer-Division*. From time to time, the signal system of the *Heeresgruppe* also failed, and the accuracy of reports was sometimes questionable. He worded it thus: the officers of the division were, for the time being, "not up to the job".[194]

General der Panzertruppe Balck considered that the achievements of the *20. Panzer-Division* on that day were due, not to its commander, but to *General* Kirchner, who conducted the battle from the front line. It was also a determining factor that the Germans did not launch their attack as a frontal assault, but at an angle of 45 degrees to the direction of the Soviet offensive.[195] Thus the hastily established anti-tank positions could not fill their role effectively.

Elements of *Panzergrenadier-Regiment 98* and *Panzer-Aufklärungs-Abteilung 8* launched their attack from the area of Kürt toward the south and southwest; at the same time, they repelled almost all company- and battalion-sized assaults launched by the Soviets from the southeast. Nevertheless, the Soviet 409th Rifle Division recaptured Szentisztvánpuszta.

The *211. Volksgrenadier-Division* attacked Németszőgyén and Bart with two battalions and 10 armoured fighting vehicles. However, Soviet counterattacks drove the Germans back to their points of departure. At Bart two operational tanks and two self-propelled guns of the 27th Guards Tank Brigade took part in repelling the German attacks.

The totally exhausted 4th Guards Mechanized Corps, whose total operational tank strength on that day was 23 tanks, launched an attack at 0900 hours together with elements of the 72nd Guards Rifle Division north from Németszőgyén, but their advance bogged down within half an hour when the Germans counterattacked with two German armoured fighting vehicles, three armoured personnel carriers and infantry the size of two companies.[196]

In the afternoon, forces of the 6th Guards Airborne Division attacked the positions of the German division with battalion and regiment-sized infantry forces, as well as with strong tank support, but they only achieved insignificant ground gains, while taking Érsekkéty. The German *211. Volksgrenadier-Division* claimed to have knocked out six Soviet tanks[197]. The troops of the division almost completely eliminated the Soviets who

194 HM HIM *Hadtörténelmi Levéltár (Budapest) microfilm archives, Kriegstagebuch Ia der Heeresgruppe Süd, Kriegstagebuch vom 11. 1. 1945* (roll no. 627. image no. 7212100).

195 HM HIM *Hadtörténelmi Levéltár (Budapest), Tanulmányok és visszaemlékezések gyűjteménye* (Collection of studies and recollections) nr. 3085, *Hermann Balck német tábornok visszaemlékezése és naplója a magyarországi harcokról és a fegyverszünetről.* (Recollections and diary of *General* Hermann Balck of the battles in Hungary and of the armistice), p.5.

196 Summarized report of the 4th Guards Mechanized Corps of the combat activity fought between 31 December 1944–16 January 1945 (copy owned by the author), p.5.

197 On 11 January the forces of the *Korpsgruppe "Kirchner"* – according to a correction made the next day – knocked out a total of eight Soviet armoured fighting vehicles, two were rendered immobile, and seized an M4A2 tank and a German *Jagdpanzer* that had been lost earlier.

had penetrated Csata.

During the day, the 5th Air Army of the 2nd Ukrainian Front flew a total of 38 sorties in the area northeast of Komárom. The majority of these were ground attack- or fighter missions.[198]

On **12 January**[199], at dawn, the German counteroffensive continued. East of Komárom, the forces attached to the German *8. Panzer-Division* advanced 3km toward Izsa. The 53rd Rifle Division suffered heavy losses in this fighting.

At about 0200 hours, the 5th Guards Tank Corps more or less completed the regrouping it had started the day before. Its formations prepared for further missions: the 22nd Guards Tank Brigade (with 11 T–34 tanks) was 3km southwest of Búcs, the 6th Guards Motorized Rifle Brigade[200] was at the creek between point no. 121 and Szilasháza, the 21st Guards Tank Brigade (with 10 T–34s[201]) was in the northeastern part of Szilasháza, and weak forces of the 20th Guards Tank Brigade[202] were in the area northwest of Búcs. The 46th Guards Tank Brigade and the 31st Guards Mechanized Brigade of the 9th Guards Mechanized Corps were operationally attached to the 5th Guards Tank Corps, and awaited orders in the northwestern part of Szilasháza.[203]

The order of Major General Savelyev, that was issued at 0300 hours on 12 January, contained instructions for further assaults. Madar was to be attacked by the 22nd Guards Tank Brigade (reinforced by 391st Guards Anti-Tank Artillery Regiment), the 6th Guards Motorized Rifle Brigade (reinforced by the 454th Guards Mortar Regiment, the 1426th Light Artillery Regiment and the 127th Guards Mortar Artillery Battalion), as well as the 21st Guards Tank Brigade. After the recapture of Madar, these forces were to take Komáromszentpéter by the end of the day. The 46th Guards Tank Brigade, the 31st Guards Mechanized Brigade and the 301st Independent Anti-Tank Artillery Regiment were first to take Hetény, then, by the end of the day, they were also to capture the southwestern part of Komáromszentpéter.

The artillery reserve of the corps consisted of the 870th Light Artillery Regiment/202nd

198 HM HIM *Hadtörténelmi Levéltár (Budapest), Szovjet iratmásolatok gyűjteménye a Budapest körüli harcokról. A 2. Ukrán Front hadijelentései. 1945/43*, and HM HIM *Hadtörténelmi Levéltár* (Budapest) microfilm archives, *Kriegstagebuch Ia der Heeresgruppe Süd, Kriegstagebuch vom 11. 1. 19 45* (roll no. 627. image no. 7212092).

199 The morning was dim, extremely windy, although the temperature remained above freezing point. During the day the temperature rose to 5° Celsius. Occasionally it rained, and visibility was considerably impaired.

200 The 6th Guards Motorized Rifle Brigade had the following vehicles and resources available: 148 riflemen, with 81 submachine gunners, 27 machine gunners, 179 artillerymen, 160 mortar-crew and 57 anti-tank riflemen.

201 Originally the 21st Guards Tank Brigade launched the operation on 6 January with T–34/85 tanks. Unfortunately, the after-action report of the 5th Guards Tank Corps does not make clear how the T–34 tanks equipped with 76.2mm guns were incorporated into the strength of the corps. In our opinion the course of events could be this: after the brigade lost all of its armoured strength, the amount of armoured fighting vehicles remaining with the 22nd Guards Tank Brigade was equally divided between the two brigades.

202 The 20th Guards Tank Brigade did not have any armoured fighting vehicles at all; it only had 32 (!) riflemen, four American M17 self-propelled four-barrelled anti-aircraft heavy machine guns from the anti-aircraft company, and one 82mm mortar battery.

203 After-action report of the 5th Guards Tank Corps, 1-31 January 1945 (copy owned by the author), p.8.

Light Artillery Brigade and the 57th Guards Mortar Artillery Regiment. The 4th Guards Signal Battalion and the anti-aircraft company of 20th Guards Tank Brigade defended the southwestern part of Búcs. The forces involved were to be prepared to attack by 0900 hours.[204]

2km north of the mouth of the Nyitra, around Gyulatelep and the guardhouse on the embankment, the Soviet 375th Rifle Division/25th Guards Rifle Corps attempted to cross over to the western bank of the river with a battalion-sized unit, but two German *"Gneisenau"* battalions repulsed them. These forces, together with 20 armoured fighting vehicles of the right flank of the *20. Panzer-Division*[205], took the Ógyalla railway station and Bagota. The *"Gneisenau"* battalions turned south in order to link up with the *8. Panzer-Division,* which was attacking from the direction of Komárom.

At 0200 hours, the right flank *Kampfgruppe* of the *8. Panzer-Division* continued its attack east to relieve the German defenders of Komáromszentpéter. At 1100 hours the Soviet forces launched their renewed attack against Madar and Komáromszentpéter. They attacked the towns from the southwest, southeast and northeast.

The 1st and 3rd Battalions/6th Guards Motorized Rifle Brigade advanced in the first wave, the 2nd Battalion advanced in the second, with fire support provided by the reinforcing artillery units. Because of the German counterattacks, by 1600 the advance was only able to approach from the southwest to within 250 metres of Madar. Therefore, following further artillery preparations, a new attack was launched at 1900 hours, but it only advanced some 100 metres again, so it went over to the defensive on the ground it had already gained.

The 22nd Guards Tank Brigade attacked on the right flank of the 6th Guards Motorized Rifle Brigade, but 1.5km southeast of Madar it met one of the armoured *Kampfgruppen* of the *20. Panzer-Division,* which contained three *Panthers,* four *Panzer* IVs, a number of armoured personnel carriers, two infantry companies and a *Flak* company. The Soviet brigade, with six tanks, engaged the Germans, and sent one platoon (with three tanks) circling round Hills 136 and 216 against the northwestern part of Madar, in order to join the 391st Guards Anti-Tank Artillery Regiment in striking a blow against the German supply lines. However, the Germans destroyed one of the T–34s at Hill 216. The other two were abandoned by their crews, who joined the main body of the brigade on foot. After this, the tank brigade went over to the defensive in the area of Hill 136 together with 6th Guards Motorized Rifle Brigade.

On the left flank of the Motorized Rifle Brigade, the 21st Guards Tank Brigade advanced, but its advance was also brought to a halt within a short time. By 1330 hours the forces of the 46th Guards Tank Brigade and the 31st Guards Mechanized Brigade had approached to within 1km of Komáromszentpéter from the south, but there ran into 20-25 German tanks and *Jagdpanzers,* 30 armoured personnel carriers and strong artillery fire, and were, therefore, similarly, forced to go over to the defensive.

In the fighting on 12 January, the 5th Guards Tank Corps came up against a total of 15 German armoured fighting vehicles and 20 armoured personnel carriers. In these actions the corps claimed destruction of four enemy tanks, two *Jagdpanzers,* one machine gun and more than 150 soldiers. Its own losses consisted of one tank destroyed and three knocked

204 After-action report of the 5th Guards Tank Corps, 1-31 January 1945 (copy owned by the author), p.9-10.
205 The regrouping of the *20. Panzer-Division* (with a total of 70 trains) was finished that day.

out, two 120mm mortars, and approximately 40 men.[206] The Germans, at the same time, claimed to have knocked out six Soviet tanks during the tank battle.[207]

The commander of 6th Guards Tank Army reinforced the units fighting around Komáromszentpéter with an artillery regiment from his own reserves; the regiment was equipped with 100mm 1944 M BS-3 anti-tank guns.[208]

The armoured *Kampfgruppe* of the *20. Panzer-Division* that spent the night at Madar was running out of fuel, because Soviet forces managed to cut the *Kampfgruppe*'s supply lines with an attack carried out the day before from Perbete toward Újgyalla. In the course of the night, the German supply vehicles got stuck in the snowy-muddy terrain, since they could not use the roads controlled by the Soviets

Despite the insufficient fuel supplies, after the armoured *Kampfgruppe* repulsed the tank-supported attacks launched against Madar from the southwest and east, it continued its advance toward Bátorkeszi with *Panzer-Aufklärungs-Abteilung 20*. German reconnaissance reported only small forces in the village. The Germans therefore planned to take Bátorkeszi and then turn toward Dunamocs.

The 18th Guards Mechanized Brigade/9th Guards Mechanized Corps held Perbete against the attack of 8-10 tanks and 12 armoured personnel carriers of the *20. Panzer-Division*. The 30th Guards Mechanized Brigade prepared to defend Bátorkeszi.[209]

According to German sources, a *Kampfgruppe* of the Hungarian Division "*Szent László*", with a combat strength of only 125 men, still fought around Kürt in the defence of the German blocking position.[210]

North of Németszőgyén, at 0900 hours, after an artillery preparation, the 14th Guards Mechanized Brigade and the 36th Guards Tank Brigade/4th Guards Mechanized Corps launched an attack toward Kollerpuszta, which was captured by the 36th Guards Tank Brigade in bitter fighting. At 1130 hours the Germans counterattacked with four armoured fighting vehicles, three armoured personnel carriers and two companies of infantry, but were repulsed. Soviet troops also penetrated Bart for a short time, but the *211. Volksgrenadier-Division* carried out countermeasures and eliminated the attempt.

The Soviet forces had reached the end of their strength. At 1500 hours the troops of the 24th Guards Rifle Corps went over to the defensive. At 1700 hours the 4th Guards Mechanized Corps received the pertinent order from the 6th Guards Tank Army.[211] Thus

---

206 After-action report of the 5th Guards Tank Corps, 1-31 January 1945 (copy owned by the author), p.10. *Major* Hein, commander of the *II. Bataillon/Panzergrenadier-Regiment 112* was also wounded during that day's fighting.

207 On 12 January, *LVII. Panzerkorps* claimed to have knocked out a total of nine Soviet armoured fighting vehicles.

208 Zavizion & Kornyushin, 1967, p.149. The projectile could penetrate 185mm thick armour at a range of 1000 metres at a 60 degree angle of impact. This was sufficient to destroy any German armoured fighting vehicle. 591 of these guns were produced during the Second World War. Of these, 185 were in the field in January 1945. An anti-tank artillery regiment at full strength had 16 such guns.

209 After-action report of the 9th Guards Mechanized Corps of the operations in the direction of Komárom–Érsekújvár in January 1945 (copy owned by the author), p.21.

210 HM HIM *Hadtörténelmi Levéltár* (Budapest) microfilm archives, *Kriegstagebuch Ia der Heeresgruppe Süd, Kriegstagebuch vom 12. 1. 1945* (roll no. 627. image no. 7212114). Although this is not confirmed by Hungarian sources, situation maps of the German *OKH* indicate the division's presence, even after 7 January.

211 Summarized report of the 4th Guards Mechanized Corps of the combat activity fought between 31 December 1944–16 January 1945 (copy owned by the author), p.5.

the blocking position of *211. Volksgrenadier-Division* held out.

On **13 January**[212], elements of the *153. Feldausbildings-Division/LXXII. Armeekorps*[213] and the *"Gneisenau"* battalions continued their attacks from Ógyalla toward the south. These forces overcame weak Soviet resistance and captured Kiskonkoly and Nagykonkoly along the Komárom – Érsekújvár railway line, then, during the afternoon, joined the forces of *8. Panzer-Division*[214] at Kolos farm that were advancing in the direction of Komárom. Elements of *Panzergrenadier-Regiment 28* attacked north-east with the support of three *Panther* tanks of the *I./Panzer-Regiment 10*, and destroyed two Soviet heavy tanks.[215] The main body of the *8. Panzer-Division* and elements of *Panzer-Abteilung* [216] were in combat west of Izsa. With this, the Germans managed to establish a continuous front line between Érsekújvár and Komárom.[217]

Starting at 1200 hours, the Soviet 5th Guards Tank Corps resumed the attack on Madar. The German defenders –seven armoured fighting vehicles and infantry amounting to two companies – claimed to have knocked out two of seven Soviet tanks that attacked the village. After three and a half hours of fighting, the 22nd Guards Tank Brigade was engaged 500 metres north of Hill 136, the 6th Guards Motorized Rifle Brigade was engaged in the southern outskirts of Madar, and the 21st Guards Tank Brigade was engaged 1km east of Újpuszta. The losses of the corps on that day included five knocked out T–34s (of which two had been destroyed), and battle casualties of six dead and 19 wounded. The Soviets claimed to have destroyed two German tanks, two *Jagdpanzers*, four armoured personnel carriers, and 100 German soldiers.

By 1630 hours, the troops of the 46th Guards Tank Brigade and 31st Guards Mechanized Brigade had reached the southeastern outskirts of Komáromszentpéter, but German armoured fighting vehicles and *Panzergrenadiers* halted their advance there. An hour later, 25 German tanks and *Jagdpanzers* launched a counterattack to drive the Soviet units back to the east. In this action, three M4A2 tanks of the 46th Guards Tank Brigade

212 In the morning the temperature was around 0° Celsius, the sky was clear. In some places the sun was also shining for short periods during the day.

213 The *153. Feldausbildungs-Division* had, on that day, four battalions of its own (two of medium strength, one average and one weak), one weak battalion formed from a non-commissioned officer training course (with a total infantry combat strength of approximately 1000 men), a weary and exhausted *Pionier* battalion, *Bataillon 7 "Gneisenau"/XVIII* (with a combat strength of approximately 300 men), the *Landeschützenbataillon 885* (with a combat strength of approximately 200 men), a heavy anti-tank gun and two light artillery batteries from the *357. Infanterie-Division*.

214 Almost all units of the *8. Panzer-Division* had been attached to the *20. Panzer-Division*. The forces of *Generalmajor* von Roden included the following units: the exhausted *II. Bataillon/Panzergrenadier-Regiment 93* and the *Maschinengewehr-Bataillon "Sachsen"*, the *Bataillon 16 "Gneisenau"/XVII* (with a combat strength of approximately 100 men), the *Bataillon 2 "Gneisenau"/XVIII* (with a combat strength of approximately 400 men), a Hungarian alarm-battalion (with a combat strength of approximately 300 men), two combat-ready own *Panzer* IVs and three *Panther* tanks, five combat-ready *Panzer* IV/70 (V) *Jagdpanzers* from *Panzerjäger-Abteilung 13*, the forces of *Panzer-Abteilung 208*, two light batteries of the *II. (Abteilung)/Panzer-Artillerie-Regiment 80*, and one weak and one strong battery of *Artillerie-Abteilung 6*. The infantry combat strength was approximately 900 men.

215 Haupt, 1987, p.384. These heavy tanks were, presumably, some of the still operational IS–2 heavy tanks of the 49th Guards Heavy Tank Regiment/6th Guards Tank Army.

216 Di Giusto, 2010, p.148.

217 In the evening, fighting was going on 5-6km from the northern part of Komárom.

were knocked out.[218]

32 submachine gun infantrymen and four M17 self-propelled anti-aircraft heavy machine guns of the Motorized Rifle Battalion/20th Guards Tank Brigade – altogether, the tiny reserve of the corps – prepared defence positions in the northwestern outskirts of Búcs. The 15th Guards Motorcycle Battalion was stationed at Bátorkeszi, the 4th Guards Signals Battalion and the 21st Guards Engineer Battalion at Búcs.

In the early hours of 13 January, the armoured *Kampfgruppe* of the *20. Panzer-Division*[219] encountered bitter resistance from the Soviet 409th Rifle Division, 2km east of Madar, and was thus forced to turn north. After this the German armoured *Kampfgruppe* – according to Soviet forces, 42 tanks and 20 armoured personnel carriers – knocked out a tank and eliminated the Soviet defenders in Szentisztvánpuszta; the Germans turned southeast, captured Antalháza and point no. 188 south of there.

It is typical of the bitterness of the fighting that the commander of *Panzer-Regiment 21, Oberstleutnant* Voß, was also wounded (the division lost 12 other officers: three were killed, and nine wounded).

At the same time, a German *Panzergrenadier Kampfgruppe* pushed east through the wood north of Madar, thereby cutting the supply lines of the Soviet forces defending Perbete (among others the 18th Guards Mechanized Brigade). The Germans learned from an intercepted Soviet radio message that the troops defending the village[220] were going to try to break out and escape to the east during the night. The 18th Guards Mechanized Brigade, together with the 458th Guards Mortar Regiment and the 388th Guards Anti-Aircraft Artillery Regiment, did, indeed, carry out the anticipated escape, and retreated to Antalháza along the road to Bátorkeszi. In the course of the breakout the Soviets lost nine dead, 19 wounded[221], one 45mm gun and one anti-tank battery's equipment.

Panzergrenadier-Regiment 98 launched an attack from the area of Kürt toward the south in order to join the armoured *Kampfgruppe* of the *20. Panzer-Division*; then, with combined forces, they were to attack toward Bátorkeszi.

Only one Soviet attempt was launched with a company-sized unit against the front line of the *211. Volksgrenadier-Division*[222], north of Németszőgyén, but this was repelled

218 After-action report of the 5th Guards Tank Corps, 1-31 January 1945 (copy owned by the author), p.11.

219 The *20. Panzer-Division* had, on that day, two still combat-ready *Panzer* III command tanks, 28 *Panzer* IV and 21 *Panther* tanks, two *Flak-Panzer* IV anti-aircraft armoured vehicles, 14 heavy anti-tank guns and 12 *Jagdpanzer* IV tank destroyers. Of the latter, five armoured fighting vehicles were attached to the *211. Volksgrenadier-Division*. The four own *Panzergrenadier* battalions and one *Panzer-Aufklärungs-Abteilung* of the division had a total of approximately 1300 men combat strength. The *Panzer-Pionier-Abteilung* had approximately 400 soldiers. The four *Panzergrenadier*-battalions and one *Panzer-Pionier-Abteilung* that were attached to the *8. Panzer-Division* did not have more than 400 men combat strength. The artillery of the division consisted of three light and four heavy batteries, three *Wespe* and *Hummel* self-propelled howitzers of the *8. Panzer-Division*, two of the five 15cm towed field howitzers and two 10cm guns.

220 Besides the 18th Guards Mechanized Brigade the following units were engaged in battle here: 1st Battalion/675th Rifle Regiment of the 409th Rifle Division, 2nd Battalion/677th Rifle Regiment of the 409th Rifle Division, the training Company of the division, and the 1243rd Rifle Regiment/375th Rifle Division.

221 Colonel Denisov, commander of the 1243rd Rifle Regiment was also wounded.

222 The *211. Volksgrenadier-Division* had six *Grenadier* battalions, one rifle battalion, an exhausted *Pionier*-battalion and the training battalion, totalling no more than 1300 men. *Panzer-Aufklärungs-Abteilung 6* was fighting with approximately 200 men. Besides the attached *Jagdpanzers* there were seven heavy anti-tank guns in combat-ready condition available for the formation. Its own artillery consisted of nine light

by the defenders.

On **14 January**[223], the forces attached to the 8. *Panzer-Division/LXXII. Armeekorps* attacked east from the Komárom bridgehead, broke through an anti-tank position on the front line of the 53rd Rifle Division, then recaptured Izsa and Patpuszta (the latter without enemy contact). The Soviet forces quickly retreated and evacuated the area between Ó-Zsitva and the Danube. *Panzer-Abteilung 208* pursued them, but was forced to stop at the south bank of the Ó-Zsitva, because the retreating Soviets had demolished the bridge.[224]

During the afternoon, the *153. Feldausbildungs-Division* recaptured Hetény from the northeast, together with elements of the *"Gneisenau"* battalions and then continued to advance to the east. Northwest of Marcelkeszi the Soviet 375th Rifle Division stopped the Germans, who were equipped with 10 armoured fighting vehicles and a battalion-sized infantry unit.

As ordered by the Staff of the Soviet 5th Guards Tank Corps, during the night of 13/14 January the elements set up a firm defensive line running Miklósházapuszta-Hill 163-southwestern slope of Hill 216-Hill 136-2km southeast Madar.

By 1400 hours in the afternoon, the forces had taken their positions on the designated areas. The 21st Guards Tank Brigade (seven tanks and a combat strength of 42 men) was defending in the northern outskirts of Bátorkeszi with front lines facing north and northwest. The 22nd Guards Tank Brigade (eight tanks and 15 men) prepared for further combat 1.5km east of Hill 165 and on the hill with a front line facing east, with the mission of preventing the Germans from entering Bátorkeszi.

The 6th Guards Motorized Rifle Brigade organized for defence with 316 men[225], four 76.2mm guns, three 45mm anti-tank guns, two 120mm and 16 82mm mortars, nine 14.5mm anti-tank rifles, one Maxim machine gun and 11 light machine guns. The brigade was reinforced by the 1426th Light Artillery Regiment, the 454th Guards Mortar Regiment and the 127th Guards Mortar Artillery Battalion. The brigade's defensive line ran Hill 216-point no. 136-2kms southeast of Madar, in order to cover the Madar-Bátorkeszi road.

The 15th Guards Motorcycle Battalion (with four operational tanks on their strength) also defended Bátorkeszi. The 32 submachine gunners of the Motorized Rifle Battalion/20th Guards Tank Brigade, the four M17 self-propelled heavy machine guns of the Anti-Aircraft Company/20th Guards Tank Brigade, as well as the 4th Guards Signals Battalion (with two tanks) were still in Búcs, and the 21st Guards Engineer Battalion was stationed in Muzsla.[226]

By the morning of 14 January the *20. Panzer-Division* captured Perbete and Újgyalla. During this mission, the formation claimed to have knocked out four Soviet armoured fighting vehicles and captured one. The formation's armoured *Kampfgruppe* shattered the Soviet anti-tank front line northwest of Bátorkeszi, and destroyed 16 Soviet anti-tank guns.

and two heavy batteries.

223 The temperature dropped in the morning to –5° Celsius. Combat activity was hindered occasionally by fog. During the day the sky was bright with no clouds, but the fog and the damp vapour remained.

224 Volleth, 1975.

225 Of this 89 were riflemen, 41 machine gunners, 12 submachine gunners, 35 anti-tank riflemen, 139 mortar and gun crew.

226 After-action report of the 5th Guards Tank Corps, 1-31 January 1945 (copy owned by the author), pp.11-12.

The Soviets had established this anti-tank position to cover the withdrawal of the 18th Guards Mechanized Brigade breaking out of Perbete.

The armoured fighting vehicles of the *20. Panzer-Division* established communications with the *Kampfgruppe* of *Panzergrenadier-Regiment 98/8. Panzer-Division* along the line Madar southeastern edge – Antalháza southeast Hill 188 – Kürt southeast.[227]

In the latter half of the day, 35 German tanks and a battalion of *Panzergrenadiers* attacked toward Bátorkeszi from the direction of Hill 165, but the counterattack of Soviet artillery and tanks repulsed this attempt. According to Soviet sources, the *20. Panzer-Division* suffered serious losses: five knocked out tanks, two destroyed armoured personnel carriers and heavy battle casualties. At around 1430 hours, a German *Panzergrenadier* company and three tanks attempted to attack again from point no. 216. However, after losing two tanks they were driven back to their point of departure.[228]

In the early morning hours, according to German sources, the armoured *Kampfgruppe* of the *8. Panzer-Division* (including the *Panther* tanks of the *I. Abteilung/Panzer-Regiment 10*), was attacked southeast of Antalháza by 40 Soviet armoured fighting vehicles[229] coming from the area of point no. 188. The concentrated fire of *Panzer-Artillerie-Regiment 80* repelled the attack, and the Germans knocked out one tank. After this, the Soviet tanks abandoned the fight and retreated to the east; then they distributed themselves evenly along their designated line of defence.

At 1120 hours, upon receiving the order to go over to the defensive, the 9th Guards Mechanized Corps defended the northern and western parts of Kisújfalu with its 18th Guards Mechanized Brigade, the western edges of the small wood north of Köbölkút with its 31st Guards Mechanized Brigade, and Köbölkút with its 30th Guards Mechanized Brigade and 14th Guards Motorcycle Battalion.

The 46th Guards Tank Brigade handed over all its remaining M4A2 tanks to the 84th Guards Tank Regiment/30th Guards Mechanized Brigade, and its personnel marched to Ipolykiskeszi.

According to Soviet sources, the reconnaissance unit of the 14th Guards Motorcycle Battalion pushed the Germans out of Antalháza, where they counted eight German tanks that had been knocked out earlier, 11 destroyed armoured personnel carriers and 300 German soldiers.[230]

Korpsgruppe "Kirchner" was now fighting on a continuous front line against the forces of the Soviet 6th Guards Tank Army and the 7th Guards Army. Behind the German lines the elimination of the trapped fragments of the scattered Soviet units also began. *LVII. Panzerkorps* wanted to establish a securing line between Dunamocs and Madar in order to prevent fire on the refineries at Komárom. Dunamocs, however, was not yet in German hands, and it seemed that the Soviets were working on a new blocking position between the

227 HM HIM *Hadtörténelmi Levéltár* (Budapest) microfilm archives, *Kriegstagebuch Ia der Heeresgruppe Süd, Kriegstagebuch vom 14. 1. 1945* (roll no. 627. image no. 7212151).

228 After-action report of the 5th Guards Tank Corps, 1-31 January 1945 (copy owned by the author), p.12. The heavy German losses suffered that day are confirmed by the unit history of the *20. Panzer-Division*, but unfortunately no exact data are given. See Hinze, 1991, p.330.

229 This would only have been possible if all of the armoured fighting vehicles of the 21st Guards, the 22nd Guards, the 46th Guards Tank Brigades and the 31st Guards Mechanized Brigade had been deployed at the same time.

230 After-action report of the 9th Guards Mechanized Corps of the operations in the direction of Komárom–Érsekújvár in January 1945 (copy owned by the author), pp.24-24/a.

village and Bátorkeszi.

On this day, the right flank forces of the *211. Volksgrenadier-Division* prepared to clear the wooded terrain northwest of Németszőgyén.

During the day, the Soviet 5th Air Army flew 725 sorties, but the majority of these were not aimed at the area of the tank battle around Komárom. The Soviets observed 40 enemy aircraft sorties over the front line of the 2nd Ukrainian Front's sector, and claimed to have shot down eight aircraft, besides suffering two losses of their own.[231]

On **15 January**[232], the commander of *LVII. Panzerkorps,General der Panzertruppe* Kirchner, ordered his two *Panzer* divisions to carry out an attack with limited objectives.

The regrouped elements of *Panzergrenadier-Regiment 28* and *98/8. Panzer-Division*, together with *Panzer-Aufklärungs-Abteilung 8* – according to Soviet sources, with 30-40 tanks and *Jagdpanzers*[233] – launched an attack from the area of Komáromszentpéter toward the southeast. The Germans recaptured Szilasháza, entered Marcelkeszi, and reached the area 2km east of the latter.[234] A *Panzer* IV tank of the *3. Kompanie/Panzer-Abteilung 208* was knocked out by the Soviets at Szedmerőcpuszta between Marcelkeszi and Hetény; the tank burnt out. A number of *Panzer* IV/70 (A) *Jagdpanzers* of the *1. Kompanie* slipped off the icy road.[235]

A group of German armoured fighting vehicles advanced into the area of point no. 140 (Basa Hill), 2.5km north of Vértpuszta, which was defended by the units of the Soviet 53rd Rifle Division.

During the day the 22nd Guards Tank Brigade was ordered by the commander of the 5th Guards Tank Corps to turn over its front line sector and its remaining tanks to the 21st Guards Tank Brigade, and then regroup at Búcs. The latter large military unit established defensive positions together with the 391st Guards Anti-Tank Artillery Regiment 1.2km east of Hill 165 and in the northern outskirts of Bátorkeszi.

The armoured *Kampfgruppe* of the *20. Panzer-Division*[236] (15 tanks and armoured personnel carriers) set off from the western outskirts of Madar toward Bátorkeszi, but was engaged by 15 tanks of the 21st Guards Tank Brigade 3km southeast of Madar.

During the day, the following units were attached to the *20. Panzer-Division*: the two *Panzergrenadier*-regiments and *Panzer-Aufklärungs-Abteilung 8/8. Panzer-Division*, the *I. Bataillon/Grenadier-Regiment 717* of the *153. Feldausbildungs-Division*, and *Bataillon 14. "Gneisenau"/XVII.*

231 HM HIM *Hadtörténelmi Levéltár (Budapest), Szovjet iratmásolatok gyűjteménye a Budapest körüli harcokról. A 2. Ukrán Front hadijelentései. 1945/58-59.*

232 In the early morning the temperature was –10°, but warmed up to –2° Celsius. The weather was still foggy.

233 The *8. Panzer-Division* had on that day four *Panzer* IIs (of this, 1 was combat-ready), 15 (three) *Panzer* IVs, 37 (eight) *Panther* tanks, two (one) *Panzer* III command tank and four (one) *Panzer* IV command tanks. One *Bergepanzer* III and three (two) *Bergepanthers* served as armoured recovery vehicles. The strength of the attached *Panzer-Abteilung* 208 consisted of the following: 20 (16 combat-ready) *Panzer* IV tanks and nine (seven) *Panzer* IV/70 (A) *Jagdpanzers*.

234 Haupt, 1987, p.384.

235 Di Giusto, 2010, pp.200, 206.

236 The *20. Panzer-Division* had in its strength the following armoured fighting vehicles: 37 (of these, 25 were in combat-ready condition) *Panzer* IVs, 34 (22) *Panther* tanks, one (one) command *Panzer* III tank, six (four) command *Panzer* IV tanks, and four (two) *Flak-Panzer* IV armoured anti-tank vehicles. Two *Bergepanzer* IIIs and two *Bergepanthers* served as armoured recovery vehicles.

At about 1400 hours the Germans launched a fruitless attack with the strength of one and a half battalions and 10-15 armoured fighting vehicles against the positions of the 6th Guards Motorized Rifle Brigade. Soviet losses totalled one dead, two wounded men and three knocked out cars.

The *II. Bataillon/Panzergrenadier-Regiment 112* launched three consecutive attacks against Bátorkeszi with support of three to four tanks, but was repelled each time by the fire of the anti-tank positions established by the Soviet 391st Guards Anti-Tank Artillery Regiment on the northeastern edge of the town.

The 5th Guards Tank Corps claimed to have knocked out a total of three German tanks and to have destroyed one on 15 January. On the same day the corps' own 1458th self-propelled Artillery Regiment also arrived, with 18 operational SU–76M self-propelled guns. These armoured fighting vehicles were ordered to Búcs, for the time being, where they were put into the corps reserve.[237]

At 2035 hours in the evening, *Generalleutnant* Grolman told the Chief of Staff of *Armeegruppe "Balck"* that, in consequence of the rapid advance of Soviet forces between the Vistula and the Oder, he could expect the withdrawal of *20.* and *8. Panzer-Divisions*, which would, possibly, be transferred to the front lines where needed. These forces were to be relieved by the *44. Reichsgrenadier-Division "Hoch und Deutschmeister"*, that is, by an infantry formation detached from the *2. Panzerarmee.*[238] Considering, also, the departure of the majority of armoured forces, this would have meant the end of the German counteroffensive.

During the night of **15/16 January**[239], the forces attached to the *8. Panzer-Division* – according to Soviet sources, 20 tanks and *Jagdpanzers* – repelled an attack by the 375th and the 53rd Rifle Divisions/25th Guards Rifle Corps at the right flank of the Soviet Corps against the area bordered by the line Óriáspuszta – Hill 165 – point no. 136 – point no. 121 line, and against the area bordered by point no. 115 – Vértpuszta on the left flank. By morning, the German units occupied Vértpuszta.

Behind the left flank of the 53rd Rifle Division, the 18 SU–76M self-propelled guns of the 1458th self-propelled Artillery Regiment established firing positions along the line point no. 125 – Szentjánospuszta – point no. 120. Theseven T–34s of the 21st Guards Tank Brigade from Bátorkeszi were ordered there as well. A tank/self-propelled gun formation was formed from the armoured fighting vehicles and was placed under command of Guards Lieutenant Colonel I.K. Ostapenko.

The armoured *Kampfgruppe* of the *20. Panzer-Division* launched an attack with artillery support at 0730 hours – according to Soviet sources, they had 20 tanks and 10 armoured personnel carriers – against the 6th Guards Motorized Rifle Brigade/5th Guards Tank Corps. The Germans captured Hill 216 and point no. 136, and pushed the Soviet infantry troops back down their eastern slopes.

Following this, the armoured *Kampfgruppe*, coming from the southwest, reached

237 After-action report of the 5th Guards Tank Corps, 1-31 January 1945 (copy owned by the author), p.12.

238 HM HIM *Hadtörténelmi Levéltár* (Budapest) microfilm archives, *Kriegstagebuch Ia der Heeresgruppe Süd, Kriegstagebuch vom 15. 1. 1945* (roll no. 627. image no. 7212161).

239 During the day the temperature was –8° Celsius, the sky was generally bright, but fog reduced visibility in certain locations.

the north bank of the Danube. At 1130 hours two German battalions and 10 tanks, with artillery support, attacked toward Dunamocs, and soon captured Szentjánospuszta, near the village, in bitter fighting. The armoured fighting vehicles of Guards Lieutenant Colonel I.K. Ostapenko, however, carried out countermeasures and forced the Germans back.

The forces of the armoured *Kampfgruppe* of the *8. Panzer-Division* also reached the north bank of the Danube from the direction of Szilasháza. They then turned west and occupied Dunaradvány; according to Soviet sources, they had 35 tanks and *Jagdpanzers*, as well as 10 armoured personnel carriers. At about 2030 hours, 12 tanks set off from the village toward Dunamocs. Another 10 armoured fighting vehicles and an infantry unit the size of a regiment advanced again toward Szentjánospuszta. The elements of 53rd Rifle Division immediately retreated. The tanks and self-propelled guns of Guards Lieutenant General I.K. Ostapenko, which the German Grenadiers almost encircled, as they were lacking infantry support, chose to withdraw to the area 500 metres northeast of Dunamocs.

The Soviets knocked out one of the *Panzer* IV tanks of the *Panzer-Abteilung 208* that were attached to the *8. Panzer-Division*. One crew member was killed, four wounded. Two other tanks transported them to the rear.[240]

From the after-action report of the *Heeresgruppe Süd* and the history of the *20. Panzer-Division* it can be determined that, on this day, Dunamocs was also taken by the Germans, although this was not reported by the 2nd Ukrainian Front until a day later.[241]

At the end of the day, the 6th Guards Motorized Rifle Brigade/5th Guards Tank Corps was fighting on the line Bátorkeszi north-northwest – southeastern slope of point no. 136 – 2km southeast of Madar. The 21st Guards Tank Brigade defended the northern outskirts of Bátorkeszi with 10 T–34 tanks and the 391st Guards Anti-Tank Artillery Regiment, and was fighting in the area of Szentjánospuszta and Dunamocs with seven tanks and the 1458th Self-Propelled Artillery Regiment.

On this day, the Soviet corps lost three knocked out SU–76M self-propelled guns (of which one was destroyed), one 45mm and two 76.2mm anti-tank guns, one machine gun, five dead and 16 wounded men. The Soviets reported that they had caused the loss of three destroyed *Jagdpanzers* and approximately 100 men.[242]

During the day, German infantry attacking from the west recaptured Marcelkeszi and continued to advance to the east. In these combat actions the Germans captured 10 artillery pieces and one anti-tank gun.

The Soviets launched an unsuccessful counterattack 3km south of Madar. They carried out an attempt with a battalion-sized unit west of Bátorkeszi, which was also supported by armoured fighting vehicles, but this had no results either. South of Kürt the Germans gained approximately 2km of ground.

The German fighter and ground attack aircraft of the *I. Fliegerkorps/4. Luftflotte* again supported the attack of *Armeegruppe "Kirchner"*. Soviet reports state that formations of 6-18 aircraft carried out approximately 100 sorties against the combat forces of the 7th Guards Army and 6th Guards Tank Army, as well as Soviet forces crossing the Garam at

240 Volleth, 1975.

241 HM HIM *Hadtörténelmi Levéltár* (Budapest) microfilm archives, *Kriegstagebuch Ia der Heeresgruppe Süd, Kriegstagebuch vom 16. 1. 1945* (roll no. 627. image no. 7212372), and Hinze, 1991, p.331. See also HM HIM *Hadtörténelmi Levéltár (Budapest), Szovjet iratmásolatok gyűjteménye a Budapest körüli harcokról. A 2. Ukrán Front hadijelentései. 1945/70.*

242 After-action report of the 5th Guards Tank Corps, 1-31 January 1945 (copy owned by the author), p.13.

Kémend and Kőhídgyarmat. The Soviet 5th Air Army carried flew 532 sorties and claimed to have shot down 22 enemy aircraft as opposed to the loss of two of its own.[243]

At 1400 hours, *Armeegruppe "Balck"* received a telegram order to relieve the two *Panzer* divisions of *LVII. Panzerkorps* as quickly as possible in exchange for the *44. Reichsgrenadier-Division "Hoch und Deutschmeister"*, and to transport them as soon as possible to *Heeresgruppe A,* which was in an extraordinarily difficult situation.

Assuming the possibility of entraining six trainloads per day, the grenadier division could not have been expected to completely arrive before 22 January at the earliest. At 1930 hours *Generalleutnant* Grolman ordered *Armeegruppe "Balck"* to prepare for the withdrawal of the *20. Panzer-Division* in the evening of 17 January. The first unit to be relieved was *Panzerjäger-Abteilung 92*, elements of *Panzer-Pionier-Bataillon 92* and an *Abteilung* of *Panzer-Artillerie-Regiment 92*.[244]

Early in the morning **of 17 January**[245], the armoured *Kampfgruppen* of the *8*. and *20. Panzer-Division*s continued their attacks. This time the armoured fighting vehicles pushed forward from Dunamocs toward the northeast but did not get far. Although, initially, the German attack went well[246], a counterattack by Soviet forces stopped their advance directly east of the village; they also encountered a large number of armoured fighting vehicles. According to German reports, 20 Soviet armoured fighting vehicles outflanked the the Germans on their left and launched an assault from the northwest toward Dunamocs. The manoeuvre, however, failed when the Germans claimed to have destroyed 11 Soviet armoured fighting vehicles without losing any of their own vehicles. Of these, four were destroyed by the *Panzer* IV/70 (A) *Jagdpanzers* of the *1. Kompanie/Panzer-Abteilung 208* that was securing at Szentjánospuszta.[247]

According to the unit history of the *20. Panzer-Division*, on this day its elements knocked out 15 Soviet armoured fighting vehicles, among them M4A2s. According to German observations, the Soviet crew members did not trust the American tanks, and, on more than one occasion, abandoned the vehicles when they were hit by rounds that did not even penetrate the armour.[248]

Although German losses were not heavy, many of the armoured personnel carriers of *Panzer-Aufklärungs-Abteilung 8* were rendered unfit for combat, and one of the most effective officers of the *I. Abteilung/Panzer-Regiment 10, Leutnant* Carl Loos, was seriously

243 HM HIM *Hadtörténelmi Levéltár (Budapest), Szovjet iratmásolatok gyűjteménye a Budapest körüli harcokról. A 2. Ukrán Front harcjelentései 1945/67.*

244 HM HIM *Hadtörténelmi Levéltár* (Budapest) microfilm archives, *Kriegstagebuch Ia der Heeresgruppe Süd, Kriegstagebuch vom 16. 1. 1945* (roll no. 628. image no. 7212378).

245 During the day the temperature was –9° Celsius. The sky was covered with thick layers of clouds, and it occasionally snowed.

246 According to a report given at 0925 hours, the two armoured *Kampfgruppen* had already knocked out three tanks and seized 16 anti-tank guns, 14 mortars and 40 machine guns. The Germans counted the bodies of 800 dead Soviet soldiers. See HM HIM *Hadtörténelmi Levéltár* (Budapest) microfilm archives, *Kriegstagebuch Ia der Heeresgruppe Süd, Kriegstagebuch vom 17. 1. 1945* (roll no. 628. image no. 7212387). This – excluding the tanks – could be losses of the 53rd Rifle Division, which was retreating in a disorganized manner.

247 Di Giusto, 2010, p.206.

248 Hinze, 1991, p.331.

wounded.[249]

According to German data the infantry that were attached to the *8. Panzer-Division* took a farm 2.5km northwest of Dunamocs after heavy fighting. The Soviets committed 20 tanks and self-propelled guns to try to recapture this cluster of buildings, but the Germans prevented them, knocking out five armoured fighting vehicles.

The Soviets initiated company- and battalion-sized attacks northwest of Bátorkeszi (as well as north-northwest of Németszőgyén). However, the Germans repulsed them, and knocked out one of the supporting tanks.[250]

The after-action report of the 5th Guards Tank Corps discusses the details of these combat actions around Bátorkeszi, rather than the tank battle around Dunamocs. According to that, the Germans – presumably units of *Panzergrenadier-Regiment 112/20. Panzer-Division* – attacked the right flank of the 6th Guards Motorized Rifle Brigade and the positions of the 1243rd Rifle Regiment/375th Rifle Division[251] on their left at about 0900 hours in the morning. The attack was launched 1km northwest of Bátorkeszi with 150 infantry soldiers and four tanks.

As a result of this battle the 1243rd Rifle Regiment was forced to retreat to the northwestern part of the town, and the right flank of the 6th Guards Motorized Rifle Brigade was also pushed back 300 metres. At 1100 hours, the 6th Guards Motorized Rifle Brigade counterattacked with two tanks of the 15th Guards Motorcycle Battalion and with artillery and mortar fire support. It more or less recovered its previous positions, holding them against the new attempt by the German tanks at about 1600 hours.

Of the combat activity on the left flank of the corps, the after-action report only provides information from the afternoon, when the mixed tank/self-propelled gun formation of Guards Lieutenant Colonel I.K. Ostapenko was attacked by seven German tanks and a company-sized infantry unit at about 1630 hours, however, the Soviet armoured units beat off the attack. Within one and a half hours, the Germans again attacked from Dunamocs, this time forcing Ostapenko's armoured group back to the area of the woods north of the village and to the vineyards 1km northeast of point no. 125. The point fell into German hands. On the same day, six self-propelled guns (three of which burnt out) and 16 men were lost by the 1458th Self-Propelled Artillery Regiment of Guards Lieutenant Colonel I.K. Ostapenko.[252]

Following this, the German armoured *Kampfgruppe* continued its attack toward Búcs, but, at about 2300 hours, its vehicles were stopped by the fire of Soviet artillery at the northern edge of the woods, 2.5km north of Dunamocs. The defenders from 5th Guards Tank Corps claimed destruction of four German tanks and four *Jagdpanzers*.[253]

The commander of the 9th Guards Mechanized Corps had already ordered the

249 Haupt, 1987, pp.384-385. *Leutnant* Loos knocked out a total of 11 armoured fighting vehicles during the fighting east of Komárom. For this, see Kindel, 2007, p.623.

250 A day later, the war diary of *Heeresgruppe Süd* indicated 14 Soviet armoured fighting vehicles knocked out for 17 January. See HM HIM *Hadtörténelmi Levéltár* (Budapest) microfilm archives, *Kriegstagebuch Ia der Heeresgruppe Süd, Morgenmeldung vom 18. 1. 1945* (roll no. 627. image no. 7213011). Soviet sources do not mention such losses of their own in this period.

251 The after-action report mentions the "43rd Rifle Regiment" two times on that day. However, this unit belonged to the 106th Rifle Division, and never fought in Hungary. It is more likely that this is a typing error, and the entries concern the 1243rd Rifle Regiment/375th Rifle Division.

252 After-action report of the 5th Guards Tank Corps, 1-31 January 1945 (copy owned by the author), p.14.

253 After-action report of the 5th Guards Tank Corps, 1-31 January 1945 (copy owned by the author), p.14.

strengthening of the defences of Búcs. The 30th Guards Mechanized Brigade and the 697th Self-Propelled Artillery Regiment were ordered to move by forced march from Köbölkút to Búcs, where the defence was already organized as early as approximately 0700 hours on 17 January with southern and western facing front lines.[254]

During the day, *Korpsgruppe "Kirchner"* adjusted its internal boundaries. The following sector boundaries came into existence: between *LXXII. Armeekorps* and the *20. Panzer-Division*: the boundary now ran from Komáromszentpéter north to Madar south and Búcs north, and between the *20. Panzer-Division* and the *211. Volksgrenadier-Division* from Csúz to Köbölkút.

On the northern front of the Soviet bridgehead there had been no significant combat activity for several days. The two brigades of the 4th Guards Mechanized Corps (with its eight remaining T–34/85s) – with the 72nd Guards Rifle Division/24th Guards Rifle Corps on the right flank, and with the 6th Guards Airborne Division on the left – held their positions with the support of the seven operational T–34s and two SU–85s of the 27th Guards Tank Brigade. They faced the German *211. Volksgrenadier-Division*.[255] The eight tanks of the 36th Guards Tank Brigade/4th Guards Mechanized Corps were fighting in the following positions:

- Two tanks at Hill 177, 4km east of Németszőgyén;
- Four tanks at the northern edge of Bart;
- Two tanks at Hill 157 (Öreg Hill), 3km southeast of Bart.

On **18 January**[256] the *Schwerpunkt* of *Armeegruppe "Balck's"* endeavours was again transferred to the Dunántúl (Transdanubia), where Operation *"Konrad 3"* had just begun. The defenders in besieged Budapest had evacuated Pest. However, this did not mean that the Germans north of the Danube were abandoning the counteroffensive of *Korpsgruppe "Kirchner"*.

During the night of 17/ 18 January, elements of *8. Panzer-Division* were engaged in bitter fighting to clear the stretch of wooded terrain east and northeast of Dunamocs. This was essential in order to secure the supply lines of the armoured *Kampfgruppen*.

It was not until about 1000 hours in the morning that the two armoured *Kampfgruppen* resumed their attack. The *8. Panzer-Division* moved out with 15 tanks and *Jagdpanzers*, 10 armoured personnel carriers and a battalion-sized infantry unit toward Bátorkeszi. The Germans attacked with the 10 tanks of the *I./Panzer-Regiment 10* and a battalion-sized infantry unit from the *153. Feldausbildungs-Division*, and captured Lukavinipuszta, 3.5km northeast of Dunamocs in heavy fighting, after forcing back elements of of the 53rd Rifle Division. Six tanks of the Soviet 21st Guards Tank Brigade then began a counterattack from three directions, but were defeated, and the Germans knocked out three tanks. The remaining 12 T–34s of the Soviet Tank Brigade then defended the road from Dunamocs to Bátorkeszi, and Bátorkeszi itself, together with the 6th Guards Motorized Rifle Brigade,

254 After-action report of the 9th Guards Mechanized Corps of the operations in the direction of Komárom–Érsekújvár in January 1945 (copy owned by the author), p.25.

255 Summarized report of the 4th Guards Mechanized Corps of the combat activity fought between 31 December 1944.–16 January 1945 (copy owned by the author), p.3.

256 The temperature was -5° Celsius, clouds filled the sky, in places it snowed lightly.

the 391st Guards Anti-Tank Artillery Regiment and the 13 SU–76M self-propelled guns of the 1458th Self-Propelled Artillery Regiment. During that day's combat activities, six tanks of the 5th Guards Tank Corps were knocked out (four of the six were destroyed).[257]

The armoured *Kampfgruppe* of the *20. Panzer-Division* advanced east with 35 tanks and *Jagdpanzers*, 30 armoured personnel carriers and an infantry unit the size of a regiment. The Germans had to cross a minefield and an improvised anti-tank ditch.

At about 1500 hours, 21 tanks of the armoured *Kampfgruppe* and the supporting infantry occupied Mária farm and point no. 124. Then, at about 1700 hours, 20 tanks of *Panzer-Regiment 21* also recaptured Karva, Nagypuszta and Kollerpuszta from the 53rd Rifle Division with *Panzergrenadier* and *Panzer-Pionier* support. A platoon equipped with 2cm four-barrelled anti-aircraft cannon also took part in these combat activities, as well as flamethrowers of the *Panzer-Pioniers* and the armoured personnel carriers of the *Panzergrenadiers*. Where necessary, Soviet soldiers that had been left behind and were hiding in the buildings were "smoked out" with *Panzerfäuste*.

According to German sources the Soviet defenders suffered heavy losses of men and material around Karva. The attackers claimed to have knocked out, among others, 40 anti-tank guns and 16-18 armoured fighting vehicles.[258]

The advance troop of the armoured *Kampfgruppe* advanced in the Csenke wood, 5km east of the village. At the same time eight German tanks and six armoured personnel carriers pushed north, but they were soon halted by the six M4A2s and two 2 Valentine Mk IXs tanks of the 30th Guards Mechanized Brigade/9th Guards Mechanized Corps[259] and the 16 SU–76M self-propelled guns of the 697th Self-Propelled Artillery Regiment. The Soviet armoured fighting vehicles defended the southern outskirts of Búcs. The 14th Guards Motorcycle Battalion was assigned defence of Szentgyörgyhalom west of Muzsla.[260]

At about 1900 hours in the evening, the 27th Guards Tank Brigade (with seven operational T–34s and two SU–85 self-propelled guns) which was at Bart was transferred to the Csenke area for attachment to the 25th Guards Rifle Corps and to help the defenders eliminate the penetration by the German armoured *Kampfgruppe*.[261]

That, same day, the first elements of the 20. *Panzer-Division* began to be transported out of Hungary in five trains. Initially the *Führungsabteilung* [command section], *Panzer-Nachrichten-Abteilung 92*, *Panzer-Pionier-Bataillon 92*, elements of *Panzer-Artillerie-Regiment 92* and the supply elements departed.

After 2100 hours in the evening, in the course of a phone conversation with *Generalleutnant* Grolman, *General der Panzertruppe* Balck brought up the idea that the withdrawal and transfer of the *8.* and *20. Panzer-Divisions* might be postponed until a successful advance would provide possibilities of significantly reducing the Soviet bridgehead. Grolman conveyed Balck's suggestion to the *Oberkommando des Heeres*, and Guderian finally sent his approval via *General* Wöhler. The next unit to leave was *Flak-Abteilung 295/20. Panzer-Division*, then, according to the plans, the *Panzergrenadier*

257 After-action report of the 5th Guards Tank Corps, 1-31 January 1945 (copy owned by the author), p.14.

258 Hinze, 1991, p.331.

259 Full combat strength of the 30th Guards Mechanized Brigade was as little as 100 men.

260 After-action report of the 9th Guards Mechanized Corps of the operations in the direction of Komárom–Érsekújvár in January 1945 (copy owned by the author), p.25.

261 See Reports of the commander of the tank and mechanized units of the 7th Guards Army from January 1945 (copy owned by the author), Report nr. 018, 18 January 1945

regiments were to follow.[262]

That same day, *Heeresgruppe Süd* notified all of its three attached armies to follow the standard actions to be carried out when encountering knocked out Soviet armoured fighting vehicles:

> Your attention is called to the order that all enemy armoured fighting vehicles seized by our troops are to be destroyed, unless they can be towed away for repair and reuse by us or have been completely destroyed.[263]

This was especially important, as it meant that, in case the Soviets managed to recapture these vehicles in the course of a counterattack, they would not find any of their own vehicles that had been disabled but were repairable.

On **19 January**[264], *Korpsgruppe "Kirchner"* was disbanded. *LXXII. Armeekorps* was detached from*Armeegruppe "Balck"* and attached to the German *VIII. Armeekorps*. Thus, *General* Kirchner commanded only the operational activities of the *LVII. Panzerkorps*.

The armoured *Kampfgruppe* of the *20. Panzer-Division* – according to Soviet sources they had 50 tanks and *Jagdpanzers*, 20 armoured personnel carriers and a regiment-sized infantry unit – pushed further along the north bank of the Danube northeast from the Karva area, and reached Csenke. For the time being, Soviet resistance was limited to mortar, artillery and anti-tank gun fire.

The German armoured fighting vehicles turning north were already within 1.5km southwest of Muzsla, when they ran into a Soviet anti-tank position – presumably the position of the recently transferred 34th Anti-Tank Artillery Brigade. Soon they were also hit by a tank-supported counterattack. The Soviet 30th Guards Mechanized Brigade and 697th Self-Propelled Artillery Regiment, holding Kollerpuszta and Búcsipuszta, penetrated into the Csenke woods from the north, and got into the rear of the German armoured *Kampfgruppe*. They drove the Germans back to the area 1km east of Karva.

The attack of the armoured *Kampfgruppe* of the *20. Panzer-Division* was halted. The 30th Guards Mechanized Brigade lost five tanks, but claimed to have knocked out four German tanks and two *Jagdpanzers*, and to have caused 200 battle casualties on the German side.[265]

The same day, the 15th Guards Motorcycle Battalion (with four tanks), the 4th Guards Signal Battalion (with two tanks) and the 21st Guards Engineer Battalion were stationed in Muzsla. Five operational tanks and two self-propelled guns of the 27th Guards Tank Brigade went into defence on the southwestern edge of the village.

Certain elements of the *8. Panzer-Division* and parts of the *153. Feldausbildungs-Division* advanced northeast from the northern outskirts of Dunamocs and from Lukavinipuszta with 12 tanks and *Jagdpanzers* and infantry units the size of two battalions,

262 *Kriegstagebuch der Heeresgruppe Süd, Kriegstagebuch vom 18. 1. 1945* (roll no. 628. image no. 7212400).

263 *Kriegstagebuch der Heeresgruppe Süd, Ia 879/45 geh. vom 18. 1. 1945* (roll no. 628. image no. 7212649).

264 The highest temperature of the day was -4° Celsius, the sky was cloudy, in the afternoon light snowfall occurred.

265 After-action report of the 9th Guards Mechanized Corps of the operations in the direction of Komárom–Érsekújvár in January 1945 (copy owned by the author), p.26.

and managed to gain 3km.

The two T–34s of the 21st Guards Tank Brigade[266] that were guarding the road to Búcs, together with the 1458th Self-Propelled Artillery Regiment, attempted to force the Germans out of the newly captured areas, but they held their new positions firmly. One of the T–34s of the 21st Guards Tank Brigade was knocked out, a Soviet soldier was killed and another one was wounded. The 5th Guards Tank Corps reported German losses as two knocked out tanks, two *Jagdpanzers*, three armoured personnel carriers and 100 men.[267]

The *1. Kompanie/Panzer-Abteilung 208,* which took part in the attack, swiftly took the cluster of houses on the point no. 108 2km southeast of Búcs, and destroyed a number of Soviet anti-tank guns and SU–76M self-propelled guns.[268]

For the defence of Kisújfalu, the commander of the 9th Guards Mechanized Corps left only the 1st Motorized Rifle Battalion/18th Guards Mechanized Brigade and the 458th Guards Mortar Regiment. The main body of the brigade and the 34th Anti-Tank Artillery Brigade were transferred to the area of Búcsperespuszta and Szentgyörgyhalom.[269] In all probability, these were the forces that the armoured *Kampfgruppe* of the *20. Panzer-Division* ran into southwest of Muzsla, during the morning.

Generalleutnant Grolman called the attention of *Armeegruppe "Balck"* to the fact that their planned assault against the hills stretching west of Muzsla carried the risk that they might be unable to break through the hardening Soviet defence, in which case the armoured units would have to be regrouped, which would mean time was wasted. In this case it would be necessary to transfer *Panzergrenadier-Regiment 112*, which was then fighting northwest of Bátorkeszi. However, commitment of the regiment would require approval of the *Armeegruppe*! The reason for this was that the withdrawal and transfer of the *Panzer* divisions to *Heeresgruppe A* had been given priority over elimination of the Soviet bridgehead over the Garam.

In the early afternoon, *LVII. Panzerkorps* requested the transfer of *Panzergrenadier-Regiment 112*, but then *Armeegruppe "Balck"*, itself, saw that the deployment of the *Panzergrenadiers* would not change the operational situation developing north of the Danube significantly, and that their deployment "was not worth" the risk caused by the delayed transport. The Germans wanted to avoid the unnecessary loss of combat value caused to the *20. Panzer-Division*. The *Armeegruppe* did not completely abandon the idea of a further attack, but it would be carried out by the *44. Reichsgrenadier-Division "Hoch- und Deutschmeister"*, which was en route to the place.

However, by evening, *Armeegruppe "Balck"* had to admit that, after the withdrawal of the *Panzer* divisions, *LVII. Panzerkorps* would not have sufficient forces to eliminate the Soviet bridgehead. Thus, from then on, the *Armeekorps* was to defend the territory gained and to secure the north bank of the Danube, thus guarding the essential supply lines of the German *I. Kavalleriekorps* that was established at Lábatlan.[270]

During the day, another six trains left Hungary carrying various units of the *20. Panzer-Division*: units of the *Führungsabteilung*, *Panzer-Nachrichten-Abteilung 92*,

266 The other 10 tanks of the 21st Guards Tank Brigade were defending Bátorkeszi.

267 After-action report of the 5th Guards Tank Corps, 1-31 January 1945 (copy owned by the author), p.15.

268 Di Giusto, 2010, p.207.

269 After-action report of the 9th Guards Mechanized Corps of the operations in the direction of Komárom–Érsekújvár in January 1945 (copy owned by the author), p.26.

270 *Kriegstagebuch der Heeresgruppe Süd, Kriegstagebuch vom 19. 1. 1945* (roll no. 628. image no. 7212416).

Panzer-Pionier-Bataillon 92, elements of *Panzer-Artillerie-Regiment 92* and more of the supply train elements. On that day it became possible for certain units of *Panzerjäger-Abteilung 92* (equipped with *Jagdpanzer* IV tank destroyers) to be transported, because, in the meantime, *Panzerjäger-Abteilung/211. Volksgrenadier-Division* had received its 14 *Jagdpanzer* 38(t)s.[271]

At the same time, six trains arrived bringing elements of the *44. Reichsgrenadier-Division "Hoch- und Deutschmeister"*, intended to relieve the two *Panzer* divisions of *LVII. Panzerkorps*; the trains brought *Aufklärungs-Abteilung 44, Reichsgrenadier-Regiment "Hoch- und Deutschmeister"*, with elements of *Artillerie-Regiment 96* and *Panzerjäger-Abteilung*[272].

General der Panzertruppe Balck considered that, even after the transfer of the two *Panzer* divisions, the elimination of the Soviet bridgehead at the Garam should still be insisted upon.

The fifth stage of the battle: The end of the German counteroffensive (20-22 January 1945)

At dawn on **20 January**[273], the situation of the armoured *Kampfgruppe* of the *20. Panzer-Division* further worsened. The previous night, at about midnight, the Soviets launched an attack with ten 10 T–34s of the 21st Guards Tank Brigade, the 30th Guards Mechanized Brigade, and parts of the 18th Guards Mechanized Brigade 4km south of Búcs, thereby reaching the road that stretched along the northern bank of the Danube, west of Karva. Therefore, the relief of the assigned elements of the division could not be carried out by the troops of the *8. Panzer-Division*[274]. In the morning, elements of *Feldausbildungs-Bataillon* [275] were only able to repulse the Soviet forces that were thrusting against the flank of the *8. Panzer-Division* by a massive counterattack.

The previous day, at 2300 hours, the *8. Panzer-Division* attempted an attack from Mária farm toward Kollerpuszta with 10 tanks and a battalion-sized infantry-unit. The

271 Of the *Jagdpanzers,* 11 were in combat-ready condition on 20 January.

272 On 16 January, *Panzerjäger-Abteilung 46* had 12 combat-ready *Jagdpanzer* 38(t) tank destroyers and eight *Marder* II and III tank destroyers.

273 Mild frost, generally cloudy sky, restricted visibility conditions, only occasional sunshine; roads were ice-covered and hardly passable because of the fresh snow.

274 The *8. Panzer-Division* had its own *Panzer-Aufklärungs-Abteilung* with a combat strength of approximately 300 men; two of its *Panzergrenadier* battalions were attached to the *20. Panzer-Division*. Furthermore, *Generalmajor* von Roden had the following units and armoured fighting vehicles: the weak *II. Bataillon/Panzergrenadier-Regiment 93*, the exhausted *Bataillon 14 "Gneisenau"/XVII*, the *Maschinengewehr-Bataillon "Sachsen"*, which had also been seriously depleted, the *I. Abteilung/Panzer-Regiment 10* with two of its combat-ready *Panzer* IV tanks and seven *Panther* tanks, *Panzerjäger-Abteilung 43* with six combat-ready *Jagdpanzer* IV tank destroyers, *Panzer-Abteilung 208* with its 16 combat-ready *Panzer* IV tanks and *Panzer* IV/70 (A) *Jagdpanzers, Panzerjäger-Abteilung 13* with six combat-ready *Panzer* IV/70 (V) *Jagdpanzers*, one 7.5cm anti-tank gun and with two of its own light artillery batteries, furthermore, one light and one heavy battery of the *20. Panzer-Division* and the *Bataillon 6 "Gneisenau"/XVIII*, respectively. The division had an infantry combat strength totalling no more than 500 men. Regarding armoured strength, see *Bundesarchiv–Militärarchiv* (Freiburg im Breisgau), *RH 2 Ost Karte 5316 (Panzer-Lage am 20. Jan. 1945)*.

275 *Feldausbildungs-Bataillon 153* had three weak and one exhausted battalions of its own, and the exhausted *Landeschützenbataillon 885* (with an infantry combat strength of approximately 400 men altogether). Its anti-tank armament consisted of only two 76.2mm anti-tank guns seized from the Soviets. Its artillery comprised two light batteries of the *357. Infanterie-Division*.

attempt was repulsed by the forces of the 21st Guards Tank Brigade and the 30th Guards Mechanized Brigade – according to their own report, by destroying two German tanks.

At 0830 hours of that same day, the armoured *Kampfgruppe* of the division[276] renewed the attack with 30 tanks, *Jagdpanzers* and armoured personnel carriers.

The Soviet forces also repulsed this attempt, with the support of the 1458th Self-Propelled Artillery Regiment, although four SU–76Ms were destroyed in the action. According to the claims of the 5th Guards Tank Corps, the Germans lost six *Jagdpanzers* and six armoured personnel carriers, four guns, two light machine guns, one machine gun and 130 men.[277]

Since they had no other option, the cut-off armoured *Kampfgruppen* of the two *Panzer* divisions attacked west from around Karva, shattered the Soviet forces blocking the highway along the riverbank, and established a new front line northwest of Dunamocs. With the recapture of Karva, the Soviets could once again engage the German supply route by fire at Lábatlan.

The two armoured *Kampfgruppen* departed with 60 tanks, *Jagdpanzers* and armoured personnel carriers to recapture Karva. However, their efforts were unsuccessful. *LVII. Panzerkorps* claimed to have knocked out a total of 10 Soviet armoured fighting vehicles on this day.

By now the 6th Guards Tank Army had just 43 armoured fighting vehicles left.[278] However, the majority of these were not tanks, but SU–76M self-propelled guns, which had relatively low combat value compared to practically all the Germans' tanks and *Jagdpanzers*.

At about 1900 hours in the evening, the 10 T–34s of the 21st Guards Tank Brigade, together with 30th Guards Mechanized Brigade, stood between Likavinipuszta and point no. 108, ready to attack toward Dunamocs and Szentjánospuszta, and then farther to the west.[279]

During the day, it turned out that the staff of *LVII. Panzerkorps* was also to be transferred to *Heeresgruppe A*. Soon after, command and control of the forces north of the Danube was turned over to the staff of the *IV. Panzerkorps* (*General der Panzertruppe* Ulrich Kleemann). After 1900 hours, an order from the *Oberkommando des Heeres* arrived, according to which all armoured vehicles of the *20. Panzer-Division* – regardless of the attack against Karva – must be withdrawn, and directed via Perbete to the Érsekújvár railway station to entrain and be transported away.[280]

The withdrawal of the armoured *Kampfgruppe* was a huge loss to *LVII. Panzerkorps*, since, according to the data from that day, it weakened the German forces fighting in the area of Dunamocs and Karva by 25 combat-ready *Panzer* IV tanks and five *Panthers*.[281] The German armoured fighting vehicles leaving the area under cover of darkness experienced a strange situation:

276 The armoured *Kampfgruppe* comprised the main body of the *I. Abteilung/Panzer-Regiment 10* equipped with *Panther* and *Panzer* IV tanks, *Panzer-Aufklärungs-Abteilung 8*, elements of *Panzerjäger-Abteilung 43*, elements of *Flak-Abteilung 286* and a number of guns of *Panzer-Artillerie-Regiment 80*.

277 After-action report of the 5th Guards Tank Corps, 1-31 January 1945 (copy owned by the author), p.15.

278 *A második világháború története 1939–1945. Tizedik kötet.* (History of the Second World War 1939-1945. Volume 10) (Budapest, 1981), p.264.

279 After-action report of the 5th Guards Tank Corps, 1-31 January 1945 (copy owned by the author), p.15.

280 *Kriegstagebuch der Heeresgruppe Süd, Kriegstagebuch vom 20. 1. 1945* (roll no. 628. image no. 7212430).

281 *Bundesarchiv–Militärarchiv* (Freiburg im Breisgau), *RH 2 Ost Karte 5316 (Panzer-Lage am 20. Jan. 1945).*

"Our armoured forces passed by at least 20 T–34s in the darkness. Both sides avoided taking any action, even without any sort of previous negotiations. Both were equally exhausted and worn out, and neither had more ammunition or fuel than the other. There was an unspoken agreement between the two forces, arising out of pure necessity. That was more than rare, especially on the Eastern Front."[282]

While the Germans were gradually withdrawing their armoured fighting vehicles from the battle, the Soviets concentrated every remaining operational armoured fighting vehicle to reinforce the defences of their infantry. At 1600 hours, five T–34s and three SU–85s of the 27th Guards Tank Brigade were transferred from Muzsla and Ebed to reinforce the defenders of Búcs.[283]

During the night of 19/20 January, *Panzergrenadier-Regiment 112/20. Panzer-Division*, which was fighting in the area of Bátorkeszi, was relieved by the *II. Bataillon/ Reichsgrenadier-Regiment "Hoch- und Deutschmeister"*, which was, together with *Aufklärungs-Abteilung 44*, attached to the *Panzer*-division. The Soviets tried to obstruct these movements by pushing forward company-sized attacks from east of Madar, northwest of Bátorkeszi and south of Kürt, but the Germans repelled them. The main body of the *Panzergrenadier*-regiment and the elements of *Flak-Abteilung 295* set off toward Upper Silesia in nine trains that same day.

The northern section of the front line of the forces of the *Kampfgruppe* of the *8. Panzer-Division* was taken over by the *153. Feldausbildungs-Division.*[284]

At about 1740 hours, the *211. Volksgrenadier-Division* launched an attack with regiment-sized forces between Hills 156 and 238 and cleared the wooded terrain 3km northwest of Magyarszőgyén of the Soviet 17th Airborne Rifle Regiment/6th Guards Airborne Division, which retreated to the road leading to Magyarszőgyén.[285]

On **21 January**[286], at around 0900 hours, after a heavy artillery preparation, Guards Lieutenant Colonel Ostapenko's tank-self-propelled gun formation drove the Germans out of Szentjánospuszta, 4km northeast of Dunamocs. However, the advance of the Soviet tanks along the bank of the Danube was halted, so they established defence positions in the northwestern outskirts.

The German *Kampfgruppe* of the *8. Panzer-Division* soon recaptured Szentjánospuszta – according to Soviet data with 10 tanks and a battalion-sized infantry force. The Soviets maintained heavy resistance, but the Germans knocked out four SU–76Ms of the 1458th Self-Propelled Artillery Regiment. In the afternoon, the Soviets again tried to recapture the cluster of buildings, but when they approached the new German MLR, another two of their self-propelled guns took fatal hits. Guards Lieutenant Colonel Ostapenko therefore

282 Panzer-Regiment 21 im Ostfeldzug, manuscript, 1959, p.226.

283 See Reports of the commander of the tank and mechanized units of the 7th Guards Army from January 1945 (copy owned by the author) Report nr. 020, 20 January 1945

284 The *II. Bataillon/Grenadier-Regiment 176*, *Füsilier-Bataillon 153* and the *Alarmtruppen* of *Grenadier-Regiment 717*. The *I. Bataillon/Grenadier-Regiment 716* and the *II. Bataillon/Grenadier-Regiment 717* were securing the lines along the Zsitva.

285 Summarized report of the 4th Guards Mechanized Corps of the combat activity fought between 31 December 1944.–16 January 1945 (copy owned by the author), p.4.

286 Mild frost, fog and vapour during the morning, occasionally snowing, sunshine and little cloud cover during the afternoon.

withdrew his force back to Hill 124.

In the meantime, the hill was also assaulted by 10 German tanks, eight armoured personnel carriers and a company-sized infantry unit from Lukavinipuszta.

Guards Lieutenant Colonel Ostapenko's formation had dwindled to two T–34s and three SU–76Ms of the 1458th Self-Propelled Artillery Regiment (during the day six self-propelled guns had been knocked out, two of which burnt out). According to Soviet sources the Germans lost two tanks knocked out, four guns, two machine guns and 80 men in these actions.

In the meantime, the other eight tanks of the 21st Guards Tank Brigade and the 391st Guards Anti-Tank Artillery Regiment continued to defend the northwestern outskirts of Bátorkeszi; five repaired tanks also arrived there in the latter part of the day from the maintenance units. From this total of 13 T–34s, seven were sent by the commander of the 5th Guards Tank Corps to Guards Lieutenant Colonel Ostapenko's formation, while the 15th Guards Motorcycle Battalion (with four operational tanks in their strength) reinforced the 6th Guards Motorized Rifle Brigade.[287]

In the late night hours, a Soviet armoured group (presumably the tanks and self-propelled guns of Guards Lieutenant Colonel Ostapenko) captured Szentjánospuszta again; the soldiers of the *1. Kompanie/Panzer-Abteilung 208*, securing in positions on the northwestern edge of Dunamocs, observed 15-20 armoured fighting vehicles.[288]

Although Karva was again in Soviet hands after three days of heavy fighting, the 53rd Rifle Division had still not managed to entirely regain its former positions on the perimeter around Dunamocs.

During the three days of combat, the forces of the 9th Guards Mechanized Corps that had been committed here had 114 battle casualties (dead and wounded), and lost 13 tanks, 11 SU–76M self-propelled guns, two armoured personnel carriers of British-American origin, an armoured reconnaissance vehicle and six prime movers; at the same time, the 21st Guards Tank Brigade/5th Guards Tank Corps and the 1458th Self-Propelled Artillery Regiment/5th Guards Tank Corps lost 10 tanks and five SU–76 self-propelled guns. The majority of the 39 Soviet armoured fighting vehicles that were knocked out burned out.[289]

An interesting contribution this day was that the 1st Tank Battalion/46th Guards Tank Brigade of the 9th Guards Mechanized Corps, which had already withdrawn earlier, was alerted and ordered (with 11 newly received M4A2s) to the area of Csepel island, Halásztelek-Tököl-Szigetszentmiklós. This suggests the Soviets feared that forces of the *IV. SS-Panzerkorps*, attacking within the course of Operation *"Konrad 3"*, would shortly cross the Danube east of Ercsi.[290]

The hill that had been cleared the previous day on the front line of the *211. Volksgrenadier-Division*, 1.5km northwest of Németszőgyén, went into Soviet hands again at dawn.

That same day, all units of the *20. Panzer-Division* were withdrawn from combat, and marched to the railway stations to be loaded and transported away. The commander of the *44. Reichsgrenadier-Division "Hoch- und Deutschmeister"*, *Generalleutnant* Hans-Günther

287 After-action report of the 5th Guards Tank Corps, 1-31 January 1945 (copy owned by the author), p.16.

288 Di Giusto, 2010, p.207.

289 After-action report of the 9th Guards Mechanized Corps of the operations in the direction of Komárom–Érsekújvár in January 1945 (copy owned by the author), p.28.

290 Loza, 1996, p.72.

von Rost, assumed command over the previous sectors of the *Panzer*-division as well. The *Aufklärungs-Abteilung*, the majority of its two *Grenadier*-regiments, the *Pionier*-, battalion, the *Mörser Abteilung*, the main body of the artillery regiment, elements of the *Panzerjäger-Abteilung*, and parts of the *Nachrichten-Abteilung* and the supply units also arrived.

Because of the ever worsening operational situation of *Heeresgruppe A*, at 1125 in the morning, Guderian pressed for the withdrawal of *LVII. Panzerkorps* and the two *Panzer* divisions, especially the *Panzer* regiments, as soon as possible. The loading and transfer of the tanks ran into railway technical difficulties, but these were overcome during the day.

On **22 January**[291] the staff of the *Panzerkorps* took over command of *LVII. Panzerkorps* from General Kirchner. [Editor's Note: As mentioned above, *General* Kirchner had previously commanded *Korpsgruppe Kirchner*, which had included both *LXXII AK* and *LVII AK*. *Korpsgruppe "Kirchner"* was disbanded on 19 January, leaving him in command of just *LVII. Panzerkorps*. At this point the staff of *LVII. Panzerkorps* resumed command of the *Korps* without subordination to *General* Kirchner.] The first serial departed on the same day toward Upper Silesia. The first four serials of the *Kampfgruppe* of the *8. Panzer-Division* also set off, containing the *Führungsabteilung*, the *I. Bataillon/Panzergrenadier-Regiment 28*, and the main body of *Flak-Abteilung 286*.

However, the main body of the *Kampfgruppe* was still engaged in battle. That is, during the night of 21/22 January, at about midnight, Guards Lieutenant Colonel Ostapenko's 11 T–34 tanks and three SU–76M self-propelled guns, with mounted infantry on the tanks, broke through the German MLR southwest of Búcs, then thrust into Baloghpuszta, and reached the northern and western outskirts of Dunamocs.

Parallel with this, the 27th Guards Tank Brigade attacked with its seven operational tanks and four self-propelled guns. By 1700 hours they reached point no. 124, 2.5km southwest of Búcs. During these combat actions, the Germans knocked out one of the T–34s of the brigade.[292]

During the morning, the 6th Guards Tank Army concentrated its remaining forces in order to continue its attack and recapture Dunamocs. Colonel General Kravchenko had the following forces with which to achieve this objective:[293]

Table 9 – Armoured fighting vehicle strength of 6th Guards Tank Army, 22 January 1945

Unit	Combat strength	Tanks	Self-propelled guns
18th Guards Mechanized Brigade	116	2	–
30th Guards Mechanized Brigade	142	2	–
14th Guards Motorcycle Battalion	118	1	1

291 The temperature stayed below -6° all day, partly cloudy sky with restricted visibility, partly clear weather.

292 See reports of the commander of the tank and mechanized units of the 7th Guards Army from January 1945 (copy owned by the author) Report nr. 022, 22 January 1945

293 After-action report of the 9th Guards Mechanized Corps of the operations in the direction of Komárom–Érsekújvár in January 1945 (copy owned by the author), p.29.

697th Self-Propelled Artillery Regiment	–	–	10
21st Guards Tank Brigade	–	9	–
1458th Self-Propelled Artillery Regiment	–	–	1
Total	376	14	12

The 25 tanks and *Jagdpanzers* of *Panzer-Abteilung 208*, supported by a battalion-sized infantry unit, destroyed the Soviet armoured fighting vehicles that had been broken through earlier and restored the front line with a perfectly executed counterattack. At 1100 hours the *Panzer* IV/70 (A) *Jagdpanzers* of the *1. Kompanie* recaptured Szentjánospuszta in a surprise attack supported by artillery fire, during which they destroyed nine Soviet tanks and anti-tank guns.[294]

After the heavy fighting was over, the Germans claimed destruction of 17 armoured fighting vehicles. Of these, elements of the 5th Guards Tank Corps lost 11 T–34 tanks and two SU–76M self-propelled guns (five tanks and the self-propelled guns were burnt out). According to Soviet data, the Germans lost four knocked out tanks, five armoured personnel carriers, two heavy armoured cars, two guns, a machine gun and approximately 100 men.[295]

The clash of armoured troops northwest of Dunamocs on 22 January was the last episode of the tank battle for Komárom. On the next day, the still engaged units of the *8. Panzer-Division* were withdrawn, and, on 26 January, the last trainload of this formation left Hungary.[296]

On 25 and 26 January the weakened remnants of the 6th Guards Tank Army also quit the battlefield. After turning over their front line sector to the 25th Guards Rifle Corps/7th Guards Army, Kravchenko's units went into the reserve of the 2nd Ukrainian Front.

After this, along the front line German *grenadiers* and Soviet infantry faced off against each other, conducting only minor operations to secure more favourable positions for their lines. The real assault forces had left the north bank of the Danube when the tanks departed.

Symbolic significance may be ascribed to the fact that, on 25 January, 10 newly repaired T–34 tanks of 21st Guards Tank Brigade which had taken part in the tank battle for Komárom were ordered by Colonel General A.V. Kurkhin, commander of the tank and mechanized forces of the 2nd Ukrainian Front, to be turned over to forces besieging Budapest.[297]

When the Komárom battle reached its conclusion, the third tank battle of Székesfehérvár, which had developed during the course of Operation "*Konrad 3*", was already raging with maximum intensity. There was a momentary period of calm north of the Danube, although all the horrors of the past weeks of fighting were felt everywhere in the countryside. As one eyewitness experienced this:

> The civilians were ordered out to bury the dead. But it was impossible to bury them in the wintry conditions of January. So they stacked the bodies up like cordwood. Bodies

294 Di Giusto, 2010, p.207.
295 After-action report of the 5th Guards Tank Corps, 1-31 January 1945 (copy owned by the author), p.17.
296 Haupt, 1987, p.386.
297 After-action report of the 5th Guards Tank Corps, 1-31 January 1945 (copy owned by the author), p.19.

> of men burnt to death, body parts lay everywhere – here a hand, there a leg – bore witness to the horrors of war. But the most horrible sight was the bank of the Danube. They hauled the now useless Soviet tanks to the former [Komárom – the author] market place. In one of them sat the driver. In his right hand he held the control stick, in his left some hair, but he had no head. This sight – for me – marked the end of the January offensive of the Soviets.[298]

The heavy fighting caused great destruction and suffering, not only on the front lines, but also behind the front. The Hungarian Komárom I. Grade Police authority prepared a report which sheds light on the ordeals the civilian population of the villages occupied by the Soviet forces had to endure during the Komárom tank battle:

> [..] The signs of the battlefield being near were already visible at the crossroads of the Izsa and Érsekújvár highways, because from there all the way to the village of Izsa Russian tanks and armoured fighting vehicles, destroyed by the German military, were scattered on both sides of the road. The demolition work was finished on that very day, and our vehicle could reach Izsa only by blowing up some five tanks.
>
> Along the highway at the edge of Izsa village lay the bodies of two Soviet soldiers. It would be appropriate [sic.] to call the attention of the village authorities to bury them.
>
> Of what the assistant town clerk, the local magistrate and other official persons related in the village hall and in the village of the conditions and experiences during the seven days of Soviet occupation, it could be stated that the Soviet army's discipline was seriously disintegrating. This is proven by the fact that the Soviet 'officials'[299] had absolutely no authority anymore, because the common soldiers raised their weapons against them, indeed, they even hit them. Eyewitnesses had seen a common soldier wrestling with a Soviet 'official'. This was natural, because the common soldiers had seen the 'officials' and officers perpetrating the vilest deeds, the officers joined the soldiers in committing outrages, this united them and the officers' authority was completely destroyed. The Soviet officer did not dare to give orders to the enlisted men, because he feared that they might denounce him for his crimes.
>
> The rape of Hungarian women, regardless of age, also began here, and on the day before the last of the seven days of their rule they asserted to everyone, in front of the Russian-speaking interpreters, that on one or another of the following evenings, every female in the village would be raped, because there were already 6,000 of their soldiers in the village. A good example of these rapes is supplied by a senior officer, a 23-year-old Soviet major, who raped a young woman. The woman wanted to make a complaint to the highest-ranking officer in the village, whose quarters were pointed out to her by another 'official'. When the woman, with a male relative, stepped into the major's room, she saw her attacker in front of her. They turned back without a word, and, after this, the rest of the 'officials' just laughed at them.
>
> At one place in the village, Soviet soldiers were looting one of the homes and when they [the members of the household – the author] looked for the officer in charge, apparently he arranged something, but when they carried on, he laughed and waved

298 Cited by Szénássy, 2000, pp.171-172.

299 Officers.

at them to go on. It also happened that the officer turned the conversation toward the most insignificant thing, to a wristwatch, and excused the soldiers by saying that they needed it.

The village was predominantly agricultural, and naturally there were complaints about that too. They carried off all of the horses. Of the cattle, four cows were butchered. Pigs were also taken, but because of shortage of time they were unable to take many. However they plucked most of the poultry, since during the week of their stay they mostly ate geese and chickens.

The general opinion was that the Soviet soldiers were overwhelmed by the riches that they found and that they wasted and destroyed everything.

They took away beds, bedclothes, and covers from the populace and transported them even to the squad's line [sic.],[300] and the artillery commanders lay in bed in the cold and directed the fire from bed.

Although in many places there was chopped firewood, they burned furniture instead. If they couldn't take furniture away, they smashed it up, so that it couldn't be used [by the local people – the author].

The flesh of the butchered livestock was not rationed out systematically, but was wasted. Thus, for instance, if they butchered a cow, they didn't split it up equally among the groups, rather the men of a group would cut off a piece for themselves, and what was left would be thrown on the dungheap.

They were also lavish with their cooking. They cooked three or four times as much as even the largest appetite of the group needed, and what was left, they threw on the rubbish tip.

On the sixth day of the occupation, stuck here with his family as a result of the village being encircled, Chief Police Inspector *vitéz* Dr. Gy. T.[301] was summoned by a Soviet police senior lieutenant, who interrogated him for three hours without any mistreatment. Soviet soldiers took all the belongings from *vitéz* Dr. Gy. T. and his 18-year-old son, leaving them only the clothes they were wearing. One of these so-called Soviet officers admiringly picked up *vitéz* Dr. Gy. T.'s police cap, declaring that it suited him very well. They also took his police uniform. However they did not interfere with any belongings of his wife and daughter, not even Mrs T's astrakhan coat, among many other things.

I shall mention that the real offences against women did not happen by day, it was only when night fell that they went into the houses and cellars and dragged them out. They dishonoured them in front of their own husbands and children or in front of strangers. Of course all this went on by threatening the women with handguns or machine guns.[302]

The general opinion was that the Soviet soldiers were constantly drunk and drank the coarsest and nastiest spirits, distilled liquors, methylated spirits, eau de cologne and vodka. This was the main cause of the vandalism.[303]

300 Accurately into the first line.

301 The document refers to the person's entire name. However, we did not deem this to be necessary here.

302 Accurately: submachine gun.

303 HM HIM *Hadtörténelmi Levéltár* (Budapest), *M. kir. rendőrség országos felügyelője iratai, 667/1945. Magyar királyi rendőrség komáromi I. fokú rendőrhatósága, 8/1945 biz. sz. jelentése.*

Conclusion

In the 17-day series of battles, the forces on the left flank of the 2nd Ukrainian Front suffered an unambiguous defeat. They did not capture the Danube crossing points at Komárom, nor did they get into the rear of *IV. SS-Panzerkorps* as it headed for Budapest.

Although the Soviets had neither operational surprise nor sufficient infantry troops, thanks to the tank and mechanized forces, the territorial gains of the first two days were significant.

The surprise attack reaching the immediate outskirts of the city is remembered thus by a former Hungarian policeman:

> [...] I would like to remark, that on 7 January the Soviet armoured wedges approached Komárom so closely that the German and Hungarian soldiers could only stop them 1km from the city. The signs and traces of battle are here now, since the knocked out or destroyed armoured fighting vehicles are left scattered on the road. Among the tanks were American-made *Schermanns* [M4A2 or Sherman tanks – the author], and two such tanks fell into German hands intact, since they slipped into the [flood defence embankment – the author] drainage ditch and couldn't get out. This attack at Komárom happened so suddenly that the people only learned about the danger the next day.
>
> There was constant air activity in the area. During the night of 21 December Soviet aircraft dropped 46 bombs on the city of Komárom. Not much damage was caused by the enemy air raids.
>
> In the city, only a small number of soldiers could be seen, and they mainly belonged to the combat formations. In the city district, the police maintained order to the complete satisfaction of the populace.[...][304]

Thus the Soviets rapidly gained ground toward the west, yet they could not get through the blocking position of the *211. Volksgrenadier-Division* – not even after committing the 4th Guards Mechanized Corps and the 24th Guards Rifle Corps. Because of this, the 6th Guards Tank Army that hurried forward to the Vág-Danube could only have a narrow, almost trap-like, corridor for itself in the German—Hungarian defences, and which was bounded on three sides by water obstacles.

The Soviet forces were committed in a widely separated manner, and this further diminished the force of the intended strike. The 25th Guards Rifle Corps/7th Guards Army closed up behind the armoured fighting vehicles extraordinarily slowly. Thus the tanks and self-propelled vehicles, lacking infantry support and the appropriate engineering and technical units, were unable to cross the Vág-Danube, or to capture Komárom or Érsekújvár.

Although the Soviets could not at first cope with the German counterattacks, they finally managed to slow them down, and then bring them to a halt. It is interesting that, in the defensive battles, the Soviet forces – with powerful support of the artillery units – demonstrated the greatest steadfastness, even with ever-diminishing strength; not, as had been the case in the course of attacks carried out initially, with a threefold superiority in

304 HM HIM *Hadtörténelmi Levéltár (Budapest), M. kir. rendőrség országos felügyelője iratai, 667/5/1945. M. kir. rendőrség politikai rendészeti osztálya szombathelyi kirendeltsége, 1945. január 31-én kelt 7/1945. pol. rend.biz. sz. jelentés* p.14.

armoured fighting vehicles.

This does not apply to the infantry of the 7th Guards Army, who, with a few exceptions, were equally feeble in attack and in defence. Among the causes for this we can find matters regarding discipline, which the Hungarian experiences quoted above also throw some light on. At the same time, the infantry were heavily dependent on their artillery support, because, lacking appropriate handheld anti-tank weapons[305], they were very sensitive to German armoured attacks.

Because of the adverse weather, the Soviet air support was not as effective as had been intended.

Although, by the end of the fighting, about half of the territory taken by the Soviets remained in their hands, they paid heavy losses for a small extension of the Párkány bridgehead.

An interesting phenomenon was that the Soviet forces suffered their heaviest armoured losses in the first three and in the last four days of the combat.

The 6th Guards Tank Army was practically annihilated. It is true, though, that on 6 January, at the start of the assault, it was far from being at full strength. According to the data of the 9th Guards Mechanized Corps, they lost 723 dead and wounded, 63 tanks and self-propelled guns, two armoured cars, 35 cars, 14 guns, three mortars and two rocket-launchers.[306] By way of personnel losses, this amounted to a 46.5% loss ratio compared to its infantry strength reported on 6 January. Its armoured strength suffered an even more serious blow: 89% of their armoured fighting vehicles were knocked out by the Germans.

The 5th Guards Tank Corps joined the attack with 91 tanks, and, during the battle, received a further 23 armoured fighting vehicles (18 self-propelled guns and five repaired tanks). Nevertheless, by the evening of 22 January it only had a total of four operational tanks and self-propelled guns.[307] Based on these figures, the corps lost 110 armoured fighting vehicles, which constitutes a 120% (!) combat loss. Because the majority of the repairable tanks that were not burnt out and the self-propelled guns remained in the territory recaptured by the Germans, those were counted as losses for Colonel General Kravchenko.

The 4th Guards Mechanized Corps had eight tanks left at the end of the battle, thus they lost at least 20 armoured fighting vehicles in action. The 27th Independent Guards Tank Brigade had to count their total losses as 10 T–34s and three SU–85 self-propelled guns (51% of its initial operational strength).[308]

Reliable records of the losses of 6th Guards Tank Army's army-level tank and self-propelled artillery units are not available, but it can reasonably be assumed that these units also lost the majority of their armoured fighting vehicles in the heavy combat.

305 The Soviet forces were equipped with the RPG-43 high explosive anti-tank (HEAT) hand grenade which could be thrown for approximately 20 metres and were able to penetrate 75mm thick armour. The German disposable *Panzerfäuste*, on the other hand, penetrated 200mm thick armour from a distance of 60-100 metres, and the reloadable *Panzerschreck* penetrated 160mm thick armour from a distance of 180 metres.

306 After-action report of the 9th Guards Mechanized Corps of the operations in the direction of Komárom–Érsekújvár in January 1945 (copy owned by the author), p.34.

307 After-action report of the 5th Guards Tank Corps, 1-31 January 1945 (copy owned by the author), p.17.

308 Compare: Reports of the commander of the tank and mechanized units of the 7th Guards Army from January 1945 (copy owned by the author) Report nr. 005, 5 January 1945 and Report nr. 022, 22 January 1945

The Soviet forces launched the attack on 6 January with 202 armoured fighting vehicles. In the course of the action they committed the approximately 30 tanks of the 4th Guards Mechanized Corps, as well as the total of 34 self-propelled guns of the 1458th and 697th Self-Propelled Artillery Regiments. Thus we can calculate that a total of least 266 Soviet armoured fighting vehicles were employed in the engagement.

Of this number – as stated above – by 20 January, there remained 43 operational tanks and self-propelled guns. By the end of the three-day engagement around Dunamocs, the 6th Guards Tank Army had a mere 24 functioning armoured fighting vehicles left. According to Soviet sources, the tank army joined the battle with an average of 72 (!) tanks and self-propelled guns between 6-13 January 1945.[309] In our opinion this was a direct result of the extremely heavy armoured losses in the first two days.

Based on the above, the Soviets lost at least 240 of their armoured fighting vehicles in the Komárom tank battle.[310] This constituted 90% (!) of the total committed armoured strength of the Soviet forces.

Not every disabled tank was destroyed, but if we calculate the average destruction ratio of 75% which was applied for the Eastern Front,[311] this nevertheless means 180 burned-out tanks (not counting repairable tanks that fell into German hands).

In the absence of accurate data, the battle losses of the Soviet forces can only be estimated. If we start from the assumption that the rest of the major military formations that were committed (one tank and one mechanized corps, as well as seven rifle divisions[312]) suffered at least the same scale of losses as the fragmented 9th Guards Mechanized Corps, then we get a figure of approximately 7,200 Soviet dead and wounded. Considering that the 53rd Rifle Division, in all probability, suffered heavier losses than 9th Guards Mechanized Corps – and not including either the losses suffered by Soviet corps and battle losses of other army-level units, which remain unknown to this time, nor Soviet soldiers taken prisoner, we may take this loss of 7,200 men to be a low-end estimate.

The Germans – initially with significant Hungarian support – prevented the Soviets achieving their operational aims and halted them, without significantly weakening the *Panzer* units that were fighting south of the Danube.

The continuous defence presented by the Germans slowly eliminated the Soviet superiority in tanks and self-propelled guns. Thus by the time that the counteroffensive was launched on 10 and 11 January, with regard to combat-ready armoured fighting vehicles, the Germans already had a slight advantage in tanks:[313]

309 Minasyan, M. M., "Délkelet-Európa népeinek felszabadítása (részlet)" in: *Hazánk felszabadulása.* (Minasyan, M. M., The liberation of the peoples of Southwestern Europe (excerpts). In: Liberation of our country) (Budapest, 1970), p.95.

310 However, the 6th Guards Tank Army was not immobile for long. On 21 February 1945 the troops of Colonel General Kravchenko again had 224 tanks and self-propelled guns.

311 According to analysis of Soviet data, 10% of the armoured fighting vehicles damaged in combat could be repaired by the troops, 15% could be repaired in the homeland, within factory conditions. However, 75% of the knocked out tanks and self-propelled guns suffered irrecoverable damage. See Winchester, Charles, *Ostfront. Hitler's War on Russia 1941–45* (Oxford, 1998), p.89.

312 The 72nd Guards, the 81st Guards and the 93rd Guards Rifle Divisions joined the fight in the course of the battle. On the issue of the amount of the Soviet rifle divisions deployed between the Garam and the Nyitra, see Minasyan, 1970, p.95.

313 Only the combat-ready armoured fighting vehicles. On the German side we did not consider the *Panzer* II light tanks and the *Marder* tank destroyers. See the sources for the data in the main text.

Table 10 – Comparative strength of armoured fighting vehicles, 6-20 January 1945

Date	Soviet forces			German—Hungarian forces		
	Tanks	Self-propelled guns	Totals	Tanks	*Jagdpanzers*	Totals
6 January 1945	186	16	**202**	20	48	**68**
11 January 1945	72	0	**72**	66	37[1]	**103**
20 January 1945	43		**43**	90		**90**

1 On 1 January the existing tank strength (21 T–34s) of the Brigade was distributed between the other two Tank Brigades.

The majority of the German tanks were *Panzer* IV tanks with the long-barrelled 7.5cm gun. This type was equivalent in performance to the T–34 tanks generally used by the Soviets, but its performance was slightly inferior to the T–34/85 version. On the other hand the German *Panther* tanks and *Panzer* IV L/70 *Jagdpanzers* were equipped with 7.5cm guns whose firepower surpassed that of the 85mm guns of the T–34/85 tanks.

On the Soviet side, the standard tank-gun calibre was 7.62mm, because only a third of the deployed Soviet tanks were T–34/85s. The US-made tanks and the SU–76M self-propelled guns had less combat effectiveness than the T–34s.

General Kirchner could only commit infantry units consisting of *Volksgrenadier*, *Feldausbildungs-* and *Alarm*-units, which, in terms of equipment, combat experience and armament, could not be compared with veteran first line units. Nevertheless, these units did hold up well in the battles. The *211. Volksgrenadier-Division,* with its attached assault guns and *Jagdpanzers,* resisted the attacks of three Soviet Rifle Divisions, two Guards Tank and one Guards Mechanized Brigades. In so doing, the German formation lost more than 1500 men.

After a brief period of wavering – and after its commander was replaced – the *8. Panzer-Division* fought outstandingly well. During the Soviet breakthrough, its *Panzergrenadiers* destroyed numerous tanks by *Panzerfäuste* and *Panzerschrecks*, contributing significantly to slowing down the Soviet offensive.

Panzer-Abteilung 208 and *Panzerjäger-Abteilung 13* provided effective support to the weakened forces of the *8. Panzer-Division.*

The newly-reconstituted *20. Panzer-Division*, transferred with extreme haste to the Hungarian battlefield, counterattacked with considerable success. At the same time, however, *Panzer-Regiment 21* was unable to properly integrate the new recruits into its ranks, and this frequently limited the effectiveness of the armoured fighting vehicles during battle.

Luckily, the after-action report of the 9th Guards Mechanized Corps contains summarized data on the German—Hungarian losses. According to these, between 6 and 22 January, the German—Hungarian forces of *Korpsgruppe "Kirchner"* lost 4,200 men dead or wounded, 973 prisoners, 83 knocked out tanks, *Jagdpanzers*, self-propelled guns and self-propelled howitzers, 69 armoured personnel carriers, four self-propelled anti-aircraft cannon, 82 cars, two aircraft, 62 artillery-, anti-aircraft- and anti-tank guns, five mortars and 70 machine guns.[314] This seems a reasonably accurate set of figures, the more so in terms of battle casualties, if we compare these with the battle casualty reports of the German *Heeresgruppe Süd*:[315]

Table 11 – *Heeresgruppe Süd* casualties, 6-22 January 1945

Unit	Officers killed	Officers wounded	Officers missing	NCOs & enlisted men killed	NCOs & enlisted men wounded	NCOs & enlisted men missing	Total
8. Panzer-Division	3	9	9	112	573	73	779[1]
20. Panzer-Division	3	26	–	134	634	25	822
153. Feldausbildungs-Division	–	3	–	159	697	48	907
211. Volksgrenadier-Division	4	33	5	250	1074	191	1557
Total	10	71	14	655	2978	337	4065

1 The unit history of the *8. Panzer-Division* (Haupt, 1987, p.386) provides a much larger loss ratio. Eight officers, 48 non-commissioned officers and 164 enlisted were killed; 16 officers, 89 non-commissioned officers and 494 men were wounded; nine officers, 21 non-commissioned officers and 228 men went missing. This means a total loss of 1077 men (excluding the sick). It is not impossible, though, that this – in spite of the author's statement – does not refer to the period of the armoured battle in the Komárom area but means the losses of the whole month of January, including the battle casualties of the later battles around Ratibor and Olomouc.

However, the above-mentioned numbers do not include the battle casualties either of the Hungarian forces, or of the German independent units and *"Gneisenau"* battalions. According to recollections, one of the Hungarian alarm companies deployed at Komárom lost 180 men.[316] Thus it seems justified to take the above-mentioned Soviet estimates as being reasonably accurate.

According to the data as of 1 January 1945, the German—Hungarian forces committed in the tank battle for Komárom – including *20. Panzer-Division* and *Panzer-Abteilung 208*, which were employed later – had a total of 290 tanks, *Jagdpanzers* and assault guns; however, only a fraction of these were in combat-ready condition.

314 After-action report of the 9th Guards Mechanized Corps of the operations in the direction of Komárom–Érsekújvár in January 1945 (copy owned by the author), p.33. The document does not mention that this data would cover the German—Hungarian losses caused by this corps. Moreover, the forces of the 9th Guards Mechanized Corps were fighting from the third day of the battle until 22 January as partly attached to the 5th Guards Tank Corps, on a joint front line shared with the divisions of the 25th Guards Rifle Corps. Therefore the reports of the damages caused were most probably intermingled on corps and army levels. This is why the data of the 9th Guards Mechanized Corps are necessarily summarized.

Another contemporary Soviet source, created after the battles, provides data of the German—Hungarian losses as 10,000 soldiers, 191 armoured fighting vehicles and 133 guns. Such a large loss ratio, however, is not confirmed by the sources in German—Hungarian archives. We cannot exclude the possibility that, because of their own failure, the Soviets projected their own losses onto their enemies.

315 HM HIM *Hadtörténelmi Levéltár* (Budapest) microfilm archives, *Kriegstagebuch Ia der Heeresgruppe Süd, Anlagen* (roll no. 629. image no. 7213786-7213788)

316 Szénássy, 2000, p.169. The surviving official data concerning losses, however, does not confirm this.

Captain (later Major) Edömér Tassonyi mentions a total of 32 German—Hungarian armoured fighting vehicles lost during the first two days of the battle, referring to German sources.[317] As is clear from the Soviet report referred to earlier, German—Hungarian forces lost 83 armoured fighting vehicles during the 17 days of the battle, 28.6% of the total number of such vehicles. However, the majority of these were only disabled and still repairable. As, at the end of the engagement, the battlefield remained mostly in German hands, maintenance units could tow away those vehicles that had not burned out and repair them.

Nevertheless, seven *Jagdpanzer* 38 (t) tank destroyers of the Hungarian 20th Assault Artillery Battalion, four from Assault Artillery Battalion "Bernolák"[318], and five *Panzer* IV tanks of the Hungarian 3rd Tank Regiment were destroyed in the course of the fighting or seized by the Soviet troops (mainly on 6 January).

The two German *Panzer* divisions each lost about 8-10 irreparably damaged *Panzer* III, *Panzer* IV and *Panther* tanks. *Panzer-Abteilung* [319] had to write off five *Panzer* IV tanks and one *Panzer* IV/70 (A) *Jagdpanzer* as total loss from its strength, while *Panzerjäger-Abteilung 13* wrote off five total losses of *Panzer* IV/70 (V) *Jagdpanzers*[320]. Thus, a total of 16 Hungarian and 32 German armoured fighting vehicles were counted as total losses in action. This is 16.5% of the total number of the armoured fighting vehicles committed.

After summarizing the losses, it can be seen that there is not much difference between the two sides in terms of battle casualties. However, as far as armoured fighting vehicle losses are concerned, substantial differences may be observed. It can therefore be stated that the Soviet tank and mechanized forces suffered heavily for the attack they launched toward Komárom.

Table 12 – Comparative losses, 6-22 January 1945

Tank battle of Komárom	Soviet troops	German-Hungarian troops	Loss ratio
Battle casualties	Approx. 7200 men	Approx. 5100	1.4 : 1
Armoured losses (repairable and total)	Min. 240	83	2.9 : 1

Naturally, the tank battle for Komárom does not rival the battle of Kursk in terms of grandiose scales; nor can it be compared to the number of armoured fighting vehicles involved in Operation "*Konrad 3*", or to the importance of the tank battles fought on

317 *Tassonyi Edömér 1982. január 12-én kelt levele Pályi Györgyhöz*, p.4. In: *HM HIM Hadtörténelmi Levéltár (Budapest), Tanulmányok és visszaemlékezések gyűjteménye* (Collection of studies and recollections), nr. 3063 Pályi Görgy: *A Szent László hadosztály repülő lövészezredének története, 1944. október–1945. december.* (György Pályi: History of the Air Force Rifle Regiment of the Division *"Szent László"*, October 1944–December 1945). These are also confirmed by the Soviet archive data: the troops claimed to have knocked out 29 enemy armoured fighting vehicles on 6 January, and three on the following day.

318 Compare: *Bundesarchiv–Militärarchiv* (Freiburg im Breisgau), *RH 2 Ost Karte 5263 (Panzer-Lage am 1. Jan. 1945)* and HM HIM *Hadtörténelmi Levéltár (Budapest), a "Szent László" hadosztály tüzérparancsnokának naplója és mellékletei. 1944. 12. 23.*

319 See Di Giusto, 2010, p.191.

320 Compare *Bundesarchiv–Militärarchiv* (Freiburg im Breisgau), *RH 2 Ost Karte 5263 (Panzer-Lage am 1. Jan. 1945)* and *RH 2 Ost Karte 5316 (Panzer-Lage am 20. Jan. 1945).*

the Great Hungarian Plain. This battle was no more important, nor more violent, than a number of other more or less "nameless" tank battles, the majority of which have still not yet been adequately studied, which the Germans and Soviets fought on the Eastern Front from the summer of 1943 until the spring of 1945. Nevertheless, the battle for Komárom was fought on Hungarian soil, with the aim of seizing the Hungarian capital, therefore it constitutes an integral part of our military history.

3

Operation "*Südwind*" (17-24 February 1945)

German plan for the elimination of the Garam bridgehead

Following the 108-day battle for Budapest, the Soviet Supreme High Command planned a major attack in the Hungarian theatre of war as a secondary strike aiding the assault launched in the direction of Berlin, on 12 January 1945. The Supreme High Command of the Armed Forces of the Union of Soviet Socialist Republics (*Stavka*) issued a directive on 17 February 1945 in which it ordered the staffs of the 2nd and 3rd Ukrainian Fronts to prepare a massive attack in the strategic direction of Vienna and Bratislava-Brno. The objectives of the Vienna operation were as follows:

- Elimination of the German *Heeresgruppe Süd*;
- Deprivation of the German war industry of its last Austrian and Hungarian natural oil resources and industrial war production areas;
- Prevention of German troops from withdrawing into the "Alpine Fortress" (*Alpenfestung*);
- Cutting off the German forces in the Balkans and in Northern Italy from their supplies;
- Closing the German forces fighting on Czech and Slovak ground in from the south;
- Assisting the advance toward Berlin and the advance into the southern German areas.

In light of the huge losses suffered during the battle for Budapest[1], the Soviet forces received a month to replenish the strength of the troops, resupply armament and prepare for the attack. The offensive was to be launched on 15 March 1945.[2]

---

1 With the fall of the Hungarian capital, on 13 February, the battle for Budapest, which had lasted for 108 days, ended. In the course of this battle, the Soviet troops lost, according to their own data, 320,082 soldiers (of this, 80,026 dead and missing), 1,766 tanks and self-propelled guns, 4,127 guns and mortars, and 293 aircraft. See Krivosheev, G. F. (ed.), *Soviet Casualties and Combat Losses in the Twentieth Century* (London, 1997), pp.152, 263.

According to German data, in the battle for Budapest during just the period between 24 December 1944 and 10 February 1945, the Soviet 2nd and 3rd Ukrainian Fronts lost, apart from the losses caused by the *Luftwaffe*, 20,132 dead, 5,138 prisoners, 1,981 tanks and self-propelled guns, 946 artillery guns, 273 mortars and 1,700 anti-tank guns. The opposing German forces lost, in the same period (from 24 December 1944 to 10 February 1945), 1,111 officers, 32,997 non-commissioned officers and enlisted men (total of battle casualties – dead, wounded and MIA). The German materiel losses are on the low side. The latter data can be found in the final German report of the battle for Budapest. This is included, among others, in Maier, 1985, pp.520-521.

2 Malakhov, 1960, pp.109-110; Zakharov, 1973, p.273; Száva Péter (szerk.), *Magyarország felszabadítása. Tanulmányok hazánk felszabadításának történetéből.* (Péter Száva (ed.): The liberation of Hungary. Studies from the history of the liberation of our country) (Budapest, 1975), p.288.

On the Western Hungarian front, the German High Command had also devised a large-scale attack against the Soviet formations holding Budapest and the eastern part of Dunántúl (Transdanubia). Its objective was to secure the resources (oil, bauxite, manganese) found in the Dunántúl region, to provide provisions and a staging area, to prevent the realization of Soviet objectives described above (of which the German High Command was aware), and to eliminate the large Soviet bridgehead on the west bank of the Danube. The strategic plan consisted of multiple phases, and was given the code name "*Frühlingserwachen*" ("Spring Awakening"). The German *6. Panzerarmee* was assigned the primary role in the offensive. It had suffered serious losses during the Battle of the Bulge, and was being reconstituted continually, although extremely slowly; the *I.* and *II. SS-Panzerkorps*, as well as the command and the *Heer* units, were "smuggled" into Hungary with utmost care and secrecy.[3]

The planned German attack was threatened by more than just the faltering materiel supplies and the lack of infantry troops apparent in the German army since the end of 1942.[4] The 7th Guards Army of the 2nd Ukrainian Front held a 17km deep bridgehead on the west bank of the Garam, northwest of Esztergom; this bridgehead seemed to be appropriate as a starting point for a Soviet offensive which (exposing the left flank of the German—Hungarian forces south of the Danube), in the case of commitment of larger forces, would be able to reach the oil refineries around Komárom, and would make possible the advance of Soviet troops toward Bratislava. Besides all the above-mentioned aspects, the bridgehead fixed considerable forces of the German *8. Armee*.

General der Infanterie Otto Wöhler, commander in chief of the German *Heeresgruppe Süd*, after returning to his command post in Eszterháza from discussions held at Hitler's Headquarters and the *OKH* (*Oberkommando des Heeres* – Supreme High Command of the Land Forces) on 10 February 1945, started preparations for an attack aimed at the elimination of the Soviet bridgehead at the Garam.[5] Because of the scope of this book, we are not able to discuss the details of this plan.

The written strategic order of the command of the *8. Armee* of 13 February 1945 states, in connection with the elimination of the bridgehead at the Garam, that according to information gathered by reconnaissance units, the Soviets had established defence positions in the bridgehead. They assumed that the armoured units of the Soviet 4th

3 Maier, 1985, pp.134-141. The combat and support units of the two *Panzer* divisions of the *I. SS-Panzerkorps* (*1. SS-Panzer-Division "Leibstandarte SS Adolf Hitler"*, *12. SS-Panzer-Division "Hitlerjugend"*) were continually arriving from the end of January to the beginning of February, in the first supply echelon; although they were far from fully reconstituted. Before departure and during the transport, the units were ordered to remove their cuff titles (*Ärmelstreifen* in German) worn on the lower left sleeve of their jackets, depicting the names of their units, and the tactical signs on the vehicles were also painted over, because Soviet reconnaissance might have identified them by these signs and numbers. Because of keeping this information confidential, the units of the *6. Panzerarmee* bore codenames down to the level of battalions (!): the *I. SS-Panzerkorps* was codenamed *"SS-Abschnittsstab Süd"*, the *1. SS-Panzer-Division "Leibstandarte SS Adolf Hitler"* was codenamed *"SS-Ersatzstaffel Totenkopf"*, the *12. SS-Panzer-Division "Hitlerjugend"* was codenamed *"SS-Ersatzstaffel Wiking"*. For this, see Tiemann, Ralf, *Die Leibstandarte. Band IV/2* (Osnabrück, 1987), p.225, and Meyer, Hubert, *Kriegsgeschichte der 12. SS-Panzerdivision "Hitlerjugend"* Band 2 (Osnabrück, 1999), 4th edition, p.480.

4 It is interesting that enough German infantry could be gathered for the attack against the Soviet bridgehead at the Garam, although it was exactly the average German infantry formation which had the lowest combat strength in the Hungarian theatre of war.

5 Maier, 1985, p.142.

Guards Mechanized Corps were gathering within the depths of the bridgehead, but the 9th Guards Mechanized Corps and the 5th Guards Tank Corps of the 6th Guards Tank Army were still being reconstituted in the area east of the Garam. Their commitment, as well as the possible commitment of units of the "Pliev" Group (1st Guards Cavalry Mechanized Group) was anticipated.[6]

According to the orders received, after a short artillery preparation, the commander of the German *8. Armee* (*General der Gebirgstruppe* Hans Kreysing) was to attack from the north and eliminate the Soviet bridgehead at the Garam on the appointed day, at 0500 hours, with all available infantry and armoured forces, with the commitment of the *I. SS-Panzerkorps*, which was directed into the area by deliberately weakening other front line sections; the formation was also ordered to establish eastern bridgeheads on the Garam at Garamkövesd, Kőhídgyarmat, Kéménd and Bény.

The following detailed tasks were assigned to the German forces. According to the time plan prepared, *Panzerkorps "Feldherrnhalle"* (*General der Panzertruppe* Ulrich Kleemann) was to gather the main body of the committed forces of the *46. Infanterie Division* (*Generalmajor* Erich Reuter), the *44. Reichsgrenadier-Division "Hoch- und Deutschmeister"* (*Generalleutnant* Hans-Günther von Rost) and the *211. Volksgrenadier-Division* (*Generalleutnant* Johann Heinrich Eckhardt) and withdraw them to be concentrated in the area of Für – Csúz – Nagyölved – Érsekkéty. The armoured group of the *Armeekorps* was assembling in the area of Farnad.

Following the start of the attack, the *Armeekorps* was to advance at full speed in the direction of Magyarszőgyén and Bart, and to take the hills and point no. 190, south of Magyarszőgyén, a village in the central direction of the attack, as well as the area south of Bart, in order to make possible the attack of the *I. SS-Panzerkorps*, which was to be committed later. The villages of Magyarszőgyén and Bart were to be occupied by the encircling forces from the rear. The forces had to take care not to let the first phase of the attack be delayed by the battle going on for the occupation of these villages.

1. SS-Panzer-Division "Leibstandarte SS Adolf Hitler" (*SS-Gruppenführer und Generalleutnant der Waffen-SS* Hermann Priess) was to close up behind the infantry of *Panzerkorps "Feldherrnhalle"*, and, starting as ordered by the *Armee*, was to occupy the hills south of the Párizs Canal and east of Köbölkút in order to provide the prerequisites for a new attack in the direction of Esztergom. Fighting for the village of Köbölkút had to be avoided, and the airfield southeast of the village was to be captured as well (Phase II).

Depending on the evolving situation, *I. SS-Panzerkorps* was to continue the attack, together with the infantry divisions, toward the area between Muzsla and Béla, where the infantry was to occupy the hills east and southeast of Béla (Phase III).

The divisions that were remaining in their positions were to join the attack as ordered by *Panzerkorps "Feldherrnhalle"*, as soon as it was successful (Phase IV).

A reinforced *Regimentsgruppe* of the German *6. Armee*, attacking from the south bank of the Danube, was to establish a bridgehead on the northern bank of the river on the first day of the attack in order to cooperate with German forces attacking from the north and

6 The commander of the Soviet 2nd Ukrainian Front, Marshal Malinovski, reinforced the defence of the bridgehead with a Cavalry Corps of the 1st Guards Cavalry Mechanized Group and a further rifle corps from the reserves of the Front, while the German attack was already in progress. The Cavalry Corps had their own tanks and self-propelled guns, too. See *A Nagy Honvédő Háború története, 1941–1945. Ötödik kötet*. (History of the Great Patriotic War, 1941-1945. Book V) (Budapest, 1967), p.249.

the west.

Panzerkorps "Feldherrnhalle" was to carry out a deception manoeuvre on the front line section of the *271. Volksgrenadier-Division* (with the forces of this division) on the night preceding the start of the attack, by creating a smaller German bridgehead on the Garam.[7]

A document dated 14 February 1945 contained the exact dates for the attack, which had, in the meantime, been given the codename "*Südwind*" ("South Wind"): the attack was to begin at 0500 hours, at dawn, on 17 February.[8]

The regrouping of *Panzerkorps "Feldherrnhalle"* began on 12 February, as well as the transport of the elements that had arrived of the *I. SS-Panzerkorps*, to the assembly area east of Érsekújvár. However, the ground was drenched by the melted snow and this considerably slowed down the advance of the motorized columns. The extremely unfavourable terrain conditions threatened to delay the deployment of the armoured troops. The tracked vehicle transports continually arriving by train from the west were sent, after reloading, toward the area of Farnad via Győr.[9] Despite the difficulties faced by the troops, by 16 February they had taken up their assembly positions and were prepared to attack. In order to deceive the Soviets the points of departure were not occupied until the evening hours of 16 February.

In the meantime, units of the Soviet 7th Guards Army were continually fortifying their positions. Although Soviet military intelligence did not have definite information or exact data about the assembling German armoured formations, or the anticipated attack, they nevertheless sought to strengthen the Garam bridgehead by distributing the available forces the best possible way; the bridgehead constituted one of the points of departure for the planned offensive toward Vienna.[10]

The bridgehead was held by the forces of the 7th Guards Army (commander: Colonel General M. S. Sumilov).[11] On the north side of the bridgehead elements of the 24th Guards Rifle Corps (Major General A. J. Kruze) established their positions:

- 81st Guards Rifle Division (Colonel M. A. Orlov);
- 72nd Guards Rifle Division (Major General A. I. Loshev);
- 6th Guards Airborne Division (Major General M. N. Smirnov).

The west side of the bridgehead was defended by the 25th Guards Rifle Corps (Lieutenant General G. B. Safiulin). The following units had been attached to it:

7 The document is included in its entirety in Maier, 1985, pp.531-532. The names of the different settlements are included here in their exact forms.

8 HM HIM *Hadtörténelmi Levéltár* (Budapest) microfilm archives, *Kriegstagebuch Ia der Heeresgruppe Süd* (roll no. 629. image no. 7213521).

9 Tiemann, 1987, pp.231-232.

10 The Soviet command had only disclosed the forces gathering in the vicinity of the Balaton during the German attack that was launched on 17 February, although they had already received news of the German units' relocation eastward via Colonel Brinkmann, leader of the British military mission. See Tóth Sándor, *A szovjet hadsereg felszabadító harcai Magyarországon*. (Sándor Tóth: Liberating battles of the Soviet Army in Hungary) (Budapest, 1965), p.324.

11 Unfortunately, apart from Zaharov, the "embarrassed" Soviet recollections and military historical works usually depict the loss of the bridgehead at the Garam only with some short sentences. Therefore, they contain neither Tables of Organization and Equipment nor combat values. Therefore, we have to rely primarily on German reconnaissance data, although this entails the possibilities of inaccuracy and mistakes.

- 409th Rifle Division (Major General J. P. Grechaniy);
- 375th Rifle Division (Major General V. D. Karpukhin);
- Elements of the 53rd Rifle Division (Colonel D. V. Vasilyevskiy).

The 36th Guards Tank Brigade (Colonel P. S. Zhukov) and the 14th Guards Mechanized Brigade (Colonel N. A. Nikitin) of the 4th Guards Mechanized Corps were concentrated in the depths of the bridgehead, around Bart, in the sector of the 24th Guards Rifle Corps with a total of 19 T–34/85 tanks and one self-propelled gun. The majority of the tanks were positioned, one by one, in the directions where danger threatened.[12] Of the forces of the 4th Guards Mechanized Corps, apart from the latter, only the 527th Mortar Regiment, the 740th Anti-Aircraft Artillery Regiment, the 129th Independent Guards Mortar (rocket launcher) Artillery Battalion and the 138th Independent Engineer Battalion were stationed in the bridgehead. All the other troops were being reconstituted elsewhere.[13]

The 27th Independent Guards Tank Brigade, attached to the 7th Guards Army, had been waiting in defensive positions on 27 January between the western side of Karva and Hill 114 (2km northwest of Karva). There were seven operational T–34 tanks and four SU–85 self-propelled guns in its strength.[14]

North of the bridgehead, on the east bank of the Garam, stood the 141st, 243rd and the 303rd Rifle Divisions of the 27th Guards Rifle Corps. According to data pertaining to 1 February, the 93rd Guards Rifle Division was attached to the 7th Guards Army. The army-level artillery was provided by the 41st Guards Artillery Brigade, the 2nd and 11th Independent Anti-Tank Artillery Brigades, the 114th and 115th Guards Anti-Tank Artillery Regiments, the 263rd, 290th and the 493rd Mortar Regiments, and the 670th, 743rd, 1119th and the 1181st Anti-Aircraft Artillery Regiments of the 5th Anti-Aircraft Artillery Division. Also present were the 60th Engineer Brigade, the 176th Independent Flamethrower Company and the 38th Armoured Train Battalion.[15]

According to German air reconnaissance, as of 15 February, the Soviets had established a deeply echeloned system of defences. Thus, for example, they continued to build infantry positions northwest of Bart, and the anti-tank block position west of the village was reinforced by mortars. A continuous system of trenches was prepared extending from Ebed through Muzsla and Béla to Bart.[16]

In spite of the above-mentioned preparations, the Soviet troops were only able to carry out limited defensive measures, because the rifle divisions had received few reinforcements and, therefore, would be unreliable in combat. Furthermore, reconnaissance by both 2nd Ukrainian Front and the 7th Guards Army failed to identify any of the German regrouping

12 HM HIM *Hadtörténelmi Levéltár* (Budapest) microfilm archives, *Kriegstagebuch Ia der Heeresgruppe Süd* (roll no. 630. image no. 7213813) and Zaharov, 1973, p.367. For the command staff see the Appendices of Zaharov's cited work.

13 Tolubko, V. F. & Barisev, N. I., *Na yuzhnom flange. Boyevoy puty 4-go gvargyeskovo mehanishirovannogo corpus (1942–1945)* (On the southern flank. The combat path of the 4th Guards Mechanized Corps 1942-1945) (Moscow, 1973), p.369.

14 Combat reports of the commander of the tank and mechanized troops of the 7th Guards Army (copy owned by the author), Report no. 027, 27 January 1945.

15 *Boyevoy sostav sovetskoy armii. Casty V (yanvar-sentyabr 1945)* (Combat composition of the Soviet Army, Part V (January-September 1945) (Moscow, 1990), p.56.

16 Data published by Meyer, 1999, pp.484-485.

that was going on at the front line of the bridgehead between 7 and 16 February. The staff of the Army was unable to identify the forces facing them until the fourth day of the battle.[17]

The German units assigned to the offensive consisted of the following forces, as of 17 February 1945:

The *44. Reichsgrenadier-Division "Hoch- und Deutschmeister"* of *Panzerkorps "Feldherrnhalle"*, had three medium-strength, three average and one weak *Grenadier* battalions (with a total combat strength of 1600 men), a medium strength *Feld-Ersatzbataillon* (300 men) and an average *Pionier*-battalion (200 men), with 17 7.5cm heavy anti-tank guns, nine light and heavy artillery batteries. There was, in addition, a heavy artillery battery attached to it. The *Panzer-Aufklärungs-Zug/Panzerjäger-Abteilung 46* of the division had Italian light armoured cars, *Marder* tank destroyers in the *1. Kompanie*, *Jagdpanzer* 38(t) tank destroyers in the *2. Kompanie* and self-propelled automatic anti-aircraft guns in the *3. Kompanie*. The mobility of the division was 85%, and 58% for the motorized units. The division was only fit for limited offensive measures.

The combat strength of the *46. Infanterie Division* consisted of three medium strength and two average *Grenadier* battalions(with a total combat strength of 1800 men), a strong *Feld-Ersatz-Bataillon* (400 men), an average *Pionier* battalion (200 men) and 22 7.5cm heavy anti-tank guns. The following units were attached to it: a medium strength battalion of the *13. Panzer-Division* and an average battalion of *Panzer-Division "Feldherrnhalle"* with three heavy anti-tank guns, as well as three strong Hungarian battalions with a combat strength of approximately 1200 men, although this latter element was still in training. Its artillery comprised eight light and one heavy artillery batteries, and four light batteries attached to it from the Hungarian 23rd Reserve Division. The mobility of the formation was 90%, and 50% for the motorized units. The division was only fit for limited offensive measures.

The combat strength of the *211. Volksgrenadier-Division* consisted of two weak and two worn out *Grenadier* battalions (with a combined combat strength of 1000 men), a weak *Feld-Ersatz-Bataillon* (100 men) and an average *Pionier* battalion (200 men) with eight 7.5cm heavy anti-tank guns. A medium strength and a strong *Grenadier* battalion of the *271. Volksgrenadier-Division* were attached to it, as well as six Hungarian heavy anti-tank guns without their prime movers. Its artillery consisted of nine light and two heavy artillery batteries and the three light batteries of the *357. Infanterie Division*. *Panzerjäger-Abteilung 211* had a company of *Jagdpanzer* 38(t) tank destroyers. The mobility of the formation was 95% and 65% for the motorized units. The division was fit for only limited offensive missions.[18]

The armoured *Kampfgruppe* of *Panzerkorps "Feldherrnhalle"*, which was assembling at Farnad, consisted of the following elements (the combat-ready armoured fighting vehicles in brackets):

- *Schwere Panzer-Abteilung "Feldherrnhalle"* (25 *Tiger B* heavy tanks);
- *Panzer-Abteilung 208* (19 *Panzer* IVs and eight *Panzer* IV/70 [A] *Jagdpanzers*);
- *Marschbataillon* of *Panzer-Division "Feldherrnhalle"*;
- *II. Bataillon/Panzergrenadier-Regiment "Feldherrnhalle"*;

17 Zaharov, 1973, p.366.

18 HM HIM *Hadtörténelmi Levéltár* (Budapest) microfilm archives, *Kriegstagebuch Ia der Heeresgruppe Süd* (roll no. 630. image no. 7213718).

- *II. Bataillon/Panzergrenadier-Regiment 93*;
- *Panzerjäger-Abteilung 13* (approximately 15 *Panzer* IV/70 [V] *Jagdpanzers*);
- *3. Kompanie/Panzer-Pionier-Bataillon "Feldherrnhalle"*.[19]

The commander of the armoured *Kampfgruppe* was *Stabs Oberstleutnant* Hans Schöneich. The remnants of the two *Panzer* divisions of *Panzerkorps "Feldherrnhalle"* had the following armoured fighting vehicles available (although not all of them were in combat-ready condition):

Table 13 – Strength of the two *Panzer* divisions of *Panzerkorps "Feldherrnhalle"*, beginning of Operation "*Südwind*"

Unit	Tanks	*Jagdpanzers*	Armoured personnel carriers	Other	Total
13. Pz. Div.[1]	2 *Pz IIs*, 1 *Pz III*	17*PzIV L/70s*	6 *Sd.Kfz 250s* 34 *Sd.Kfz. 251s*	2 observation tanks 1 *Hummel* self-prop. howitzer	63
Pz. Div. "FHH"[2]	2 *Panthers*	–	5 *Sd.Kfz 250s* 14 *Sd.Kfz. 251s*	1 *Hummel* self-prop. howitzer	22
Total	5	17	59	4	85

1 Nevenkin, 2008, p.344.
2 Nevenkin, 2008, p.654.

The *I. SS-Panzerkorps,* under code name *SS-Abschnittsstab Süd,* provided the *Schwerpunkt* for the attack.

The commander of *SS-Ersatzstaffel Totenkopf* (*1. SS-Panzer-Division "Leibstandarte SS Adolf Hitler"*) was *SS-Brigadeführer und Generalmajor der Waffen-SS* Otto Kumm[20]. The total strength of the formation was 19,055 men. Its armament included:[21]

- 158 (of this, 146 combat-ready) MP 44 assault rifles
- 229 MG 42 light machine guns
- 306 MG 34 light machine guns (a total of 366 combat-ready MG 34 and MG 42 machine guns)
- 38 (20) heavy machine guns
- 55 (13) mortars
- 18 (18) 15cm *Nebelwerfer*
- 6 (6) 21cm *Nebelwerfer*
- 24 (5) flamethrowers

19 See Di Giusto, 2010, p.149.
20 Kumm assumed command of the division on 15 February 1945 from *SS-Brigadeführer und Generalmajor der Waffen-SS* Wilhelm Mohnke. Earlier, between 12 July 1941 and 1 May 1943 he was commander of the *Regiment "Der Führer"/SS-Panzer-Division "Das Reich"* on the Eastern Front, then on 30 January 1944 took over the command of the *7. SS-Freiwilligen-Gebirgs-Division "Prinz Eugen"*.
21 Tanks and *Jagdpanzers* are included in a different table.

- 21 (10) 7.5cm heavy anti-tank guns
- 840 (840) *Panzerfäuste*
- 32 (32) *Panzerschrecks*
- 14 (8) infantry guns (of this, five [3] self-propelled)
- 67 (50) anti-aircraft cannon
- 18 (14) 8.8cm anti-aircraft guns
- 17 (12) towed and one self-propelled light field howitzers
- 15 (8) towed heavy field howitzers
- 4 105mm guns
- 13 (4) heavy reconnaissance armoured cars
- 34 (12) light and 101 (72) medium armoured personnel carriers.[22]

The commander of *SS-Ersatzstaffel Wiking* (*12. SS-Panzer-Division "Hitlerjugend"*) was *SS-Brigadeführer und Generalmajor der Waffen-SS* Hugo Kraas. The total strength of the formation was 16,845 men. Apart from the armoured fighting vehicles, its armament included:

- 34 towed and two self-propelled light field howitzers
- nine towed heavy field howitzers
- three 10cm cannon
- 24 150mm *Nebelwerfer*
- eight 7.5cm heavy anti-tank guns
- 18 8.8cm anti-aircraft guns
- 22 automatic anti-aircraft guns and two 2cm self-propelled four-barrelled automatic anti-aircraft guns.[23]

There is no further general data regarding armament available. However, as a comparison, we provide here the armament, combat strength and vehicle strength of the *II (Bataillon)/SS-Panzergrenadier-Regiment 26*, four days prior to the assault. The combat strength of the battalion consisted of eight officers, 42 non-commissioned officers and 351 men (altogether 401 men). Their armament included the following: 76 handguns, five signal pistols, 192 carbines, four rifle grenade-launchers, seven semi-automatic rifles, 22 submachine guns, 33 MP 44 assault carbines, 27 MG 42 machine guns, five MG 34 machine guns, six other type machine guns, three 7.5cm heavy anti-tank guns, four 12cm heavy mortars, 61 *Panzerfäuste*, nine magnetic hollow charges and nine anti-tank mines. Their mobility was provided by two *Volkswagens*, four cars, two *Fiat* and two *Opel-Blitz* trucks, one armoured personnel carrier, one motorcycle, one prime mover, a half-track truck (*"Maultier"*) and one ambulance car.[24] The other battalions had approximately the same strength.

22 Tiemann, 1987, p.505, Appendix 11. The data refers to the situation on 12 February 1945, and that means the armament of the units not yet arrived in Hungary was also included in the list. The combat-ready armament is included in parentheses. The number of combat-ready armoured fighting vehicles is summarized in the next table.

23 Meyer, 1999, pp.481-482. The data refers to the situation on 1 February 1945. The number of combat-ready armoured fighting vehicles is summarized in table 1.

24 Meyer, Hubert, *Kriegsgeschichte der 12. SS-Panzerdivision "Hitlerjugend"* Band 2 (Osnabrück, 1987), 2nd edition, pp.815-817.

The German units taking part in the attack within the framework of the Operation "*Südwind*" on 17 February 1945 had the following available combat-ready armoured strengths:

Table 14 – Armoured strength of German units participating in Operation "*Südwind*", 17 February 1945

Unit	*Panzer IV*	*Panther*	*Tiger B*	*Panzer IV L/70*	*Jagdpanther*	*Jagdpanzer 38(t)*	Total
1. SS-Pz. Div.	21	26	19 [1]	7	–	–	73
12. SS-Pz. Div.	30	44	–	22[2]	4[3]	–	100
44. Reichsgren. Div. "HuD"	–	–	–	–	–	17[4]	17
46. Inf. Div.	16[5]	–	–	–	–	–	16
211. Volksgren.Div.	–	–	–	–	–	9	9
Pz. Gruppe "FHH"	19	–	25	23	–	–	67
Total	86	70	44	52	4	26	282

1 *Tiger B* heavy tanks of the *schwere SS-Panzer-Abteilung 501* assigned as the *II. (Abteilung)/ SS-Panzer-Regiment 1.*

2 Of these, nine *Panzer IV/70 Jagdpanzers* were part of the strength of the *schwere Panzerjäger-Abteilung 560* subordinated to the Division.

3 These *Jagdpanzers* were the vehicles of the *schwere Panzerjäger-Abteilung 560.*

4 Of these, nine *Jagdpanzer 38(t)* tank destroyers belonged to the *Panzerjäger-Kompanie 1335.*

5 *Panzer IV* tanks and *Panzer IV/70 Jagdpanzers* of the *Panzer-Abteilung 208* together.

At 0100 hours on 16 February 1945, as an introduction to the Operation "*Südwind*", on the left flank of *Panzerkorps "Feldherrnhalle"*, a reinforced regimental group of the *271. Volksgrenadier-Division* launched an attack northwest of Léva in order to cross the Garam in a diversion operation, establish a bridgehead on the east bank of the river, and, starting from this point, reach the Léva – Alsószecse railway line. Soviet counterattacks, launched during the early morning hours, had been effectively met by German ground-attack aircraft raids and were repelled, without exception.[25]

German preparations for the attacks went smoothly, and it became possible to launch the attack one hour earlier than originally planned (0500 hours). With this, the cover of darkness, which provided a considerable advantage, could be exploited for an additional hour. Finally, the time for the start of the attack was set for 0400 hours in the morning. Because of flooding in the area of the Párizs Canal, plans were also prepared for the armoured units to bypass to the west. *OKH* was informed of all this only three hours prior to the launch of the attack.[26]

25 Maier, 1985, p.148.

26 Maier, 1985, p.148.

On 13 February, the first trainloads of tanks for *schwere Panzer-Abteilung "Feldherrnhalle"* arrived through Komárom, and unloaded at Perbete. The area of Csúz was set as the assembly area for the formation.[27] There were not enough train carriages available for the transport of the vehicles, therefore the *3. Kompanie* had to wait until all of the empty carriages returned back to Mór on 15 February.

On 14 February the *Pionier* platoon of the *Abteilung* arrived to the area of Kürt to instal grousers for the *Tiger B* tanks to let the tanks climb to the otherwise barely accessible points of departure.[28]

On 15 February, the *Abteilung* commander studied the area of the prospective offensives around Kürt together with the company commanders, and contacted the commanders of the *Grenadier* units positioned along the MLR stretching from the north toward the south, on the eastern side of Kürt.

The company commanders then contacted each tank commander personally to brief them on their own company sectors of the front line section, thereby avoiding drawing unnecessary attention.[29]

According to the plan, the attack was to be launched in the area north of the road leading from Kürt toward the east. Due to the unfavourable terrain, the Soviets were less likely to expect a counterattack from there. However, reinforced anti-tank positions and minefields were identified on the road itself. Further difficulties were expected to unfold as the heavy tanks approached the hill.

The *Pionier* platoon of the *Abteilung* prepared a solid route that would also be usable for the *Tigers*, however, it was not a safe and secure undertaking for the heavy tanks to climb up this track under cover of darkness.[30] The *Abteilung* had 14 combat-ready *Tiger B* tanks that day.[31]

At 0200 hours on 17 February, reveille was ordered for the *Abteilung*. The independent unit, having, in the meantime, 25 combat-ready *Tiger B* tanks[32] (six to eight *Tiger Bs* in each company, two command *Tiger Bs* and armoured personnel carriers), set off at 0230 hours via Für and Kürt toward the vineyards north of Kürt. The tanks had to manoeuvre in complete darkness without any source of light to get to their points of departure.

The first phase of the German attack (17-19 February 1945)

At 0400 hours at dawn on **17 February**[33] – with an approximately two-hour artillery preparation – Operation "*Südwind*" began. Melting of snow thoroughly soaked the ground, and the Párizs Canal was flooded, forming considerable obstacles for the assaulting

27 Schneider, Wolfgang, *Tigers in Combat Volume 1* (Winnipeg, 1994), p.170.

28 Diary of Nordewin von Diest-Korber. In: Lochmann, Dr. Franz-Wilhelm, Richard Freiherr von Rosen, Alfred Rubbel & Rolf Sichel (hrsg.), *Erinnerungen an die Tiger-Abteilung 503 1942-1945* (Bassum, 1990), p.394.

29 The black uniform of the German armoured soldiers was practical on one hand, because the oil stains and other dirt were not visible on it; however it was extremely salient when the soldiers were inspecting the area of the anticipated attack on foot. The enemy could draw the necessary conclusions.

30 Lochmann, Freiherr von Rosen, Rubbel & Sichel (hrsg.), 1990, p.353

31 Schneider, 1994, p.170.

32 *Hauptmann* von Diest-Koerber remembers approximately 22 tanks. Lochmann, Freiherr von Rosen, Rubbel & Sichel (hrsg.), 1990, p.395; Schneider, 1994. The author includes this data on p.170.

33 Daily weather: temperature 5° Celsius, sky bright. The roads with solid surfaces were passable, the cart roads were passable only for tracked vehicles, wheeled vehicles moved with considerable difficulties.

Germans, especially for the armoured fighting vehicles that wrestled with the extremely disadvantageous terrain conditions. The Soviet units in defence in the deeply echeloned system of positions, packed with blocking positions and anti-tank obstacles, further slowed the pace of the attack down.

Schwere Panzer-Abteilung "Feldherrnhalle" (*Hauptmann* Nordewin von Diest-Koerber) set off at 0420 hours; tanks from the *3. Kompanie* advanced in the center of its battle formation[34]. The armoured fighting vehicles of the *2. Kompanie* drove forward on the left and the armoured fighting vehicles of the *1. Kompanie* advanced on the right. Under cover of their own artillery's fire preparation, the heavy tanks passed the preparatory positions. The artillery of the Soviet defence soon joined the battle. The supporting *Grenadiers* of the *44. Reichsgrenadier-Division "Hoch- und Deutschmeister"* suffered heavy losses in the raging shellfire.

One of the tanks of the *Abteilung* ran on a mine after having passed a Soviet trench. The *Pionier* platoon of the *Abteilung* arrived in the area in armoured personnel carriers and cleared a corridor through the mine defences.

The *Tiger B* advancing on the right of the tank of the *Abteilung* commander ("I") was knocked out and set aflame. By the light of the blazing fires the German tanks provided excellent targets to the Soviet anti-tank artillery.

When the *grenadiers* caught up, the advance continued. As the command tank passed another Soviet trench, a Soviet anti-tank grenade hit the side of its turret. As did every other tank commander during movements in darkness, out of pure necessity, in order to better navigate, the *Abteilung* commander drove with his head above the open hatch. A grenade fragment struck the back of his head. He had enough composure to turn over command to *Leutnant* Heerlein by radio. He was then transported to the rear in an ambulance armoured personnel carrier.

Not too long after these events, the attacking *Tiger B*s overran and destroyed a Soviet heavy artillery battery; after this, the Soviet defence quickly collapsed. At the end of the day, *Hauptmann* Wiegand assumed command of the *Abteilung*. The tank with turret number 112 had knocked out two Soviet anti-tank guns and two trucks.[35]

The *44. Reichsgrenadier-Division "Hoch- und Deutschmeister"*, starting from the area between Für and Kürt on the front line sector of *Panzerkorps "Feldherrnhalle"*, came up against heavy resistance of the Soviet 6th Guards Airborne Division. At 0420 hours the *Reichsgrenadier-Regiment "Hoch- und Deutschmeister"* and the soldiers of the *II. Bataillon/ Grenadier-Regiment 131* assaulted the Soviet positions and drove back the opposing forces. However, this could only be attained at the cost of heavy losses inflicted on them. *Grenadier-Regiment 132* was involved in the same kind of heavy combat. Its assaulting companies were temporarily halted at the wooded area around point no. 265 by the heavy Soviet machine gun, anti-tank gun and mortar fire.

After elimination of the remaining Soviet weapons pits, *Grenadier-Regiment 132* advanced from the west toward Magyarszőgyén and Németszőgyén, and, at about 1300 hours, after heavy fighting, thrust into the village. *Aufklärungs-Abteilung 44* and *Panzerjäger-Abteilung 46*, which were attached to the regiment, attacked from the north

34 The majority of the *3. Kompanie* did not arrive in time at Perbete, and, thus, could not join the attack until 18 February.

35 Diary of Hans Welsch, crew member of the tank with turret no. 112. (Typed manuscript, copy owned by the author, p.13).

and further increased pressure on the Soviets; in this way the attack soon gained ground and the villages were taken and held by the Germans. The regimental command post was established 100 metres west of the local church.

However, the Germans were yet to face an unpleasant surprise. Two *Marder* tank destroyers of the *1. Kompanie/Panzerjäger-Abteilung 46* and a self-propelled 2cm automatic anti-aircraft cannon of the *3. Kompanie* were driving along the forked main road of the village. Two soldiers were going ahead of the armoured fighting vehicles in order to spot mines in time. Suddenly fire was heard and they were seen lying on the ground. The self-propelled automatic anti-aircraft cannon opened fire at the church tower, approximately 500 metres away. Its fire incapacitated the Soviet observer. By firing a signal pistol at the last moment, the commander of the armoured fighting vehicle also managed to prevent the German *Fw* 190 ground-attack aircraft from attacking their own troops. As they moved forward, the self-propelled anti-aircraft cannon knocked out another truck and helped destroy an anti-tank gun, too.[36]

Other elements of the division (*II. Bataillon/Reichsgrenadier-Regiment "Hoch- und Deutschmeister", II. Bataillon/Grenadier-Regiment 131*), supported by the *Tiger B* heavy tanks of *schwere Panzer-Abteilung "Feldherrnhalle"*, advanced into the wooded area northwest of Magyarszőgyén during the afternoon hours, then charged through Ivánhalmapuszta and Aradpuszta and reached the Párizs Canal northeast of Kisújfalu. In the meantime, the Germans captured a number of enemy soldiers and seized a number of anti-tank guns.[37] During the attack, the commander of the *II. Bataillon/Reichsgrenadier-Regiment "Hoch- und Deutschmeister", Major* Günther Knoll, exercised command of the battle from a *Tiger B* heavy tank.[38]

The *46. Infanterie Division*, concentrating southeast of Nagyölved, fought in the centre, and advanced to the area approximately 3km southeast of Németszőgyén. This movement forced the surprised Soviets back out of their main line of resistance; the division advanced via point no. 190, reinforced by an anti-tank section, and reached the Párizs Canal west of Gyiva. The battle was effectively supported by the tanks and *Jagdpanzers* of *Panzer-Abteilung 208* and aircraft of the *Luftwaffe*.[39] *Panzer-Abteilung 208* (*Hauptmann* Loytved), however, suffered heavy losses while engaged in battle with the Soviet anti-tank guns. *Hauptmann* Jürgen von Stülpnagel, commander of the *3. Kompanie*, fell 4km southeast of Németszőgyén.[40] The *Panzer* IV/70 (A) *Jagdpanzers* of the *1. Kompanie* reached Köbölkút, where the armoured fighting vehicle of the commander of the III. *Zug* was knocked out by the Soviets.[41]

The *211. Volksgrenadier-Division* attacked from the area of Érsekkéty toward Bart, and its leading elements reached the valley southwest of Bart. However, the constantly increasing Soviet resistance did not let the division continue the attack toward Bart from

36 Agis, Hermann, *Das Ende am Plattensee. Die 44. Infanterie-Division "Reichsgrenadier-Division Hoch- und Deutschmeister" im Endkampf* (Nürnberg, 2006), p.107.

37 HM HIM *Hadtörténelmi Levéltár* (Budapest) microfilm archives, *Kriegstagebuch Ia der Heeresgruppe Süd* (roll no. 631. image no. 7214040), and Schimack, A., *Die 44. Infanterie-Division. Das Tagebuch der Hoch- und Deutschmeister* (Wien, 1969), pp.334-336.

38 Agis, 2006, p.108.

39 Maier, 1985, p.149, and HM HIM *Hadtörténelmi Levéltár* (Budapest) microfilm archives, *Kriegstagebuch Ia der Heeresgruppe Süd* (roll no. 631. image no. 7214040).

40 Volleth, 1975.

41 Di Giusto, 2010, p.150.

the southwest until the late afternoon hours. East of the village, the advance of one of its regimental groups was stopped and held up by a surprise counterattack of the Soviets. The other elements of the division established blocking positions facing south-east during the rest of the day.[42]

The forces of the *1. SS-Panzer-Division* closed up behind the assault formation of the *46. Infanterie Division*.

The forces of the *1. SS-Panzer-Division "Leibstandarte SS Adolf HItler"* that had already arrived were divided into two *Kampfgruppen*. The *Infanterie-Gruppe* of the division, commanded by *SS-Obersturmbannführer* Max Hansen[43], occupied points of departure north of Kural. The *Kampfgruppe* consisted of elements of SS-*Panzergrenadier-Regiment 1* and *2*, elements of *SS-Panzer-Aufklärungs-Abteilung 1*, the *1. Kompanie/SS-Panzerjäger-Abteilung 1* (seven *Panzer* IV/70 *Jagdpanzers*) and two batteries of 3.7cm automatic anti-aircraft guns.[44]

The *Panzer-Gruppe* that was in position southeast of Farnad, commanded by *SS-Obersturmbannführer* Jochen Peiper, commander of *SS-Panzer-Regiment 1*, prepared to exploit the successes of the *46. Infanterie Division*. The *Kampfgruppe* consisted of the following units: *SS-Sturmbannführer* Werner Poetschke's *I.* (mixed) *(Abteilung)/SS-Panzer-Regiment 1* (*1. Kompanie*: 12 *Panthers*; *2. Kompanie*: 13 *Panthers*; *6. Kompanie*: 10 *Panzer* IVs; *7. Kompanie*: 11 *Panzer* IVs), *schwere SS-Panzer-Abteilung 501* of *SS-Obersturmbannführer* Heinz von Westernhagen (the unit was employed as *II. Abteilung* of the *Panzer-Regiment*) (staff: two *Tiger Bs*, *1. Kompanie*: six *Tiger Bs*; *2. Kompanie*: 14 *Tiger Bs*; *3. Kompanie*: 14 *Tiger Bs*[45]; *4. Kompanie*: eight 2 and 3.7cm automatic anti-aircraft guns mounted on *Panzer* IV chassis), the III (armoured) *Bataillon/SS-Panzergrenadier-Regiment* 2 commanded by *SS-Sturmbannführer* Jupp Diefenthal, and the *I.* (self-propelled) *Artillerie-Abteilung/SS-Panzer-Artillerie-Regiment 1* and the *3.* (armoured) *Kompanie/SS-Panzer-Pionier-Bataillon 1*.[46]

After the *grenadiers* of the *46. Infanterie Division* had broken through the tactical depths of the Soviet defence, they came up against a reinforced Soviet anti-tank sector southeast of Németszőgyén and their advance was halted. The *Waffen-SS Kampfgruppen* had also moved out in the early morning hours.

Panzer-Gruppe "Peiper", followed by *Kampfgruppe "Hansen"*, set off from Serespuszta and, at about noon, closed up to the order of battle of the *46. Infanterie-Division*. The tanks and armoured personnel carriers – avoiding the difficult terrain – advanced on the road between Farnad and Németszőgyén. The *Panther* heavy tanks of the *1. Kompanie/SS-Panzer-Regiment 1* led the way; after a while they took over the task of securing the right flank of the group. During their advance, they came under badly directed Soviet mortar fire, but did not suffer any losses. After a brief position assessment, the group took positions on the left side of the road leading to Németszőgyén in a deeply echeloned inverted wedge

42 HM HIM *Hadtörténelmi Levéltár* (Budapest) microfilm archives, *Kriegstagebuch Ia der Heeresgruppe Süd* (roll no. 631. image no. 7214040).

43 Hansen was the commander of SS-*Panzergrenadier-Regiment 1*.

44 The Germans used their automatic anti-aircraft cannon as often against infantry and weakly armoured ground targets as against aircraft. Their firepower, especially against Soviet infantry mass attacks, was destructive.

45 Of the remaining 36 heavy tanks 19 were in combat-ready condition.

46 Tiemann, 1987, pp.232-233 and Agte, Patrick, *Jochen Peiper. Kommandeur Panzerregiment Leibstandarte* (Berg am Starnberger See, 1998), p.344.

formation (the *Panther* and *Tiger B* heavy tank companies on the flanks, followed by the *Panzer* IV companies and the *III. Bataillon/SS-Panzergrenadier-Regiment 2*, equipped with armoured personnel carriers). In front of Németszőgyén the *Panzer-Gruppe* came under heavy anti-tank gun fire.

Upon this, the vehicles accelerated, exploiting the cover offered by the terrain, and assembled to attack behind a slope. Their preparations were constantly interfered with by heavy mortar and rocket launcher-fire. *SS-Obersturmbannführer* Peiper sent five *Tiger Bs* to the hill, and, protected by their thick armour, the vehicles started to knock out the Soviet anti-tank guns, one by one. After elements of *SS-Panzergrenadier-Regiment 1* also joined in (*Kampfgruppe "Hansen"* was supporting the fight of the *46. Infanterie-Division* until then), the tanks and armoured personnel carriers, firing all of their available firearms, even signal pistols, poured over the edge of the hill and engaged the Soviet anti-tank positions in a blaze of fire. The concentrated tank gun, automatic anti-aircraft cannon and machine gun fire did its bit: the Soviets retreated with their numerous heavy weapons. The road was free toward the Párizs Canal. *Panzer-Gruppe "Peiper"* and elements of the *46. Infanterie-Division* reached the canal east and west of Sárkányfalva in the evening. As the Soviets were destroying the bridges there, the wedge formations had to stop until, in the darkness, they could force the crossing to the other bank.[47]

The *12. SS-Panzer-Division "Hitlerjugend"* launched its attack in the afternoon hours. Its forces lined up west of the *1. SS-Panzer-Division "Leibstandarte SS Adolf Hitler"*, on the right side, behind the *46. Infanterie-Division*. *SS-Panzergrenadier-Regiment*[48] attacked on the right flank and *SS-Panzergrenadier-Regiment 26*[49] on the left. By 2100 hours, in the night, the *I. Bataillon/SS-Panzergrenadier-Regiment 26* occupied a small bridgehead on the south bank of the canal, southeast of Párizspuszta. As the *II. Bataillon/SS-Panzergrenadier-Regiment 26* was closing up, the bridgehead was soon widened. At 0045 hours on 18 February, the *II. Bataillon/SS-Panzergrenadier-Regiment 26* had already reached the road junction 800 metres southeast of Párizspuszta. The battalions of *SS-Panzergrenadier-Regiment 26* established temporary defence positions on the areas already captured.[50]

In the evening of 17 February, the Germans took advantage of the fact that the Soviets had ordered the 93rd Guards Rifle Division, until then in defence on the northern bank of the Danube, to launch a counterattack against the German forces that had broken through, and, thereby, weakened their defence in that area. *Kampfgruppe "Hupe"* (*Grenadier-Regiment 284, II. Bataillon/Grenadier-Regiment 287,* with fire support from the *2.* and *3. Batterie* of *Sturm-Artillerie-Brigade 239,* with 20 *StuG.* IIIs and *StuH.* 42s) of the German *96. Infanterie-Division,* started the crossing manoeuvre from the area of Tát to the sector of Ebed on the northern bank of the Danube, in order to support the German groups that were attacking and prevent the Soviets from holding a reduced bridgehead by leaning on Muzsla.[51]

A number of *StuH.* 42 assault howitzers of *Sturm-Artillerie-Brigade 239* (commanded by *Oberleutnant* Senkpiel) occupied firing positions in Esztergom, near the basilica, and

47 Tiemann, 1987, pp.235-237, and HM HIM *Hadtörténelmi Levéltár* (Budapest) microfilm archives, *Kriegstagebuch Ia der Heeresgruppe Süd* (roll no. 631. image no. 7214040).

48 The commander was *SS-Obersturmbannführer* Siegfried Müller.

49 The commander of the regiment was *SS-Obersturmbannführer* Bernhard Krause.

50 Meyer, 1999, p.487.

51 Maier, 1985, p.149.

engaged the Soviets tanks and self-propelled guns that were assembling in the Párkány area. [52]

The German *Armee* artillery shelled Nána and Kőhídgyarmat during the day.[53] The *Luftwaffe* supported *Panzerkorps "Feldherrnhalle"* with 90 ground-attack and fighter aircraft, and raided the Bény area with 30 bombers.[54]

At about 2300 hours, during the night, the Germans crossed the Párizs Canal at two points and held two lesser bridgeheads on the south bank. They found a crossing point northeast of Köbölkút where the armoured fighting vehicles were also able to cross.[55]

The 7th Guards Army claimed to have knocked out and/or destroyed 54 German armoured fighting vehicles on the first day of the operation. Of these, 11 were knocked out by one battery (Guards Lieutenant Rodin) of the 155th Guards Artillery Regiment/72nd Guards Rifle Division near point no. 177, 3km southwest of Bart.[56]

The Soviet Front Command noticed that the centre of the German attack was directed at the boundary between the 25th Guards and the 24th Guards Rifle Corps. The swift breakthrough of the attacking forces toward the south and southeast, and the encirclement of the two divisions of the 25th Guards Rifle Corps were possible because the two corps commanders did not do all that was needed in order to organize effective defence by the troops.[57]

On **18 February** [58], the German attack continued. On the right flank of *Panzerkorps "Feldherrnhalle"*, *Kampfgruppe "Staubwasser"* (*I.* and *II. Bataillon/Grenadier-Regiment 945, II. Bataillon/Grenadier-Regiment 946* and *Maschinengewehr-Bataillon "Sachsen"*) closed up to the left flank of the *44. Reichsgrenadier-Division "Hoch- und Deutschmeister"*, occupied Óriáspuszta, and advanced further toward Bátorkeszi.[59]

After *Artillerie-Regiment 96* displaced toward Für, the *44. Reichsgrenadier-Division "Hoch- und Deutschmeister"* managed to cross the canal at Kisújfalu, and, in the course of the afternoon, occupied the village of Köbölkút and the wooded area northeast of it. Elements of the division reached the Bátorkeszi – Köbölkút road 3.5km northeast of Bátorkeszi. [60]

The *Tiger B* heavy tanks of *schwere Panzer-Abteilung "Feldherrnhalle"*, attached to the division, after breaking through a Soviet anti-tank block position reinforced with tanks northwest of Kisújfalu, advanced further with the support of the mounted *grenadiers* via point no. 129 (2.5km south of Köbölkút) along the railway toward Párkány, toward the southeast. Their advance was slowed down at various points by minefields. One of

52 Kurowski & Tornau, 1978, pp.283-284.

53 Maier, 1985.p.150.

54 HM HIM *Hadtörténelmi Levéltár* (Budapest) microfilm archives, *Kriegstagebuch Ia der Heeresgruppe Süd* (roll no. 630. image no. 7214041).

55 Maier, 1985, p.150.

56 Zaharov, 1973, p.367.

57 Zaharov, 1973, p.367.

58 Weather that day: mild frost at night, 6° Celsius during the day, slightly cloudy, sunny. The roads remained unchanged.

59 HM HIM *Hadtörténelmi Levéltár* (Budapest) microfilm archives, *Kriegstagebuch Ia der Heeresgruppe Süd* (roll no. 631. image no. 7214043. and 7214049).

60 Schimack, 1969, p.337, HM HIM *Hadtörténelmi Levéltár* (Budapest) microfilm archives, *Kriegstagebuch Ia der Heeresgruppe Süd* (roll no. 631. image no. 7214049).

the liaison officers of the German artillery, as the sixth member of the crew, directed fire support by radio from one of the heavy tanks. Before darkness fell, the *schwere Panzer-Abteilung* received orders from the *Grenadier-Division* by radio to continue its advance to Béla. En route, it repeatedly came under fire from Soviet tanks and self-propelled guns deployed in delaying combat. At about midnight the *schwere Panzer Abteilung* saw white signal rockets, indicating the positions of *Panzer-Gruppe "Peiper"* of the *1. SS-Panzer-Division "Leibstandarte SS Adolf Hitler"*, which had advanced to the Muzsla area.[61]

After the advance of the heavy armament of the *46. Infanterie Division*, in the afternoon, the formation attacked toward the east, but stumbled upon Soviet positions that put up a fierce defence. In spite of this, the German force managed to advance into the area north of Libád.[62]

Even though it had the support of the *2. Kompanie/Panzer-Abteilung 208* [63], the repeated attacks of the *211. Volksgrenadier-Division* were unsuccessful against the Soviet troops defending Bart, and the Germans were forced to go over to the defensive. Followed by this, the German division had to repel a number of Soviet reconnaissance missions.[64]

The 36th Guards Tank Brigade was engaged in dynamic battle with the German armoured fighting vehicles supporting the German infantry that were defending in the sector of the 72nd Guards Rifle Division around point no. 153, and knocked out five of them.[65] The 292nd Guards Self-Propelled Artillery Regiment/4th Guards Mechanized Corps soon arrived to reinforce the tank brigade, with a strength of 20 SU–76M self-propelled guns.[66]

Kampfgruppe "Hansen", of the *1. SS-Panzer-Division "Leibstandarte SS Adolf Hitler"*, established a bridgehead on the two sides of Sárkányfalva with the support of units of the *46. Infanterie Division*. The bridgehead was further broadened by attacking south in the morning, in the face of strong Soviet resistance. The Soviets lost four T–34s in the urban combat going on in the southern part of Sárkányfalva (two were knocked out by the *Panzerbüchse-Zug /6. Kompanie* of *SS-Panzergrenadier-Regiment 1* with *Panzerschreck*[67]). There was a Soviet anti-tank position located on the hill south of the village, which was overrun by the *SS-Panzergrenadiers* supported by fire of the *Panzer* IV/70 *Jagdpanzers* of the *1. Kompanie/SS-Panzerjäger-Abteilung 1* at about noon. After this, the unit dug itself in and waited for the armoured fighting vehicles of *Panzer-Gruppe "Peiper"*.

At 1250 hours, the armoured fighting vehicles started crossing over to the other bank on the pontoon bridge constructed by the *Pioniers*, and, having completed the crossing,

61 HM HIM *Hadtörténelmi Levéltár* (Budapest) microfilm archives, *Kriegstagebuch Ia der Heeresgruppe Süd* (roll no. 631. image no. 7214049), and Számvéber, Norbert, A német 503. nehézpáncélososztály magyarországi harcai 1944-1945. Szakdolgozat. (Norbert Számvéber: Combat history of the schwere Panzer-Abteilung 503 in Hungary 1944-45. Thesis) (Budapest, 1999), p.83.

62 HM HIM *Hadtörténelmi Levéltár* (Budapest) microfilm archives, *Kriegstagebuch Ia der Heeresgruppe Süd* (roll no. 631. image no. 7214049).

63 Di Giusto, 2010, p.150.

64 HM HIM *Hadtörténelmi Levéltár* (Budapest) microfilm archives, *Kriegstagebuch Ia der Heeresgruppe Süd* (roll no. 631. image no. 7214049).

65 Zaharov, 1973, p.367.

66 Tolubko & Barisev, 1973, p.372.

67 The *Panzerschreck* was a recoilless, reusable handheld anti-tank rocket launcher, which penetrated 160mm armour from a distance of 150-180 metres. Although German and Hungarian regulations prohibited the use of the *Panzerschreck* against infantry and strongpoint targets, due to shortage of ammunition, they were often used in such manner during urban combat with destructive effect.

continued their attack toward the south. The fire of a number of lesser anti-tank blocking positions and the mass raid by aircraft of the Soviet Air Force interfered with their advance; however, the air raids were of no effect for the time in question. The *SS-Panzers* rounded Béla from the left. During the evening they reached the Köbölkút – Párkány road, and then the hills northeast of Muzsla. As information regarding the enemy positions was scarce and indefinite, the night was spent in all-around ("hedgehog") defence on the two sides of the roads leading to Köbölkút and Párkány.[68]

The *Panzergrenadier* regiments of the *12. SS-Panzer-Division "Hitlerjugend"* were regrouping when a Soviet counterattack was launched against them in the dawn hours with a battalion-sized unit, which was also supported by two T–34 tanks and some anti-tank guns. The attack was repulsed by the Germans. After this, the *II. Bataillon/SS-Panzergrenadier-Regiment 26* established positions on the hill 350 metres south of the road junction.

During the afternoon, *SS-Panzergrenadier-Regiment 25*, supporting the elements of the *44. Reichsgrenadier-Division "Hoch- und Deutschmeister"* in occupying Köbölkút, thrust into the eastern part of the village and to the hill north of it. To the left of the *Grenadier-Division*, and north of the village, the *III* (armoured) *Bataillon /SS-Panzergrenadier-Regiment* [69] attacked with its armoured personnel carriers, elements of which had already carried out reconnaissance in the area during the preceding night and had lost two armoured personnel carriers. The supporting artillery and the machine guns, 2cm triple-barrelled cannon and mortars mounted on armoured personnel carriers, concentrated their fire. The Soviet anti-tank gun and mortar positions were eliminated, and the sector occupied. In the meantime, the *I. Bataillon/SS-Panzergrenadier-Regiment 26* occupied the eastern part of Köbölkút, the *II. Bataillon/SS-Panzergrenadier-Regiment 26* continued its attack south, occupied point no. 186, advanced further toward the Köbölkút – Párkány railway and established securing positions there facing toward the south and southeast.[70]

Based on the events of the day, the German high command assumed that the Soviets would attempt to establish a new MLR along the blocking line Bart – Libád – northern Danube. According to German assessment, the centre of the Soviet defensive efforts (and a possible starting point for a Soviet counterattack) was the area between Bény and Bart, where the Soviet Air Force attempted to create an air blockade. In light of all this, the units of the German *8. Armee* faced the following tasks:

- *1. SS-Panzer-Division "Leibstandarte SS Adolf Hitler"* was to get in the rear of the Soviet blocking position established between Béla and Muzsla;
- *46. Infanterie Division* was to advance eastward on both banks of the Párizs Canal and was to occupy the hills east of Libád and west of Kéménd;
- *211. Volksgrenadier-Division* was to remain in the area of Bart in order to contain and repel the anticipated flank attack by the Soviets.

In order to accomplish this last aim, the German *8. Armee* considered evacuating its own bridgehead that had been established northwest of Léva in order to reinforce the considerably weakened *211. Volksgrenadier-Division* with the two battalions withdrawn

68 Tiemann, 1987, pp.238-240 and Maier, 1985, p.151.

69 Its commander was *SS-Sturmbannführer* Hermann Brandt.

70 Meyer, 1999, p.488.

from there. The Germans were surprised to be able to identify only one Soviet assault formation: they found a unit north of Nána with approximately 30 armoured fighting vehicles.[71] In our opinion, this observed Soviet tank formation was the 27th Independent Guards Tank Brigade (Colonel N. M. Brizhinev).

Besides all the above-mentioned aspects, it was also important that communication be established with *Kampfgruppe "Hupe"* of the *96. Infanterie-Division*, which was fighting in the Ebed area, because that was the only way that forces needed for the attack against Bart and the advance to the Garam line could be freed up.[72]

The four *StuH.* 42 assault howitzers of *Sturm-Artillerie-Brigade 239* (commanded by *Leutnant* Marx) that were attached to *Kampfgruppe "Hupe"* had already been engaged in combat since 0400 hours, at dawn, north of the Danube toward Ebed. The *3. Batterie* of the brigade (*Oberleutnant* Kettl) was being transported by the German *Pioniers* to the north bank of the Danube since 0700 hours in the morning, and the *2. Batterie* (*Leutnant* Linder) was likewise being transported, starting at 1100 hours. By evening the German assault guns had knocked out a Soviet T–34 tank.[73]

The *4. Luftflotte* of the *Luftwaffe* attacked the Garam crossing points and the bridge at Bény in 140 sorties that day, on which one hit was recorded, according to the reports. It was able to do even less to counter the Soviet ground-attack and fighter aircraft activity.[74]

On **19 February**[75], the situation of the Soviet troops in the southern sector of the bridgehead became catastrophic. In the early morning hours, *Kampfgruppe "Staubwasser"* occupied the villages of Búcs and Bátorkeszi and cleared the surrounding areas of the remnants of the shattered Soviet units.[76]

The *44. Reichsgrenadier-Division "Hoch- und Deutschmeister"* advanced from the Köbölkút area south to the Danube, in order to clear the area south of the Búcs – Muzsla line of the remnants of Soviet units. *Aufklärungs-Abteilung 44* advanced toward Bátorkeszi with the support of the *Tiger B* heavy tanks of *schwere Panzer-Abteilung "Feldherrnhalle"*, the *Jagdpanzer* 38(t) tank destroyers of *Panzerjäger-Abteilung 46* and the *Panzerjäger-Kompanie 1335*, but the village had already been captured by *Kampfgruppe "Staubwasser"*.[77]

Kampfgruppe "Hupe", of the *96. Infanterie Division*, was fighting in the Ebed area. At 0600 hours in the morning, Soviet tanks launched a counterattack from the north with the aim of retaking the village, and, in the meantime, two *StuH.* 42 assault howitzers of *Sturm-Artillerie-Brigade 239* were knocked out by 0900 hours. The commander of the *2. Batterie/Sturm-Artillerie-Brigade 239*, *Leutnant* Theodor Linder, was killed, together with

71 Maier, 1985, p.151.

72 Maier, 1985, p.152.

73 From a letter of Dr. Willy R. Jaitner, a former *Oberleutnant* of *Sturm-Artillerie-Brigade 239* to András Palásthy, dated 27 February 1988. Copy owned by the author.

74 HM HIM *Hadtörténelmi Levéltár* (Budapest) microfilm archives, *Kriegstagebuch Ia der Heeresgruppe Süd* (roll no. 630. image no. 7214050).

75 The weather that day: frost at night, 6° Celsius during the day, generally bright and sunny. The cart tracks were drying up.

76 HM HIM *Hadtörténelmi Levéltár* (Budapest) microfilm archives, *Kriegstagebuch Ia der Heeresgruppe Süd* (roll no. 631. image no. 7214056).

77 Schimack, Wien, 1969, p.337, and HM HIM *Hadtörténelmi Levéltár* (Budapest) microfilm archives, *Kriegstagebuch Ia der Heeresgruppe Süd* (roll no. 631. image no. 7214056).

his crew.[78]

In the early morning hours, the *46. Infanterie Division* occupied the hills southeast of Libád in a perfectly executed manoeuvre, and, with this, gained observation of the Garam river. Subsequently, the assault of armoured *Kampfgruppe "Schöneich"*, attached to the division at Kéménd, was repulsed by the Soviet defence. The division, supported by the attached *Panzer-Gruppe* (mainly *Panzer-Abteilung 208* and *Panzerjäger-Abteilung 13*), launched an attack in the evening to take Kőhídgyarmat, but the attempt failed.[79]

Panzer-Abteilung 208, attacking toward Kéménd, found itself in an extremely difficult situation that day in the Bibitpuszta sector. This was the consequence of the German infantry's failure to follow the *Panzer* IV tanks and *Panzer* IV/70 (A) *Jagdpanzers* into the Soviet artillery and anti-tank gun fire. At the same time, the Soviet infantry launched counterattacks. In this way, the German troops suffered heavy losses and were forced to abandon their vehicles, if only for a short time, and retreat on foot. Later a German counterattack recaptured the area and the armoured fighting vehicles were then towed away; a number of them were damaged. One of the command tanks of the *Abteilung* staff burnt out and therefore was rendered inoperable. Following this, the extremely weakened *Panzer-Abteilung* played no further part in the operation.[80]

One of the gunners of the 1st Battalion/Soviet 36th Guards Tank Brigade fighting in the Kéménd area, Guards-Corporal V. J. Tolstov, knocked out a total of nine armoured fighting vehicles, five armoured personnel carriers and 11 mortars from his ambush position while defending the crossing point on the Garam. Later he was awarded the Hero of the Soviet Union for his deed.[81]

In the early morning, the *Panzer-Gruppe* of the *1. SS-Panzer-Division "Leibstandarte SS Adolf Hitler"* advanced further from its positions northeast of Muzsla toward Párkány, in order to reach the mouth of the Garam. They were to cross a stone bridge over a creek before reaching Muzsla, but the first few *Panzer* IV and *Panther* tanks ran over mines and were rendered immobile. The other tanks and armoured personnel carriers crossed at a less steep area, but a few more armoured fighting vehicles stalled, and needed towing. With this, there were already eight temporarily immobile tanks lost at the bridge. After the soldiers of the *9. (Panzer-Pionier) Kompanie/SS-Panzer-Regiment 1* cleared the mines, the stone bridge was again available for use.[82] Not long after this, Soviet ground-attack aircraft attacked the armoured fighting vehicles and caused considerable damage (a number of armoured fighting vehicles were damaged, some personnel were wounded).

In the meantime, the Germans noticed three Soviet tanks trying to retreat toward the Párkány railway station on the other side of the Párkány railway embankment. Seven *Panther* tanks of the *1. Kompanie/SS-Panzer-Regiment 1* led the German *Panzer-Gruppe* pursuing them. The armoured fighting vehicles found the going difficult on the deep, soggy ground. Suddenly the Soviet tanks moved out from the cover of the embankment and attacked the side of the exposed right flank of the company. A *Panzer V* was instantly

78 Kurowski & Tornau, 1978, p.284.

79 HM HIM *Hadtörténelmi Levéltár* (Budapest) microfilm archives, *Kriegstagebuch Ia der Heeresgruppe Süd* (roll no. 631. image no. 7214056).

80 Di Giusto, 2010, p.150.

81 Malakhov, M. M., *Osvobozhdeniye Vengrii i Vostochny Avstrii* (The liberation of Hungary and Eastern Austria) (Moscow, 1965), p.168.

82 *Der Freiwillige 1995/2*, pp.20-21.

knocked out (the crew got out of the vehicle in time). Meanwhile two *Panthers* reached the railway station, and took cover behind a locomotive stand. At that moment, one of them (the tank of the leader of the *III Zug/1. SS-Panzer-Kompanie*) was again hit and set aflame. In the cover provided by the burning tank, the other one drove around the locomotive stand and shot the Soviet T–34 in the side from a range of 50 metres, which also set the T–34 alight. The second round fired by the *Panther* tore off the turret of the tank. The arriving *Tiger B* heavy tanks and the *Panthers* of the *2. Kompanie/SS-Panzer-Regiment 1* knocked out two more T–34s. The third Soviet tank turned round and fled to the other side of the railway.

In the meantime, an element of *Kampfgruppe "Hansen"* was occupied with clearing Béla, where the *Panzerjäger-Zug* of the *6. Kompanie/SS-Panzergrenadier-Regiment 1* knocked out another T–34.

Panzer-Gruppe "Peiper" advanced farther toward the southeast, and its attack gained considerable ground. It eliminated minor Soviet anti-tank blocking positions in front of Kismuzslapuszta, Muzsla and Párkány. Another Soviet ground-attack aircraft raid caused losses to the *Kampfgruppe*. Despite this, the *I. (Abteilung)/SS-Panzer-Regiment 1*, with the *1. Komnpanie* in the lead, exploiting the support of the *Tiger B* heavy tanks and the *Panzer-Gruppe* of the *12. SS-Panzer-Division "Hitlerjugend"*, thrust into the north-eastern part of Párkány at about 1300 hours. At the same time, the assault guns supporting *Kampfgruppe "Hupe"* also launched their attack and advanced into the south-western part of the village. North of Esztergom, an assault group of the *711. Infanterie Division* attacked toward Párkány and forced its way into the innermost parts of the town. [83]

During the fighting for Párkány, the *III.* (armoured) *Bataillon/SS-Panzergrenadier-Regiment 2*, commanded by *SS-Sturmbannführer* Jupp Diefenthal, launched an attack to occupy Nána and soon cleared the village of Soviet troops. The battalion was supported by the *Panzer* IV tanks of the *6. Kompanie/SS-Panzer-Regiment I*.[84]

The *Panzer-Gruppe* of the *12. SS-Panzer-Division "Hitlerjugend"* (the *II. (Abteilung)/ SS-Panzer-Regiment 12* and the *III. Bataillon/SS-Panzergrenadier-Regiment 26*) was located southwest of Köbölkút, when, south of the Köbölkút – Muzsla road, the Soviets attempted to retake the ground lost the day before. The local incursions were eliminated by the two *Panzergrenadier* regiments of the division. The *Panzer-Gruppe* launched its attack at 0530 hours through the lines of the *Panzergrenadier-Bataillone*. The armoured personnel carrier battalion was in the lead, on both sides of the road connecting Köbölkút and Muzsla. The *Panzer-Abteilung* of *SS-Hauptsturmführer* Hans Siegel followed on the road itself because of the danger of mines.

The armoured personnel carriers of the *III. Bataillon/SS-Panzergrenadier-Regiment 26* soon came under anti-tank gun and artillery fire from the direction of Muzsla. The *Panzer-Abteilung*, moved to the fore and eliminated the Soviet resistance by dawn with the help of the *2. Kompanie*, managing to secure the village. The surrounding area was cleared by the soldiers of the *I.* and *II. Bataillon/SS-Panzergrenadier-Regiment 26*. The

83 Agte, 1998, p.347. The German units captured 43 tanks of various type and manufacture, but not Soviet made, at the Párkány railway station, and another 35 at the north-western edge of the village. The majority of the armoured fighting vehicles had Hungarian markings. For this, see HM HIM *Hadtörténelmi Levéltár* (Budapest) microfilm archives, *Kriegstagebuch Ia der Heeresgruppe Süd* (roll no. 630. image no. 7213813).

84 Agte, 1998, p.347.

latter battalion was assigned the task of establishing contact with *Kampfgruppe "Hupe"* by attacking through Ebed in the direction of Párkány. *SS-Panzergrenadier-Regiment 25* ran into considerable Soviet resistance during its attack north of the Köbölkút – Muzsla road. Therefore, the support of the *Panther* tanks that were coming from the direction of Muzsla was very useful. With their help, the regiment was able to close up to the main body of the division by about 1200 hours.

The *Panzer-Gruppe* regrouped before the assault on Párkány. In the meantime, *SS-Panzergrenadier-Regiment 26*, driving from Muzsla toward Ebed, came under rocket launcher-fire, in consequence of which the commander of the regiment, *SS-Obersturmbannführer* Bernhard Krause, was mortally wounded.[85]

The attack of the *Panzer-Gruppe* was launched at about 1200 hours. In the urban combat that ensued, the *II. (Abteilung)/SS-Panzer-Regiment 12* managed to knock out a number of T–34 and T–34/85 type Soviet tanks. The *9. Kompanie/III. Bataillon* of *SS-Panzergrenadier-Regiment 26* lost two armoured personnel carriers during the engagement.[86]

Despite the fact that German fighter aircraft shot down six Soviet aircraft and did everything they could to provide cover for their own troops against superior numbers of enemy machines, the Soviets won nearly absolute control of the air on that day. Their ground-attack aircraft formations attacked without pause and caused heavy losses to the armoured wedge formations of the *1. SS-Panzer-Division "Leibstandarte SS Adolf Hitler*, and the anti-aircraft weapons of the ground troops, mounted on barrels, provided little shelter against the attackers.[87]

However, control of the air could not save the southern sector of the Soviet bridgehead either. The troops of the completely smashed 25th Guards Rifle Corps abandoned their positions in the evening of 19 February without being ordered to do so by the commander of the 7th Guards Army and fled to the east bank of the Garam. Consequently, the defence of the remaining bridgehead was conducted by the 24th Guards Rifle Corps.[88]

In light of what had been achieved to date, the German *8. Armee* planned to regroup its troops in order to carry out the tasks of the next few days. The *1. SS-Panzer-Division "Leibstandarte SS Adolf Hitler"* was to occupy Kőhídgyarmat from the south. The *12. SS-Panzer-Division "Hitlerjugend"* and the *44. Reichsgrenadier-Division "Hoch- und Deutschmeister"* had to withdraw their units from the positions held to this time in the front line and had to direct them into the area of Bart. With this, the battalions that were relieved after the elimination of the bridgehead at Léva could be used to reinforce the left flank of the *8. Armee*. At last, the decision was made to eliminate the area of the remaining bridgehead with a single attack in the night of 20 February. The task contained in the original plan, that is, that following the crossing over the Garam the troops were to advance to the Ipoly, was changed by Hitler in order to complete Operation "*Südwind*" as soon as possible: bridgeheads were to be established on the eastern bank of the Garam (this was

85 Command of theregiment was taken over by the commander of the *I. Bataillon/SS-Panzergrenadier-Regiment 26, SS-Sturmbannführer* Kostenbader. See Meyer, 1999, p.488.

86 Meyer, 1999, p.488.

87 Maier, 1985, p.153

88 Zaharov, 1973, p.367. German reconnaissance detected the withdrawal of two divisions from the southern sector of the bridgehead, which retreated, leaving the majority of their heavy weapons behind, only saving their soldiers. For this, see Maier, 1985, p.155.

also contained in the original plan), which, then, were to fix lesser Soviet forces, or possibly reserves, too.[89]

Regrouping of forces (20 February 1945)

On 20 February[90], the regrouping of German divisions began. *Kampfgruppe "Hupe"* of the *96. Infanterie Division*, which was still in action that day, was finally withdrawn and, to the entire satisfaction of *Armeegruppe "Balck"*, it returned to its parent division, south of the Danube. The elements of the *12. SS-Panzer-Division "Hitlerjugend"* were gradually relieved by the *44. Reichsgrenadier-Division "Hoch- und Deutschmeister"* and the *SS* units set off for their new assembly area northwest of Bart. Their movement was slowed down by ceaseless attacks from Soviet ground-attack aircraft. Only lesser march columns or lone vehicles could feel safe from them. The exhausted troops could finally get some rest. Soon they also received ammunition, food and fuel supplies, too.[91]

During the night, the *6.* and *7. Kompanien* of the *Panzer-Gruppe* of the *1. SS-Panzer-Division "Leibstandarte SS Adolf Hitler"*, equipped with *Panzer* IV tanks (advancing on both sides of the Párkány – Kéménd road), attacked from the west, while part of the *46. Infanterie-Division* attacked from the west against Kőhídgyarmat; however they were stalled by the fire of the Soviet defence in the early morning hours, just like another *Kampfgruppe* of the *46. Infanterie-Division* which was attacking toward Kéménd.

The operation became catastrophic on 20 February for *Panzer-Abteilung 208*. Five of their armoured fighting vehicles were knocked out by the Soviets at dawn. The unit, which had only 11 combat-ready tanks and *Jagdpanzers* left, was stuck in a valley. Wherever they tried to get out, the Soviets pounded them with anti-tank guns and mortars. At about 1200 hours, the *Panzer-Abteilung* repelled a Soviet infantry attack. After this, at about 1430 hours, fire resumed from the anti-tank guns and mortars. Additional armoured fighting vehicles were set aflame. The unit soon lost the last of its combat-ready armoured fighting vehicles, and the situation worsened second by second. At that time, *Hauptmann* Bohn, commander of *Panzer-Abteilung 208*, ordered the crews to detach the trigger mechanisms of the guns and the machine guns of the armoured fighting vehicles, and attempt to fight their way back to the command post of the *Abteilung* on foot. This movement was successful, though two soldiers went missing during the manoeuvre.[92]

Kampfgruppe "Hansen" of the *1. SS-Panzer-Division "Leibstandarte SS Adolf Hitler"* closed up to the armoured units stalled in front of Kőhídgyarmat, and went over to the defensive in the area held. In the meantime, the main body of *Panzer-Gruppe "Peiper"* was in Párkány filling the armoured fighting vehicles up with fuel and ammunition, besides carrying out the most necessary repairs.[93]

The combat-ready armoured fighting vehicle-strength of the Germans was considerably diminished by 20 February. The situation of the independent armoured troops is shown in the table below:[94]

89 Maier, 1985, p.153.

90 Weather that day: frost at night, temperature: 7° Celsius during the day, slightly cloudy, sunny, fog in certain areas. Unpaved roads passable only by night.

91 Maier, 1985, p.153, HM HIM *Hadtörténelmi Levéltár* (Budapest) microfilm archives, *Kriegstagebuch Ia der Heeresgruppe Süd* (roll no. 631. image no. 7214061).

92 Volleth, 1975.

93 Tiemann, 1987, p.244, and Maier, 1985, p.153.

94 HM HIM *Hadtörténelmi Levéltár* (Budapest) microfilm archives, *Kriegstagebuch Ia der Heeresgruppe*

Table 15 – Armoured strength of independent German units participating in Operation "*Südwind*", 20 February 1945

<table>
<tr><th>Unit</th><th>Panzer IV</th><th>Panzer IV L/70</th><th>Tiger B</th><th>Jagdpanther</th><th>Total</th></tr>
<tr><td>s. SS Pz. Abt. 501</td><td>–</td><td>–</td><td>6</td><td>–</td><td>6</td></tr>
<tr><td>s. Pz.Jg.-Abt.560</td><td></td><td>9</td><td>–</td><td>4</td><td>13</td></tr>
<tr><td>Pz. Abt. 208</td><td colspan="2">11[1]</td><td>–</td><td>–</td><td>11</td></tr>
<tr><td>s. Pz-Abt. "FHH"</td><td>–</td><td>–</td><td>7</td><td>–</td><td>7</td></tr>
<tr><td>Total</td><td>11</td><td>9</td><td>13</td><td>4</td><td>37</td></tr>
</table>

1 *Panzer IV* tanks and *Panzer IV/70 Jagdpanzers* together.

Soviet troops claimed to have knocked out eight German armoured fighting vehicles. The remaining bridgehead was 10km wide and 4km deep. This was defended by the 24th Guards and 27th Guards Rifle Corps, and part of the 4th Guards Mechanized Corps.[95]

The Soviets kept the German assembly areas under incessant artillery and mortar fire from their artillery that was concentrated on the east bank of the Garam. The effect was further increased by the low-altitude raids by Soviet ground-attack aircraft that attacked under cover of fighter aircraft.[96]

The 150 aircraft of the German *Luftflotte 4* flew approximately 220 sorties against the Soviet artillery positions, and Soviet tank assembly areas that had been identified on the east bank. However, extremely heavy Soviet anti-aircraft gunfire prevented observation of the effects.[97]

Not only the German but the Soviet command, too, regrouped its forces. March columns totalling 3600 motor vehicles were identified driving from the Budapest area toward Balassagyarmat and Ipolyság. Those German assessments that anticipated a Soviet counterattack proved to be too pessimistic. The Soviet command, "falling for" a captured German officer who told them, for sure, that four *Panzer* and four infantry divisions were to be expected from the other bank of the Garam[98], and, because of the situation that appeared to support this in the Garam bridgehead, thought only of stopping the German attack.[99]

Süd (roll no. 630. image no. 7213747).

95 Zaharov, 1973, p.368.

96 Maier, 1985, p.153.

97 HM HIM *Hadtörténelmi Levéltár* (Budapest) microfilm archives, *Kriegstagebuch Ia der Heeresgruppe Süd* (roll no. 630. image no. 7214062).

98 Maier, 1985, p.154.

99 According to the directive issued on 17 February regarding the assault operation against Vienna, the 2nd and 3rd Ukrainian Fronts that were preparing for the offensive committed the reinforcements according to the sector borders and the operational aims specified in the directive. The 6th Guards Tank Army, being reconstituted east-southeast of the Garam, would not be risked in a counterattack, since the Soviets had learned a bitter lesson on 10 January about the capabilities of just one reinforced German *Panzer* division carrying out a well-timed counterattack. The aim was rather to retain the remaining bridgehead, or, in case that proved impossible, to defend the line of the Garam. At least this is what seems to be plausible from the assessment of Soviet sources. Acceptance of the statement by the German officer was confirmed by interrogation of Soviet prisoners-of-war one day later, but it is also remarkable that, for

As the regrouping of the *12. SS-Panzer-Division "Hitlerjugend"* was delayed by the air activity of the Soviet Air Force, the German *8. Armee* provided the following orders for its units:

- *1. SS-Panzer-Division "Leibstandarte SS Adolf Hitler"* was finally to occupy Kőhídgyarmat together with the *46. Infanterie Division.*
- *12. SS-Panzer-Division "Hitlerjugend"* was to eliminate the remaining Soviet positions on the Bart – Kéménd – Bény line with a night attack, together with the *211. Volksgrenadier-Division* and parts of the *Infanterie Division*, attacking from the direction of northwest and west.
- The last remaining elements of *Kampfgruppe "Hupe"* were to be transported back to the southern area of the Balaton.[100]

The second phase of the German attack (21-22) February 1945)

At dawn on **21 February**[101], the *1. SS-Panzer-Division "Leibstandarte SS Adolf Hitler"* (*Panzer-Gruppe "Peiper"*[102] with the mounted *SS-Panzergrenadiers* of *Kampfgruppe "Hansen"*) and the appointed *Kampfgruppen* of the *46. Infanterie Division* advanced into Kőhídgyarmat from the south and west; the village was protected with minefields; however, the troops reached its southern edge and the centre of the village. The Soviets concentrated tanks, flamethrowers and numerous anti-tank guns in order to establish an effective system of fire. The fierce Soviet defence stopped the German attack, and the Germans were forced to go over to the defensive. Strong Soviet artillery and mortar fire and low-level attacks by Soviet ground-attack aircraft caused considerable losses to the Germans. The attack northwest of the village gained practically no ground.[103]

As darkness fell, the *1. SS-Panzer-Division "Leibstandarte SS Adolf Hitler"* and forces of the *46. Infanterie Division* renewed their attack on Kőhídgyarmat. During the night battle that raged again, the Germans managed to drive the Soviets out of the village by 2100 hours and take possession of the entire village.[104] Only then could clearing commence.

At 2230 hours in the night, when the *Grenadier* battalions of the *44. Reichsgrenadier-Division "Hoch- und Deutschmeister"* joined the *Panzer-Gruppe* consisting of *schwere Panzer-Abteilung "Feldherrnhalle"*[105] and a number of *Jagdpanzers* and armoured personnel carriers, they attacked the Soviet positions south of Bart. The aim of the attack was partly to cover the rear of the German troops occupying Kőhídgyarmat, and partly to cover the elements of the *12. SS-Panzer-Division "Hitlerjugend"* (assigned to be part of the attack to be launched the next dawn) that were assembling west of Bart, occupying their points of departure. The attacking German armoured fighting vehicles had considerable difficulties

example, in Malakhov, 1960, p.110. four (!) attacking German *Panzer* divisions are mentioned.

100 Maier, 1985, p.154.

101 Weather that day: frost at night, temperature 5° Celsius during the day, bright sky. The condition of the roads was constantly improving.

102 By then, the majority of the armoured fighting vehicles of the *Panzer-Gruppe* had dropped out of further combat, mainly because of mechanical problems. For example, the *1. Kompanie/SS-Panzer-Regiment 1* had only five *Panthers* by that time.

103 Maier, 1985, p.154, Tiemann, 1987, p.245 and HM HIM *Hadtörténelmi Levéltár* (Budapest) microfilm archives, *Kriegstagebuch Ia der Heeresgruppe Süd* (roll no. 631. image no. 7214066).

104 Tiemann, 1987, p.246.

105 By that time, *schwere Panzer-Abteilung "Feldherrnhalle"* had only six combat-ready *Tiger B* heavy tanks.

with the minefields. The Germans were also engaged by Soviet T–34 tanks and self-propelled guns, but the engagement was rather short and one-sided – they knocked those out without any losses inflicted upon themselves. Their way was soon blocked by a Soviet anti-tank area comprising 25 anti-tank guns. As this was impossible to eliminate, they retreated after suffering the loss of three *Tiger B*s.[106]

In light of the day's accomplishments and the anticipated total elimination of the Soviet bridgehead on the Garam, agreement on plans regarding the imminent large German offensive gained primary importance. As the *6. Panzerarmee* was concerned because of the ever-increasing losses of the *SS-Panzer* divisions fighting at the Garam, it had already been insisting for days that the units be withdrawn immediately. However, *Heeresgruppe Süd* did not approve of this until now; it only ordered the withdrawal schedule to be prepared, which was turned in by the *6. Panzerarmee* on this day.[107]

The *Luftwaffe* supported the ground forces with 290 sorties carried out on this day.[108]

As of the morning of **22 February**[109], the Soviets put up extremely heavy resistance in their remaining bridgehead.

The *1. SS-Panzer-Division "Leibstandarte SS Adolf Hitler"* and the elements of the *46. Infanterie Division* that were clearing Kőhídgyarmat eliminated the Soviet resistance pockets both in the village and on the west bank of the Garam. An armoured *Kampfgruppe* of the *1. SS-Panzer-Division "Leibstandarte SS Adolf Hitler"* (units of the *I. (Abteilung)/ SS-Panzer-Regiment 1* and the *III. Bataillon/SS-Panzergrenadier-Regiment 2*) advanced farther north and occupied the road junction between Kéménd and Kőhídgyarmat on the bank of the Párizs Canal.[110]

The main body of the *46. Infanterie Division*, reinforced by *Kampfgruppe "Schöneich"*, occupied Bibitpuszta and the road section 1km from there after heavy fighting.[111]

The elements of the *12. SS-Panzer-Division "Hitlerjugend"* that had moved into positions during the previous night with considerable difficulties[112] launched their assault at 0445 hours against Bart from the north. *SS-Panzergrenadier-Regiment 25* attacked on the right flank, and *SS-Panzergrenadier-Regiment 26* on the left flank. The *II. Bataillon/ SS-Panzergrenadier-Regiment 26* was assigned the task of following the main body of the regiment on the left and securing the left flank of the division from Bény. The *Panzer-Gruppe* of the division stood in readiness behind *SS-Panzergrenadier-Regiment 26*.

106 Schimack, Wien, 1969, p.337.

107 Maier, 1985, p.155.

108 HM HIM *Hadtörténelmi Levéltár* (Budapest) microfilm archives, *Kriegstagebuch Ia der Heeresgruppe Süd* (roll no. 630. image no. 7214069).

109 Weather that day: frost at night, temperature 6° Celsius during the day. Alternating sunny and cloudy periods, little rain. The roads were drying up.

110 Tiemann, 1987, p.246.

111 HM HIM *Hadtörténelmi Levéltár* (Budapest) microfilm archives, *Kriegstagebuch Ia der Heeresgruppe Süd* (roll no. 631. image no. 7214074).

112 The soldiers of the *I. Bataillon/SS-Panzergrenadier-Regiment 26* had been engaged by the machine guns of their own tanks coming behind them while marching into their points of departure, because the armoured fighting vehicles, manoeuvring only a couple of hundred metres away from the Soviet positions, lost contact with the infantry. They did not notice the red light of the flash-lamps on the backs of the *Panzergrenadiers* marching at the rear either, and assumed that they were Soviet infantry. The unnecessary battle casualties amounted to five dead and eight wounded. For this, see Meyer, 1999, p.490.

The *Panzer-Gruppe* spearheaded the attack with support from artillery batteries, mortars and *Nebelwerfer*. Even before they could reach the first Soviet positions, the armoured fighting vehicles ran into a Soviet minefield. A number of tanks, including the command tank of the *II. (Abteilung)/SS-Panzer-Regiment 12*, were damaged. The torn off tracks had to be repaired while under heavy Soviet fire. The armoured fighting vehicles sought shelter, and joined the battle against the Soviet anti-tank guns. The heavy Soviet artillery, mortar and rocket launcher fire caused heavy losses to the *Panzergrenadiers*.

The armoured personnel carriers of the *9. Kompanie/III. Bataillon* of *SS-Panzergrenadier-Regiment 26* attacked from the east, through the minefield. Although they were hit by anti-tank gun fire from the left, they combined their speed and the firepower of the (single and triple-barrelled) 2cm cannon of the *II.* and *III. Zugs*, and contained the Soviets while they stormed through their positions. The other armoured personnel carriers attacked toward Bart. Some of them soon bogged down in the bed of a watercourse but three armoured personnel carriers managed to push on into the village. The assault was effectively supported by their own tanks. The armoured fighting vehicles that were already in the village advanced toward the church, and then further on toward the southeast edge of the settlement. The village was full of Soviet vehicles. The effect of the mass impact of the incoming rounds of 2cm tracer fragmentation shells was horrible. The majority of the houses were practically ruined. However, the firepower was soon restricted when the T–34 and T–34/85 type Soviet tanks forced the armoured personnel carriers to seek shelter. One of the *SS* armoured personnel carriers was soon knocked out. The Soviet tanks, abandoned by their infantry, at last departed toward Bény.

SS-Panzergrenadier-Regiment 25, fighting on the right flank, could not arrive at its point of departure in time, and, in consequence, could only join the *II. (Abteilung)/SS-Panzer-Regiment 12* and the *I. and III. Bataillon/SS-Panzergrenadier-Regiment 26*. The regiment occupied the western part of Bart.

In order to relieve the defenders, a Soviet counterattack was launched in the morning from the direction of Bény along the road leading toward Bart, but the *II. Bataillon/SS-Panzergrenadier-Regiment 26* repelled the assault, even as it was engaged in mortar fire. During the morning hours, the Germans managed to fully clear the village of the remnants of the Soviet units. Bart was held by *SS-Panzergrenadier-Regiment 25*. The elements of *SS-Panzergrenadier-Regiment 26* were withdrawn. Bart was one of the strongest points of the Soviet defence on the Garam. The Soviets left two combat-ready T–34s, six heavy howitzers, a number of anti-tank guns, mortars and other vehicles in the village. The number of Soviets captured reached 80; among them was a colonel.[113]

A Soviet counterattack was launched in the evening hours in the direction of Bibitpuszta, which was also supported by tanks; consequently, the Soviets again occupied the area.[114]

With this, the bridgehead still held by the Soviets on the western bank of the Garam was narrowed down to the section between Kéménd and Bény. The *SS-Panzer* divisions, which were fighting effectively although suffering heavy losses, were largely involved in the planned offensive; the subordination relations and the withdrawal of the units caused much disagreement among the members of the German high command.[115]

113 Meyer, 1999, pp.490-491.

114 HM HIM *Hadtörténelmi Levéltár* (Budapest) microfilm archives, *Kriegstagebuch Ia der Heeresgruppe Süd* (roll no. 631. image no. 7214079).

115 Because of the losses suffered at the Garam, two *SS-Panzer* divisions needed considerable reinforcements

Further German regroupings (23 February 1945)

On 23 February[116], time was spent with the repeated regrouping of the German forces. The manoeuvres of and the route taken by the supply columns were continuously hindered by the Soviet artillery harassing fire from the eastern bank. Visibility was poor, therefore air activity was low on both sides. Consequently, ground traffic could go on during the day, with specified spacing between vehicles for security and employment of small vehicle groups. The evening before, a German ground-attack aircraft formation appeared in the area of Kéménd and Bény with 85 aircraft and attacked artillery positions, field fortifications and vehicle columns in the east. According to the German reconnaissance data, the Soviet forces in the bridgehead were reinforced by elements of a new Mechanized Brigade of the 4th Guards Mechanized Corps.[117] This, however, is not confirmed by Soviet sources.

The Germans prepared to launch a night assault in order to eliminate the remaining Soviet bridgehead between Kéménd and Bény. In this situation, the night attack had better chances for success because the German troops attacking under cover of darkness could only be met by inaccurately directed fire (there was not any possibility to observe the effect of the impacts). The Soviet anti-tank guns and field artillery that were hunting the German armoured fighting vehicles[118] by direct fire were in disadvantageous positions too. The Soviet artillery crew could only direct their fire based on the muzzle flashes, although this method resulted in considerable inaccuracies. The Soviets could, of course, count on only a fraction of the number of ground-attack aircraft they originally had, not mentioning the psychological effect exerted on the Soviet infantry in their positions coming from the hundreds of tracer rounds from machine guns and automatic cannon.

The attack aimed at the complete elimination of the bridgehead was scheduled to 0200 hours on 24 January; the German troops taking part in the mission had the following tasks assigned to them:

- *1. SS-Panzer-Division "Leibstandarte SS Adolf Hitler"* and elements of the *44. Reichsgrenadier-Division "Hoch- und Deutschmeister"* were to attack from the south;
- Elements of the *46. Infanterie-Division* were to attack Kéménd from the southwest, in order to occupy the village and the Soviet positions on the hills west of Kéménd;
- *12. SS-Panzer-Division "Hitlerjugend"* was to cooperate with the forces of the *211. Volksgrenadier-Division* and was to occupy Bény by attacking from west and north.

The attack was to be launched without any kind of lengthy artillery preparation. The task of the artillery was to keep the bridges at Kéménd and Bény under constant fire and

again. However it was questionable to what extent these units could be reinforced before the launch of the new offensive. Another problem was that the *Panzer* divisions were temporarily subordinated to the *Panzerkorps "Feldherrnhalle"* by the command of the German *8. Armee*, and this was highly disapproved by the *Waffen-SS*. Of this, see more in Maier, 1985, pp.155-157.

116 Weather that day: temperature 6° Celsius, it was cloudy, around noon the clouds parted. The road conditions did not improve.

117 Maier, 1985, p.158.

118 Although a number of works on the subject mention the issue of infrared night-vision devices on some of the *Panther* tanks of the *SS-Panzer* divisions during the battles fought on the Hungarian theatre of war, up to now there is no conclusive evidence as to the existence of these devices.

destroy any attempts at the concentration of forces.[119] According to Soviet sources, the German artillery engaged the area of the remaining bridgehead by fire for six hours before the launch of the final assault.[120]

The complete elimination of the Soviet bridgehead (24 February 1945)

At 0200 hours, at dawn on 24 February[121], following a short artillery firestrike, the elimination of the remaining Soviet bridgehead began.

The *46. Infanterie-Division* captured Kéméndipuszta during an eventful battle and then advanced further east.[122]

The *Panzer-Gruppe* of the *1. SS-Panzer-Division "Leibstandarte SS Adolf Hitler"* attacked Kéménd from the south; it was followed by the formations of *Kampfgruppe "Hansen"*, among them elements of *SS-Panzergrenadier-Regiment 2* of *SS-Obersturmbannführer* Bernhard Siebken. According to Soviet sources, the German units attacked Kéménd with a total of 100 armoured fighting vehicles. The 36th Guards Tank Brigade, fighting in the sector of the 24th Guards Rifle Corps had 16 operational T–34/85 tanks on that day.[123]

The well-established Soviet trench system, defended by remnants of the 24th Guards Rifle Corps, was covered by a number of anti-tank strongpoints. One of them comprised 37 heavy anti-tank guns. *Panzer-Gruppe "Peiper"*, supported by one of the *Kampfgruppen* of the *44. Reichsgrenadier-Division "Hoch- und Deutschmeister"*, broke through the Soviet anti-tank sector, and advanced into Kéménd during an extremely heavy battle.

Occupation and clearing of the village was the task of *SS-Panzergrenadier-Regiments 1* and *2*. After they took point no. 150, 2km northwest of Kéménd, in bitter fighting, following a new firestrike from the German artillery, the forces assaulted Kéménd from the south and west. *Panzergrenadier* squads, equipped with MP-44 assault rifles, led the way in front of the *Sturmabteilungen*, and the companies were positioned behind them. At first, they were only met by rifle fire, but they soon ran into heavy machine gun, mortar and rocket-launcher fire. The fight went on from one house to another. The German companies were stuck at one point, then, after concentrating their forces, thrust forward again. At last, by late afternoon, they managed to completely clear the village of the Soviets.

The defence of the crossing point on the Garam at Kéménd was assigned to three T–34/85 tanks of one of the platoons of the 36th Guards Tank Brigade (Junior Lieutenant I. S. Dyeputatov). The tank of the Junior Lieutenant was positioned in the centre of the battle formation. 50 metres to its right stood the tank of Junior Lieutenant I. F. Borisov, and 40 metres to its left, the tank of Lieutenant K. P. Tulupov stood in firing position. The three Soviet tanks – in cooperation with the rifles and the artillery – claimed to have knocked out a total of 26 German armoured fighting vehicles and 12 armoured personnel carriers on 23 and 24 February. On 24 February, the tank of Tulupov was knocked out by the Germans, two members of the crew were killed, and the Lieutenant himself was wounded. Later all three tank commanders, together with their gunners, received the Hero

119 Maier, 1985, p.158.

120 Zaharov, 1973, p.368.

121 Weather that day: temperature 6 Celsius, thick layers of clouds, raining in certain places. The unpaved roads and the open terrain were muddy and hardly passable even for the tracked vehicles because of the sudden melting.

122 HM HIM *Hadtörténelmi Levéltár* (Budapest) microfilm archives, *Kriegstagebuch Ia der Heeresgruppe Süd* (roll no. 631. image no. 7214084).

123 Zaharov, 1973, p.368.

of the Soviet Union decoration.[124]

The Garam bridge east of Kéménd was held for a little time, but then it was destroyed by the Soviets, who retreated from the area. The Soviet artillery that was in position on the east bank fired heavy barrages on the crossing points, without regard for their own retreating troops, in order to impede the attempts of the Germans to cross.[125]

According to the data provided by air reconnaissance, the left flank units of the Soviet 27th Guards Rifle Corps established perfectly camouflaged light machine gun and heavy machine gun nests, and anti-tank gun positions on the front line sector of the *12. SS-Panzer-Division "Hitlerjugend"* at Bény, on the eastern side of the north-west railway embankment. The Soviets also included the flood control dams in their defence system. There was a minefield stretching along the railway crossing of the Érsekkéty – Bény road.

The attack was to be carried out by the *Panzer-Gruppe* of the division, together with the *I. and II. Bataillon* of *SS-Panzergrenadier-Regiment 26. SS-Panzergrenadier-Regiment 25* secured around Bart. The two *SS-Panzergrenadier-Bataillone* stood on both sides of Érsekpuszta (right flank: *I. Bataillon/SS-Panzergrenadier-Regiment 26*, left flank: *II. Bataillon/SS-Panzergrenadier-Regiment 26*). The *Panzer-Gruppe* occupied its points of departure east of the *puszta*. In order to cover up the noise of the engines and tracks, the division's artillery laid down harassing fire. Prior to the start of the attack the mine sweeping groups of *SS-Panzer-Pionier-Bataillon 12* attempted to clear the minefield positioned in front of the railway crossing, but they were noticed by the Soviets, who covered the area with fire.

To maintain surprise, there was no artillery preparation or fire by heavy weapons prior to the attack through point no. 157 (Őr Hill). Despite this, the Soviets alerted their forces and fired barrages, in which the *1.* and *3. Kompanie/SS-Panzergrenadier-Regiment 26* suffered heavy losses. The *II. Bataillon/SS-Panzergrenadier-Regiment 26* was brought to a halt when it received heavy infantry fire in its flank. In the meantime, the *II. (Abteilung)/ SS-Panzer-Regiment 12* brought its forces forward. Two two-tank elements advanced along the road connecting Érsekkéty and Bény and, in the spare light of dawn, engaged the Soviet anti-tank guns that had been identified on the railway embankment. Meanwhile, the *2. Kompanie/SS-Panzergrenadier-Regiment 26* approached to within 200 metres of the railway crossing. Under cover of artillery support and fire of heavy infantry weapons, the company crossed the railway embankment and, by using hand grenades and submachine guns, eliminated the hidden Soviet positions in close combat.

The *II. Bataillon/SS-Panzergrenadier-Regiment 26* also closed up, then broke into the Soviet positions. In the meantime, the tanks engaged the Soviet anti-tank guns and also knocked out a number of T–34s. The 2cm cannon of the armoured personnel carriers of the *II. Bataillon/SS-Panzergrenadier-Regiment 26* provided perfect support for the *Panzergrenadiers* attacking on foot, and they also eased their own manoeuvres. The battle for the control of Bény finally ended at about 0830 hours. The Germans occupied the village and the Soviets retreated to the east bank of the Garam. When the *SS-Panzergrenadiers* were approaching the bridge at Bény, the Soviets blew it up. The clearing of the village lasted until noon; then, the battalions took up securing positions at the eastern edge of Bény. The Soviets that were defending around point no. 120, 2km southwest of Bény, were destroyed

124 Zaharov, 1973, pp.369-370.

125 Tiemann, 1987, pp.248-249, Agte, 1998, p.347 and HM HIM *Hadtörténelmi Levéltár* (Budapest) microfilm archives, *Kriegstagebuch Ia der Heeresgruppe Süd* (roll no. 631. image no. 7214084).

by the German tanks attacking from the north.[126]

The *211. Volksgrenadier-Division*, in the wake of the successes of the *12. SS-Panzer-Division "Hitlerjugend"*, occupied Leándpuszta during the morning.

Before the front line sector of the *44. Reichsgrenadier-Division "Hoch- und Deutschmeister"* fortified works were observed on the eastern bank of the Garam. A strong *Alarm-Gruppe* of the division closed the bridge 2kms southeast of Kéménd. The division then occupied the hill and the road junction 2km northwest of Kőhídgyarmat and then advanced toward Kéménd. The Soviets put down heavy harassing fire during the whole day from the eastern bank, concentrating on the area of Kéménd and Bény.[127]

On the night preceding 25 February the remnants of the Soviet troops crossed to the eastern bank of the Garam. As described in the book of Marshal M. V. Zaharov:

> Our soldiers crossed the Garam through the ice and the ford, because the bridge [at Kéménd – the author] had been destroyed by the enemy.[128] This retreat was organized by the Front High Command. Considering the fact that the 7th Guards Army was exhausted from the heavy fighting of the last eight days, and was incapable of holding the bridgehead, their retreat was approved as of the evening of 25 February [in the dawn of 25 February – the author] and it was ordered that a solid defence was to be established on the western bank of the Garam.[129]

Conclusion

Operation "*Südwind*", aimed at the elimination of the Soviet bridgehead at the Garam, had ended. *Heeresgruppe Süd* received a report from the German *8. Armee* at 1720 hours reporting the complete elimination of the bridgehead, and this was forwarded to the *OKH* by the *Heeresgruppe* at 1745 hours.[130]

According to Soviet data, between 17 and 24 February 1945, the 7th Guards Army lost 8194 soldiers, 54 destroyed tanks and self-propelled guns, and 459 other guns (of these, 374 76mm or greater calibre guns).[131]

According to German data, the Soviets suffered the following main types of losses in the period between 17 and 22 February 1945:

Table 16 – Soviet losses according to German reports, 17-22 February 1945

Losses[1]	**Sector of *Armeegruppe "Balck"*** [2]	**Sector of German *8. Armee***	**Total**
Captives (POW)	92	445	537

126 Meyer, 1999, pp.491-492, and HM HIM *Hadtörténelmi Levéltár* (Budapest) microfilm archives, *Kriegstagebuch Ia der Heeresgruppe Süd* (roll no. 631. image no. 7214084).

127 HM HIM *Hadtörténelmi Levéltár* (Budapest) microfilm archives, *Kriegstagebuch Ia der Heeresgruppe Süd* (roll no. 631. image no. 7214084).

128 According to the Germans these had been blown up by the Soviets in order to prevent the enemy crossing the river.

129 See Zaharov, 1973, p.368.

130 Maier, 1985, p.159.

131 See the directive no. 11036 of the Main Command of the Armed Forces of the Union of SSR (*Stavka*) issued on 6 March 1945. In: *Ruski Arhiv: Velikaya Otechestvennaya. Stavka VKG: Dokumenti i materiali 1944–1945*. T. 16 (5-4) (Moscow, 1999), p.207. It should be noted that Minasyan, 1970, p.107, mentions 8800 soldiers as the number of the battle casualties of the 7th Guards Army, however, no data is communicated regarding the material losses.

Losses[1]	**Sector of *Armeegruppe "Balck"*** [2]	**Sector of German *8. Armee***	**Total**
Deserted	–	2	2
Counted battle casualties	621	1448	2069
Estimated battle casualties	200	650	850
Battle casualties total	821	2098	2919
Destroyed armoured fighting vehicles	6	65	71 [3]
Armoured reconnaissance vehicles	5	2	7
Anti-tank guns	No data	289[4]	289
Rocket launchers	–	4	4
Artillery guns	2	43	45
Anti-aircraft guns	–	12	12
Mortars	6	33	39
Machine guns	8	107	115
Aircraft	1	2	3

1 HM HIM *Hadtörténelmi Levéltár* (Budapest*)* microfilm archives*, Kriegstagebuch Ia* der *Heeresgruppe Süd* (roll no. 630. image no. 7214078.). The table mainly contains the data summarized on 22 February 1945. According to the Germans the number of the Soviet prisoners at the end of the operation probably reached 700, the number of the dead exceeded 4000; they lost 334 (all types) of guns and the Germans knocked out approximately 90 Soviet tanks and self-propelled guns. See Maier, p.160. The *I. (Abteilung)/SS-Panzer-Regiment 1* inflicted the following losses on the Soviets: it knocked out 25 T–34 tanks, 18 artillery guns, destroyed and seized 164 anti-tank guns; destroyed eight anti-tank rifles, 55 trucks and 32 horse-drawn wagons, seized 30 (Hungarian, Italian, British and German) tanks, killed 280 Soviet soldiers in action. See Agte, 1998, p.348.

2 Losses inflicted by the units of the *96.* and *711.* I*nfanterie-Divisions* deployed here.

3 This number only contains the knocked out Soviet tanks, because at Párkány alone, the German units retook 78 tanks that were "foreign" to the Soviets.

4 The number of artillery devices was deducted from the total number of knocked out and seized guns.

The German troops fighting for the elimination of the bridgehead suffered extremely heavy losses, which could, subsequently, barely be made good. The number of combat-ready armoured fighting vehicles showed particularly large differences compared to the situation on 17 February, although other types of armament showed considerable losses too.[132]

132 Two *Panzer* divisions of the *I. SS-Panzerkorps* (apart from the armoured vehicles and devices) temporarily lost 825 *Kar* 98k carbine rifles, 50 *Gew* 43 rifles, four *Kar* 98k sniper rifles with telescopic sight, 388 9mm handguns, 85 *MP* 38/40 submachine guns, 135 *MP* 44 assault rifles, 47 rifle grenade launchers, 136 *MG* 34/42 light machine guns, four *MG* 42 heavy machine guns, 12 tank machine guns, four *MG* 81 machine guns, one *MG* 151/15 triple-barrelled machine gun, three *MG* 151/20 triple-barrelled automatic cannon, two 2cm *Flak* 38 anti-aircraft automatic cannon, two 3.7cm *Flak* 37 anti-aircraft automatic cannon, one 8.8cm *Flak* 37 anti-aircraft gun, two 8cm *GrW* 34 mortars, one 12cm *GrW* 42 mortar and one 7.5cm heavy anti-tank gun. Of the armament on the tanks one 7.5cm *KwK* 40 (*Panzer* IV) tank gun, four 7.5cm

The following table shows the situation of the German troops fighting on the western bank of the Garam as of 24 February:

Table 17 – Strength and combat readiness of German formations fighting on the western bank of the Garam, 24 February 1945

24 February 1945	Combat strength of the *Infanterie*	Number of heavy anti-tank guns	Combat value[1]
44. Div. "HuD"	1700 men	20	II.
46. Inf. Div.	1100 German 1200 Hungarian	20	III.
211. Volksgr.Div.	1100 men	8	IV.
1. SS-Pz.Div.	1700 men	10	II.
12. SS-Pz.Div.	1800 men	12	II.

1 II.: limitedly suitable for attack; III.: suitable for defence without limitations; IV.: limitedly suitable for defence.

Battle casualties of the German troops were also large. This was, in part, due to the fact that it was not the armoured fighting vehicles, but the *Grenadiers* and the *Panzergrenadiers* that were the first to assault the well-organized and strongly defended front line of the Soviets, making way for the *Panzer-Gruppen*. In addition, urban warfare was prevalent during the whole course of the operation, and this method of fighting also took its toll on both sides. Battle casualties of the German troops are summarized in the following table:

Table 18 – German battle casualties, 17-22 February 1945

Battle casualties	Dead	Wounded	MIA	Total
I. SS-Pz. Armeekorps	413 men	1923 men	653 men	2989 men
44. Reichsgren. Div. "HuD".	128 men	739 men	21 men	888 men
46. Inf.Div.	288 men	1178 men	127 men	1593 men
211. Volksgr.Div.	140 men	761 men	100 men	1001 men
Total	969 men	4601 men	901 men	6471 men

The combat-ready armoured strength of the Germans, on 24 February 1945, is shown in the following table:[133]

KwK 42 (*Panther*) tank guns and three 8.8cm *KwK* 43 (*Tiger B*) tank guns were damaged. See HM HIM *Hadtörténelmi Levéltár* (Budapest) microfilm archives, *Kriegstagebuch Ia der Heeresgruppe Süd* (roll no. 630. image no. 7214495. and next image).

133 HM HIM *Hadtörténelmi Levéltár* (Budapest) microfilm archives, *Kriegstagebuch Ia der Heeresgruppe Süd* (roll no. 630. image no. 7213824 and next image).

Table 19 – German combat-ready armoured strength, 24 February 1945

Unit	*Panzer IV*	*Panther*	*Tiger B*	*Panzer IV/70*	*Jagdpanther*	*Jagdpanzer 38(t)*	Total
1. SS-Pz.Div.	11	2	2	17	–	–	32
12. SS-Pz.Div.	19	7	–	27	8	–	61
44. Reichsgren. Div. "HuD"	–	–	–	–	–	12	12
Pz.Gruppe "FHH"	2	2	5	5	–	–	14
211. Volksgr. Div	–	–	–	–	–	4	4
Total combat-ready	32	11	7	49	8	16	123

According to Soviet data, the troops of the 7th Guards Army knocked out and/or destroyed at least 87 armoured fighting vehicles in the period between 17 and 24 February 1945.[134] The majority of these (54) were knocked out on the first day, when the firepower of the defenders of the bridgehead was at its greatest.

According to its own account, the German *1. SS-Panzer-Division "Leibstandarte SS Adolf Hitler"* counted only two *Panzer* IVs, two *Panthers* and five armoured personnel carriers as total losses. Furthermore, one *Panzer* IV, five *Panthers* and two *Tiger Bs* had to be transported back to Germany for factory repair.[135] This would mean the loss of a total of 12 tanks and five armoured personnel carriers in the two SS-*Panzer* divisions, together. The newly published German data, however, more or less supports the numbers given by the Soviets. The detailed armoured strength of the *I. SS-Panzerkorps* is shown in the following table[136]:

Table 20 – Armoured strength of *I.SS-Panzerkorps* before and after Operation "*Südwind*", 1945

Armoured fighting vehicle	Before the operation[1]		After the operation[2]		Difference		Total
	1. SS-Pz. Div.	***12. SS-Pz.Div.***	***1. SS-Pz. Div.***[3]	***12. SS-Pz.Div.***[4]	***1. SS-Pz. Div.***	***12. SS-Pz.Div***	
Panzer IV	24/21 [+10]	20/12 [+14]	30/21	34/21	-4	–	-4
Panther	36/34 [+5]	28/20 [+16]	28/25	30/9	-13	-14	-27
Tiger B	26/15 [+19][5]	–	33/9	–	–	–	–

134 Zaharov, 1973, pp.367-368. There is no data available concerning the days 21 and 22 February 1945.

135 See HM HIM *Hadtörténelmi Levéltár* (Budapest) microfilm archives, *Kriegstagebuch Ia der Heeresgruppe Süd* (roll no. 630. image no. 7214495).

136 Data source: Nevenkin, 2008, pp.788-789, 910. The first numbers denote the existing armoured fighting vehicles, the second numbers denote the combat-ready ones. The brackets contain the numbers of armoured fighting vehicles in transport to the units as supplements.

Armoured fighting vehicle	Before the operation[1]		After the operation[2]		Difference		Total
	1. SS-Pz. Div.	*12. SS-Pz.Div.*	*1. SS-Pz. Div.*[3]	*12. SS-Pz.Div.*[4]	*1. SS-Pz. Div.*	*12. SS-Pz.Div*	
Panzer IV/70	11/8 [+10]	29/12[6] [+23]	20/17	31/13[7]	-1	-7	-8
Jagdpanther	–	6/3[8] [+10]	–	7/2	–	–	–
Total	97/78 [+44]	83/47 [+62]	111/72	102/45	-18	-20	-39
Sd.Kfz. 250	33/15	21/15	29/24	No data	-4	No data	No data
Sd.Kfz. 251	72/64 [+63]	106/95	125/97	No data	-10	No data	No data
Total	105/79	127/110	154/121	No data	-14	No data	No data

1 Data from 8 February 1945.
2 In the case of *1. SS-Panzer-Division* the data refers to 5 March 1945, and in the case of the *12. SS-Panzer-Division* the data refers to 1 March 1945.
3 Apart from these, the Division had a further three (two) assault guns, 11 (seven) *Flak-Panzer IV* anti-aircraft armoured fighting vehicles, four (one) *Panzer IV* artillery observer armoured vehicles and 13 (five) heavy reconnaissance armoured cars.
4 Apart from these, the *12. SS-Panzer-Division* had further eight (five) *Flak-Panzer IV* anti-aircraft armoured fighting vehicles too. On 1 March 1945 the *schwere Panzerjäger-Abteilung 560* had 14 (six) *Panzer IV/70*s and seven (two) *Jagdpanther* tank destroyers, and eight (eight) *Flak-Panzer IV* anti-aircraft armoured fighting vehicles.
5 of the arriving 19 supplementary *Tiger B* tanks were finally received by the *schwere Panzer-Abteilung 506* and not by the *schwere SS-Panzer-Abteilung 501/1. SS-Panzer-Division.*
6 Together with the armoured fighting vehicles of the s*chwere Panzerjäger-Abteilung 560.*
7 On 1 March 1945 the heavy *Panzerjäger-Abteilung 560* had a further 14 (six) *Panzer IV/70*s and seven (two) *Jagdpanther* tank destroyers, and eight (eight) *Flak-Panzer IV* anti-aircraft armoured fighting vehicles.
8 The armoured fighting vehicles of the s*chwere Panzerjäger-Abteilung 560.*

According to the data above, the *1. SS-* and *12. SS-Panzer-Divisions* had the following total losses: a total of at least 39 armoured fighting vehicles and 14 armoured personnel carriers during Operation "*Südwind*". Based on the remaining German data, though partial, it can be assumed that the total loss of the *Panzer-Gruppe* of *Panzerkorps "Feldherrnhalle"* might have been at about the same ratio:

- *Schwere Panzer-Abteilung "Feldherrnhalle":* one *Tiger B* heavy tank;
- *Panzer-Abteilung 208:* six *Panzer* IV tanks and six *Panzer* IV/70 (A) *Jagdpanzers*[137];
- *Panzerjäger-Abteilung 13:* nine *Panzer* IV/70 (V) *Jagdpanzers;*
- Thus, a total of 22 armoured fighting vehicles.
- The *44. Reichsgrenadier-Division "Hoch- und Deutschmeister"* and the *211.*

137 See Di Giusto, 2010, p.150.

Volksgrenadier-Division had only five less *Jagdpanzer* 38(t) tank destroyers, each, as compared to the 17 and nine combat-ready vehicles respectively, that were in combat-ready condition at the start of the Operation "*Südwind*". Unfortunately, we do not have exact data, and we cannot calculate how many of these were a total loss.

The total losses (repairable and irrecoverable) of German armoured fighting vehicles, based on the available combat-ready vehicles before and after Operation "*Südwind*", can be estimated as approximately 130 tanks and *Jagdpanzers*. This is almost 150% of the Soviet losses. However, it should be noted that the majority of the German armoured fighting vehicles were rendered immobile only temporarily because of mines, hits from various weapons, mechanical problems or being stuck in the ground (for a maximum of three weeks). At the same time, the *1. SS*-and *12. SS-Panzer-Divisions* had almost the same combat-ready armoured strength at the beginning of the new offensive operation, "*Frühlingserwachen*", as they had before Operation "*Südwind*", because of the supplies that were continually arriving for the troops.

As opposed to this, the Soviet armoured fighting vehicles that were knocked out in the Garam bridgehead were destroyed during the battle, or remained damaged in the areas occupied by the Germans, and were eventually blown up by the German *Pioniers*. The seized Soviet tanks faced the same fate, or were "enlisted" into the German tank destroyer units; or they ended their earthly career as targets on the practice fields of German tank destroyer training grounds behind the lines.

Despite their losses the German armoured units could rest assured that they could fight "in their own manner and pace" on the Hungarian front, even in the sixth year of the war, despite the superiority of the Soviet Air Force, whose superiority was often fruitless. The *SS-Panzer* divisions that were fighting against the Allies in Normandy, and then in the Ardennes, had less to fear from low-altitude raids by enemy fighter and ground attack aircraft on the Eastern Front. Here they again had enough space to use their combat formations, combat tactics and superior armoured combat methods that had been well proven on the tactical level. The overwhelming superiority of the Soviets in artillery and anti-tank firepower was, however, effectively balanced only by night assaults.

The commander of the *44. Reichsgrenadier-Division "Hoch- und Deutschmeister"*, *Generalleutnant* von Rost also wrote down his experiences in the fighting in the Garam bridgehead:

> 1. The enemy: The Soviet infantry showed strong resistance in their positions and in tight situations. The reason for this can be attributed to their fear of being shot down if captured. This is the reason why there are no incidents of going over to the enemy. Although the officers disengage from the enemy too early, nevertheless, their command is strict and adaptable so long as the front line is not shaken.
>
> The fire of heavy weapons was used *en masse*, and the fire thereof was directed and concentrated extremely well, especially at the beginning of the battles.
>
> Retreat was executed perfectly. They were not obsessed with hanging onto terrain, but evacuated the area in order to save their troops from being cut off.
>
> In the rear areas, there were cases of "base wallah" behaviour, where officers were sometimes captured in their sleep or while intoxicated.

Construction of positions: [constructed] very skilfully, exploiting the natural defences and camouflages. There was no special MLR, only a very deeply echeloned main defensive area, with massive employment of anti-tank guns in anti-tank blocking positions with as many as 30 guns in a depth of as much as 10km.

The enemy air force joined the combat with ongoing ground-attack aircraft raids as early as the first day of the battle. The raids were concentrated almost exclusively in the vicinity of the front line.

After the telephone lines were no longer available, the unencoded radio traffic of the enemy provided us with valuable insights into the enemy situation. Commitment of our reserves and armoured fighting vehicles to force a breakthrough was ordered twice based on unencoded radio messages containing reports of critical situations; both deployments were flawlessly successful.

We did not observe any new weapon or device or new combat tactics.

2. Proposed [German] deception manoeuvres for the planned armoured attack: general noise by *Raupenschlepper Ost* [half-tracked lorries] in sectors where appearance of armoured fighting vehicles could be anticipated [by the enemy]; attack with armour in terrain unfavourable for armoured fighting vehicles. The attack positions of the armoured fighting vehicles must be located at least 5km back from the main front line. Thus, the clatter of the tracks would not be easily recognized and detected by the enemy. The roads from the assembly positions to the [German] MLR should be painstakingly maintained and must be marked in order that the troops should be able to complete the move at night in a single manoeuvre. The moment of surprise must be safeguarded at all times and must be secured at all costs, otherwise the enemy would regroup his anti-tank weapons in time. Assaults against enemy anti-tank blocking positions proved to be almost hopeless.

3. Attacking at night in pitch black darkness is impossible. However, night attacks in even the slightest moonlight are extremely successful and this possibility must be utilized at all times in light of the enemy firepower.

Employment of armoured fighting vehicles at night is limited in its effectiveness. The most successful attempts utilized the attack of our infantry in the early morning hours. Thus the initial objective lines can be reached while still under cover of darkness. At daybreak the *Panzer-Gruppe* passes through the lines of our own infantry to break through.

If the attacking forces have already spent a long time in the attack areas and have a considerable amount of reconnaissance data about the enemy infantry positions and heavy armament, even in the depths of the defensive positions, then night attacks [can be launched] with artillery preparation. For this, a large number of aerial photographs are needed, because the majority of the enemy nests cannot be detected by ground observations (cleverly positioned nests on reverse slopes).

If the attacking forces are brought forward just before the beginning of the manoeuvre, then the night attack [is to be launched] without artillery preparation, because then [lacking detailed reconnaissance data] the effect [of the artillery barrage] would be extremely low, as has been proven in a number of cases.

4. The cooperation of the division's artillery with the infantry has worked well, even in a battle of movement.

5. Using of smoke shells in wooded areas and against armoured fighting vehicles, with

the aim of blinding the anti-tank blocking positions, was extremely successful.
6. The main task of the *Pioniers* in case of deploying armoured fighting vehicles is to eliminate deeply echeloned enemy minefields. Half of our own armoured losses were caused by mines.
7. At least at the beginning of the attack, during the breakthrough of the defensive belt, the armoured fighting vehicle formations must take into consideration the slow pace of the following infantry and, initially, suppress the enemy infantry. Following the breakthrough of the defensive belt, the armoured fighting vehicles must advance through the depth of the enemy lines, otherwise, the success achieved in intense fighting by the infantry at the cost of heavy losses would be lost, and the enemy would gain time to stabilize their positions. A necessary prerequisite for this would be that armoured infantry elements are needed for these manoeuvres (armoured personnel carrier battalion).

For example, on the second day of the attack, the first breakthrough of the division to Köbölkút could not be fully utilized because there was no second wave of armoured fighting vehicles with mounted infantry, or this was deployed in separate assaults in other areas.
8. Direct cooperation with the *Luftwaffe* is only possible if the officer controlling the aircraft is provided with an armoured all-terrain vehicle. The place of this officer is with the *Schwerpunkt* regiment, following the successful breakthrough by the *Panzer-Gruppe*.
9. Aerial photographs taken before the attack again arrived too late. Also, the [aerial photo] sorties were flown too far prior to the attack. The enemy had, since then, regrouped his forces. Aerial photographs must be delivered immediately, eliminating all delays in courier service, in order not to avoid loss of the advantage that could be provided by good aerial photos.
10. Our own signal system, most importantly due to the uninterrupted functioning of the telephone network and the radio system, sufficed completely for direction and control of the attack operations.

Target maps and radio code tables made it possible to pass the orders and reports in a matter of minutes.

It is absolutely essential that the artillery forward-observer be in an armoured fighting vehicle, even if that results in one less tank being available for combat.
11. Supply of the troops was extremely difficult during the whole operation, because the order of battle of the 1945-type infantry division is completely insufficient for this type of employment.[138]

The results of the operation were not entirely clear. It clearly stabilized the southern flank of the German *8. Armee* and practically deprived the Soviet main command of one of the most important points of departure for the attack operations in the direction of Pozsony – Vienna (not to speak about the significant Soviet losses). The *6. Panzerarmee*, however, had been "smuggled" to the Hungarian front line via extremely comprehensive and thorough conspiratorial methods. The surprise that had been planned in using its forces for the subsequent major attack was lost by the premature employment of these

138 Cited by Agis, 2006, pp.114-116.

forces in missions devised and launched to reach limited objectives. Moreover, the German troops that were committed, as well as the German *SS-Panzer* divisions, suffered losses that could never be fully replaced. The reconstituted strength and equipment of one of the groups involved in the main effort in the planned German spring offensive, the *1. SS-Panzer-Division "Leibstandarte SS Adolf Hitler"*, was lost: the units were forced to begin everything again.

In our opinion, Operation "*Frühlingserwachen*", and the ensuing German combat activity, would have collapsed more quickly and tragically if the Soviet bridgehead at the Garam had not been eliminated. It might not have been launched at all, because, in this case, it might have been feared that the Soviets would attack the German forces gathering south of the Danube by breaking though the exhausted *8. Armee*, as they had attempted to do in early January, and, in this case, the remnants of the German *6. Panzerarmee* would not have been able, in any way, to avoid encirclement.

Operation "*Südwind*", launched with the aim of eliminating the Soviet bridgehead at the Garam, although with limited goals, was the last of the operation of the *Waffen-SS* during the Second World War that was successful and went according to the initial plans.

4

Attack of the Soviet-Romanian forces in the direction of Bratislava–Brno (25-31 March 1945)

After 24 February, *schwere Panzer-Abteilung "Feldherrnhalle"* was directed into the area of Csúz, where the *Abteilung* used the period of temporary calm for repairs and refitting. On 1 March, the unit again had 11 combat-ready *Tiger B* tanks ready for action.[1]

On 6 March, fuel usage was restricted at the *Abteilung*, because there was no chance that the unit would receive supplies soon. At 1200 hours it was notified that the *Abteilung* was to relocate to Verebély the next day.

On 7 March, the *Abteilung* marched to Verebély via Érsekújvár, where it was attached to the (mixed) *Panzer-Regiment 4*, which was still in the process of activation.[2] The regiment was an element of the *13. Panzer-Division*, which was, at that time, composed only of a mixed *Panzer-Abteilung* (two *Panzer* IV-companies, two *Panther* companies) and an armoured personnel carrier battalion.

On 8 and 9 March, the vehicles of the *Abteilung* were continually arriving at Verebély.[3]

On 10 March, the *Abteilung* was standing in *Korpsreserve* with 15 combat-ready *Tiger* B tanks.

On 11 March, five new *Tiger B* tanks arrived at the formation.[4]

On 15 March, 19 combat-ready heavy tanks and seven repairable within a short period of time were available for the *Abteilung*.[5] Two of the seven anti-aircraft armoured fighting vehicles were in combat-ready condition.[6]

In the meantime, the *Abteilung* was reorganized, based on the 1945-type, so-called "free system". The overall required strength in vehicles was decreased, however, the previously-designated number of tanks was retained. Nevertheless, as it was impossible to replace losses, the so-called emergency required strength (*Notsoll*) was established as 31 *Tiger* B tanks.

On 18 March, *schwere Panzer-Abteilung "Feldherrnhalle"* was still in Verebély. There

1 Schneider, 1994, p.171.

2 The remnants of the *Panzer* regiment were assigned into *Panzer-Division "Feldherrnhalle 2"*, in existence from 20 February 1945, organized from the remnants of the *Panzer-Abteilung 13. "Feldherrnhalle"*; the commander was *Oberst* (*Generalmajor* from April) Dr. Franz Bäke until the end of the war. From then on it was called *gemischtes Panzer-Regiment "Feldherrnhalle 2"*, and consisted of the former *II. Abteilung* (renamed as *I. Abteilung*)/*Panzer-Regiment 4*, and the *II.* (armoured personnel carrier) *Bataillon*/former *Panzergrenadier-Regiment 93*.

3 Diary of Hans Welsch, p.13.

4 Schneider, 1994, p.171.

5 Schneider, 1994, p.171.

6 Jentz, Thomas L., *Die deutsche Panzertruppe* Band 2 (Wölfersheim-Berstadt, 1999), p.247.

were 170 men, 15 combat-ready *Tiger* B tanks, three anti-aircraft armoured fighting vehicles with 3.7cm automatic anti-aircraft cannon, two 2cm self-propelled automatic anti-aircraft cannon, and six armoured personnel carriers on its strength.[7]

On 20 March, an armoured personnel carrier-company from the *13. Panzer-Division* was ordered to join *Panzer-Gruppe "Feldherrnhalle"*, consisting of the *schwere Panzer-Abteilung* stationed in the Verebély area, and *Panzerjäger-Abteilung* [8], in order to provide opportunities for the crew to learn cooperation with armoured fighting vehicles in an accelerated manner, by joining the armoured units.[9]

On 25 March, north of the Danube, the 7th Guards Army of the Soviet 2nd Ukrainian Front, its 1st Guards Cavalry-Mechanized Group and 53rd Army launched their attack toward Pozsony (Bratislava) and Trencsén.

There was a total of 365 operational tanks and self-propelled guns in the strength of the 2nd Ukrainian Front. Of this, the 4th Guards and 6th Guards Cavalry Corps of the 1st Guards Cavalry-Mechanized Group (Lieutenant General I. A. Pliev) had a total of 22 T–34s, 41 Mk IX Valentines and 20 M3 Stuart tanks, 63 SU–76M self-propelled guns, giving a total of 146 operational armoured fighting vehicles.[10] There were a total of five tank regiments and two self-propelled artillery regiments.

The 27th Independent Guards Tank Brigade was also attached to the Soviet 7th Guards Army; it had a mere 11 T–34 tanks and SU–85 self-propelled guns, although only nine of these were in operational condition at the beginning of the operation. The 27th Guards Rifle Corps of the army was also supported by the Romanian 2nd Tank Regiment (Colonel Stan Zătreanu), which had the following armoured strength on 11 March 1945:[11]

Table 21 – Armoured fighting vehicle strength of 2nd Romanian Tank Regiment, 11 March 1945

Type	Available	Operational
T–4 [*Panzer* IV] tank	8	7
Renault R–35/45 tank	32	24
T–38 [*Pz.* 38(t)] tank	10	9
R–2 [*Pz.* 35(t)] tank	2	0
TA [*StuG.* III] assault gun	13	8
TACAM R–2 tank destroyer	5	0
Total	70	48

The order of battle for the Romanian 2nd Tank Regiment was as follows in March

7 HM HIM *Hadtörténelmi Levéltár* (Budapest) microfilm archives, *Kriegstagebuch Ia der Heeresgruppe Süd* (roll no. 630. image no. 7214939).

8 The *Panzerjäger-Abteilung 13* was a unit of the *13. Panzer-Division* under the process of reorganization. The *Abteilung* had 20 *Jagdpanzer* 38(t) tank destroyers. However it was not combat-ready yet, because the crews had to be retrained to this new type as they had been fighting with *Panzer* IV/70 *Jagdpanzers* before.

9 HM HIM *Hadtörténelmi Levéltár* (Budapest) microfilm archives, *Kriegstagebuch Ia der Heeresgruppe Süd* (roll no. 630. image no. 7214987).

10 Kolomjec, M. & Mosanszkij, I., *Tanki Lend-Liza* (Lend-lease tanks) (Moscow, 2000), p.60.

11 Domanski, Jacek & Janusz Ledwoch, *Wien 1945* (Warsaw, 2006), pp.38-39 and Sinescu, Maria "The Romanian Tank Troops in the approach to Vienna" in: *Romania in World War II 1941–1945* (Bucharest, 1997), pp.295-296.

1945:

1. Reconnaissance Company: eight *Sd.Kfz.* 222 armoured cars and five *Sd.Kfz.* 251s;
2. 1st Tank Battalion: one (T 4) tank company and two (TA) assault gun companies;
3. 2nd Light Tank Battalion: two R 35 tank companies (R 35 and R 35/45), one T 38 tank company and one TACAM battery;
4. Reconnaissance Tank Group: two R 2 tanks;
5. Anti-Aircraft Battery: 4 x 20mm *Gustloff* model 1938 anti-aircraft guns;
6. Command Company: radio communications platoon, cable communications platoon and an engineer platoon.[12]

In the period between 25 March and 1 April 1945 the German *8. Armee* had the following elements during the battles fought on Hungarian soil, on both banks of the Danube and along the Garam: the weak *Kampfgruppen* of the *711., 96., 357., 153., 76.* and *15. Infanterie-Divisions*, the remnants of the *211., 46.* and *271. Volksgrenadier-Divisions*, the *8.* and *101. Jäger-Divisions*, the *182. Reserve-Division*, *Panzergrenadier-Brigade 92*, *Kampfgruppe* "Ameiser" of the *37. SS-Kavallerie-Division*, *Heeres-Sturmgeschütz-Brigaden 228, 286* and *325*, *Heeres-Sturmartillerie-Brigade 239*, *Pionier-Brigade 52*, independent *Panzerjäger-Abteilungen 662* and *721*, four machine gun battalions, two *Landeschützen-Bataillone*, two *Sicherungs-Bataillone*, parts of the Hungarian 20th, 23rd and 24th Infantry, 27th Light and 5th Reserve Divisions, and the 151st Rocket Launcher Artillery Battalion.

On 24 March, the German *8. Armee* had a total of approximately 200 tanks, assault guns and *Jagdpanzers*[13], but only a portion of these were in combat-ready condition.

The following units were defending the Hungarian sector of the Garam on 24 March, attached to *Panzerkorps "Feldherrnhalle"*[14] (from the northern left flank toward the Danube):

Table 22 – Units defending the Hungarian sector of the Garam attached to *Panzerkorps "Feldherrnhalle"*, 24 March 1945

Divisions and defensive belts	Daily strength	Combat strength	Combat-ready armoured fighting vehicles	Field artillery	7.5cm anti-tank guns
357. Inf. Div. Slovak border- Sáró north	11,288 men	6,010 men	12 *Jg.Pz.* 38(t)s	9 light batteries 2+2 heavy batteries	10+11
46. Volksgren. Div. Sáró north- Kőhídgyarmat	9,303 men	4,600 men[1]	8 *StuG.* IIIs[2]	11+6 light batteries 1 heavy batteries	23

12 See Nitu, Victor, The Tanks http://www.worldwar2.ro/arme/?article=24 (accessed 10 April 2012).

13 Rauchensteiner, Manfred, *Krieg in Österreich 1945* (Wien, 1970), p.151.

14 HM HIM *Hadtörténelmi Levéltár* (Budapest) microfilm archives, *Kriegstagebuch Ia der Heeresgruppe Süd* (roll no. 630. image no. 7215108. and next image).

Divisions and defensive belts	Daily strength	Combat strength	Combat-ready armoured fighting vehicles	Field artillery	7.5cm anti-tank guns
211. Volksgren. Div. Kampfgruppe Kőhídgyarmat south-Danube south bank	8,771 men	4,229 men	7 *Jg.Pz.* 38(t)s	3 light batteries 2 heavy batteries	11
Pz. Div. "FHH 2"[3]	3,230 men	1,013 men	16 *Panthers* 20 *Panzer* IVs[4] 12 *Jg.Pz.* 38(t)s	–	4
Pz. Div. "FHH 1" Komárom bridgehead south of the Danube	6,530 men	2,861 men	13 *Panthers* 15 *Panzer* IVs 2 *Panzer* IV/70s (A)	2 light batteries	1
Total	39,122 men	18,713 men	105 armoured fighting vehicles	31 light batteries 7 heavy batteries	60

1 Approximately 1200 men of this were from three battalions of the Hungarian 13th Infantry Regiment.

2 According to our opinion these vehicles were partly or in whole the armoured fighting vehicles of the *Sturmgeschütz-Brigade 286* subordinated to the *46. Volksgrenadier-Division*.

3 On 23 March 1945 the P*anzer-Division "Feldherrnhalle" (Kommandeur: Generalmaj*or Günther Pape) was renamed *"Feldherrnhalle 1"*, and the *13. Panzer-Division (Kommandeur: Ober*st Franz Bäke, from 20 April 1945, *Generalmajor*) receive*d* the name *"Feldherrnhalle 2"*. The different units of the Divisions also took the names, respectively. The *Panzer-Division "Feldherrnhalle 2"* composed the *Korpsreserve*. The two *Panzer* divisions have partly been under the process of establishment.

4 On 21 March 1945 the Division also had a further eight *Panzer IV/70 (V) Jagdpanzers* from the past; these were, according to our opinion, intended for the 4. *Kompanie/Panzer-Abteilung 2110*.

Schwere Panzer-Abteilung "Feldherrnhalle", with 15 combat-ready *Tiger B* heavy tanks, five *Flak-Panzer* IV anti-aircraft armoured fighting vehicles and six armoured personnel carriers was also part of the armoured reserve for *Panzerkorps "Feldherrnhalle"*.

In the early morning hours of **25 March 1945,** following a mere 15 minute-long artillery preparation fire, the 27th Guards Rifle Corps of the Soviet 7th Guards Army established bridgeheads on the west bank of the Garam, in the sector of the German *357. Infanterie-Division* at Alsóvárad, Nagykálna, Kiskálna and Újbars. Attacking from the direction of Alsóvárad, the Soviet troops occupied Bajka and the eastern part of Barsendréd in the morning hours. Approximately 300 Soviet infantry also thrust into the eastern part of Nagysalló. In the area of Garamszentgyörgy, German reconnaissance identified 36 moving armoured fighting vehicles, 17 guns and a number of trucks.

Only containing attacks were launched against the positions of the *46. Volksgrenadier-Division*, but the Soviets, attacking from the eastern bank, managed to capture Kőhídgyarmat from the *Kampfgruppe* of the *211. Volksgrenadier-Division*.

The *Panzer-Gruppe* of *Panzerkorps "Feldherrnhalle"* (*schwere Panzer-Abteilung "Feldherrnhalle"*, *Panzerjäger-Abteilung "Feldherrnhalle 2"*, and an improvised armoured personnel carrier company), together with the *Schützen-Regiment* and the *Alarm* companies of the *Panzerkorps* that were brought up from Verebély, was employed in the area of Garamlök, and along the road leading from Nagykálna toward the southwest. Parts of the *Panzer-Gruppe* temporarily recaptured Nagykálna and Kiskálna in a counterattack, despite heavy Soviet artillery fire and constant raids by Soviet ground-attack aircraft.[15]

Schwere Panzer-Abteilung "Feldherrnhalle" advanced toward Töhöl and then carried out a counterattack toward Nagykálna, which, in the meantime, had again been taken by Soviet troops. The *Tiger B* heavy tanks, without any support, tried all night to break into the village, but eventually failed. Soviet wedge formations were advancing westward on their left and right too.

The *I. Bataillon/Panzergrenadier-Regiment 66/Panzer-Division "Feldherrnhalle 2"* arrived on the same day in the area of Libád and Béla, where it was sent into reserve.

Late at night, the Soviet 1st Guards Cavalry-Mechanized Group has also crossed the river southwest of Léva with its 146 tanks and self-propelled guns. Early, at dawn the next morning, the troops of Lieutenant General Pliev started to complete the breakthrough of the German tactical defence and pursuit of the fleeing enemy.[16]

On **26 March 1945**, the rifle troops of the Soviet 7th Guards Army occupied a number of lesser bridgeheads on the western bank of the Garam.

Southwest of Léva, the Soviet 27th Guards Rifle Corps was supported by the Romanian 2nd Tank Regiment. The 1st Tank Battalion with its *Panzer* IV tanks and *StuG.* III assault guns, of German origin, attacked with the regiments of the Soviet 375th Rifle Division toward Felsővárad–Ény–Zsitvagyarmat. The 2nd Tank Battalion, with R–35/45 tanks and TACAM R–2 tank destroyers, supported the 93rd Guards Rifle Division in its advance toward Barsendréd, Barsbese and Komját. In the meantime, the Romanian tanks contacted German *Tiger B* and *Panther* tanks. The regiment claimed to have destroyed two 15cm guns and 12 7.5cm anti-tank guns during that day's fighting, but it also suffered heavy losses.[17]

During the day, *schwere Panzer-Abteilung "Feldherrnhalle"* was ordered back to Töhöl, where a desperate defensive battle was going on. While the *Tiger B* tanks launched a new counterattack, almost all of the German units were in retreat from the area, since the Soviets had already advanced to the outskirts of Verebély. Under heavy Soviet artillery and mortar fire, the armoured fighting vehicles were firing at anything that moved. The

15 HM HIM *Hadtörténelmi Levéltár* (Budapest) microfilm archives, AOK 8 Ia. Nr. 437/45 g. Kdos. (roll no. 630. image no. 7215119), and *Tagesmeldung vom 25. 03. 1945* (roll no. 630. image no. 7215461).

16 Pliev, I. A., *V bojah za osvobozhdenyie Ruminii, Vengrii, Czehoslovakii* (The battles for Romania, Hungary, Czechoslovakia) (Moscow, 1985). See www. http://militera.lib.ru/memo/russian/pliev_ia3/04.html (accessed 6 April 2012).

17 The regiment lost 12 dead and five wounded, besides, at least one tank of the 2nd Tank Battalion was knocked out. See *România in războiul antihitlerist, 23.8.1944-9.5.1945* (Bucuresti, 1966), pp.527-528.

engagement continued, even after darkness fell; the tank with turret no. 112 knocked out a Soviet anti-tank gun.[18]

Elements of the Soviet 6th Guards Cavalry Corps were engaged in heavy artillery and mortar fire in the area of Fakóvezekény and Cseke. In addition, they ran into a minefield. The 154th Tank Regiment, the advance troop of the corps, was engaged in night combat near Cseke, in which the Germans, from their ambush positions, knocked out a number of Soviet tanks with *Panzerfäuste*.[19]

That day there were a total of 15 Romanian and Soviet armoured fighting vehicles knocked out in the sector of the German *Panzerkorps "Feldherrnhalle"*.[20]

At dawn on **27 March 1945,** *schwere Panzer-Abteilung "Feldherrnhalle"* was ordered back from Töhöl to Verebély in order to prepare for new counterattacks. Some of the heavy tanks established defences on the eastern side of Verebély, while another of their groups, commanded by the *Abteilung* commander, secured the possible roads of retreat to be used by their elements toward the Nyitra, in the direction of Kalász. The *Abteilung* also maintained contact with the repairing station, established back in the rear.

The *Tiger B* tanks held the eastern edge of Verebély throughout the day. In the night, *Hauptmann* von Diest-Koerber retreated with the *Abteilungsstab*, a number of tanks, and the supply units toward Kalász without orders to do so, where they established themselves in hedgehog position.

In the evening, the elements remaining in Verebély came under heavy Soviet artillery fire, in which *Leutnant* Fürlinger was killed when stepping out of the cover of a house.[21] Following this, the group retreated toward Kalász as requested by the *Abteilung* commander.[22]

The *Panzerjäger-Abteilung* of *Panzer-Division "Feldherrnhalle 1"* received 21 *Jagdpanzer* 38(t) tank destroyers in March 1945. The *Abteilung* was first to be retrained to this type. Earlier they had fought with *StuG*. III assault guns. The *Abteilung* was transported by train to Köbölkút by 1900 hours on 25 March, then it marched to Gyiva, and arrived there at about 2300 hours. On 26 March, two *Jagdpanzer*-companies of the *Panzerjäger-Abteilung* (both with a supporting *Grenadier-Zug* of their own) were attached to the *Kampfgruppe* of the *211. Volksgrenadier-Division* and stood in reserve.

On 27 March, the *Jagdpanzers* supported the counterattack of the infantry in the sector of the *211. Volksgrenadier-Division* east of Gyiva, via the Teknyős Valley toward Kőhídgyarmat. In the evening, the Germans had to retreat. The rearguard was composed of the *1. Kompanie/Panzerjäger-Abteilung "Feldherrnhalle 1"* with its *Jagdpanzers*.[23]

In the period between 20 and 27 March, *Kampfgruppe "Pape"* of *Panzerkorps*

18 Diary of Hans Welsch, p.13.

19 Pliev, 1985.

20 HM HIM *Hadtörténelmi Levéltár* (Budapest) microfilm archives, *Kriegstagebuch Ia der Heeresgruppe Süd, Morgenmeldung vom 27. 03. 1945* (roll no. 630. image no. 7215477).

21 The *Leutnant* had earlier assumed command of the *1. Kompanie*, when the former commander of the company, *Oberleutnant* Oemler was assigned to *schwere Panzer-Abteilung 509*.

22 Diary of Hans Welsch, p.13, and the diary of von Diest-Koerber in: Lochmann, Freiherr von Rosen, Rubbel & Sichel (hrsg.), 1990, p.397.

23 Letter from Hans Schwanke von Bargen, former *Leutnant* of *Panzer-Division "Feldherrnhalle 2"* to András Palásthy, dated 4 March 1992. Copy owned by the author.

"Feldherrnhalle" (mainly the armoured elements of the *Panzer-Divisions "Feldherrnhalle 1"* and *"Feldherrnhalle 2"*) was fighting south of the Danube, in the outskirts of Komárom, to defend the crossing points of the Danube. These armoured fighting vehicles were evacuated not evacuated until 27 March; then were ordered back to the Felvidék (Upper Hungary), to the area of Érsekújvár.

In the early morning hours of 27 March, the *Panzer-Abteilung* of the *Panzer-Regiment "Feldherrnhalle 2"* knocked out a total of 20 armoured fighting vehicles of the 4th Guards Cavalry Corps/1st Guards Cavalry-Mechanized Group between Pozba and Kisbelleg.[24] The 134th Tank Regiment of the 10th Guards Cavalry Division lost six of these vehicles.[25] However, the German armoured fighting vehicles were still unable to hold up the advance of the Soviet cavalry troops between Hull and Újlót.[26]

In this way, on 27 March the *I. Abteilung* of the *Panzer-Regiment* of *Panzer-Division "Feldherrnhalle 1"* (*2. Kompanie*) repelled three tank-supported attacks from Soviet infantry elements 7.5kms east of Érsekújvár, at the edge of Udvard. The German armoured fighting vehicles engaged in street combat with the attackers on the night preceding 28 March, and then retreated west during the course of the day.[27]

On **28 March 1945,** Soviet troops occupied Udvard. The Germans observed the movements of 25-25 Soviet armoured fighting vehicles east and northeast of Nagysurány, respectively. A *Panzer-Gruppe* of *Panzerkorps "Feldherrnhalle"* was in heavy combat, 5km northwest of Verebély, in the area of Kalász and Babindál.[28]

At 0130 hours, at dawn, the *Jagdpanzer* 38(t) tank destroyer*s* of the *Panzerjäger-Abteilung* of *Panzer-Division "Feldherrnhalle 1"* retreated to Für. Then, at 0800 hours in the morning, they launched a counterattack from the garden of the mansion, flanking the Soviet troops from the left. Following the successful mission the *Jagdpanzers* returned to the garden of the mansion.[29]

That same day, *schwere Panzer-Abteilung "Feldherrnhalle"* relocated to the area of Nyitra, crossing the borders of contemporary Hungary.

On **29 March 1945,** the Soviet 6th Guards Airborne Division/24th Guards Rifle Corps of the 7th Guards Army occupied Nagysurány in heavy combat, and the 93rd Guards Rifle Division/27th Guards Rifle Corps occupied Komját.

24 Between 25 March and 1 April, the German *8. Armee* claimed to have knocked out as few as 37 Soviet armoured fighting vehicles north of the Danube (a further 21 were knocked out by the Komárom bridgehead defended south of the river). See HM HIM *Hadtörténelmi Levéltár* (Budapest) microfilm archives, *Kriegstagebuch Ia der Heeresgruppe Süd* (roll no. 630. image no. 7215182). Thus, this armoured battle was probably the most important among the engagements fought between armoured fighting vehicles on the Felvidék (Upper Hungary) in March 1945.

25 Pliev, 1985.

26 HM HIM *Hadtörténelmi Levéltár* (Budapest) microfilm archives, *Kriegstagebuch Ia der Heeresgruppe Süd, Kriegstagebuch vom 27. 03. 1945* (roll no. 630. image no. 7214788).

27 Di Giusto, 2010, p.209.

28 HM HIM *Hadtörténelmi Levéltár* (Budapest) microfilm archives, *Kriegstagebuch Ia der Heeresgruppe Süd, Tagesmeldung vom 28. 03. 1945* (roll no. 630. image no. 7215490).

29 Letter from Hans Schwanke von Bargen, former *Leutnant* of the *Panzer-Division "Feldherrnhalle 2"* to András Palásthy, dated 4 March 1992. Copy owned by the author.

The *Kampfgruppe* of the commander of *Panzer-Division "Feldherrnhalle 1"*, *Generalmajor* Pape, temporarily stopped the advance of the Soviets west of Ürmény.[30]

Three assault guns of the German *1. Batterie/Sturm-Artillerie-Brigade 239* retreated to the northern bank of the Danube, and three *StuG.* III assault guns of the Hungarian 7th Assault Artillery Battalion were directed to Vágsellye by the *Stab* of the German *8. Armee.*[31]

On **30 March 1945,** Soviet troops occupied Nyitra, Érsekújvár and Komárom, then crossed the Vág river, in order to be able to continue their attack toward Bratislava, and toward the northwest.

On **31 March 1945** the Soviet 4th Guards Cavalry Corps/1st Guards Cavalry-Mechanized Group broke through the weak German securing line, and reached the Hidaskürt–Diószeg line. Elements of the 10th Guards Cavalry Division occupied Galánta. The Soviet troops advancing from the Diószeg area toward the north and northeast were repelled by the units of the regrouped *Panzer-Division "Feldherrnhalle 1"*.[32]

The same day, *Panzer-Division "Feldherrnhalle 1"* had nine *Panzer* IV and eight *Panther* tanks, besides, one *Panzer* IV/70 (A) and nine *Jagdpanzer* 38(t) tank destroyers in combat-ready condition.[33] *Panzer-Division "Feldherrnhalle* 2" had 10 combat-ready *Panzer* IV tanks and *Panzer* IV/70 (V) *Jagdpanzers*, and 12 *Panther* tanks.

The two *"Feldherrnhalle" Panzer-Divisions* retreated gradually toward the northwest. By the last day of March combat activities involving the armoured units and larger military formations had practically ended on the Felvidék (Upper Hungary) area, then part of contemporary Hungary.

30 HM HIM *Hadtörténelmi Levéltár* (Budapest) microfilm archives, *Kriegstagebuch Ia der Heeresgruppe Süd, Tagesmeldung vom 29. 03. 1945* (roll no. 630. image no. 7215499).

31 Letter of Dr. Willy R. Jaitner, a former *Oberleutnant* of the *Sturm-Artillerie-Brigade 239* to András Palásthy, dated 27 February 1988. Copy owned by the author.

32 HM HIM *Hadtörténelmi Levéltár* (Budapest) microfilm archives, *Kriegstagebuch Ia der Heeresgruppe Süd, Tagesmeldung vom 31. 03. 1945* (roll no. 630. image no. 7215521).

33 Nevenkin, 2008, pp.347, 657.

Appendix I

Order of battle of the Division "*Szent László*" as of 21-22 December 1944

Commander of the Division: Staff Colonel *vitéz* Zoltán Szügyi
Division Staff Commander: Staff Major Árpád Lajtos
Division Artillery Commander: Colonel Vilmos Dárday
Chief of Detachment Ia (operations): Staff Captain Lajos Győry
Operational adjutant: Captain *vitéz* János Iványi
Chief of Detachment Ib (intelligence and counter-espionage): Lieutenant (on specialized duty) Colonel József Bodor
Chief of Detachment Ic (supplies): Staff Captain Jenő Rutkay
Chief of the Staff Company: Captain András Szabolcs
Catholic military chaplain: military chaplain rev. István Senye
Protestant military chaplain: military chaplain rev. László Csaba

- Grenadier-Regiment (Lieutenant Colonel Valér Stefán)
    - bicycle platoon;
    - anti-tank gun platoon (three 7.5 cm Pak 40s);
    - sapper platoon;
    - signal platoon;
    - 1st Grenadier Battalion (Captain Sándor Pálfi): 27 light machine guns, eight machine guns, two heavy rifles, 14 8 cm mortars + one tank destroyer platoon (with *Panzerfäuste* and *Panzerschreck*);
    - 2nd Grenadier Battalion (Captain Miklós Békássy): 17 light machine guns, eight machine guns, two heavy rifles, 10 8 cm mortars + one tank destroyer platoon (with *Panzerfäuste* and *Panzerschreck*).

Total regimental strength: 50 officers, 1782 non-commissioned officers and enlisted men.

- Air Force Rifle Regiment (Lieutenant Colonel István Heinrich)
    - bicycle platoon;
    - anti-tank gun platoon (three 7.5 cm Pak 40s);
    - sapper platoon;
    - signal platoon;
    - 1st Air Force Rifle Battalion (Captain György Pályi): 24 light machine guns, 12 8 cm mortars + one tank destroyer platoon (with *Panzerfäuste* and *Panzerschreck*);
    - 2nd Air Force Rifle Battalion (Major Frigyes Freyer): 24 light machine guns, 12 8 cm mortars + one tank destroyer platoon (with *Panzerfäuste* and *Panzerschreck*).

Total regimental strength: 46 officers, 1782 non-commissioned officers and enlisted men.

- 1st Parachute Regiment (Captain Edömér Tassonyi)
  - bicycle platoon;
  - anti-tank gun platoon (three 7.5 cm Pak 40s);
  - sapper platoon;
  - signal platoon;
  - 1st Battalion/1st Parachute Regiment (Captain Zoltán Kiss): 27 light machine guns, 12 machine guns, four heavy rifles, 11 8 cm mortars + one tank destroyer platoon (with *Panzerfäuste* and *Panzerschreck*);
  - 2nd Battalion/1st Parachute Regiment (1st Lieutenant Henrik Sanna): 27 light machine guns, 12 machine guns, six heavy rifles, three 5 cm grenade launchers, eight 8 cm mortars + one tank destroyer platoon (with *Panzerfäuste* and *Panzerschreck*).

The strength of the 2nd Battalion/1st Parachute Regiment was approximately 500 men. Data for the 1st Battalion/1st Parachute Regiment is missing.
(Each battalion of the three regiments consisted of three rifle companies and one heavy weapons company. There were three platoons within each rifle companies, each with three squads.)

- Tank Destroyer Battalion *"Szent László"* (commander ?):
  - two companies, only one had towed anti-tank guns (seven 7.5 cm Pak 40s). Strength: 17 officers, 350 non-commissioned officers and enlisted men.

- Reconnaissance Battalion *"Szent László"* (Captain László Takács):
  - sapper platoon;
  - signal platoon;
  - anti-tank gun platoon (without the guns);
  - mortar platoon (four 8 cm mortars);
  - cavalry squadron (nine light machine guns);
  - bicycle company (three light machine guns);
  - armoured anti-aircraft platoon (three combat ready *Nimród* armoured self-propelled anti-aircraft guns);
  - light tank platoon (one combat ready *Turán* tank).

Strength: 12 officers, 300 non-commissioned officers and enlisted men.

- VIII Towed Field Artillery Battalion (Lieutenant Colonel László Bobiss-Selmeczy (?)):
  - three batteries, each with four 15 cm heavy field howitzers. Strength: unknown.
- 1st Mortar Artillery Battalion (Captain Roderig Rapaics):
  - three batteries, each with eight 12 cm mortars. Strength: unknown.
- 9th Field Artillery Battalion (commander ?):
  - three batteries, each with four 8 cm field guns. Strength: unknown.
- 76th Field Artillery Battalion (commander ?):

    - three batteries, each with four 10.5 cm light field howitzers. Strength: unknown.

- 20th Assault Artillery Battalion (Major József Henkey-Hőnig):
    - Staff Battery;
    - three assault artillery batteries.

Strength: 15 officers, 550 non-commissioned officers and enlisted men. 25 Jagdpanzer 38(t) Hetzer *Jagdpanzers* allocated and taken over from the Germans at Kővágóőrs. Crew in training in Győr.

- 53rd Pioneer Battalion (Lieutenant Colonel Ernő Koppányi):
    - three companies (five light machine guns, four machine guns, five 8 cm mortars).

Strength: 21 officers, 930 non-commissioned officers and enlisted men.

- Signal Battalion *"Szent László"* (Lieutenant Colonel András Baráth):
    - Radio Company;
    - Field Telephone Company.

Strength: 21 officers, 600 non-commissioned officers and enlisted men.

- Division *"Szent László"* supply troops (5 officers, 200 non-commissioned officers and enlisted men)

Appendix II

Armoured strength of the Hungarian 2nd Armoured Division, December 1944[1]

Armoured fighting vehicle	**7 December 1944**		**28 December 1944**		**Difference of "available"**
	Available	**Combat ready**	**Available**	**Combat ready**	
Nimród armoured self-propelled AA gun	26	7	1	1	-25
Csaba armoured car	8	3	No data	No data	No data
Turán 40 tank	35	–	4	–	-31
Turán 75 tank	8	–	5	–	-3
Toldi (20 mm) tank	16	5	–	–	-16
Panzer III tank	1	–	–	–	-1
Panzer IV tank	20	2	10	10	-21[1]
Panther tank	4	–	1	–	-3
StuG. III	1	–	–	–	-1
Total	119	17	21	11	-101

1 On 21 December 1944, there were 21 *Panzer* IVs in the strength of the *Division*, and a further 10 tanks were received at the end of December. Thus, 10 of the total of 31 *Panzer* IVs has remained by 28 December.

1 Based on summarized German archival data.

Bibliography

Unpublished sources

The bulk of the book has been researched from original combat reports and other documentation produced by German, Hungarian and Soviet formations. Precise details of this material can be located in the footnotes present throughout the book.

Published sources

A Nagy Honvédő Háború története, 1941–1945. Ötödik kötet. ('History of the Great Patriotic War, 1941-1945 Book V') (Budapest, 1967)

Agis, Hermann, *Das Ende am Plattensee. Die 44. Infanteriedivision "Reichsgrenadier-Division Hoch- und Deutschmeister" im Endkampf* (Nürnberg, 2006)

Agte, Patrick, *Jochen Peiper. Kommandeur Panzerregiment Leibstandarte* (Berg am Starnberger See, 1998)

Armstrong, Richard N., *Red Army Tank Commanders – The Armored Guards* (Atglen PA, 1994)

Bárczy, János, *Zuhanóugrás* ('Sky-diving') (Budapest, 1981)

Boyevoy sostav sovetskoy armii. Casty V (yanvar-sentyabr 1945) ('Combat composition of the Soviet Army, Part V (January-September 1945)') (Moscow, 1990)

Di Giusto, Stefano, *Panzer-Sicherungs-Kompanien and Panzer-Abteilung 208–I./Panzer-Regiment Feldherrnhalle. Italy 1943–1944. Hungary –Slovakia–Moravia 1944–1945* (Erlangen, 2010)

Domanski, Jacek & Janusz Ledwoch, *Wien 1945* (Warsaw, 2006)

Haupt, Werner, *Die 8. Panzer-Division im Zweiten Weltkrieg* (Friedberg, 1987)

Hinze, Rolf, *Hitze, Frost und Pulverdampf – Der Schicksalweg der 20. Panzer-Division* (Meerbusch, 1991)

Hősök. A Sovietunió Hősei a magyarországi felszabadító harcokban 1944-1945. ('Heroes. Heroes of the Soviet Union during the liberation battles in Hungary') (Budapest, 1981)

Jentz, Thomas L., *Die deutsche Panzertruppe* Band 2 (Wölfersheim-Berstadt, 1999)

Kindel, Richard, *Die 8. Panzer-Division der Deutschen Wehrmacht 1939-1945*, Band 2 (Wuppertal, 2007)

Kolomjec, M. & Mosanszkij, I., *Tanki Lend-Liza* (Lend-lease tanks) (Moscow, 2000)

Kregel, Heiko, *Geschichte des Panzer-Regiments 10, 1938–1945* (Berlin, 2010)

Krivosheev, G. F. (ed.), *Soviet Casualties and Combat Losses in the Twentieth Century* (London, 1997)

Kurowski, Franz & Tornau, Gottfried, *Sturmgeschütze – "Die Panzer der Infanterie"* (Würzburg, 2008)

Lochmann, Dr. Franz-Wilhelm, Richard Freiherr von Rosen, Alfred Rubbel & Rolf Sichel (hrsg.), *Erinnerungen an die Tiger-Abteilung 503 1942-1945* (Bassum, 1990)

Loza, Dimitry Fjodorovich, "A szovjet csapatok felszabadító harcai Nógrád megyében", ('Liberating battles of the Soviet troops in Nógrád county. December 1944') in: *Hadtörténelmi Közlemények,* issue 1967/4

Loza, Dimitry, *Commanding the Red Army's Sherman Tanks* (Lincoln NE, 1996)

Lykow, Iwan Semjonowitsch, *In bedrohlicher Stunde* (Berlin, 1987)

Maier, Georg, *Drama zwischen Budapest und Wien* (Osnabrück, 1985)

Malakhov, M. M., "A Balatontól Bécsig (részlet)" in: *Fejezetek hazánk felszabadításának történetéből* ('From Lake Balaton to Vienna') (excerpt) in: 'Chapters from the history of the liberation of our country') (Budapest, 1960)

Malakhov, M. M., *Osvobozhdeniye Vengrii i Vostochny Avstrii* ('The liberation of Hungary and Eastern Austria') (Moscow, 1965)

Martin, Kornél & István Ugron, "Fejezetek a Szent László hadosztály történetéből. I. rész." ('Chapters from the history of the Division *"Szent László"*, Part I') in: *Hadtörténelmi Közlemények*, issue 1995/3

Meyer, Hubert, *Kriegsgeschichte der 12. SS-Panzerdivision "Hitlerjugend"* Band 2 (Osnabrück, 1987, 2nd edition)

Meyer, Hubert, *Kriegsgeschichte der 12. SS-Panzerdivision "Hitlerjugend"* Band 2 (Osnabrück, 1999, 4th edition)

Minasyan, M. M., "Délkelet-Európa népeinek felszabadítása (részlet)" in: *Hazánk felszabadulása*. ('The liberation of the peoples of Southwestern Europe (excerpts). In: Liberation of our country') (Budapest, 1970)

Nevenkin, Kamen, *Fire Brigades – The Panzer Divisions 1943–1945* (Winnipeg, 2008)

Paul, Wolfgang, *Brennpunkte. Die Geschichte der 6. Panzerdivision (1. leichte) 1937–1945* (Krefeld, 1977)

Pliev, I. A., *V bojah za osvobozhdenyie Ruminii, Vengrii, Czehoslovakii* ('The battles for Romania, Hungary, Czechoslovakia') (Moscow, 1985)

Rauchensteiner, Manfred, *Krieg in Österreich 1945* (Wien, 1970)

Schadewitz, Michael, *Panzerregiment 11/Panzerabteilung 65 1937–1945, Panzerersatz- und Ausbildungsabteilung 11 1939–1945* (Lünen, 1987)

Schimack, A., *Die 44. Infanteriedivision. Das Tagebuch der Hoch- und Deutschmeister* (Wien, 1969)

Schneider, Wolfgang, *Tigers in Combat Volume 1* (Winnipeg, 1994)

Schneider, Wolfgang, *Tiger im Kampf. Band II* (Uelzen, 2001)

Senger und Etterlin Jr. v. F. M. Dr., *Die 24. Panzer-Division vormals 1. Kavallerie-Division 1939–1945* (Neckargemünd, 1962)

Sinescu, Maria "The Romanian Tank Troops in the approach to Vienna" in: *Romania in World War II 1941–1945* (Bucharest, 1997)

Száva, Péter (ed.), *Magyarország felszabadítása. Tanulmányok hazánk felszabadításának történetéből.* ('The liberation of Hungary. Studies from the history of the liberation of our country') (Budapest, 1975),

Szénássy, Zoltán, *Komáromi m. kir. 22. gyalogezred.* ('Hungarian 22nd Infantry Regiment at Komárom') (Komárom, 2000)

Szepesvári, Vitéz Béla, *A Hazáért mindhalálig. Vitéz Szepesvári Béla háborús naplója. Magánkiadás, é.n.* ('For the Motherland, until the end. Wartime diary of Vitéz Béla Szepesvári') (self-published, n.d.)

Tiemann, Ralf, *Die Leibstandarte. Band IV/2* (Osnabrück, 1987)

Tolubko, V. F. & Barisev, N. I., *Na yuzhnom flange. Boyevoy puty 4-go gvargyeskovo mehanishirovannogo corpus (1942–1945)* ('On the southern flank. The combat path of the 4th Guards Mechanized Corps 1942-1945') (Moscow, 1973)

Tóth, Sándor, *A szovjet hadsereg felszabadító harcai Magyarországon.* ('Liberating battles of the

Soviet Army in Hungary') (Budapest, 1965)

Traditionsverband d. Div., *Geschichte der 3. Panzer-Division Berlin-Brandenburg 1935–1945* (Berlin, 1967)

Volleth, Karl, "Die Kompanie Honstetter. Der Weg der alten 3./Pz. Rgt. 35 nach dem Ausscheiden aus dem Regiment" in: *Panzernachrichten. Kameradschaft ehem. Panzer-Regiment 35 e.V. Nr. 45,* April 1975

Vopersal, Wolfgang, *Soldaten, Kämpfer, Kameraden. Marsch und Kämpfe der SS-Totenkopfdivision. Band Vb* (Bielefeld, 1991)

Wegmann, Günter (Mitarb.), *"Das Oberkommando der Wehrmacht gibt bekannt ..."* (Osnabrück, 1982)

Winchester, Charles, *Ostfront. Hitler's War on Russia 1941–45* (Oxford, 1998)

Zaharov, M. V., *A 2. és a 3. Ukrán Front felszabadító hadműveletei Délkelet- és Közép-Európában, 1944–1945* ('Liberating operations of the 2nd and 3rd Ukrainian Fronts in Southeastern and Central Europe, 1944-1945') (Budapest, 1973)

Zaloga, Steven J. & Ness, Leland S., *Red Army Handbook 1939–45* (Stroud, 1998)

Zavizion, G. T. & Kornyushin, P.A., *na Tiknom okeane...* ('To the Pacific Ocean') (Moscow, 1967)

Index

Index of People

Index of Places

Note: A Hill (*magaslat* in Hungarian) is a geographical category, but a Point (*magassági pont* or *háromszögellési pont* in Hungarian) is a topographical category. Both are used by military organisations for Command and Control and for reporting, hence both appear in the index below.

Index of German Military Units

Command Functions

Heeresgruppen

Armeegruppen

Armies

Corps

Divisions

Brigades

Kompanie

Miscellaneous

***Luftwaffe* Formations**

Index of Hungarian Military Units

Armies

Divisions

Divisions

Brigades

Regiments

Battalions

Companies

Aviation Units